TRADITIONS AND CELEBRATIONS FOR

THE

BAT MITZVAH

TRADITIONS AND CELEBRATIONS FOR THE

BAT MITZVAH

edited by Ora Wiskind Elper

The Sadie Rennert Women's Institute for Torah Studies

URIM PUBLICATIONS
Jerusalem • New York

Traditions and Celebrations for the Bat Mitzvah
Edited by Ora Wiskind Elper

Copyright © 2003 by MaTaN: The Sadie Rennert Women's Institute for Torah
Studies, Jerusalem

Some articles appearing in this book were translated from the Hebrew book:
Bat Mitzvah: Kovetz Ma'amarim, edited by Sara Friedland Ben Arza (MaTaN, 2002).

First Edition
ISBN 965-7108-52-7

Urim Publications, P.O. Box 52287, Jerusalem 91521 Israel

MaTaN, 30 Rashbag Street, Jerusalem 91080 Israel
www.matan.org.il

Lambda Publishers Inc.
3709 13th Avenue Brooklyn, New York 11218 U.S.A.
Tel: 718-972-5449 Fax: 718-972-6307
Email: mh@ejudaica.com

www.UrimPublications.com

"In all their ways they knew God,
Who guided their righteous paths."

On the occasion of Keren Golda Greenberg's entrance into the
life of *mitzvot*,

this book is dedicated to her grandmothers,
Shirley Schachter and Blu Greenberg.

Their lives incorporate the heart of Jewish Womanhood:

In thought and action, in wisdom and lovingkindness,
in love of God and love of all God's creatures.

Dedicated to the memory of

J.J. Greenberg,

who fulfilled with his life the model of Aharon HaKohen
אוהב את הבריות ומקרבן לתורה

He loved his fellow human beings,
and brought them close to the Torah.

CONTENTS

II. "And Above All, Study Torah"

On Women and the Feminine

Halakhic Issues Concerning Women

PREFACE

זה היום עשה ה׳ נגילה ונשמחה בו
"This day has been granted to us by Hashem –
let us celebrate and rejoice in it!"
(Psalms 118:24)

Happiness abounds as the children of our friends and families, as well as our own children, mark the vital passage into maturity. *Bar and Bat Mitzvah* initiates a young person into a new stage of life and has an effect on many levels – halakhically, intellectually and emotionally. The transition experienced by young women as they reach *bat mitzvah* age is truly a crucial one, yet Jewish tradition includes no long-standing or universally accepted practices to mark the event. In recent years, as the Jewish world has awakened to the riches Torah learning and observance offer women, the desire to prepare for and celebrate *bat mitzvah* in a meaningful and lasting way has grown tremendously. Many families of young women, and young women themselves, sense this need keenly, yet questions abound: What sort of preparatory study material will speak to the young woman, and where can this material be found? Is there a learning framework in which she will feel comfortable and where she will be able to grow personally? What sort of celebration is halakhically acceptable, and what type should be avoided? Can one hold a *seudat mitzvah*, make a *siyyum*? Should the girl, or additional participants, give a speech? Are there other creative alternatives?

This volume evolved from a profound sense that many members of the community feel at a loss when attempting to prepare for and mark their daughters' passage into Jewish maturity. *Traditions and Celebrations for the Bat Mitzvah* is an attempt to respond to this need – to provide readable and accessible material that addresses the central issues surrounding *bat mitzvah*, to share the views of qualified rabbinical authorities from many generations on relevant halakhic questions, to describe models of successful programs, and to offer ideas, thoughts and encouragement.

Years of experience with young women and their families who have anticipated upcoming *bat mitzvot* have convinced me that, as *Hazal* say, "One can learn Torah only from that place that draws one's heart."[1] If we wish to instill a lasting love of Torah and *mitzvot* in the souls of our daughters and to secure within them a rooted sense of Jewish identity, *bat mitzvah* can certainly be a precious opportunity to move the heart of each girl in a most personal way. And thus *Hazal* understand the verse (Psalms 1:2):

כי אם בתורת ה׳ חפצו ובתורתו יהגה יומם ולילה

("But his delight is in the Torah of the Lord, and in His Torah he meditates day and night") as an assurance that if one invests one's unique essence in establishing a connection with the "Torah of the Lord," the learning gained becomes transformed into one's own most authentic "Torah," a lasting companion throughout life. The months leading up to *bat mitzvah* and the event itself are essential experiences of finding individual forms of expression that hold great potential benefits for the family, the community as a whole, and for the *bat mitzvah* girl herself.

It is my sincere hope that *Traditions and Celebrations for the Bat Mitzvah* will be a source of guidance and aid, helping to make *bat mitzvah* a more meaningful and memorable event in all of our lives. Special gratitude is due to the community of Ra'anana, Israel, who provided continual faith in, and inspiration for, this project and accompanied it to fruition.

Oshra Koren
Director of MaTaN Hasharon, Ra'anana, 5763 (2003)

---

[1] *Avodah Zarah* 19a:.אמר רב אין אדם לומד תורה אלא ממקום שלבו חפץ

EDITOR'S INTRODUCTION

As MaTaN Women's Institute for Torah Study in Jerusalem entered its twelfth year of activity, it seemed appropriate for MaTaN to take on a new *mitzvah*. In addition to those to which MaTaN was already committed – Torah learning and acts of *hesed* – MaTaN accepted the challenge of compiling a collection of essays about contemporary *bat mitzvah* celebrations. That collection, initiated by Oshra Koren and edited by Sara Friedland Ben Arza, was published in Hebrew in 2002. The highly positive response it met aroused interest in providing a similar volume in English, in the hope of aiding Jewish communities outside of Israel as well in enriching their daughters' *bat mitzvah* experiences.

The essays in this collection fall into three general categories: Part I, Marking the Day and Celebrating the Event, presents the opinions of *posekim*, encouraging and opposing aspects of the *bat mitzvah* celebration itself. *Responsa* received from rabbis and educators who were asked for their views on appropriate ways to mark the *bat mitzvah* day are also included here. Other, specific issues concerning the *bat mitzvah* celebration considered in this section are the suitable locale and participants, a celebratory meal and its halakhic status as a *seudat mitzvah*, the parents' blessing *baruch she-petarani* marking the young woman's acceptance of *mitzvot*, and *bat mitzvah* speeches, or *derashot*.

In effect, the *bat mitzvah* celebration itself is but a part of an extended process, in which the young woman prepares herself intellectually and emotionally for new social, personal and halakhic responsibilities. The experiences she gains in that important period before her *bat mitzvah* will continue to accompany her after the event as well, and aid her in future stages of her life. Part II, And Above All, Study Torah contains essays exploring a rich variety of sources that can be studied with *bat mitzvah* girls. These essays are not geared for adolescents; rather, they have been collected here with the idea that their content may be of special interest to young women of *bat mitzvah* age. Teachers and parents can profitably use them as materials to be adapted and made relevant at an individual level, to respond to the specific tastes and concerns of their students and daughters. They may also serve as a basis for organized study in preparation for *bat mitzvah*, and afterwards. Finally, a wealth of ideas and directions for *bat mitzvah* speeches may be gleaned from them as well. This section begins with essays concerning prominent female persona of Jewish tradition, from biblical figures to modern women of valor. The second section addresses certain halakhic issues of particular relevance to women – observance of *Rosh Hodesh*, candle lighting, Torah study, *Megillah* reading and *zimmun*.

The guiding force in the conception of this anthology was the desire to seek out and discuss sources concerning women that could enrich the learning experience and Jewish identity formation of young women as they approach their *bat mitzvah*. In awareness of the crucial importance of a personal encounter with the sources, we have compiled Part III, Meaningful Preparation Through Active Participation. These essays offer practical suggestions, guidelines and descriptions of actual frameworks within which the contents of this book can be implemented. Such contexts include the dynamic of a women's *beit midrash*, mother-daughter *hevruta* guided learning programs, tutor-student learning partners, composition of family booklets, and the unique nature of women's Torah learning in general.

Most of the essays in this volume were written for the anthology itself. Many of them first appeared in the Hebrew edition and are published in English translation here; others are original English contributions and are published here for the first time. A minority of essays was first published elsewhere in another form. These appear with editorial changes and original publication information.

This collection of essays is variegated not only in the subjects raised. The views voiced in it are heterogeneous as well, expressing a plurality of approaches within the Orthodox Jewish community to the status of women and related subjects. Styles and genres of composition vary here too, ranging from academic discussion to more traditional yeshivah-style discourse; from spoken presentations to poetic evocation; from halakhic *responsa* of rabbis to personal meditations of parents and educators.

וִיהִי נֹעַם ה׳ אֱלֹקֵינוּ עָלֵינוּ וּמַעֲשֵׂה יָדֵינוּ כּוֹנְנָה עָלֵינוּ כּוֹנְנוּ יָדֵינוּ וּמַעֲשֵׂה יָדֵינוּ כּוֹנְנֵהוּ

May the labor and concern of all those who contributed here be established for a blessing.

Ora Wiskind Elper and Sara Friedland Ben Arza
Jerusalem 5763 (2003)

Acknowledgements

Special recognition is due to Oshra Koren for her original conception of this anthology in Hebrew, her enthusiasm and dedication to the project as it took form and throughout its transformation into this English edition. Recognition is also due to Sara Friedland Ben Arza – her wisdom, vision and creativity were invaluable in bringing the Hebrew version into existence. Much gratitude to MaTaN and its director, Malke Bina, whose generous spirit and openness enriches everyone around her, for her wholehearted contributions to this book. To Gina Junger for her endless efforts in raising the community's consciousness of the importance of *bat mitzvah* education. Generous financial support was given by Jean Ehrenberg, Lynn and Steven Farber, Mindy and David Greenberg and Mindy and Avrum Tokayer. The efforts of our translators – Gershon Clymer, Etka Liebowitz, Dov Lapin, Zipporah and Jonathan Price, Miriam Weed and Judith Weil – are greatly appreciated, as well as the efficiency and good will of publisher Tzvi Mauer and the editorial staff of *Urim Publications*. Finally, we are indebted to the devoted founders of MaTaN: Lili Weil, Suzanne Hochstein, Colette Kahn, Judith Kaufman Hurwich *ᵶ"l* and Micheline Treves *ᵶ"l*. Without their efforts, this institution would not exist.

JOURNEY TO HERSELF

Baruch Kahana

"*Bat mitzvah*" – we might consider three different aspects of this concept: first, the age in question – the beginning of adolescence; second, the individual – the future young woman; third, the *mitzvah* – the spiritual and *halakhic* world we put before the girl and hope, in its light, to educate her. Before I talk about the whole picture, I'd like to spend a few minutes on each of these components.

1.

In the 1950s Erik Erikson, a prominent psychoanalytic thinker, began to speak of adolescence as the period of "identity formation."[1] We could say that our identity is our innermost response to the question "Who are you?" A person can respond to that question using a variety of social parameters – age, profession, family status, cultural affiliation, gender. I think we would all agree that any such definition would be partial and superficial; having a certain profession surely doesn't express my entire essence. I'm characterized more by the way in which I fulfill my professional role, by my unique style. The same is true of the other components of identity we mentioned (and innumerable others as well). When we know a person, we can recognize the mark of her unique personality in everything she does, in the way – which no one else can reproduce – she fulfills each social role, in marriage, parenting, etc.

How, then, should we describe an individual's identity, that profound and unique aspect of the self? Maybe the best way is to think of it as a wondrous work of art, created by the individual out of a variety of social materials. Just as an artist takes raw materials and instills in them something

---

* translated by Ora Wiskind Elper

[1] Erik Erikson, *Identity, Adolescence and Crisis* (W.W. Norton: New York, 1968).

of his own soul, so each of us gathers the 'components of identity' from the cultural environment in which we live and invests them with original content of our own.

Anyone who knows children is aware that each of them, almost from birth, bears a distinct personality. What, then, is unique about adolescence? Are people devoid of identity until that time? Another question: the process of identity formation never ends; every change in familial or professional situation, every element we learn and internalize affects our identity. If we have some pre-established uniqueness, and our identity develops throughout our lives, what occurs in adolescence, and not earlier or later?

The answer may be found in the understanding of identity I suggested above as creation. From the moment of birth each child is undeniably an independent and unique creation. The creative process in which the self takes form clearly never ends, but at a certain stage of life, the question emerges: Who is the creator? The young person begins to feel mature enough to take the whole creative process, that is, her life, into her own hands. The parents are suspicious. After all, they put their souls into this child, lovingly shaping her in light of their highest values and worldview. How can they entrust such a young and inexperienced person with such a precious investment? All the small and exhausting arguments ("When are you coming home?") are but the external, technical side of the real struggle for freedom and identity.

The process is necessary, although it may occur in varying degrees of intensity. Paradoxically, for example, deep love felt on both sides might actually make the confrontation more severe (especially when it isn't accompanied with respect for the young person's uniqueness and with real trust). A high-quality youngster, who senses the presence of her creative abilities, may be an especially obstinate rebel. On the other hand, a youngster fearful of losing his parents' love may not rebel at all (and pay for it later in his life). Erikson speaks of the danger of identity dissipation threatening those who do not undergo this process. That is the situation of the young person who doesn't know who she is, who is unable to influence the course of her own life. She seems to be unable to take charge of her destiny, to shape it according to her will; rather, she lets herself be carried along through life. The sense of independence – that she saves for those moments after school or work is over, sitting with friends or letting time go by idly. Only then does she feel somewhat free. What to do, though – that she doesn't know.

Psychology in our post-modern age added another concept to the idea of identity: the narrative, which describes the personal story of each individual. Every person has a characteristic life story expressing his or her unique qualities, his or her relationship to their surroundings, etc. The difference between a psychically "healthy" and a "pathological" individual comes to the fore by comparing their life stories. Prof. Hayyim Omer describes a "good" life story as one that enables one to construct one's own life and feel it is one's own.[2] In that sort of story, a person can say, "I am the hero of that story" and that it is "a story with a future."

In light of these concepts, we can return to our consideration of adolescence as the age of "identity acquisition." It is then that the youth feels ready to be the author and heroine of her own story. She's no longer willing to define herself only as a member of her family, a secondary character in her parents' story. Instead, she's about to become the central figure in her own narrative, a new story.

I'd like to suggest one more concept, that of the "search for the essential self" in the teaching of R. Avraham Yitzhak Hacohen Kook.

"The breath of our nostrils, the anointed of the Lord" – that might and glory is not external to us, it is our own the breath…. We must seek our "I," our own selves, seek and we shall find.[3]

This idea, of course, is fundamental to R. Kook's worldview.[4] Hidden in each of us is a special, divine light, containing nuances present in no other individual; each of us bears sole responsibility for realizing the particular hues within us. Through that effort, each of us participates in our personal redemption, as well as in the redemption of the Jewish nation and the entire world.

---

[2] H. Omer and N. Alon, *Ma'aseh haSippur ha-Tippuli*, 1997, p. 133.

[3] R. Avraham Yitzhak Hacohen Kook, *Orot Ha-kodesh* (Jerusalem, 1964), vol. 3, p. 140.

[4] And in Hasidic thought as well, but this is beyond the realm of our discussion.

How is this related? That whole spectrum of divine light is present in the individual from birth. Only at a later stage, though, does he or she become aware of their personal obligation to bring their sublime soul from potentiality to actualization, sometimes in full opposition to the demands of their environment. It is at that moment he or she comes to feel the "hero" of their life story, to form his or her identity themself according to that "essential I" he or she seeks. The moment is adolescence, and this may explain why a battle of such tremendous internal force takes place then.

2.

As we said, our concern is not with adolescence in general, abstract terms, but with the maturation of young girls. Is there a special maturation process characteristic to girls in particular?

I've described adolescence as a process in which people begin to form their identity, to take various social elements and imprint them with a personal stamp emerging from the deepest parts of the soul. The gender of the individual is one of the most decisive of those elements. Existence as a man or as a woman colors one's life with bold strokes, imposes a burden of tasks that may contradict one's inner sense ("Start acting like a man!" "Be a little more feminine!"), sets behavioral guidelines, and binds one to gender-specific rituals.

A maturing girl is acutely aware of her feminine genes bursting out of the hidden reaches of her body and giving it new form. She knows that new body is meant for certain roles that will accompany her throughout her life – as partner and as mother. That awareness fills her with excitement, but also with profound anxiety. Her soul is "a place of joy and trembling" (after Psalms 2:11).

In extreme cases, such as anorexia, worry can lead to a desperate attempt to restore the little girl's body she once had, devoid of sexual signs. But anxiety is most often mixed with happiness, expressed with moderation. At this age, girls tend to be preoccupied with their external appearance, fall into depression over pimples, daydream about their chances of finding the right person to marry. They compare themselves endlessly with one another, whisper and giggle as if they were party to some secret that can't be divulged – and in a sense, they're right!

Boys, at the very same time, become slightly drunk with the physical strength their bodies are gaining. They group together, too, but not in whispers. With rowdy shouts, they beat their chests like a band of chimpanzees.

At their root, these phenomena – sensed by boys and girls alike with ceaseless amazement – are catalyzed by intense physical changes beyond their control. We could compare them to someone on a thrilling, frightening roller coaster ride, soon to be thrown into cold water and begin swimming. Why shouldn't they shout?

Let's think a bit more about that water into which the young lady will imminently be tossed. Inarguably, femininity is more than a physical quality; it also includes a social element called "female status." The revolution in the status of women is perhaps the most profound of all the revolutions of the twentieth century. During that century, women won the right to vote and to be elected, and entered every profession formerly considered "male." Today, we take all this for granted, and find it difficult even to imagine it otherwise. What concerns us now is the final stage of the revolution: equality in salary and representation.

All this, though, is only the external aspect of the feminist revolution. In essence, it is a battle over identity. Women are tired of being a passive object in history run by men. To no lesser extent than men, women aspire to be author and heroine of their life story.

For adolescents this issue is highly relevant, especially for some of the stronger, more spiritually alert, high-quality girls. (I stress, for *some* of those girls. My intent is by no means to pass judgement on girls who live in peace with the traditional role.) Well aware of what's happening in the larger world, they reject the traditional social role given to women. Looking for challenges, like the boys, they set themselves goals once considered clearly "male." They demand the right to enter combat units in the army. Aspirations like these, of course, may lead to conflicts related to self-confidence, etc., but the same is surely true for boys.

3.

In all this, the position of Jewishly observant girls is unique. Here I'd like to quote two successful religious women in their recollections of their own adolescence:

> I was the first in my family to reach the age of taking on the *mitzvot*. They made a party for me and bought me pretty dresses. I got a lot of presents, and was quite happy… But when my brothers had their *bar mitzvahs*, they got an *aliyah* to the Torah, read the *Haftorah*, and their celebration was deeply and intrinsically connected to Torah. Mine wasn't. I knew I had reached a point of new responsibility toward the *mitzvot*, that I needed to actualize what I had learned and internalized. But I felt far from Torah. It wasn't my world. Torah didn't embrace me like it did the boys.[5]

> I still remember the deep humiliation I felt as a young girl at my first encounter with the generalizations voiced by *Hazal* [the Rabbis] on the nature of women – such as that women have feeble intellect [*da'atan kala*], or that they have no essential character…. How could my *Hazal*, whom I respected so much, talk about me in such insulting terms?[6]

Judaism in its present form, the result of a long tradition of *halakhic* rulings delegates a role for women that is marginal in the extreme. Daniel Shalit, a religious thinker, summarizes a list of encouraging and positive things the Rabbis said about women and comments:

These words of affection and respect still cannot, in and of themselves, enable the woman to establish her identity securely, because in the society in question, the man is the predominant, active one. He, moreover, is "The Person" (*ha-Adam*), while the woman looks like a person of a secondary sort.[7]

---

[5] B. Sheleg, "*Mitzvah she-hazman grama,*" *Nekudah*, Adar 1999.

[6] T. Ross, "*Hashlakhot ha-feminism al teologia yehudit orthodoxit,*" *Deot*, Nissan 5758.

[7] D. Shalit, *Ohr shivat ha-yamim*, 1999, p. 23.

Where, then, should the developing woman look to find her identity? This question would be justified if religious education were the only source on which she draws. This, though, is not and cannot be the reality. Our young girls read many different books, newspapers and magazines, meet up with a variety of people (or their friends do), watch television. Anyone who talks with them becomes aware of the extent to which they have internalized the right to their own opinions. They feel free to get angry at the "demeaning expressions" (like those mentioned above by Tamar Ross) they read in rabbinical writings and biblical commentaries. Not all of them, of course. A few just ignore such expressions. Others get into a real conflict: with humility and awe, they stand before the tremendous world of Jewish spirituality, and yet they cannot accept the marginal role in it that is assigned to them. Their entire being rebels.

The problem, it seems, gets worse and worse. If the Jewish world, or at least the widespread religious worldview, is unable to give the girl the spiritual foundations for a stable and supportive identity, she will be forced to seek them outside of it. Such a conclusion, needless to say, is very troublesome for religious education. Could it be possible, after all, to find Jewish sources that could help adolescent girls to weave the story of their lives?

4.

Mystical teaching may suggest a direction. The Kabbalists developed the concepts of "masculine" and "feminine" comprehensively and profoundly, and recognized them as metaphysical entities. The manifold permutations arising from them can serve to explain a wide range of phenomena in reality. R. Moshe Hayyim Luzzatto (Ramhal) writes:

> Masculine and feminine – they are the root source of the world's entire being and the essence of existence, and their *tikkunim* are in accordance with what is necessary for the world's continued existence.[8]

---

[8] R. Moshe Hayyim Luzzatto, *Kelah pituhei hokhmah* (Tel Aviv, 5752), sec. 116.

The masculine, in mystical thought, is the active, spiritual, creative, restoring element. The feminine is the passive, physical element, which awaits restoration.[9] As Ramhal explains, the feminine is "the mystery of *malkhut*," the passive entity ready to be "repaired" by the active masculine entity. Here, though, we discover one of the most amazing reversals in kabbalistic teaching. The masculine, precisely because of its active and creative nature, is also more likely to destroy and ruin. It is the feminine, ostensibly passive, that remains pure despite all of life's complications, pure in its hope for future redemption. This reversal is most cogently expressed in hasidic "psychological" teaching. There, the feminine dimension of *malkhut* becomes the innermost point that remains forever loyal in her longing for God, the source of all the hopes for spiritual renewal. R. Isaac of Komarna, for example, describes a series of *tzaddikim* from the prophet Jeremiah to R. Levi Yitzhak of Berditchev who envisioned the *Shekhinah* in the form of a woman. He explains the spiritual meaning of that vision:

> This means that all Jews have a pure point of Jewishness that cannot be harmed, and for it they sacrifice themselves with all their hearts for the sake of His Great Name....[10]

He continues, describing the ploys of the "evil inclination," about whose purpose is to "darken the heart, plotting against the foundation of life rooted in the feminine element (*nukba*)...." That pure point is the feminine component of the soul.

Through this perspective, Rav Kook can offer the following interpretation of the blessing, "...for not making me a woman." It is an expression of thanks offered by men for their creative power: "What great happiness and expanse there is in that good portion, in the soul's belonging to an active, creative, renewing, and broadening man."[11] Later, in discussing the blessing said by women, "...who made me according to His will," he suggests the problem inherent in that masculine creativity.

---

[9] "The material aspect of the created entities emerges from the *gevurot* in the feminine element." (*Kelah pituhei hokhmah*, sec. 115.)

[10] Cf. R. Yitzhak Isaac of Komarna, *Netiv Mitzvotekhah*, 1982, 86.

[11] R. Avraham Yitzhak Hacohen Kook, *Olat Re'ayah*, Jerusalem, 1963.

It may, at times, turn away from the highest divine intentions…. The same, however, is not true of the activated [as opposed to activating] quality of the woman…which is directed to His absolute and perfect will. Thus, the woman's blessing is a prayer of thanks for her good portion, "who made me as He willed."

Building on this interpretation, his son, R. Tzvi Yehudah Kook also related to the woman's blessing "*she-asani kirtzono*" in an essay that appeared in a Hebrew collection on women and education, published about one generation ago.

> It sounds discriminating, but really it isn't. "As He willed" – according to divine Will – this is a tremendous thing, with profound meaning: greater closeness to God. The male was created from the dust of the earth, and only after that was a divine soul breathed into him. But the material from which the female was formed was not crude earth; rather, she was taken from the body of the male already invested with a vital, divine soul…. (Thus) the woman may respond in strong recognition of her worth "Who made me as He willed" – according to His own wish – a special creation….[12]

The male's beginnings are in the raw earth, and thus he must create himself. The woman, on the other hand, is a divine creation, her essence imprinted with the *Shekhinah*, and this makes her less needful of the yoke of *mitzvot*. She is already a completed creation, of the "spiritual aristocracy," as R. Kook says, and does not need such an energetic "repair" [*tikkun*].

Experienced educators, though, can testify that these ideas don't touch the hearts of many of our girls, whose greatest desire is, in fact, to create themselves by themselves, to be the protagonist of their life stories. Even the deepest and most beautiful explanation of why they are absolved from that sort of self-creation fails to convince them.

In practice, women are conquering one field after another in religious life. Girls (again, many of the more spiritually developed among them) are

---

[12] R. Tzvi Yehudah Kook, "*Koha shel ha-ishah be-seder ha-min ha-enoshi,*" ed. B.T. Rosenfeld, *Ha-ishah ve-hinukhah,* 1980, p. 57.

not far behind them. They learn *Gemara*, dream about a career as rabbinical advocates, express views on important issues in Jewish thought, and often consolidate impressively creative and perceptive ideas. This process – like any other maturation process – cannot be arrested (except at the expense of the heavy psychic damage). It can, however, be influenced through honest dialogue. Could such a dialogue be based on essential Jewish texts?

5.

Erikson writes:

> The special dangers of the nuclear age clearly have brought male leadership close to the limit of its adaptive imagination. The dominant male identity is based on a fondness for "what works" and for what man can make, whether it helps to build or to destroy…. Maybe if women would only gain the determination to represent publicly what they have always stood for privately in evolution and in history (realism in housholding, responsibility of upbringing, resourcefulness in peacekeeping and devotion to healing), they might well add an ethically restraining, because truly supranational, power to politics in the widest sense.[13]

Erikson, although male, senses that the culture of the present, founded on masculine principles, has reached its end. He appeals to women to exert their influence. What we have here is not a *concession* to women's entering the male domain, but an *appeal*, requesting that they change that domain.

It seems to me that profound Torah ideas, like those of R. Tzvi Yehudah Kook mentioned above, could enhance this appeal to an unprecedented extent. Our tormented world so sorely lacks the revelation of the *Shekhinah*, the "eternal Feminine" that Zeitlin describes as the source of all "beauty, delicacy, softness, love, mercy, modesty, endless longing, ceaseless yearning of the soul."[14] Maybe the penetration of women into various cultural realms will come to be seen as the beginning of a deep and vital cultural change bound to enrich our existence with the unique contribution women alone can make.

---

[13] *Identity, Adolescence and Crisis*, pp. 261-262.

[14] Hillel Zeitlin, *Al gevul shnei olamot* (Yavne: Tel Aviv, 1976), p. 114.

Such a contribution, though, like any other creation, cannot emerge from treading the same old paths, or even from a path made by the most respected authorities. Creativity, by nature, must be free; it must flow from the depths of the artist's soul and not from passive reception of others' words. Every authentic creator has a personal voice. The major role of the artist's mentor is to heed that voice.

Daniel Shalit adds: "The inner meaning of the developments of our days seems to be that both genders are preparing for an ultimate integration. In that integration, each gender comes to contain some of the qualities of the other while maintaining its own root open toward the Creator…."[15]

We stand at the threshold of a culture that will be neither "masculine" nor "feminine;" rather, it will be founded on a balance between two autonomous and equal essences. Note well: these two essences will have already completed a developmental process, and will be able to contain one another. In other words, instead of stereotypical "men" facing stereotypical "women" there will be complex human beings, each of them comprised of a masculine and a feminine side existing in a harmonious balance. This sort of men and women know how to listen to one another, and how to internalize one another's uniqueness.

Here we could add the wisdom known to mystics. They teach that when the final redemption comes, the *Shekhinah* will rise from the dust and stand face to face, equal in stature, before the Holy One, blessed be He.

Thus in the last two of the seven blessings of the marriage ceremony, the first says: "Who gladdens groom and bride," while the second says: "Who gladdens the groom with the bride." For now, the bride receives from the groom, signified by [the first blessing] "Who gladdens *groom and bride*." In the time to come, though, they will be of equal stature, sharing a single crown as they did before [her] diminishment; thus, "Who gladdens the *groom with the bride*." It is also said: "The voice of the groom and the voice of the bride will be heard…." (Jeremiah 33:11), for in the future the bride, too, will have a voice….[16]

---

[15] *Or shivat ha-yamim*, p. 70.

[16] R. Shneur Zalman of Liady ["the Alter Rebbe," founder of Habad Hasidism], *Likkutei Torah* (Kehat: Brooklyn, 1987) *Shir Hashirim* 48b.

R. Nahman of Bratslav, similarly, writes: "From the stories women tell, we can know of the state of the *Shekhinah*, where she is holding right now...."[17]

Perhaps these words can offer a key to understanding the deeper historical meaning of the feminine "search for identity" we are witnessing. The future the Alter Rebbe envisions is already knocking at our door. Women demand a voice of their own. Such an understanding does not enclose the definition of feminine identity now awakening. On the contrary, it impels us to listen to that emerging voice. That, after all, is the nature of listening: we can't know ahead of time what we will hear.

Handling a process of this kind must also include a dialogue with the feminine identity awakening in our maturing daughters, despite all the roughness and immaturity which it appears, for indeed, every maturation process entails elements that have not yet ripened.

6.

How is it done? "Let us call the maiden, and ask her" (Genesis 24:57).

The process we have described is, essentially, the emergence of a profound longing for identity. It is a declaration, voiced by a whole spiritual world, of independence. Giving over old-fashioned pedagogical lessons has no place here. What we need is a continuous dialogue (one that may include things that are hard to hear, like statements by Bambi Sheleg and Tamar Ross cited above).

We must be attentive – to the full extent *halakhah* allows us – to girls' spiritual aspirations. More than that, we must listen to them, learn from them, leave the stance of "knowing all" that sometimes cages us.

Maybe, as a first small step, we can think along with them about the *bat mitzvah* celebration – it shouldn't be marginal and unimportant, but neither should it turn into a mere imitation of boys' *bar mitzvah* celebrations; thinking together, with humility and mutual respect.

Perhaps that's the first thing we need to learn.

---

[17] R. Nahman of Bratslav, *Likkutei Moharan* (Jerusalem, 1980) 1.203.

I. MARKING THE DAY AND

CELEBRATING THE OCCASION

Celebrating the *Bat Mitzvah*

COMMUNITY-DESIGNED *BAT MITZVAH* CELEBRATIONS[#]

RABBI BENNY LAU

We are fortunate to live in an era of religious awakening among Jewish women. This awakening, which comes from different directions, demands that each and every one of us give our utmost attention to the summons to active involvement in serving God, and in confronting that demand. This renaissance has met with considerable suspicion on the part of the Orthodox community and the religious establishment, for neither can be sure whether the phenomenon reflects a genuine evolution to a higher stage of Divine service, or whether it is merely the product of a battle of the sexes.[1] One subcategory of this far-reaching issue is the *bat mitzvah* celebration. In recent years, many girls (and their parents) in various communities throughout the Orthodox world have expressed the desire to infuse their *bat mitzvah* celebrations with religious content. They are no longer content with a mere party or festive dinner. They wish to link themselves with the world of the synagogue – the world of prayer and Torah reading.

Two essays discussing this subject have recently been published in Hebrew. One, by Dr. Benny Gesundheit, is "The *Bat mitzvah* Celebration";[2] the second, by Rabbi Daniel Touito, is "The *Bat mitzvah* Celebration - A

---

* translated by Dov Lapin

[#] This essay combines a critical review of previous discussions of the subject with a description of my own involvement with it in the Kibbutz Sa'ad community, where I served as Rabbi. I would like to thank my wife Noa for her remarks and editorial comments.

[1] See, for example, R. Yuval Cherlow's article, "On the Distinction Between Reform and Religious Revival" (Heb.), *Akdamut*, 7 (5759), pp. 101ff., and my response to his article in *Akdamut*, 8 (5760).

[2] On the internet: www.daat.ac.il.

study of rulings by contemporary *halakhic* authorities."[3] Each of them cites the meager available *halakhic* material on the subject. I would like to review the respective conclusions reached by the authors of these essays, and ascertain what we may learn from them with regard to the community *bat mitzvah* ceremony.

A. The *Mitzvah* in the *Bat Mitzvah* Festive Meal

One of the earliest controversies over *bat mitzvah* concerns the definition of a girl's celebration as a *simhah shel mitzvah*, the "celebration (literally, joy) of performing a *mitzvah*." The opponents of the *bat mitzvah* celebration argued that the occasion is characterized by no religious significance whatsoever.

The chief spokesman for this position is the late R. Moshe Feinstein *z"l* (of blessed memory). In his first *responsum* on this issue, R. Feinstein formulated the fundamental position that strips the celebration of any religious significance. On close reading of this *responsum* we see that R. Feinstein is troubled most of all by *bat mitzvah* celebrations held in the synagogue:[4]

> A synagogue, even one that was built conditionally,[5] is not a place for the celebration of non-essential occasions. Since the *bat mitzvah* ceremony is certainly a manner of *reshut* [an optional, as opposed to compulsory act] and entirely insignificant [from a *halakhic* point of view], there are therefore no grounds to permit its taking place in the synagogue.... This is especially the case given that the source of the practice comes from Conservative and Reform Jews. If the girl's father chooses to make a party at home, he may do so, but that is insufficient basis or grounds to consider the *bat mitzvah* an actual *mitzvah* or *seudat mitzvah*. It is no different than an ordinary birthday party.... To refrain from this practice altogether would really be preferable, although no law prohibits it.

---

[3] Originally published in an anthology by the students of the Amiel Institute for Training Teachers for the Diaspora.

[4] R. Moshe Feinstein, *Responsa Iggerot Moshe, Oreh Hayyim* 1:104.

[5] I.e., with the clear intention that it would be used for other purposes as well (trans.).

Such a celebration, however, cannot be made in a synagogue, even at night, when no prayers are held.

R. Feinstein's argument that the *bat mitzvah* celebration is not a *mitzvah* but rather "optional and insignificant" is not at all easy to accept. In practice, the **bar** *mitzvah* has indeed been recognized by many authorities – Ashkenazi as well as Sephardi – as a *seudat mitzvah*. And if the *bar mitzvah* is a *seudat mitzvah*, common sense would dictate that there is no difference between boys' and girls' celebrations (of attaining the obligation of *mitzvot*). Indeed, many authorities have disagreed with R. Feinstein. For instance, R. Ovadia Yosef writes:[6]

> It seems that it is certainly a *mitzvah* to prepare a meal and a celebration for a *bat mitzvah*. This is consistent with the ruling of Maharshal [R. Shlomo Luria, 1510–1573] in his work, *Yam Shel Shelomo* (*Bava Kama*, 7:37). He wrote, "There is no greater *seudat mitzvah* than the *bar mitzvah* meal, in which we thank and praise the Holy One, who granted this young man the good fortune to become *bar mitzvah*. Indeed, 'those who are commanded and who perform [*mitzvot*] are greater than those who are not commanded and do so.'"[7]
>
> Similarly, the *bat mitzvah* day, on which a girl becomes obligated by all those commandments concerning women and enters the category of "one who is commanded and performs" should certainly be considered a day of rejoicing. There is an element of *mitzvah* as well.

---

[6] R. Ovadiah Yosef, *Responsa Yabia Omer*, 6 (*Oreh Hayyim*), 29.

[7] This ruling by Maharshal has often been cited as a source for the *mitzvah* in the *bar mitzvah* celebration. See, for example, *Noda beYehuda* in his commentary *Dagul MeRevava*, *Yoreh De'ah*, 391 (cited by *Pit'hei Teshuvah ad loc.*); R. Yair Bakhrakh, *Responsa Havvot Ya'ir*, 70 (in which he reviews the criteria for defining a celebration as a *seudat mitzvah*); *Mishnah Berurah*, *Oreh Hayyim*, 225:6, and others. The implication of this last statement, found in *Kiddushin 32b*, according to Rashi, is that one who performs a commandment simply because he or she is required to do so (regardless of whether that individual actually wants to) is performing a more significant act of piety, and is therefore greater than one who does so out of choice.

Indeed, I saw that Ben Ish Hai [R. Yosef Hayyim ben Eliyahu, Baghdad, 1835-1909] *Parashat Re'eh,* 17, wrote, "Although it is not customary to hold a feast on the day on which a girl attains the age of obligation, she should nevertheless rejoice on that day, and wear her Shabbat garments. If she has the means, she should put on a new garment and recite the *shehehiyanu* blessing, bearing in mind that her blessing is for the joy of becoming obligated to perform *mitzvot* as well."

While Ben Ish Hai indeed wrote that (in his time) it was not the custom to prepare a feast for a *bat mitzvah,* those who do so in our time are to be commended. Ben Ish Hai's own words, moreover, suggest that when a special feast was not made in honor of a *bat mitzvah,* that was simply in deference to the prevailing custom.

I saw a similar opinion expressed by my dear friend, R. Ovadiah Hedaya, in his *responsum Yaskil 'Avdi* (sec. 28). He infers from Ben Ish Hai's words that a feast should indeed be held in honor of a girl's attainment of the age of obligation, but that the custom was simply not practiced in his community. R. Hedaya therefore concludes that in communities in which *bar mitzvah* celebrations are indeed practiced, it is certainly a desirable and commendable custom to celebrate a *bat mitzvah.* Just as a feast and celebration are held in honor of a boy who undertakes the obligation of commandments, the same should equally apply to girls undertaking that obligation, and for the same reason.

R. Feinstein himself was aware of the difficulty his statements raised. In a subsequent *responsum,* he reiterated and defended the position that, despite *Yam Shel Shelomo*'s ruling, a girl's celebration of her attainment of *mitzvah* age cannot be considered celebration of a *mitzvah*:[8]

There is no discernible difference in practice between a girl who is a minor and the same girl when she matures, unlike the case of a boy, in which the change is highly evident. From that day onward,

---

[8] R. Moshe Feinstein, *Responsa Iggerot Moshe, Oreh Hayyim,* 2, 97 (5719).

he may participate in public observation of any *mitzvah* requiring [a quorum of] three or ten men. We do not hold feasts and celebrations for mere awareness, although, in fact, [the girl] experiences essentially the same joy [as the boy].

It seems to me that the origin and evolution of R. Feinstein's objection to granting religious significance to the *bat mitzvah* stem from the perceived connection between celebrating a *bat mitzvah* and attending a synagogue without segregation between men and women. The fear of emulating the Reform movement prompted R. Feinstein and other rabbinic opponents of the *bat mitzvah* celebration as well, to divest the occasion of any religious significance. It is noteworthy that, in actual fact, all Jewish communities, with the exception of the most extreme ultra-Orthodox groups, indeed celebrate the *bat mitzvah* of their daughters in one form or another, by holding a festive meal at home or at a banquet hall.

In his discussion, Gesundheit shows that a progressive development has taken place in rabbinic attitudes toward this celebration. This ranges from regarding the *bat mitzvah* celebration as an absolute biblical prohibition (*issur de'orayeta*) (a position taken by R. Wolkin, author of *Zakan Aharon*), to deeming the celebration "insignificant" (R. Feinstein), to considering it ultimately "an admirable and worthy custom" (R. Ovadiah Yosef). The original indignation directed to offenders was mitigated and gradually replaced with concerns over girls' education. Today, hard-line positions that prohibit any celebration whatsoever of the *bat mitzvah* day are virtually unheard of. It is in cases such as these that the Rabbis instructed *halakhic* authorities to "Go out and see what the people do" in determining appropriate practice. And what we see is that the Orthodox community, which does not take *halakhah* lightly, does indeed make *bat mitzvah* celebrations!

In effect, in purely *halakhic* terms, the argument over whether a *bat mitzvah* celebration may or may not be considered a *seudat mitzvah* (a feast celebrating a *mitzvah*) really boils down to a minute and tangential point of law. What is the *halakhic* significance of whether or not a party is called a *seudat mitzvah*?

For R. M. Feinstein's position, the question is indeed invested with genuine *halakhic* significance, since he discusses *bat mitzvah* celebrations held *in the synagogue*. His means of distancing *bat mitzvah* celebrations from the synagogue is by stripping those events of any *mitzvah*-related elements. If the celebration is not held in the synagogue, though, the question of its *halakhic* significance becomes immaterial. The following *responsum*, fascinating as well as entertaining, written in Baghdad at the beginning of the twentieth century, shows just how trivial the debate really is. Although the *responsum* addresses the *bar mitzvah* celebration for boys, it applies equally to the subject at hand:[9]

A learned and wealthy man fulfilled the obligation of *pidyon haben* (redemption of the first-born son). He celebrated the occasion with a feast and invited Torah scholars to celebrate with him. They sat at the table joyful and content. And, since Torah scholars customarily discuss Torah matters, the wealthy host raised the issue of *seudat mitzvah* with some of the scholars seated near him. What constitutes a *seudat mitzvah*? They disputed whether a *bar mitzvah* feast held at the onset of a boy's fourteenth year or a housewarming party (*hanukkat habayit*) constitutes a *seudat mitzvah*. Each camp cited proofs supporting its position.

A second group of scholars seated at the rich man's table was engaged in discussion as well, but on a different topic. The wealthy host said to those scholars: "We too are discussing Torah! Why don't you join our conversation and share some new idea on the subject with us? After all, we are the larger group and you are the smaller; you should follow our lead!" One of the scholars of the second group said to him, "The subject we are debating is far greater and more fundamental than yours. The practical ramifications of the discussion of *seudat mitzvah* in general, and what constitutes *seudat mitzvah* apply solely to a minor [prohibition], virtually a voluntary act of piety. The sole *halakhic* outcome of your discussion can be that such a celebration [i.e., a *bar mitzvah* or housewarming] is considered either a *seudat mitzvah* or a *seudat reshut*

---

[9] *Responsa Torah Lishma*, 482. This collection of *responsa* is attributed to R. Yosef Hayyim, the author of *Ben Ish Hai*. Many of the *responsa* (including this one), however, were written by R. Yehezkel Kahali of Baghdad.

[an optional celebratory meal]. What bearing does that have on severe prohibitions? We, on the other hand, are deliberating the *halakhot* on a subject with critical ramifications – it concerns a severe prohibition that carries the death penalty. It would not be right to abandon our discussion and join yours!"

The host was truly ashamed at being vanquished by that scholar. He said to these seated near him, "Is there no similarly grave consequence for the matter we are discussing, relating it to a severe biblical prohibition? After all, everything in the Torah is interconnected! I would be overjoyed – and would give a donation to the yeshivah scholars as well – if one of you could discover some influence our subject bears on a severe biblical prohibition." But the scholars were unable to discover anything of that nature. Thus, we turn to your honor with the question whether some ramification of this matter can indeed be found linking it to a severe biblical prohibition. Please instruct us and may reward come from Heaven!"

The response: It is indeed possible.

One instance would be a case in which a man betrothed a woman by saying to her, "You will be consecrated to me on the condition that you eat a *seudat mitzvah* with me today." The woman then ate with him at a *siyyum* [a celebration on completion of a volume or tractate of the *Mishna* or Talmud], a housewarming party, a *bar mitzvah*, or the like. The scholars set to debating whether or not such celebrations are considered *seudot mitzvah*. If they are indeed *seudot mitzvot*, the woman is now unquestionably betrothed to him, as the condition has been fulfilled. If a second man then consecrates her, the second betrothal would be invalid. Furthermore, if she has [illicit] sexual relations with any man other than the first, both he and she would be subject to the death penalty. On the other hand, if the feast is not considered a *seudat mitzvah*, she would not betrothed [to the first man]; if the second man consecrates her, then, she would be betrothed to the second man, and would be permitted to him alone. In that case, if the first man would have relations with her, he would be guilty [of adultery with a married woman]. The practical outcome is therefore of dire consequence regarding a severe biblical prohibition, i.e., the prohibition of adultery – a capital offense punishable by death.

Even those who maintain that a *bar mitzvah* ceremony is not considered a *seudat mitzvah* do not argue that it is a sin to have one. It takes a virtuoso like the author of this *responsum* to find a *halakhic* consequence related to a severe prohibition.

B. "Your forefathers never imagined" an innovation like this *bar mitzvah*

Many of the detractors of the celebration of *bat mitzvah* found their opposition on the grounds that the *bat mitzvah* is a new, modern custom that never before existed. R. Eliezer Waldenberg collected most of these opinions in his prefatory endorsement of R. A. Zakai's Hebrew book, *A Bat Mitzvah Present*. R. Waldenberg remarks to the author – who cites all the positions in favor of the celebration:[10]

"It is inconceivable that such a significant and popular book would make no mention of the other side of the coin, i.e., the opponents – one camp against the other."

R. Waldenberg then presents a list of those authorities in opposition to the *bat mitzvah* celebration.[11] The common denominator shared by all these *responsa* is the argument that our forefathers had never heard of celebrations for *bat mitzvah* girls.

R. Weinberg, however, took issue with R. Waldenberg's conclusion:[12]

There are those who argue against the *bat mitzvah* celebration, because it goes against the tradition of generations past, who did not observe this custom. But this is not really a valid argument. In previous generations, girls' education was not an issue, because all

---

[10] R. Eliezer Waldenberg, *Tzitz Eliezer*, vol. 3:33.

[11] Cited by R. Touito; see note 3.

[12] R. I. Weinberg, *Responsa Seride Esh*, vol. 3, 93. R. Ovadia Yosef, in his *responsa Yehavve Da'at*, vol. 2, 29, cited R. Weinberg's words in full with the author's consent

Jews were God-fearing and imbued with Torah. The very air in every Jewish town was suffused with the spice and spirit of Judaism. Girls brought up in Jewish homes absorbed Jewish values effortlessly; they virtually suckled Judaism with their mothers' milk.

Today, however, times have changed drastically. The influences of the street threaten to extinguish the last spark of Judaism in the hearts of Jewish boys and girls. The girls attend Christian or secular schools, where the objective is not to imbue pupils with love of the Torah of Israel and the sacred customs and practices of authentic Judaism.

Today, all our resources must be focussed on girls' education. It is indeed tragic that, in general studies – languages, secular literature, science, and humanities – girls are educated the same as boys, while their religious education – the study of Bible, rabbinical ethical literature and education toward the practical *mitzvot*, required of Jewish women – is completely neglected. Thankfully, the great Torah sages of the previous generation were aware of this injustice and built up institutions for Torah and religious instruction for Jewish girls. The establishment of the comprehensive school system of *Beit Yaakov* has been our generation's most impressive statement. Common sense and pedagogic imperatives, then, would nearly compel us to celebrate a girl's attaining the age of obligation of *mitzvot* just as we celebrate a boy's. The discrimination that is made between boys and girls in celebrating coming-of-age ceremonies is highly offensive to the basic human sensitivities of young Jewish women, who, in other areas of life, have already been granted "emancipation," as it were.

Needless to say, R. Weinberg's view is closely linked to the reality in which he lived: in confrontation with modernity and the process of assimilation of the Jewish community (women included) with the gentile surroundings.

C. Celebration in the Synagogue Versus *Seudat Mitzvah*

At the end of his essay, R. Touito writes:[13]

> My study of the positions of the various rabbinic authorities led
> me to note, among other things, the following phenomenon. The
> position maintained by the various Sephardic Chief Rabbis of this
> century in their rulings has consistently been the most innovative –
> in terms of its leniency, in terms of its broad public perspective,
> and in terms of invoking public policy considerations in their
> rabbinical rulings. This stance befits sages who publish rulings for
> the nation dwelling in Zion.

Although R. Touito's statement does reflect a genuine trend that has
become evident in recent years, *i.e.*, the emergence of Sephardic and
Oriental rabbinic authorities as more innovative than their Ashkenazic
counterparts,[14] I do not believe that it holds true in this specific case.

Ashkenazic authorities dealt with this issue differently than the
Sephardic authorities simply because they lived in different social realities.
A close scrutiny of R. Feinstein's *responsa* shows that the point evoking his
greatest objection is the celebration *in the synagogue*.

In his earlier *responsum*, R. Feinstein specifies: "There are no grounds to
permit holding it in the synagogue... If the girl's father chooses to make a
party at home, he may do so...."[15] In a later *responsum*, R. Feinstein also
considers the issue of the synagogue. A question addressed him by a R.
Meir Kahane implicitly states that in his community, it was customary for
the *bat mitzvah* girl to deliver a speech from the *bimah* (podium) during the
service. R. Feinstein states his vehement opposition to this practice. The
only thing he found grounds to permit was having a *kiddush* after the
service, as is done on every joyous occasion; during the course of it the *bat
mitzvah* girl could say a few words in honor of her celebration.

---

[13] C.f., note 3 above.

[14] See, in particular, the extensive and important research done by Tzvi Zohar.

[15] R. Moshe Feinstein, *Responsa Iggerot Moshe, Oreh Hayyim*, 1:104, 5715.

In his question R. Kahane raised the possibility that forbidding the *derashah* in the synagogue might be harmful, while permitting it might be beneficial. R. Feinstein responded:[16]

> As for the benefit his honor suggests – the practice, on the contrary, would actually be detrimental, as it would encourage the violation of Shabbat and other things. In effect, even in the case of boys, the benefit [of the *derashah* given in the synagogue] in bringing them closer to Torah and *mitzvot* has not been proven. Even if his honor can point to a positive effect for some outstanding young lady, in the vast majority of cases it would be harmful. Thus, the modern custom of *bat mitzvah* celebrations should be discouraged rather than embraced – without conflict, however....

Unlike the above *responsa*, which deal primarily with *bat mitzvah* celebrations in the vicinity of the synagogue, the *responsa* written by Sephardic and North African authorities focus on *bat mitzvah* celebrations held at home or at banquet halls. It seems to me that this difference stems from a different reality: these authorities were not forced to contend with the influence of Reform or Conservative synagogues. Their sole interest was to deal positively with the girl and her family as she reached the milestone of accepting the *mitzvot*. The *bat mitzvah* is indeed a *seudat mitzvah*, and there is no reason to be hampered by unnecessary concerns. I would even risk saying that had authorities like Ben Ish Hai, R. Hedaya, and R. Yosef known that *bat mitzvah* celebrations could undermine synagogue practice, they would have not have been among its proponents.

If there is a *responsum* worthy to be called "innovative" and "liberal" as R. Touito does in his essay, it is the *responsum* by R. Weinberg cited above, who encouraged *bat mitzvah* celebrations *a priori* in understanding of contemporary needs.

It should be noted, however, that R. Weinberg himself was well aware of those movements that attempted to undermine traditional synagogue

---

[16] R. Moshe Feinstein, *Responsa Iggerot Moshe, Oreh Hayyim*, 4: 96.

practice; he thus expressed his reservations regarding actual celebration of the *bat mitzvah* in the synagogue:[17]

> Although my own tendency is to permit *bat mitzvah* celebrations, I agree with the *gaon* R. Feinstein's position articulated in his book *Iggerot Moshe* (*Oreh Hayyim*), that the *bat mitzvah* should not be celebrated in the synagogue, even at night, when no one is present. Rather, the celebration should be held in a private home or in a hall adjacent to the synagogue. Moreover, the rabbi [of the community] should publicly address some moving words to the girl coming of age, admonishing her to observe, from that day forward, the fundamental commandments concerning her relationship with God (i.e., *kashrut*, Shabbat, family purity). He should stress the importance of raising and educating her children, and her responsibility to encourage and support her husband's Torah learning and observance of *mitzvot;* he should remind her to seek a husband who is scholarly and God-fearing.

R. Weinberg's statement clearly articulates his concerns over attempts to undermine traditional synagogue practice and the dissolution of gender distinctions.

Life in close contact with Western society, with its tendency to imitate the Christian world and church practices, is clearly what arouses constraints and suspicions such as these. Rabbinical authorities without direct experience of Western culture did not share the same concerns at all.

D. Back to the Synagogue

As we have said, the practice to hold some form of *bat mitzvah* ceremony has been accepted by most Orthodox Jewish communities today. Even the ultra-Orthodox sector holds some kind of celebration, each community in keeping with its own character and style.

---

[17] R. I. Weinberg, *Seride Esh, ibid.*

In that sense, those sources that document a dispute belong to a bygone reality; they no longer reflect contemporary practice. Even so, a close reading of the contentions voiced by the rabbis who supported *bat mitzvah* celebrations may aid us in responding adequately to girls who express the wish to have their *bat mitzvah* celebration in the synagogue.

One of R. Weinberg's arguments, cited above, in favor of the *bat mitzvah* celebration was: "Common sense and pedagogic imperatives would nearly compel us to celebrate a girl's attaining the age of obligation of *mitzvot* just as we celebrate a boy's. The discrimination between boys and girls in celebrating coming-of-age ceremonies is highly offensive to the basic human sensitivities of young Jewish women."[18] R. Ovadia Hedaya voices the same argument:[19]

> The intent involved is clearly to grant equal rights. Since it is customary to make a celebration in honor of a *bar mitzvah*, a similar celebration was instituted in honor of a *bat mitzvah*, in order to prevent jealousy between sons and daughters.

R. Ovadia Yosef could be cited as well; he expands on Rabbi Weinberg's ruling:[20]

> To prevent *bat mitzvah* girls from holding celebrations serves to encourage people with evil intent to accuse the sages of Israel of ostensibly committing an injustice to Jewish women and discriminating between boys and girls.

All of these figures took into account the change in the social status of women in the world at large, and in the Jewish community as well. While thirty years ago, it was the *bat mitzvah* celebratory meal that was seen as an

---

[18] R. Weinberg, *Seride Esh* 3: 93.

[19] R. Ovadia Hedaya, *responsa Yaskil 'Avdi*, vol. 6. R. Touito, in his essay cited in note 3, understands from R. Hedaya's words, "not to arouse jealousy between sons and daughters," that the author considers the desire to grant "equal rights" a positive attitude.

[20] R. Ovadia Yosef, *Responsa Yabi'a 'Omer*, 2:29.

innovation generating heated controversy, today the dispute concerns the synagogue. Citing the same arguments that were proposed to allow *bat mitzvah* celebrations in the first place, Jewish families now seek something beyond the material experience of a dinner and a party. They wish to experience – together – the spiritual experience of their daughters' entrance into the world of Torah and the synagogue.

This gives rise to variety of requests: some girls wish to give a speech (*derashah*) in the synagogue; others would like to be called up to the Torah in a women's prayer group; still others want to read the *haftarah* (without its blessings), and so forth.

In many cases, the family approaches the community rabbi to check the compatibility of these requests with practical *halakhah*. The phenomenon should not be seen as an attempt to undermine or ignore the *halakhah* (although such attempts are not unheard of). Rather, it reflects a desire to initiate a dialogue between the community and its rabbi in the hope that the *halakhah* has the means enabling it to respond favorably to some of the demands.

1. Refraining from Conflict and Offense to Public Sensibilities

In his consideration of the struggle of the "Women of the Western Wall" Justice Menachem Elon wrote:"[21]

> It is an indisputable fact that the vast majority of those who pray at the Western Wall day and night belong to the camp that genuinely and sincerely believes that changes such as those demanded in the two petitions before us are a desecration of the prayer area adjacent to the Western Wall…. The prayer area before the Western Wall should not be the battleground for a "war" of acts and opinions regarding this issue…. To hold the requested prayer service would be extremely injurious to the sensitivities of the vast majority of worshippers regarding that location."

---

[21] Cited in Dr. Eliav Shochetman's Hebrew essay "More on the Questions of Women's *Minyanim*," *Tehumin* 17 (5757), p. 174.

The statement holds true not only for the Western Wall. They apply to each and every community and each and every synagogue. A community that is still unready – educationally as well as socially – to accept the active participation of women in its communal prayers may find itself embroiled in debates so fierce that they threaten to break the community apart. The process of the genuine involvement of women in worship should begin on the educational/informative plane. The community – men and women – must undergo a gradual process of accepting advancements in the status of women in religious life. It is no secret that in most Orthodox communities, such an awakening has just not occurred. Several months ago, I was invited to be a Shabbat guest at a settlement community, whose members are considered "Modern Orthodox." The women of that community are involved in all levels of community life – social, financial, and political. During one of my talks, I was "attacked" on the subject of women's status in Jewish law. In response, I pointed out to the community members the architecture of their own synagogue, and to the area they had reserved in it for the women's section. The layout of the synagogue proclaimed loud and clear that the community's women had no interest in integration in syna- gogue life – not during Shabbat services and certainly not at weekday prayers. Clearly, then, no one in that community is pressing the rabbi to respond to the needs of *bat mitzvah* girls in being integrated in serving God through prayer. The families are content to celebrate their daughters' *bat mitzvah* in the usual fashion. Indeed, in most communities, very few women feel the kind of distress that prompts them to approach the community rabbi requesting or demanding an improvement in their situation and status. To the women who do, I can only say, "Do not awaken or rouse love until the time is right"! (Song of Songs, 2:7, 3:5).

2. Rabbinic Rulings in Keeping With the Nature of the Community

Jewish communities in various places in Israel and the world over have experienced the process of internalizing the right of women to participate actively in serving God. In this respect as well, no two communities are alike. In some places the primary awakening has been with regard to Torah study. Other communities are more advanced in the realms of prayer. The developments in each community correspond with the nature of its membership. R. Yehuda Herzl Henkin, in this context, wrote:[22]

> I cannot write a ruling permitting women's prayer groups, as it is impossible to rule from a distance; one must get to know the people involved.
>
> In the context of the current religious awakening among women, then, it is very important for the rabbi to have personal contact with the community's decision-making process, and to be closely involved with the members themselves.[23]

E. Torah Reading by Women for Women

The key *halakhic* issue in the innovation of the *bat mitzvah* celebration involves the young girl's reading the Torah in the framework of a women's prayer group. A theoretical study of *halakhah* from its inception to the present day shows that all the grounds for permitting women's Torah readings have already been set out. Any specific problem that arises can be relatively easily solved, if the positive motivation is there to do so. Following are the central subjects that have been raised in this context. A woman holding the Torah Scroll during her menstrual period, the opening and reading of a Torah Scroll at a time not required by Jewish Law (according to the ruling of Ezra the Scribe), recital of prayers that require a *minyan* (*davar shebikedusha*) in the absence of ten men of *bar mitzvah* age and above, and imitation of gentiles. These arguments have already been raised, studied

---

[22] R. Yehuda Herzl Henkin, *Responsa Bene Banim*, 2:1.

[23] A religious community in Israel was recently witness to a case demonstrating the importance of this issue. During a Shavuot *tikkun* (all-night learning vigil), a woman delivered a lecture before a mixed audience of men and women. This was done with the full knowledge and consent of the local rabbi, R. Shlomo Riskin. The former Sephardic Chief Rabbi, R. Mordechai Eliyahu voiced strong objection to the practice. I would cite this as an example of social norms being rooted in the ambience of the particular community. The rabbi, of that community should therefore be the one to assess such practices *halakhically*.

and resolved by various authorities, and this is not the place to review them.[24]

To demonstrate the tensions this issue can evoke, I would like to cite a case in point from my personal experience in the Kibbutz Sa'ad community. Although the event in question is not a *bat mitzvah* celebration, the fundamental concept is the same.

Several years ago, a group of women on the kibbutz expressed the feeling that they felt left out of the kibbutz's *Simhat Torah* celebrations. These women clearly had no desire to undermine the *halakhah*. Rather, they wanted to right an injustice that exists in many communities: the men dance with the *Sifre Torah*, while the women sit on the sidelines and chat. Theirs, then, is a purely social occasion with no apparent relevance either to closeness to God or to rejoicing in the Torah. This group of women had joined together and decided that for them, *Simhat Torah* would be a day of *avodat Hashem*, of serving God. While the male members of the community circled the *bima* (during the *hakafot*), they began the day with two Torah lessons given by women. The response on the part of the community's women was overwhelming. These *shiurim* became a focal point of the holiday. A few years later, in the wake of the religious revival occurring throughout Israel and the Jewish world, representatives of the women's community approached me for aid in designing a framework for prayer and Torah reading for women. The Sa'ad community is a particularly open one (sometimes too much so), and it was clear to me that if a rabbi accompanied the process and it took form under his guidance, little opposition to it would be aroused. In accordance with my instructions (after consultation with greater rabbinic authorities than myself), the women who would be called up to the Torah did not read *birkot haTorah* early in the morning with the rest of their personal morning blessings. When they received, their *aliyah*, they could then recite *birkot haTorah* (thus avoiding the possibility of a *berakhat le-vatalah*). They refrained from saying the traditional blessings

---

[24] See R. Aryeh A. Frimer and R. Dov I. Frimer, "Women's Prayer Services – Theory and Practice," *Tradition* 32:2, 1998 and, more recently, Mendel Shapiro, "Qeriat ha-Torah by Women: A *Halakhic* Analysis"; Yehuda Herzl Henkin, "Qeriat ha-Torah by Women: Where We Stand Today"; Mendel Shapiro, "Concluding Responses to Qeriat ha-Torah for Women" www.edah.org Sivan 5761, Vol. 1, Issue 2. See also various responses to this question in this volume.

recited by men called up to the Torah, *barekhu* and the blessing after the Torah reading. As a result, they basically recited *birkot haTorah* within the framework of their ordinary, daily obligation to recite blessings over the Torah. All defining characteristics of a *minyan* – the saying of *kaddish*, *kedushah*, etc. – were left out. The service was held in a social hall and not in the synagogue. The outcome was exhilarating. Women came out of the classes and the Torah reading with the feeling of having participated in a meaningful religious experience. When *Simhat Torah* was over, though, and the story of the event circulated outside the Sa'ad community, the attacks began. What all of the attackers had in common was a total lack of familiarity with the process the community had undergone in readying themselves spiritually for that prayer service. Eminent rabbis who heard my first-hand description of the process admitted (some fully, others hesitantly) that nothing about it was *halakhically* forbidden.

The opposition to changes in women's status in communal prayer comes from two separate directions. One objection stems from confusing between women who wish to pray together with women desiring to form a *minyan*, and is thus founded on a simple error. An example of this sort of (deliberate) conflation of concepts can be found in the exchange of essays, published in the Hebrew periodical *Tehumin*, between Rivka Lubich and Eliav Shochetman.[25] It is really only experts in the field who can recognize confusion of this kind. The truth is, even the people themselves who take part in such prayer groups are often unaware of the distinction. When the organizers of women's Torah readings take care to observe *halakhic* guidelines, they make sure that the women called to the Torah do not say "*barekhu*" and that they recite *birkot haTorah* in accordance with their *halakhic* obligations, and no more. The legal status of reading the Torah together with the blessings said before reading begins is in accordance with *halakhic* criteria. Clearly, a central responsibility of the organizers and the

---

[25] Eliav Shochetman, "Women's *Minyanim* at the Western Wall" (Heb.), *Tehumin* 15 (5755), pp. 161–184; Rivka Lubich, "On Women's Prayer" (Heb.), *Tehumin* 17 (5757), p. 165, 175; Eliav Shochetman, "More on the Question of Women's *Minyanim*" (Heb.), *Tehumin* 17 (5757), pp. 168–174.

rabbi accompanying the process is to explain the *halakhic* status of the occasion to all concerned.

The second objection is connected to the serious (and legitimate) concern that permission granted to a single, specific community might lead to other communities assuming they can follow suit – their own preparation, though, may be insufficient or the context they choose may be simply inappropriate. It is unwise to "jump the gun" and permit everything that can, theoretically, be permitted. I am convinced that, given the current state of Orthodox communities, it is not advisable for rabbis whose broad public responsibilities reach beyond the confines of community rabbinics to spearhead the movement and grant over-reaching permission to all. Such indiscriminant allowances risk bringing highly destructive results in the case of a community interested in innovation alone without undergoing the spiritual process underlying and supporting it.

On the other hand, local rabbis, who are in direct dialogue with their communities, must guide the process of religious awakening among the community's women and serve as a progressive force, while simultaneously safeguarding and guiding the process in accordance with the principles of *halakhah*.

One recurrent issue in every discussion or debate on this subject is the sincerity of the petitioners: Is their primary interest in imitating men, or do they sincerely yearn to serve God in truth? In this context, I'd like to cite R. Weinberg's *responsum* mentioned above in *Seride Esh* regarding *bat mitzvah* celebrations. His words, though written long ago, are as relevant today as when they were first published:

> It depends, ultimately, on the intentions of those in favor of the new custom of *bat mitzvah* celebrations. Do they wish to fulfill a commandment or, Heaven forbid, to imitate the gentiles?
>
> I am well aware that, among God-fearing Jews, there are those who oppose the *bat mitzvah* celebration and take a strict approach. They do not even attempt to clarify the issue in the light of *halakhah*, reacting to it emotionally instead. The Jewish heart that cherishes the traditions of parents and teachers resists all change in religious practice. To individuals with such sentiments, I would

recall Maimonides' words in his commentary to *Mishna Gittin* 8:5: "These things [the Sages] enacted to engender peace [within the community]." They must, however, be aware that those in favor of permitting the modern custom of *bat mitzvah* celebrations are motivated by sincere concern for strengthening the religious education of Jewish girls. These girls, in the reality of our generation, are in great need of spiritual sustenance and moral support as they reach the age of *mitzvot*.

It is quite impossible,[26] and probably wrong as well[27] to attempt to expose the innermost motivations of the proponents of the new custom.

It would be best, I believe, for each community in which the subject arises in its naturally context, to formulate and develop its own *bat mitzvah* ceremonies in close consultation with the rabbi of the community. A rabbi who knows his community and its members needs to make every effort to listen to the voices arising from its innermost reaches. He must try to distinguish between melodies of holiness and rumblings of rebellion. He should be an active partner in preparing girls for their *bat mitzvah* celebrations. If the rabbi and community work together in mutual understanding, the potential is there for developing a worthy and joyous event that will encourage the *bat mitzvah* girl and bring her closer to God, as well as gratifying her, her parents, and our Father in Heaven.

---

[26] This is R. Cherlow's assessment; see note 1 above.

[27] On the potential distortions of seeking women's intentions in their desire to serve God, see Chana Kehat's recent Hebrew article, "Many Women Acted Valorously," *Hatzofeh*, 25 Tammuz 5760, p. 7.

CELEBRATING *BAT MITZVAH* WITH A *SEUDAT MITZVAH* – SHOULD A GIRL GIVE A *DERASHAH* OR MAKE A *SIYYUM?*[#]

YARDENA COPE-YOSSEF

The gray regularity of everyday life is illuminated from time to time by ceremonies we hold to mark important milestones in our lives. The *halakhic* details of how to celebrate such events are meant to give form to the feelings of joy we have, or to intensify awareness of its unique aspects. Events marking transitions or achievements in Jewish life are celebrated by holding a *seudat mitzvah* or festive meal. Festive meals are an integral part of weddings and the occasions of *brit milah, pidyon ha-ben* (redemption of a first-born son), and *bar mitzvah*, as well as on completion of learning a tractate of the Talmud (*siyyum massekhet*) or consecration of a new home (*hanukat ha-bayit*). In his work *Yam shel Shlomo*, R. Shlomo Luria defined it this way:

> Any meal held not simply out of happiness and friendship, but in order to offer praise and thanks to God, to announce the performance of a *mitzvah*, or to make known one's experience of a personal "miracle" *(pirsum ha-nes)* is called a *seudat mitzvah*.[1]

---

[*] translated by Ora Wiskind Elper

[#] *Derashah:* a talk on a Torah topic; *siyyum:* the formal completion of a unit of study, usually a tractate of Talmud.

[1] R. Shlomo Luria (1510–1573), *Yam shel Shlomo* on *Bava Kama* 80a. The context is a discussion of the question of the celebration of the seventh day for a boy. Rav, as we know, refused to participate in any simple meal [*seudat reshut*], one not held in honor of any *mitzvah*. R. Luria concludes that each of the possible interpretations he suggests – the meal held for a *brit milah, pidyon ha-ben*, or even one celebrating the miracle of a safe childbirth – can be considered a *seudat mitzvah* according to that definition.

It may seem, as R. Benny Lau points out in his essay in this volume, that the pure *halakhic* implications involved in whether to include the *bat mitzvah* meal in the *halakhic* category of *seudat mitzvah* are relatively minor. My feeling, though, is that we should have respect for the sensibilities of the family or the girl who might resent the thought that her *bat mitzvah* is considered by *halakhah* as just another birthday.[2]

I would like to reconsider the question of the *seudat mitzvah* as an *halakhic* form of recognizing transitions and achievements. In addition, I'd like to outline the ways in which a girl's entrance into keeping *mitzvot* may be celebrated in the *halakhically* recognized form of the *seudat mitzvah*.

A. Rabbinic sensibilities versus common practice

Let's begin by rereading the *responsa* from *Torah Lishma*,[3] cited in R. Benny Lau's essay, in a different light – as a critique of the religious establishment for not relating seriously enough to a certain wealthy man's distress over the proper definition of a *seudat mitzvah*. The following scenario is described there:

> A learned and wealthy man fulfilled the obligation of *pidyon haben* (redemption of the first-born son). He celebrated the occasion with a feast and invited Torah scholars to celebrate with him. They sat at the table joyful and content. And, since Torah scholars customarily discuss Torah matters, the wealthy host raised the issue of *seudat mitzvah* with some of the scholars seated near him. What constitutes a *seudat mitzvah?* They disputed whether a *bar mitzvah* feast held at the onset of a boy's fourteenth year or a

---

[2] As we'll see below, according to *Yam shel Shlomo*, there are ramifications from the Talmud itself concerning the definition of the nature of the meal, such as a scholar's enjoyment from that meal. The two implications most familiar to us today are the eating of meat at a *seudat mitzvah* held during the first nine days of the month of Av, and the *seudat mitzvah* held on a *taanit bekhorot*, absolving first-born sons of their obligation to fast. See Rema, *Oreh Hayyim* 551.10 and *Mishnah Berurah*, *Oreh Hayyim* 470. 15-17 and *Shaar ha-tziyun* ad loc. These two implications will be discussed in relation to the *seudat mitzvah* held upon the completion of study of a talmudic tractate. Some less well-known implications include issues such as whether those invited are required to participate in any specific way, whether someone in mourning is permitted to eat at specific *seudot mitzvah*, and whether the meal can be held at the synagogue.

[3] *Responsa Torah Lishma*, 482.

housewarming party *(hanukat ha-bayit)* constitutes a *seudat mitzvah*. Each camp cited proofs supporting its position.

A second small group of scholars seated at the rich man's table was engaged in discussion as well, but on a different topic. The wealthy host said to those scholars: "We too are discussing Torah! Why don't you join our conversation and enlighten us with some new idea on the subject? After all, we are the larger group and you are the smaller; you should follow our lead!" One of the scholars of the second group said to him, "The subject we are debating is far greater and more fundamental than yours. The practical ramifications of the discussion of *seudat mitzvah* in general, and what constitutes *seudat mitzvah* apply solely to a minor prohibition, virtually a voluntary act of piety. The only *halakhic* outcome of your discussion can be that such a celebration [i.e., a *bar mitzvah* or housewarming] is considered either a *seudat mitzvah* or a *seudat reshut* [an optional celebratory meal]. What bearing does that have on severe prohibitions? We, on the other hand, are deliberating numerous *halakhot* on a subject with critical ramifications – it concerns a severe prohibition that carries a court-inflicted death penalty. It would not be right to abandon our discussion and join yours!"

The reaction of the wealthy man at this pointed refusal is also portrayed:

The host was truly ashamed at being vanquished by that scholar. He said to these seated near him, "Is there no similarly grave consequence for the matter we are discussing, relating it to a severe biblical prohibition? After all, everything in the Torah is interconnected! I would be overjoyed – and would give a donation to the *yeshivah* scholars as well – if one of you could discover some influence our subject bears on a severe biblical prohibition." But the scholars could not find the convincing argument he sought.

And so we turn to your honor with the question: Can some ramification from this issue be found relating it to a severe biblical prohibition?

R. Yehezkel Kehali's response was:[4]

It is certainly possible. One instance would be the case in which a man betrothed a woman by saying to her, "You will be consecrated to me on the condition that you eat a *seudat mitzvah* with me today." The woman then ate with him at a *siyyum* [a celebration on completion of a tractate of Mishna or Talmud], a housewarming party, a *bar mitzvah*, or the like. The scholars set to debating whether or not such celebrations are considered *seudot mitzvah*. If they are indeed *seudot mitzvot*, the woman is now unquestionably betrothed to him, as the condition has been fulfilled. If a second man then consecrates her, the second betrothal would be invalid. Furthermore, if she has [illicit] sexual relations with any man other than the first, both he and she would be subject to the death penalty. On the other hand, if the feast is not considered a *seudat mitzvah*, she would not be betrothed [to the first man]; if the second man consecrates her, then, she would be betrothed to the second man, and would be permitted to him alone. In that case, if the first man would have relations with her, he would be guilty [of adultery with a married woman]. The practical outcome is therefore of dire consequence regarding a severe biblical prohibition, i.e., the prohibition of adultery – a capital offense punishable by death sentence inflicted by a *beit din*.

In the ensuing paragraph he cites yet another life and death issue:

...Concerning the "rebellious son" *[ben sorer u-moreh]*, who enters that category when he has eaten a *triens* of meat and drunk half a *log* of fine wine, etc. This, however, does not apply if he eats in the company of a *seudat mitzvah*....

---

[4] The *Responsa Torah Lisma* is attributed to R. Yosef Hayyim, the Ben Ish Hai, although the signature on them is that of R. Yehezkel Kehali, who lived in Bagdad in the same period as the Ben Ish Hai, in the nineteenth century.

What the host and his guest felt was a compelling problem was considered by the scholarly contingent as inconsequential. The mockery and ridicule heaped on the questioner drive him to turn to a rabbi of status to see if some significant implications may, despite everything, be found concerning his subject. Is the response here sincere or ironic? He does find two crucial implications in the decision whether or not a particular meal can be considered a *seudat mitzvah*. The first – in determining whether a woman is married or single; the second – in defining the "rebellious son." The second case indicates clearly that the implication is theoretical, when we recall that, according to most opinions, an actual "rebellious son never was and will never be."[5] The first solution he proposes, concerning marital laws [*dinei kiddushin*], also sounds more like a theoretical proposition than a real *halakhic* conclusion.

The accusing finger, here, points to the group of scholars. Those in the supposedly less learned group felt it important to define what was included in the category of *seudat mitzvah*, a question the rabbinical contingent perceived as unscholarly. Yet R. Yehezkel Kehali's response justified the former even within the rabbinical arena. The group of "simple" Jews was the victor over the vanquished rabbis on their own battleground; in the end, their "simple" reasoning found ramifications in criminal law.

R. Moshe Feinstein responded in a completely different vein when asked on three separate occasions about *bat mitzvah* celebrations. His answers leave the strong impression that R. Moshe Feinstein would have preferred not to deal with the issue of defining *bat mitzvah* at all, but because the public (or, more precisely, community rabbis) demand it, he takes up the issue in three different *responsa*.[6]

R. Lau, in his discussion, pointed to some of the socio-*halakhic* reasons that led R. Feinstein to rule as he did. An additional factor hinted in his words should also be mentioned:[7]

---

[5] The citation reads as follows, "The rebellious son never was and will never be; why, then, [did the Torah] mention him? To say: Explicate the issue and receive your reward." C.f., *Sanhedrin* 71a, *Tosefta Sanhedrin* (ed. Zukermandel) 11.6.

[6] R. Moshe Feinstein, *Responsa Iggerot Moshe, Oreh Hayyim* 1. 104; 2. 97; 4. 36.

[7] *Responsa, Oreh Hayyim* 1.104.

And if it were within my power, I would also eliminate the *bar mitzvah* celebrations done here for boys. As we all know, it has brought no one closer to Torah and *mitzvot*, not even the *bar mitzvah* boy himself, not even for a moment. Even the opposite: in many places, it leads to violation of Shabbat and other prohibitions. Things that have become customary, though, and even originate as a *mitzvah* are difficult to eliminate. But to innovate the same thing for girls…?

Beyond his consideration of the custom itself are two barbs: First, R. Moshe Feinstein protests the negative outgrowths of *bar mitzvah* celebrations in the style common in the 1950s in the United States. (These *responsa* were written in 1957–1959.) The second jab comes from R. Feinstein's approach, as a learned scholar, to the uproar surrounding the festive meals and celebrations as opposed to the benefit involved. In truth, *bar* and *bat mitzvah* celebrations in his time very often failed to mark the young person's entrance into a lifetime of Torah and observance of *mitzvot*. In effect, R. Feinstein's opposition to these meals follows a tradition of several *responsa* in which *seudot mitzah* of this sort are discussed in other circumstances as well.

B. Specific Reservations Against *Seudot* and Celebrations

A number of early *halakhic* authorities [*rishonim*] listed various sorts of *mitzvot* that are distinguished by holding a *seudat mitzvah*. Such lists were not compiled in order to delimit or define the concept of *seudat mitzvah*. Rather, they appear for the most part in the context of laws regarding mourning or vows.

1. With whom should one mingle?

One example may be found in the *Responsa Maharil Hahadashah*. There, R. Yaakov ben Moshe Molin is asked:[8] "A person who took a [religious] vow not to eat outside his home wrote me requesting a dispensation to eat at a *seudat mitzvah*. He asked what should be considered a *seudat mitzvah*." The

---

[8] R. Ya'akov ben Moshe Molin (Germany, 1360-1427), *Responsa Maharil Hahadashot*, 104.

Maharil unhesitatingly includes a *siyyum* – a meal held upon completing a talmudic tractate – in his list of *seudot mitzvah*, although the *bar mitzvah* meal is notably absent from his list.[9] Later in his comments, however, he does caution against exaggeration in regard to *seudot mitzvah*, and encourages careful selection of the *seudot mitzvot* one attends:

> *Seudat mitzvah* includes *brit milah*, *pidyon ha-ben*, *siyyum massekhet*. All who enjoy a festive meal held by a Torah scholar, it is as if they are enjoying the illumination of the *Shekhinah*, as the Sages taught regarding the meal held by Yitro (*Berakhot* 64a). It follows, then, that *Lag be-Omer* is also a *seudat mitzvah*.... In all these cases, however, although they are *seudot mitzvah*, one should check and see if those attending are like the people of Jerusalem [of good standing], for at times the people there may be rash and empty, acting light-headedly and speaking profanities [c.f., *Sanhedrin* 23a].... If so, even in the case of a wedding feast...he who guards his soul will keep a distance, for to attend – the loss exceeds the gain.

2. Too much of a good thing?

A later *halakhic* authority, R. Shlomo Luria, author of *Yam shel Shlomo*, who considered the definition of *seudat mitzvah* extensively, raises the subject in the context of a problem similar to the one implicit in R. Moshe Feinstein's criticism. Following a lengthy definition and consideration of several cases, such as a Hanukah meal, a *siyyum massekhet*, housewarming party, and *bar mitzvah seudah*, he concludes:[10]

---

[9] See below with regard to the origins of *bar mitzvah* as a *seudat mitzvah*. Opinions are divided on how ancient the custom to hold *bar mitzvah* festive meals really is. See I. Ta-Shema's Hebrew article on Jewish "consecration" ceremonies, *Tarbiz* 68. He writes (p. 594): "The primary source for [the *seudat bar mitzvah*] is commonly cited by everyone as the Maharshal's words in *Yam shel Shlomo*... But a far earlier source is extant, found in *Piskei R. Avigdor* of Vienna, who lived in Vienna in the first half of the thirteenth century, three hundred years before the Maharshal. He writes that one should hold a celebration [*mishteh*] for one's son on his thirteenth birthday."

[10] R. Shlomo Luria, *Yam shel Shlomo*, 104. He is considered among the early *aharonim*.

In any case, they should not be held so frequently that they threaten to eliminate one's regular Torah learning completely; rather, from time to time, and if they can [manage] without him – each case should be weighed separately. The God-fearing person who desires to purify himself will be guided by Heaven on the straight path of moderation.

Even when a meal is formally defined as a *seudat mitzvah* – as we will see, his definition is quite broad – a Torah scholar must still take care not to rush from one *seudah* to another at the expense of his regular learning. He warns even more urgently, like the Maharil before him, of the importance of investigating the nature of the celebration; when a meal does not have the atmosphere of a *seudat mitzvah*, he is skeptical of whether it can be considered as one.

Meals held in honor of *hinukh habayit* [housewarming party], though, are merely an expression of friendship. Especially, much to our distress, those meals and festivities held by common people nowadays – they are a disgrace, serving only to slate themselves with laughter and light-heartedness. The Maharam also rules this way.[11] In any case, it seems to me that a God-fearing person who wishes to consecrate his new home to Torah and *mitzvot*, and to offer praise to Him for all He has bestowed, does not permit drinking, games, and foolishness in it from the outset. Rather, first of all he consecrates it with a *seudah* and with words of Torah devoted to the event itself.[12] That indeed is a *seudat* mitzvah. And of this, the Torah said, "Drink, drink deep, O loving companions" (Song of Songs 5:1), [and the Sages added], "this was at the consecration [of the *Mishkan*]."

3. Is the *seudah* just a gimmick to avoid obligations?

A third and final example of the type of criticism leveled against *seudot mitzvah* concerns neither excessive numbers of meals nor their questionable atmosphere, but rather using the meal as a *halakhic* tactic to avoid performing the *mitzvot* themselves. Even though the *bar mitzvah* meal's

---

[11] *Responsa*, R. Meir of Rotenberg, 4. 605 (Prague edition).

[12] Later on, we will see how this addition helps in considering the meal as a *seudat mitzvah*, as well as its potential significance regarding the *bat mitzvah*.

status as a *seudat mitzvah* rather than an optional meal *[seudat reshut]* was well established at least since the days of R. Shlomo Luria, R. Eliezer Waldenberg writes in the latter half of the twentieth century:[13]

> Thus, it is appropriate that a boy who becomes *bar mitzvah* on the same day as a postponed fast *[taanit hanidhah]* should indeed keep the fast. And with regard to what you cite in the name of a *dayyan* from פעטס who compared the ruling of exempting a *bar mitzvah* boy from fasting on the day of his *bar mitzvah* because it is a day of personal celebration to a similar case *[Shulhan Arukh, Oreh Hayyim* 559.8], who rules that when Tisha be-Av falls on Shabbat, causing it to be postponed to Sunday, the father who makes a *brit milah* for his son is exempt from fasting, for it is a day of happiness for him. And according to *Yam shel Shlomo* on *Bava Kama* 88.37 that there is no *seudat mitzvah* greater than the *bar mitzvah* meal, I would respond as follows. Although the *Magen Avraham* [551.33] permitted eating meat at a *bar mitzvah* even on those days when eating meat is customarily forbidden...*to permit, on the same grounds, eating on a postponed Tisha be-Av fast day – this, to my mind, is highly problematic [emphasis added]*. See for yourself how difficult it is for *halalkhic* authorities to explain the leniency in the case of the father and his son's *brit milah*, which is found explicitly in the *Shulhan Arukh* itself. And they testify that the practice is not to be lenient with regard to *brit milah*.... *How, then, can we come and add yet another exemption in the case of the bar mitzvah – especially when the whole thrust of the mitzvah of having a seudah for a bar mitzvah is recognition that the boy has merited reaching the age of obligation, and "greater is he who is commanded and performs..." as the Yam shel Shlomo notes? What right, then, do we have to absolve the boy of the very first mitzvah – to fast – that he now has the opportunity to perform* [emphasis added]?

---

[13] R. Eliezer Waldenberg, *Responsa Tzitz Eliezer*, 9.27.

R. Waldenberg questions relying on the definition of the *bar mitzvah* meal as a *seudat mitzvah*, when its sole purpose is to exempt the boy from the very first *mitzvah* he has the chance to perform under obligation.

R. Waldenberg is not the only one to deliberate questions such as these. Many discussions have been devoted to the definition of a meal as a *seudat mitzvah* for the purpose of granting exemptions to individuals. Cases in point are in relation to meals held for a *siyyum*, in the context of permitting meat to be eaten during the Nine Days [from *Rosh hodesh* Av until Tisha be-Av], and absolving first-born sons from *ta'anit bekhorot* on Erev Pesach. These discussions contain audible criticism leveled against those who really seek *halakhic* tricks because they find it hard to live without meat for a week.

C. The positive potential of *seudot mitzvah*

Despite the hesitations voiced above, I believe that holding a festive event with a meal to mark the occasion of a girl's *bat mitzvah* can be a meaningful experience. This depends, first of all, on whether we will content ourselves with minimalist, technical view of the *seudah* limited to details such as simply absolving someone of something, considering whether an invitation to such a *seudah* obligates the person invited, or allowing the possibility of holding it in a synagogue. As R. Yehezkel Kehali suggested, all of this is tangential. Indeed, as we have seen, the approach that emerges from limited contexts such as these actually threatens to undermine the true significance of the celebration.

Secondly, we saw that the nature of the celebration may also alter its definition. In R. Shlomo Luria's day, as we saw, housewarmings were sometimes wild parties, complete with drunkenness and merrymaking; in R. Moshe Feinstein's generation *bar mitzvah* celebrations may have been expensive, showy affairs devoid of all religious content (worse, even occasioning transgressions), that brought no one closer to Torah and *mitzvot*. Surely, then, celebrations of a completely different nature can be held as well. The feelings of warmth and friendship surrounding my oldest daughter's *bat mitzvah* is engraved in my memory, as well as the overwhelming reaction of guests moved to tears as she spoke on the subject of *Shema Yisrael* and sacrificing one's life for the sake of the *Am Yisrael* and *Torat*

Yisrael. I'm sure all my readers can recall similar positive memories of their own.

The happiness shared at a meal celebrating a *mitzvah* bears many fruits: it transforms an individual's or family's personal event into a celebration of the entire community. If it truly corresponds, in definition and nature, with what is required of a *seudat mitzvah,* then it serves to raise the celebrating community to the level of a *havurat mitzvah* – a *"mitzvah* community."[14] Beyond that, the Talmud avers:[15]

> "And I praised happiness" [Kohelet 8:15] – that is, the joy of a *mitzvah.* "What good is happiness?" [Kohelet 2:2] – that is, joy unrelated to any *mitzvah.* Hence we learn that the *Shekhinah* dwells neither amidst jesting nor foolery nor small talk nor empty chatter, but only for the sake of the joy of a *mitzvah.*

Rashi there offers this example: "Joy of a *mitzvah* – such as *hakhnasat kalla* [a wedding]." To be sure, care must be taken that the joyful event imbued with the "joy of *mitzvah*" both in definition and atmosphere.

D. Does the *Bat Mitzvah Seudah* Fall Under the Rubric of the "Joy of *Mitzvah*"?

1. Sources for the *bar mitzvah* feast

Although there are even earlier sources,[16] the *Yam shel Shlomo* is unique in his systematic definition of the entire phenomenon of *seudat mitzvah,* in his consideration of specific cases, including the *bar mitzvah* meal, and in his presentation of sources that underlie their inclusion in that category. We cited his general definition above:

---

[14] The *havurat mitzvah* is mentioned in the *Yerushalmi, Moed Katan* 3.8 (fol. 73d): "One in mourning for all [relatives] is prohibited from attending a [festive] meal for thirty days – in the case of [a deceased] father or mother, for twelve months. If there is a *havurat mitzvah* or *kiddush ha-hodesh,* one is permitted [to attend]."

[15] *Shabbat* 30b.

[16] See n. 9 above.

Any meal held not simply out of happiness and friendship, but in order to offer praise and thanks to God, to announce the performance of a *mitzvah*, or to publicize a "miracle" *[pirsum ha-nes]* is called a *seudat mitzvah*.

In a broad interpretation of his words, offering "praise and thanks to God" seems to be a separate and sufficient condition for the event to be a *seudat mitzvah*.[17] A narrower interpretation might suggest that the meal, during which one gives praise and thanks to God would have to be held either in order to publicize a miracle or to celebrate a significant *mitzvah*. Even in this more restricted reading, we could ask whether such a definition could invite the inclusion of any *mitzvah*. The answer, apparently, is no. R. Shlomo Luria himself proceeds to examine each separate instance. In the case of a "*seudat hodayah* [meal of thanksgiving] for a safe deliverance of both mother and baby" he states,

> To publicize the miracle…thus a certain sage wrote…that the custom we have, after the birth of a boy, to enter the home on the first Shabbat night following the birth and have a taste of something, that is in fact a *seudat* mitzvah, the very same *seudah* that Rabbeinu Tam mentions.

Did he state this so that the reason for the *seudah* would correspond to his definition, or because he found a similar case in rulings by his predecessor, the author of *Terumat Hadeshen*? It's hard to say. His writings combine orderly definitions with reliable *halakhic* precedents.

In his discussion of *seudot* held during the festival of Hanukah as well, R. Shlomo Luria evokes the various precedents and the definition of his making. Here, he has to contend with the opposing precedent of the Maharam of Rotenberg that appears in the *Tur*.[18]

R. Meir of Rotenberg used to say that the *seudot* we customarily hold during Hanukah are optional *seudot (seudot reshut)* held for the purpose of

---

[17] R. Yair Bakhrakh in his *Responsa Havvat Yair*, 70.

[18] *Tur, Oreh Hayyim*, 670.

showing praise and thanksgiving and not for the purpose of joy and festivities.

The sources he presents to support his approach, in opposition to the Maharam, do not say explicitly that *seudot hanukah* fall in the category of *seudot mitzvah*. They need to be explicated to make them fit his general view. The Rambam, for instance, does call the festival of Hanukah "days of joy and praise," but does not discuss the meals held during Hanukah. His comments are cited nonetheless in support of the contention that those meals are considered *seudot mitzvah;* this is justified solely by the use of the word "joy" in speaking of the festival. Reading R. Shlomo Luria's discussion further, we have an increasing sense of the tension between his striving for consistency in the definition and his need to deal with precedents contradicting his method. After stating that a meal held to commemorate an infant son's "salvation" [*yeshua*, i.e., safe birth] is a *seudat mitzvah*, he is forced to this logical conclusion: "All the more so the days of Hanukah, which were instated to offer praise, gratitude, and proclamation of the miracle" – they too must be included in the category of *seudat mitzvah*.

In his discussion of the issue of *siyyum massekhet*, which he describes in no uncertain terms as a *mitzvah*-meal (or *siyyum sefer*, "completing a book," as he terms it), we find a moving description of an incident in which R. Luria innovated a law, based on a certain logical assumption, but later withdrew his innovation. In his mind, a *seudat siyyum* is without a doubt a *seudat mitzvah*. He writes (without citing any specific sources):[19] "A *seudat siyyum sefer* is a *seudat mitzvah* according to all views." He instructed that the blessing "*she-hasimhah be-meono*" [joy is in His dwelling] should be said at a meal celebrating completion of a book, "For there is no greater joy in the eyes of God than the happiness of Torah." His reasoning was, "It is no less than that of *pidyon ha-ben*, which is the simple announcement of performance of a *mitzvah*." But he continues:

This is what I once taught as *halakhah*. And the celebration was interrupted with great rioting, under very difficult conditions. I put

---

[19] *Yam Shel Shlomo*, ibid.

the blame on myself for having gone against the teachings of my masters, who had never heard of such a thing. Indeed, they spoke only of weddings and *pidyon haben*…. And all their words, to be sure, are received tradition, and profound secrets are contained in their every word. How, then, does one select a particular *mitzvah* and not another?

He expresses deep sorrow and regret for having violated what he received from his own teachers. We learn of his hesitation to innovate based on his own reasoning alone when this contradicts the opinions of his masters, despite his personal involvement in the subject. Later on we will make a closer consideration of his comments regarding the source for celebrating a *siyyum massekhet* by holding a meal.

On the issue of the *bar mitzvah* meal, R. Shlomo Luria also cited precedents for the custom known to him (again, without citing their sources): "The *seudat bar mitzvah* held in Ashkenazic custom – it would seem there is no greater *seudat mitzvah*, as its very name testifies." He does cite this interesting origin of the practice to mark entering the age of *mitzvot*:

A celebration is made, with praise and thanksgiving to God – that the youth has merited being a *bar mitzvah*, for "greater is he who is commanded" and that the father has merited raising him until this day; now he can bring him into the covenant of Torah in its entirety. Proof of this appears at the end of the first chapter of *Kiddushin* (31a). Rav Yosef concludes, after hearing R. Hanina state that "greater is one who is commanded and performs" and upon hearing that the law was not like R. Yehudah who said that a blind person is exempt from *mitzvot*, that he should hold a celebratory meal. Whereas in Rav Yosef's case it was simply the joy of being informed of his "commanded" status that prompted him to celebrate, it is that much more fitting to hold a celebration when the actual time arrives that a person comes of age and enters the status of being commanded.

Needless to say, he does not speak of marking a girl's acceptance of the *mitzvot*. According to his definition and reasoning, though, there need not be any difference between the two. While numerous twentieth-century *halakhic* authorities have discussed the issue, and have decided that the *bat mitzvah* is or is not a *seudat mitzvah*, almost no one, to my knowledge, has challenged the logic of equality in the status of the boy and girl in entering the obligation to keep *mitzvot*.[20]

2. Can the *Bat Mitzvah* be Compared to the *Bar Mitzvah*?

Because the *seudat mitzvah* is founded upon definition as well as custom, we see that most of its opponents based their views on statements such as "it was not the practice" or "we have not seen." They anchor their stance in the fact that it has never been the custom to celebrate *bat mitzvah* with a *seudah*. To be sure, in Europe before World War II and in the United States, marking the maturation of Jewish girls with special celebrations was not seen in a positive light. The origin of such modern ways was transparent – the desire to reproduce the confirmation ceremonies practiced in Reform congregations, which themselves stemmed from an imitation of Christian confirmations. In addition to the absence of an authentic Jewish practice, this innovation was thus rejected as an adoption of non-Jewish traditions. This contention is voiced by R. Yehiel Weinberg, author of *Seridei Esh* between the lines in a long *responsum*. R. Weinberg is even led to praise Reform Jews themselves.[21] "Even the Reform among us do so not in order to resemble [non-Jews], but to make a family celebration on the occasion of their child's reaching maturity." He also indicates the positive element seen by those who wish to introduce the practice:

---

[20] The *halakhic* basis for celebrating the *bat mitzvah* has been challenged on the grounds that a girl's taking on of the *mitzvot* is not, practically speaking, a publicly recognized event (c.f., *Iggerot Moshe, Oreh Hayyim* 2.97). A reaction to this contention may be found in *Responsa Yabia Omer* 6.29. Some authorities forbid it out of considerations of modesty or because it has no real benefit, since girls are exempt from four out of sixteen of the positive time-bound *mitzvot* commonly practiced today. An extensive survey of those for and against may be found in R. Daniel Tuito's Hebrew discussion, "*Hagigat bat mitzvah: Iyyun be-darkhei pesikatam she-hokhmei doreinu*" in *Bat Mitzvah*, ed. S. Friedland ben Arza (Jerusalem, 2002), pp. 40–68. At the beginning of his essay, R. Tuito shows that in the opinion of most authorities, there is no difference between boys and girls in terms of the basic definition of entering the age of *mitzvot* at which they become "commanded." The only difference concerns the age at which the transition takes place.

[21] R. Y. Weinberg, *Seridei Esh*, 3.93.

And our fellow Jews who have this new *bat mitzvah* custom say their purpose is to instill in the heart of the young woman, who has reached the age of obligation in *mitzvot*, feelings of love for Judaism and its commandments, and to arouse pride for her religion and her belonging to such a great and holy people. It makes no difference to us that non-Jews celebrate their own confirmation ceremonies....

Although the following comments made by the author of *Seridei Esh* may sound out-of-date in our generation, I'd like to cite them in full. They concern the ability of the *posek* to overcome the absence of a precedent custom:

There are those who oppose celebration of the *bat mitzvah* on the grounds that it goes against the practice of generations past, who did not follow that practice. Their contention, though, is really not legitimate, for previous generations did not need to deal with girls' education. Each and every Jew was full with Torah and fear of Heaven; the very atmosphere of every Jewish town was charged with the aroma and spirit of Judaism. Girls who grew up in Jewish homes inhaled the Jewish spirit effortlessly; they nearly suckled Judaism from their mothers' breasts. Now, though, the generations have changed drastically. Influences from the street uproots from the heart of every boy and girl every last glimmer of Judaism; girls learn in gentile schools.... Now it is our task to concentrate all our efforts on their education.... Straight logical reasoning and the basic principles of pedagogy nearly compel us to celebrate girls' reaching the age of obligation in *mitzvot* as well. The distinction that is made between boys and girls on the issue of celebrating their maturation deeply injures the human sensibilities of the young woman who, in other domains has already been awarded with emancipation, so to speak.

Benny Gesundheit notes[22] that R. Weinberg makes his contention less than absolute – the circumstances he describes *"nearly* compel us." Gesundheit attributes this to R. Weinberg's awareness that his call for the introduction of a new custom is based on a consideration that is not strictly *halakhic.* I would describe it as a matter of policy.[23]

R. Daniel Tuito, who reviewed the *halakhic* opinions regarding the *bat mitzvah* celebration,[24] also showed that the *posekim* who permitted it did so despite their awareness of the absence of a precedent custom. Renewal of the custom became possible due to the tremendous changes experienced in our generation and in the consciousness of maturing girls, as R. Weinberg explained.

R. Benny Lau pointed out[25] that those authorities living in Israeli who permitted *bat mitzvah* celebrations were not at all concerned with the problem of imitating the Reform movement or with the question of holding the celebration in the synagogue. Israeli *posekim* thus concentrated on the issue of whether or not there is a basis for introducing the custom of having a *seudat mitzvot* in honor of the *bat mitzvah.*[26]

A fundamental question in the *halakhic* discourse on the subject, as we have seen, is the nature of the *seudat mitzvah.* Does it correspond with the requirements of modesty; what elements of content does it have, that it not be like "those meals and festivities held by common people nowadays – a disgrace, serving only to slate themselves with laughter and pleasantry" that R. Luria, cited above, described? Rather than going into the negative elements that might be aroused in meals of this nature, I prefer to concentrate on the positive potential inherent in celebrating the *bat mitzvah* with a *seudat mitzvah.*

---

[22] On the internet: www.daat.ac.il (March 12, 2000).

[23] An interesting and complex question, which I will not investigate here, is the extent to which it is possible to exert a direct influence of the creation of new customs, and on the basis of what reasoning.

[24] See n. 21

[25] See n. 2

[26] Some Ashkenazi rabbinical authorities in Israel were exceptions to the rule. These *posekim* were not worried about direct Reform influences, but about the internalization of a custom initiated by the Reform movement. Their views can be found in R. Tuito's essay.

E. Two Suggestions for a *Bat Mitzvah Seudah*

1. A *Bat Mitzvah Derashah* Transforms the *Halakhic* Status of the Meal

In most cases, the *bar* or *bat mitzvah* is not celebrated the very day after the young person's birthday – the twelfth in the case of a girl, and thirteenth in the case of a boy.[27] R. Shlomo Luria raises the *halakhic* problem involved in holding a *seudat mitzvah* for a *bar mitzvah* before that date and offers this solution: "If the young man is taught to give a *derashah* about the event [the *bar mitzvah*], then it is not inferior to a house dedication meal *[hanukat ha-bayit]*." Regarding festive meals for a *hanukat habayit* he says: "If at the outset the meal is designated to inaugurate the house, say words of Torah, and give a *derashah* about the event, this indeed is a *seudat mitzvah.*"

R. Yair Bakhrakh goes into an extensive discussion of what this demand entails, because the simple presence of Torah scholars speaking words of Torah clearly does not transform every event into a *seudat mitzvah*. R. Bakhrakh defines the problem and the solution at the same time:[28]

> This, in my humble opinion, is the rule – in common parlance, the word *seudah* merely means that invited guests take part. A *seudat mitzvah*, however, is designated as such only when people are gathered for the celebration of a *mitzvah* or for the *derashah*. This has already been established by our predecessors, because the speech is an integral part of the meal; all those partaking of the meal listen to the speaker's words. That is how it should be – and not as the masses wrongly do; therefore, even if a handful of scholars among them do speak words of Torah, that is insufficient.

---

[27] The source for the onset of the age of obligation is *Niddah* 45b. *Yam shel Shlomo* cites the maturation signs mentioned in the Talmud there as a literal requirement regarding the celebration of entering the obligation in *mitzvot*.

[28] R. Yair Bakhrakh, *Responsa Havvat Yair,* s. 70.

In other words, for a meal to be defined as a *seudat mitzvah*, it must include a *derashah* directed to the invited guests as a group, and the contents of that *derashah* must be devoted to the event itself.

2. Is it Preferable That the *Bar/Bat Mitzvah* Give the *Derashah*?

In light of this connection between the *seudat mitzvah* and the *derashah*, we must determine whether there is a *halakhic* preference that the person in whose honor the celebration is being held should be the one to speak. R. Shlomo Luria writes only that on the occasion of a *bar mitzvah*, the young man himself should speak about the event. He does not specify how compulsory this is.

At this juncture, we might ask, regarding those who permit holding a *bat mitzvah* meal: should the young woman herself speak? Contemporary *posekim* take a number of stances.

R. Moshe Feinstein, despite his opposition to defining the meal as a *seudat mitzvah* writes:

> The girl is also permitted to say something in honor of the celebration, and this may indeed help in attaining the desired benefits you mention. Her words, though, should not be said from the altar, but at the table where *kiddush* is made.

Indeed, R. Feinstein does not consider that meal to be a *seudat mitzvah* at all, and thus the girl's speech makes no particular contribution to its status. We could note, nonetheless, that R. Moshe Feinstein does not negate the possibility itself that the girl could get up and speak before the gathering on grounds of modesty, appropriateness, etc. He even admits that it might lead to some sort of spiritual benefit, as his questioner suggests.

Similarly, R. Meshulam Rata in his *responsum* to a question posed in 1958 by R. S.Z. Kahana, Ph.D., then director of the Ministry of Religion, does not announce a new custom in the celebration of *bat mitzvah*. His answer is primarily concerned with the blessing *barukh she-patarani* ["blessed be He who has absolved me of his/her sins"].[29] On marking the day, he says:[30]

---

[29] See R. Tuito's discussion, pp. 62–68.

The event can be celebrated as a day of rejoicing and happiness amongst family and friends in her home and at the girls' school she attends. And the teacher (man or woman) may give a lecture on matters of the day, elucidating the responsibility of a daughter of Israel upon attaining the age of *mitzvot*.

The *responsum* as a whole is carefully formulated, and opens possibilities rather than recommending preferred ways to celebrate. R. Rata sees such an event as a pedagogical opportunity for the teacher, an occasion for speaking to the young woman of her obligations in reaching the age of *bat mitzvah*. His words do not suggest anything about the active participation of the girls themselves. It could be noted that his answer might have been somewhat different had the questioner been a private individual.

R. Yehiel Weinberg[31] cautiously differs with R. Moshe Feinstein's stance and permits the *bat mitzvah* celebration under certain conditions:[32]

And although my tendency is to permit *bat mitzvah* celebrations, still I concur with the view of the *gaon* R. M. Feinstein in his book *Iggerot Moshe, Oreh Hayyim*, that the festivities should not be held in the synagogue, not even at night, when no one is there. Rather, they should be held in a private home or hall adjacent to the synagogue. *And all this provided that the rabbi speak [emphasis added]* instructively to the young woman, warning her, from that day forth to keep the essential *mitzvot* between herself and God....

Like R. Rata, R. Weinberg perceives the event as a chance to educate the girl and prepare her in observance of the *mitzvot* and fear of Heaven. His

---

[30] R. Meshulam Rata, *Kol Mevaser* 2.44.

[31] *Responsa Seridei Esh* 3.93.

[32] In addition to the other conditions he goes on to enumerate, related to where the *bat mitzvah* celebration is held and to its nature, R. Weinberg adds an interesting subjective condition. After a short discussion of the issue of adopting non-Jewish practices and imitating the ways of heretics he concludes: "In effect, it depends on the intentions of those who wish to introduce the new custom of celebrating the *bat mitzvah* – whether they act for the sake of the *mitzvah* or, Heaven forbid, to imitate the sects."

comments make no mention of the young woman's own active participation in the event.

R. Ovadiah Yosef writes:[33]

> This would suggest that a young woman as well, when she reaches the age of twelve years and a day, and becomes bound by all the *mitzvot* incumbent on women...enters the category of "one who is commanded and performs" with regard to those *mitzvot*. Her entrance into the *mitzvot* should be celebrated in a meal of gratitude and joy, for in that sense there is no difference between a boy and girl in reaching the age of obligation... (provided that all standards of modesty the Torah requires are upheld...). Words of Torah should be said, as well as songs and praises to God, at the festive gathering held for the *bat mitzvah*; then it can surely be considered a *seudat mitzvah*....

R. Ovadiah does not specifically raise the issue of the speech and its contents. He reiterates the concepts and conditions we saw above regarding the *seudat mitzvah* in honor of the *bar mitzvah* boy and applies them to the *bat mitzvah* as well.

In the sources cited in A. Ahrend's essay[34] from the years 1963–1964 (5723–5724), R. Yitzhak Nissim recommends that girls celebrate their *bat mitzvah* in the company of friends and relatives, and that a rabbi should be present. He suggests that "the rabbi should speak in honor of the event, addressing the prime importance of the *mitzvot* and the rewards of keeping them.... It is appropriate for [the girl] to prepare a short talk concerning the event and the importance of the day."

R. Nissim gives the girl herself an active role. He presents the *derashah* not as a vital component that makes the meal a *seudat mitzvah,* but as a desirable act on the *bat mitzvah* day. What we have here, to my mind, is a valuable educational opportunity of greater weight than the speech directed to the girl. His comments also relate to the content of the *derashah* – the

---

[33] *Responsa Yehavve daat,* 2.29.

[34] Aharon Ahrend, "*Hagigat bat mitzvah be-fiskei haRav Yitzhak Nissim,*" *Bat Mitzvah,* ed. S. Friendland ben Arza (Jerusalem 2002), pp. 109–115.

significance of the event itself. The advance preparation he suggests enables the girl to internalize the personal meaning of her taking the yoke of the commandments upon herself. His words may allude to R. Shlomo Luria's requirement to "prepare the youth to speak at the *seudah* on the meaning of the event."

The last figure in this series, chronologically as well, is R. Shaul Yisraeli. R. Yisraeli sets specific conditions for the event, one of them being that "the Rabbi should speak words of Torah…the girl can also speak of her responsibility in keeping *mitzvot*."[35]

3. Proceeding with sensitivity

For the component of the *derashah* to give the meal the character of a *seudat mitzvah*, I would add something else beyond the *halakhic* requirement. All of us have witnessed scenes in which the young man or woman is forced, on that special day, to stand before invited guests and read a speech written by the parents, an uncle, or a rabbi, without the young person's having participated in the process or the content. Even in cases when the youth participated in composing the *derashah*, chose the subject, or even wrote it herself or himself, we have sensed the artificiality of their statements about the importance of maturity, taking responsibility, etc. Usually, these are only empty words. Another problem we have all seen – the terrible embarrassment the young speaker suffers, and the difficulty we have in hearing and comprehending the speech, regardless of the quality of the text itself.

I would like to propose a certain solution, not at all new, that may help in overcoming most of these problems. What I suggest is a special learning framework for the *bar mitzvah* boy or *bat mitzvah* girl throughout the year before the event.[36] The creative process, in which the *derashah* takes form through active efforts in Torah study, differs radically from the artificial speeches described above. The intensity of the learning experience carries over to the way the speech is delivered as well. In this manner, the learning

---

[35] R. Shaul Yisraeli, *Responsa Bemareh Habazak* (Jerusalem 5750), vol. 1, *responsum* 7.3, p. 13.

[36] For an in-depth discussion on this point, see Bryna Levy's essay later in this volume.

becomes hers. As Rabba said,[37] "In the beginning, one's learning is called God's, but later it is called one's own, as the verse says, 'His desire is for God's Torah, and upon his Torah will he meditate day and night.' [Psalms 1:2]"

It is essential that the pace of the learning, the study load she adopts, and the material studied are suited to the girl's will and ability. As we saw above, the *bat mitzvah* speech should relate in some way to the event at hand, to the meaning of her acceptance of the *mitzvot*. Needless to say, the idea that the girl herself should speak is only a suggestion; clearly, not every girl – or boy for that matter – has the inborn ability to stand before an audience and give a *derashah*. More important, to my mind, than the externalized "final product" is the learning preceding the event, the preparation for and internalization of the significance of taking the *mitzvot* upon oneself. If the girl is unwilling to give the speech herself, her mother, father, relative, rabbi, teacher, or any combination of the above can do so. In that way, as well, the event gains the status of a *seudat mitzvah*.

F. Completing a Book – Making a *Siyyum*

The custom is already widespread for boys to devote the year preceding their *bar mitzvah* to learning a tractate of the Talmud, and to complete it on the day of their *bar mitzvah*. As we saw earlier, *siyyum massekhet* [completing a tractate] is grounds in and of itself for holding a *seudat mitzvah*. And yet, for a *bar mitzvah* to attain the status of a *seudat mitzvah,* we noted that there is no *halakhic* need for a *siyyum massekhet* or speech in honor of the event. The event itself, if held on or after the birthday, is sufficient.

1. Can a woman make a *siyyum?*

How should we relate to a girl interested in completing a tractate on the day of her *bat mitzvah?* Can a woman (post-*bat mitzvah*) who completes a tractate (or other unit of learning, as we will see below) hold, on an ordinary day, an official *siyyum* that fulfills the *halakhic* criteria for a *seudat mitzvah?*

Explicit *halakhic* treatment of this question may be found in the book *She'erit Yosef.* R. Shlomo Halevi Wahrman of Kew Garden Hills, New York

---

[37] *Avodah Zara* 19a.

was asked about the following case. A woman completes a tractate and holds a *seudah* in honor of the event; are the members of her household participating in the meal permitted to meat and drink wine during the first nine days of Av (c.f., Rema, *Oreh Hayyim*, 551)?[38] The decision whether a woman's learning is sufficient reason for holding a *seudat mitzvah* on the occasion of a *siyyum* carries definite *halakhic* ramifications.[39] A separate issue to be raised in this context is what the woman should learn in order to hold a *seudah* of that sort.[40] In his response, R. Wahrman examines the *halakhic* definition of the *mitzvah* of Torah study for women.[41] He recalls the Rambam's famous statement that a woman who learns Torah is surely rewarded as "one who is not commanded yet performs." He also delineates an aspect of Torah learning to which women, in his view, are fully obligated. He proposes distinguishing between two variants. First, Torah learning considered as "And you shall teach them" [Deuteronomy 11:19 – the second part of the *Shema*], from which women are exempt.[42] Second, learning for the sake of knowing Torah, after the verse [Deuteronomy 6:6, first part of the *Shema*], "And you shall instruct them [*veshinantem*] to your

---

[38] Eating meat and drinking wine are normally prohibited from the first through the ninth of Av as part of the observance of a period of mourning in commemoration of the destruction of the Temple in Jerusalem.

[39] See n. 2 above.

[40] On this question, see R. Shlomo Borenstein, "Siyum: Celebrating the Completion of a Mitzvah," *Journal of Halacha and Contemporary Society*, vol. 28, pp. 57–61. On the matter of who can be present, and when this sort of *siyyum* should be held, see pp. 54 ff. A brief treatment of the subject may also be found through the Internet site: http://pages.nyu/edu/. In discussing the *seudat siyyum*, the issues raised by *posekim* include: 1. On what type of book can one make a *siyyum*? 2. How much must one cover to make a *siyyum*? 3. To what degree of depth must one study the book? Is there a difference in definition between a regular meal held for finishing a unit of learning, a meal that exempts participants from a *taanit bekhorot*, and a meal that enables the eating of meat during the Nine Days? In his *responsum* in *Yabia Omer* 1.26, R. Ovadiah Yosef rules that a *seudat siyyum* can be held for completing a tractate of Mishna, provided it was learned in depth and with full comprehension. R. Yosef mentions a series of *posekim* on the issue. R. Shlomo Kluger, in *Healef lekha Shlomo*, s. 386 permits holding a *seudah* on the occasion of completing one of the prophetic books of the *Tanakh*, if it was not learned solely for the sake of the *seudah* itself. R. Moshe Feinstein (*Responsa Iggerot Moshe, Oreh Hayyim* 1.157) rules similarly, on the condition the book was learned with classical biblical exegesis.

[41] On this subject, in a different context than the *seudat siyyum*, see R. Aryeh Strikovsky's essay later in this volume.

[42] C.f. *Kiddushin* 29b.

children" – that the words of Torah should be sharp [i.e., dear] in your mouth.[43] The second variant, he suggests, should be obligatory for women.[44] Having established a woman's obligation to study Torah to the extent that she becomes well versed in Torah, he concludes, "After having performed the whole *mitzvah* herself, over such a long period of time, who can imagine the happiness in her heart? Certainly there is an obligation to have a *seudah*...."

A contrary opinion is voiced by R. Shlomo Bornstein in the name of R. Hayyim Pinhas Sheinberg.[45] In his view, because women's learning as a whole falls in the category of "not commanded yet performing," a woman's completion of a unit of study does not mandate a *seudat mitzvah*.

2. Sources for Making a *Siyyum* and Their Implications

To gain a clearer view of the issue, we need to examine the source for holding a *seudah* in honor of completing a unit of Torah study. R. Shlomo Luria, as we saw above, wrote extensively about the *seudat siyyum*.[46] He cites two possible sources for the custom to hold a meal at the completion of a tractate.[47] The first reads:[48] "Abaye taught, 'I shall be rewarded, for when I see that a young Torah scholar has completed a tractate, I hold a *seudah*[49] for all the Torah scholars.'" Rashi there explains that Abaye was the head of a *yeshivah*, and would celebrate his student's completion of a *massekhet* with a festive meal. D. Golinkin[50] posits that at issue is a tractate of the Mishna, as the Babylonian Talmud was not yet a text as such in Abaye's time. However, we need not draw that conclusion. The Amoraim

---

[43] C.f. *Kiddushim* 30b and *Sifre Devarim* (ed. Finkelstein) 3–6, p. 60.

[44] R. Shlomo Halevi Wahrman, *She'erit Yosef*, 2.4.

[45] R. Hayyim Pinhas Sheinberg, who lives in Jerusalem, is a prominent rabbinical figure in the ultra-Orthodox community.

[46] *Yam shel Shlomo, Bava Kama*, end of chapter 7.

[47] The same two sources are mentioned by R. Moshe Isserles, *Shulhan Arukh, Yoreh Deah* 246.26.

[48] *Shabbat* 118b.

[49] We find the Aramaic phrase Abaye uses, *yoma tava*, in the sense of a "meal" in *Berakhot* 46a.

[50] David Golinkin, *"Teshuvah be-inyan seudat 'siyyum bekhorot' be-arvei pesahim,"* Et la-asot 1, Summer 5748, pp. 88–102.

apparently had a corpus of teachings adjacent to the Mishna that took form gradually over the years.[51] One distinct message that can be drawn from this source is that the *mitzvah* relates not only to the individual scholar who has completed a unit. As the *Yam shel Shlomo* comments, "Even someone who has not finished that tractate has the great *mitzvah* of rejoicing together with the scholar who has. Hence Abaye, although he may not have completed it himself, 'held a *seudah* for all the scholars' – in other words, he would invite others to join him." This source, cited in two places in *Yam shel Shlomo*, is apparently the principal origin for the custom to make a meal on the occasion of a *siyyum massekhet*.[52]

The second source that R. Shlomo Luria evokes appears in two talmudic contexts.[53] Why, it is asked, is Tu be-Av (the fifteenth day of the month of Av) considered a festive day for the Jewish people, *yom tov le-Yisrael?* This is one of the answers proposed: "Raba and Rav Yosef both said, 'That is the date [of the year] that trees cease to be chopped down [for use in the Temple sacrifices]."[54] Rashbam comments: "And the day they stopped, all were joyous for having completed such a tremendous *mitzvah*." R. Nissim and the *Nimmukei Yosef* elaborate: "It is indeed customary to be joyous regarding a *mitzvah;* when one has been fully performed, we have a celebration, a feast and a *yom tov*." The emphasis here is on the completion of a (great) *mitzvah*. Indeed, R. Moshe Feinstein selects this as the primary

---

[51] In fact, "young Torah scholars" or *tzorba de-rabbanan* in Abaye's phrase were individuals whose learning was considered more intensive/profound than that of the "*tannaim*" who learned and reviewed only the *mishnayot*. C.f., *Megillah* 28b. It therefore seems likely that completion of a *massekhet* by these young scholars entailed more than merely knowing the plain meaning of the Mishna.

[52] A number of reasons, beyond the scope of our discussion, underlie this. First, the explicit subject is a *yoma tova,* i.e., *seudah*, as we remarked in n. 49 above. In the next source, however, the parallel Hebrew phrase appears – "There were no better days (*yamim tovim*) for the Jews…" – but it is unclear whether here, too, the connotation is a *seudah*. Moreover, the basis suggested there for the importance of Tu be-Av is but one of six different reasons. Finally, in our first source, the central point of discussion is *siyyum massekhet*.

[53] *Ta'anit* 30b and *Bava Batra* 121a.

[54] After Tu be-Av the weather started getting cooler; the cut trees did not dry sufficiently in the sun, and there was danger that the wood might get wormy and unusable for use in the Temple sacrifices.

source for the custom of holding a *siyyum massekhet*.[55] This passage makes clear that a *yom tov* is made for the completion of other *mitzvot* as well (other than completing a book), *mitzvot* in which a person invested much energy over an extended period of time. For that reason, this source opens up the possibility of holding a *seudah* in celebration of completing study units other than a tractate of Mishna or Gemara. That is the conclusion R. Moshe Feinstein eventually reaches.

We understand now why *Yam shel Shlomo* cited both sources.[56] The first one indicates explicitly that a *seudah* was held in honor of finishing a tractate. The second one joins finishing a tractate together with the celebration of completing performance of *mitzvot* in general. I believe the *Yam shel Shlomo* sought to create a comprehensive definition of the concept *seudat mitzvah*, and to include the *seudat siyyum* in it as well.

In terms of our subject, then, it seems that a woman's completion of a *massekhet* would correspond to that definition. As we have seen: "any meal held not simply out of happiness and friendship, but in order to offer praise and thanks to God, *to announce the performance of a mitzvah [emphasis added],* or to make known one's experience of a personal "miracle" [*pirsum ha-nes*] is called a *seudat mitzvah*."

R. Sheinberg ruled that a woman who learns Torah is not doing so in fulfillment of a commandment. In that manner, he eliminated the possibility that a woman could make a *seudah* to celebrate completion of a unit of Torah. R. Wahrman, on the other hand, was motivated by the same source to find a broader basis for women's learning, a framework that would grant her learning the importance of a *mitzvah* and thereby accord her *seudat siyyum* the status of a *seudat mitzvah*.

If we base ourselves solely on the first source, Abaye's practice described in *Shabbat* 118b, there is no apparent problem with holding a

---

[55] *Iggerot Moshe, Oreh Hayyim* 1. 157.

[56] There are other potential sources for the practice. For example, the Maharsha on *Shabbat* 118b cites the midrash *Shir ha-Shirim Rabba* 1: "Immediately, '[King Shlomo] came to Jerusalem, and stood before the ark of the covenant of the Lord, and offered up burnt offerings, and offered peace offerings, and made a feast *[mishteh]* for all his servants' [1Kings 3:15]. R. Elazar said, From this we learn that a *seudah* should be held for completing a unit of Torah [*le-gomra shel Torah*]." This source is frequently cited by *posekim* as a basis for the *simhat Torah* as well as the source for celebrating a *siyyum massekhet*.

seudah in honor of a girl's *siyyum* and saying the customary accompanying text [*nusah ha-siyyum*].[57] There is no reference here to whether or not it is considered a "great *mitzvah*." On the other hand, relying on this source alone would exclude the possibility of making a *siyyum* in honor of finishing any unit other than a tractate of Mishna or Talmud. As we have seen, for some *posekim* and in some communities, this very possibility may be relevant for a good number of young women who wish to study a book of *Tanakh* in preparation for their *bat mitzvah*. In any case, R. Wahrman's definition aside, we could say that a woman's Torah learning – even if she is in the category of "not commanded yet performing" – may be considered to be a great and important enough *mitzvah* to merit holding a *seudat mitzvah* at its completion.

It should be stressed once again that, as in the case of the *derashah*, the principal value of the *siyyum* does not lie in the one-time event of the *seudah* itself. Rather, it is the culmination of a long and meaningful process for the girl, who has taken upon herself to learn the Torah and transform it into her own Torah, and has realized her goal. The importance of the ceremony is in its power to motivate and strengthen the girl to continue learning. Moreover, it may well encourage other girls (as well as other women and men) to grow in their own Torah learning. It shows an appreciation for the inner feeling of accomplishment and is an expression of the deep satisfaction that stems from her perseverance in the difficult labor of Torah. It also contains a prayer for her future, and the future of *Am Yisrael*.

> Please, Hashem, our God, sweeten the words of Your Torah in
> our mouth and in the mouths of Your People, the House of Israel,
> and may we, our offspring, and the offspring of Your people, the

---

[57] This text may be found at the end of all tractates of the Babylonian Talmud and includes the recitation of a special *kaddish*. According to some *halakhic* authorities, *kaddish* may also be said. This issue stimulated a serious disagreement over the question of whether a woman who is an only daughter is permitted to say the Mourner's *kaddish*. Among those who permit it are: R. Yaakov Risher, *Responsa Shevut Yaakov*, 2. 93; R. Eliezer Zalman Greivasky, *Sefer kaddish le-olam*, fol. 11a-12a; R. Yehuda Henkin, *Teshuvot Bnei Banim* 4; R. Shaul Yisraeli, *Responsa Bemarei habazak* 21, p. 38, *responsum* 13.1. Other *posekim* permit or forbid it with various limitations. For more on the subject, see R. Joel Wolowelsky, *Women, Jewish Law and Modernity*, pp. 84–94. All agree that *kaddish* can be said only in the presence of a *minyan* of ten adult men. C.f., *Megillah* 23b and Rambam, *Mishneh Torah, Hilkhot Tefillah u-nesiat kapayim* 8.4.

House of Israel, may all of us know Your name and study Your Torah. Your commandment makes me wiser than my enemies, for it is forever with me. May my heart be perfect in Your statutes, so that I not be shamed. I will never forget Your precepts, for through them You have preserved me.

Conclusion

We have seen that *seudot mitzvah*, particularly those held in honor of a *bar mitzvah* or *bat mitzvah*, can be an appropriate means of marking transitions. In the case of the *bat mitzvah*, the meal can mark the young woman's acceptance of the yoke of *mitzvot* in the company of her relatives and friends. The *seudat mitzvah* has the power to turn those who sit together into a *mitzvah* community and cause, through their joy in participating in a *mitzvah*, the *Shekhinah* to dwell among them. We found no *halakhic* problem in defining the *bat mitzvah* meal on par with the *bar mitzvah* meal. The value of these *seudot* depends on the content invested in them, and the meaningful preparations made before them. The process of creating a *derashah* and the learning that leads to the *seudah* in honor of completing a study unit both have tremendous potential. They can transform the *bat mitzvah* day into a memorable milestone in life of the girl itself, and a meaningful important event in the life of her community.

BAT MITZVAH CELEBRATIONS

Rabbi Joel B. Wolowelsky

Certainly, when we see women as full members of the Torah community – much as we take for granted their full membership in our everyday society – it becomes difficult to oppose the logic of the *bat mitzvah* celebration. The principle that "it is better to act out of *halakhic* obligation than personal commitment" applies to women as well as men. A religious girl should feel no less excited about finally being obligated in *mitzvot* than would a boy. As R. Yehiel Yaakov Weinberg noted, instituting *bat mitzvah* celebrations is but a logical extension of the relatively recent establishment of serious Torah schools for women.

Straight logical reasoning and the basic principles of pedagogy just about compel us to also celebrate girls reaching the age of obligation in *mitzvot*. The discrimination that we maintain between boys and girls celebrating reaching maturity deeply offends the personal feelings of the mature girl, who in other areas of life has already earned emancipation, as it were.[1]

R. Weinberg then raised the more general issue of the limits of establishing ceremonies that seem to imitate those of the non-Jewish world, deciding that any similarities between a *bat mitzvah* celebration and, say, Christian confirmation ceremonies are irrelevant. Indeed, it seems that *responsa* of the last generation opposing establishing *bat mitzvah* celebrations have little resonance in our modern Orthodox world. Imitating Christian confirmation rituals or mimicking Reform ceremonies are simply not part of our consciousness. *Bat mitzvah* celebrations in our religious community are conducted *leshem mitzvah,* for the sake of the *mitzvah* itself, and, as R. Weinberg concluded,[2] our attitude towards these celebrations should turn on the motivation of those who wish to introduce them.

---

[1] R. Yehiel Yaakov Weinberg, *Responsa Seridei Esh* (Jerusalem: Mosad HaRav Kook, 1977), 3.93, p. 297.

[2] Ibid., p. 298.

The problem, then, is how to concretize our natural inclination in this matter. Of course, some parents are simply organizing only a public show; the obligation in *mitzvot* is, for them, nothing to celebrate. The key, then, for understanding the parents' motivation in organizing a *bat mitzvah* party is in how they celebrate their daughter's becoming obliged in *mitzvot*. Local rabbis should be taking the lead in working out a proper observance. Certainly their relative inaction has nothing to do with enforcing traditional values.

The form that the *bat mitzvah* celebration takes should reflect our perspective on women's role in society. In our schools, we educate girls to express their maturity with some public performance; they learn to speak in front of their respective classes, give reports, hold school office, and so on. Our religious expression should take note of this widespread assumption and we should expect the *bat mitzvah* girl to present herself in some way as an adult. The *devar Torah* is a natural vehicle for this public adult performance; hence the growing custom of the girl's *siyyum* being the center of a *bat mitzvah* celebration. Some will finish a *massekhet* of Mishna, some a chapter of Talmud, others a book of Tanakh. Some will prefer a *devar Torah* on a specific topic of research.

There is some debate on whether the *bat mitzvah* girl should deliver her address in the synagogue proper, with repeated reference to R. Moshe Feinstein's insistence that any ceremony be kept out of the synagogue.[3] But here too it is important to note how the celebration would fit into our everyday use of the synagogue. R. Feinstein had noted that *bat mitzvah* celebrations are purely *reshut* (permitted but not obligatory) activities. As a general rule, the holiness of the synagogue *(kedushat beit hakenneset)* precludes its being used for optional activities. However, virtually all of our synagogues are now built with an explicit intention of using it for other purposes, thereby allowing them to be used for a whole range of *reshut* activities, including lectures. Thus, if women speak in the synagogue during the week, there is no reason why the *bat mitzvah* girl cannot speak from the pulpit after the services are over. (Indeed, some *shuls* that allow this make a point of asking the men to remove their *talitot* to formally indicate that the service is over.)

---

[3] R. Moshe Feinstein, *Responsa Iggerot Moshe* (New York: Moriah, 1959) *Oreh Hayyim*, 1.104, p. 170.

If we believe that reaching the age of *mitzvot* is equally significant for boys and girls alike, we should be careful not to send a contradictory message. For example, if the *bat mitzvah* girl does not speak from the pulpit, neither should the *bar mitzvah* boy. Neither youngster's *devar Torah* is part of the service and could be delivered elsewhere. The rabbi would certainly want to congratulate the *bar* or *bat mitzvah* from the pulpit, but if she is not called forward to receive a gift, neither should he be. The simplest solution would be to arrange a *seudah* and preface it with a *siyyum*. This would also be a good opportunity for the rabbi to speak and present the synagogue's gifts.

The synagogue gift chosen for presentation also sends a communal message. In general, a set of books seems right for both a *bar* and *bat mitzvah* and, indeed, there are many – such as a set of *Mishna Berurah* – that would be appropriate for both. The candlesticks that some give a *bat mitzvah* is somewhat impractical – most young girls do not follow the Lubavitch custom of lighting Shabbat candles – and involves *halakhic* problems.[4] Actually, when we think about it calmly, we realize that the real preference should be a *kiddush* cup; she is now obligated in *kiddush* just as is an adult man.[5] In many homes, only the *ba-al habayit* says *kiddush* Friday night; yet the sons at the table often have their own *kiddush* cup as a symbol of their adulthood. The same should be true of the daughters in the family who have reached the age of *mitzvot*.

While a *seudah* can be arranged for any convenient time, the *seudah shel-ishit* on Shabbat afternoon has the added advantage of being a community affair not limited to invited guests. Others have decided to make use of the community *oneg Shabbat* held in the synagogue complex after dinner Friday night. A *seudah* on a Sunday for invited guests is similarly appropriate. Halakhists might disagree whether a meal in honor of a *bat mitzvah* is in and of itself a *seudat mitzvah*. But, as R. Ovadia Yosef points out, when the meal is accompanied by appropriate *divrei Torah*, all must concede its status as a *seudat mitzvah*.[6]

---

[4] R. J. David Bleich, "Sabbath Candles for Young Girls," *Tradition*, 16:1, Summer 1976, pp. 150–155.

[5] *Shulhan Arukh, Oreh Hayyim*, 271:2.

[6] R. Ovadia Yosef, *Responsa Yabia Omer*, (Jerusalem: Porat Yosef, 1976), *Oreh Hayyim*, 6. 29, pp. 96–99.

There are those who turn to women's prayer groups as the proper venue for *bat mitzvah* celebrations. This is not the place to review the various controversies that have centered on these groups.[7] If the *bat mitzvah*'s family is a member of such a prayer group during the year, it is certainly appropriate to observe the celebration there. But if that is not the case, then – *halakhic* arguments regarding the groups themselves aside – participation there has the same non-authenticity as showing up in a *shul* for a *bar mitzvah* celebration and stumbling over the blessings. Women's prayer groups, at this time, do not enjoy widespread participation among the women of our community. *Bat mitzvah* observances should flow naturally from our everyday Torah assumptions and life-style.

Our *yeshivot* have a responsibility to educate our students in an appreciation of reaching the age of *mitzvot* without encouraging the excess all-too-often common to *bar* and *bat mitzvah* celebrations. Certainly, school bulletins and synagogue newsletters should regularly congratulate *benot mitzvah* just as they do *benei mitzvah*. But group celebrations rob each celebrant of being the appropriate focal point for the day. (One yeshivah elementary school educator conducted a "group" *bat mitzvah* celebration on a Sunday morning. All sixth-grade girls rehearsed all term for a musical cantata that included singing and dancing [but no *divrei Torah*]; each girl received candlesticks. It would be interesting to see what a parallel boys' celebration would be.) An appropriate model would be a breakfast for the girl's class following *tefillot*; the *bat mitzvah* (or *benot mitzvah*) can speak, as can the teacher, and the girl can be the focus of a simple *seudat mitzvah*. This same breakfast model would work well for *benei mitzvah* too.

A major technical *halakhic* issue associated with *bat mitzvah* celebrations is that of the blessing "*she-petarani me-onsho shel ze*" ("who has relieved me of this one's punishments"), usually said by the father of a *bar mitzvah* when the boy first gets an *aliyah* to the Torah. There are two longstanding debates concerning this *berakhah* as it is applied to a *bar mitzvah*: What does the

---

[7] See, for example, Aryeh A. Frimer and Dov Frimer, "Women's Prayer Service: Theory and Practice," *Tradition*, 32:2, Winter 1998, pp. 5–118.

blessing mean, and should it be said in full *berakhah* form (*beshem umalkhut*)?[8]

The latter question evolves from the fact that this *berakhah* is not mentioned in either Talmud. There is a general prohibition against instituting new *berakhot*; hence the reluctance to assign full status to this *berakhah*. Sephardic custom is to say it in a contracted form (*beli shem umalkhut*). (This is in accordance with general Sephardic custom of limiting whenever possible the saying of a *berakhah* that is questionable in any way.) Ashkenazic authorities differ among themselves; the Gaon of Vilna, for example, rules that it should be said as a full *berakhah*, while others side with the Sephardic custom.

There are two interpretations regarding the meaning of the *berakhah*. The first relates to the idea that a minor child can be punished for the sins of his father. When the child reaches adulthood, the father gives thanks that he will be no longer be responsible for the suffering of his son. The second interpretation is that the father is responsible for educating his minor son in the ways of Torah. If the latter sins, the former is held responsible for those transgressions. Now that the son is responsible for his own education, the father gives thanks for no longer being held responsible.

As former Israeli Chief Rabbis Yitzhak Nissim[9] and Ovadia Yosef[10] point out, both reasons apply equally to a girl who reaches the age of *mitzvot*. They therefore rule that the father should say the *berakhah* in contracted form (*beli shem umalkhut*, as is Sephardic custom) – when his daughter reaches the age of *mitzvot*.

R. Elyakim Elinson notes further that not only do these lines of reasoning apply equally to the daughter and son, they apply equally to mother and father. Indeed, he points out, the mother might have greater obligation than the father in educating a daughter. Preference, he says, should therefore be given to the mother at a *bat mitzvah* celebration (although both can

---

[8] R. Binyamin Adler, *Hilkhot ve-Halikhot Bar Mitzvah* (Jerusalem: Sefarim Or HaTorah, 5734 [1974]), pp.77–81.

[9] R. Yitshak Nissim, "*Al birkhat barukh shepetarani*," *Noam* (Jerusalem: Mahon Torah Sheleima, 5724 [1964]), vol. 7, pp. 1–5.

[10] R. Ovadia Yosef, *Responsa Yabia Omer, Oreh Hayyim*, 6.29, pp. 96–99.

say it).[11] Similarly, the mother can recite the *berakhah* at a *bar mitzvah* celebration too. R. Elinson cites Rabbis Nissim and Yosef to the effect that the *berakhah* should be said *beli shem umalkhut*, although it is unclear why those authorities who say that a full *berakhah* should be said at a *bar mitzvah* celebration would not maintain the same position for a *bat mitzvah*. Either way, just as she can say *birkhat hagommel* in the synagogue during the Torah reading, the mother can do so for this *berakhah*, although she might better recite it at the *seudat mitzvah* when she speaks. Here is another opportunity to have the mother's voice heard in our community, and it should not be lost.

---

[11] R. Elyakim G. Elinson, *Ha-isha vehamitsvot*, vol. 1 (Jerusalem: The Jewish Agency, 5734 [1974]), pp. 181–184.

THE *BAT MITZVAH* IN CONTEMPORARY LAW AND JEWISH PRACTICE*

ERICA BROWN

The ceremony that marks the *bar mitzvah* is a relatively late addition to the corpus of Jewish law and practice. For the girl, the *bat mitzvah* celebration is an even later development and, arguably, still in formation. Significantly, the Talmud makes no mention of festivities comparable to contemporaneous practice. In *Pirkei Avot* (*Ethics of our Fathers*), we read about the age of thirteen as the acceptance of the commandments but the age is only one of many in the expanse of Jewish life. "At five for Scripture, at ten for Mishna, at thirteen for *mitzvot*, at fifteen for Gemara, at eighteen for marriage…."[1] The age of thirteen is only one of several stages in a young man's spiritual and educational development. The current practice of celebration is rooted in a midrash on Genesis 25:27, "The boys grew," referring to Esav and Yaacov:

> R. Elazar said: A man must see to the needs of his son until he is thirteen, from there onwards he must say: "Blessed is He who released me from the responsibility for this one."[2]

The blessing did not evolve into an actual ceremony until much later. In the sixteenth century, R. Shlomo Luria discusses whether or not a meal on the day of the *bar mitzvah* is considered a *seudat mitzvah*, a festive meal to commemorate a commandment. He determines that it would qualify as

---

* This essay was originally published in *Jewish Legal Writings by Women* (Urim, 1998), pp. 232–258. It appears here with permission of the publisher, with minor editorial changes.

[1] *Pirkei Avot*, 5:25.

[2] *Bereishit Rabbah*, 63.10.

long as the boy gave a *halakhic* discourse during the meal.[3] Thus, the celebration was still in formation four hundred years ago which, in the span of rabbinic literature, makes this a rather late legal development.

Why the development of a male ritual rather than one for both genders evolved at this time is unclear, when the purpose for the celebration is presumably the same regardless of gender. R. Alfred S. Cohen, in his article on the topic in the *Journal of Halacha and Contemporary Society* asks this important question:

> ...the rationale for making a celebration for a boy who reaches the age of thirteen arises from the fact that a person has to give thanks for achieving a higher level of religious responsibility. Since a girl of twelve undergoes the very same elevation in status, progressing to a level where she has to observe all the *mitzvot* incumbent upon a Jewish woman, does it not follow that there should be the identical obligation to make a party for her?[4]

Jewish educational institutions and parents who express the same concern have, in the last decades, tried to create more religious depth to mark the occasion for girls. Realizing that this entrance into Jewish adulthood, if not significant, can be a farewell to Judaism — especially if compared to the opportunities offered the male at the same life interval — parents and educators have explored new and old ritual observance for the young woman. The ones currently employed by parents anxious to ensure that their daughters feel this important religious transition are usually more a matter of personal predilection than uniformly prescribed, or expected, tradition. More often than not, because no standard ceremony has been adopted in ritually observant communities, the attempt at making religion more egalitarian has led to boys and girls having the same costly party,

---

[3] R. Shlomo Luria, *Yam shel Shlomo, Bava Kama,* 7.37. For more extensive discussion of this subject, see Yardena Cope-Yossef's essay earlier in this volume.

[4] R. Alfred S. Cohen, "Celebration of the Bat Mitzvah," *Journal of Halacha and Contemporary Society,* 12 (New York, 1986) p. 8. In this article I will move from primary sources to secondary sources, the latter consisting mostly of articles reviewing various legal aspects of the *bat mitzvah* celebration. Several of these articles brought new *halakhic* sources to my attention.

sometimes devoid of spiritual content. Lisa Aiken, in her book *To Be a Jewish Woman,* mentions that in the absence of uniform ritual for the *bat mitzvah* that, "The possibilities are endless."[5] One wonders what she means by this. Even if this were the case, perhaps the range of alternatives should not be endless. While some use the ambiguity of Jewish law on the matter as an opportunity to craft unusual and poignant ceremonies, the fact that there is no consistent practice, endorsed by the rabbinic community, leaves the girl – perhaps not fully realized until much later in life – a sense that her passage is more a matter of invention than of tradition.

This paper is a plea for the Orthodox rabbinic establishment to create a *uniform* ceremony that acknowledges the significance of young women entering the adult world of *mitzvah* observance. The *halakhic* analysis that follows will try to demonstrate where, within the framework of Jewish law, there may be more room to include young women in ritual performance. Yet these represent only a few suggestions to stimulate more thought about the issue of a girl's religious development in general. When a discussion of *bat mitzvah* becomes tied to a host of other potentially explosive issues – as it has – we lose sight of the most significant question: what do we have to do as rabbis, parents, and educators to ensure that the next generation of Jewish women will be spiritually demanding, ritually observant, and fully educated?

In order properly to explore Jewish legal writings on the possibilities open for the *bat mitzvah* celebration, we will look at three customs that are central to the day of celebration: the blessing traditionally recited by the father over the son, the speech or *derashah,* and the commemorative meal or *seudat mitzvah.*[6] Then we have to put the legal discussion within a broader picture

---

[5] Lisa Aiken, *To Be a Jewish Woman* (Northvale, New Jersey: Jason Aaronson, 1992) p. 241.

[6] R. Michael Broyde brought to my attention the need for rituals that demonstrate that the girl entering Jewish adulthood can now fill the religious obligations of others. Presumably, under the general rubric of the *mitzvah* of *hinukh*, she has been observing most commandments up until this point. The *bat mitzvah* shows a change of status by filling another's responsibility for commandment performance. This can be accomplished by any number of commandments. More than any of the other observances of the day, R. Broyde feels that this is central to the meaning of the *bat mitzvah*. Although

of *halakhic* development to see the limitations on new rituals for this event, why they exist and what direction might be fruitful for a preservation of the spirit of *halakhah*, while acknowledging the changing demands placed on Jewish women today. This will be framed by a brief discussion of maturity in Jewish law, an area in which boys and girls share more similarities in Jewish law than differences.

Maturity in Jewish Law

Maturity is defined in Jewish law as the age at which an individual becomes responsible for commandment performance. This is technically defined as twelve years and one day for a girl and thirteen years and one day for a boy. A *mishna* in *Niddah* confirms this new stage of "*halakhic* maturity:"

> At eleven and one day, a girl's vows are inspected; at twelve and one day, they are valid. At twelve and one day, a boy's vows are inspected; at thirteen and one day, they are valid. Before this age, even if they were to say, "We know to whom we are vowing, to whom we are donating," their vows are not vows and their donations are not donations. After that age, even were they to say, "We do not know to whom we are vowing, to whom we are sanctifying," their vows are vows and their donations are donations.[7]

Before the prescribed ages, even were they mature enough to realize the implications of the oaths they had just taken, the children's vows would not be valid. Once they each reach a certain age respectively, regardless of their actual maturity, they are legally bound by their own words. Thus, the Mishna acknowledges that at a very definite date, children become ready to enter the legal world of adults and to assume responsibility for the way they speak and act regarding the performance of Jewish law. Maturity, however,

---

I agree in principle with his conclusion, I think there are certain accepted "norms" for the *bar mitzvah* celebration that can be meaningful and of educational value for the *bat mitzvah* as well, provided that they are *halakhically* permissible, of course. To merely point to one area to mark the occasion, such as allowing the young woman to make a blessing over bread for her guests, would be to strip the day of other aspects which have also become integral to Jewish rites of passage.

[7] Mishna *Niddah* 5:6.

is defined not only by some mental transition that translates into action at twelve and thirteen, but also by the physical transformation that is assumed will take place during early adolescence. The Mishna in *Sanhedrin* records that the onset of puberty is also significant for the observance of Jewish law.

> "A stubborn and rebellious son" (Deuteronomy 21:18) – when does he become liable to the penalty of a stubborn and rebellious son? From the time he produces two hairs until he grows a beard around [i.e., the hair of the genitals, not the face, but the Sages spoke in polite terms].[8]

The *Shulhan Arukh* describes those who can participate in a quorum as, "males, free men, adults who have [at least] two pubic hairs."[9] For males, then, there is a correlation between the onset of puberty and liability or responsibility. Maimonides makes a distinction, in the physical realm, between males and females:

> A girl, after twelve years of age, even were she not to have signs [two pubic hairs], not beneath and not above, is considered an adult. Boys are as their signs…. A boy until thirteen is termed a *katan* and *tinok* even if he has a few hairs before this time, this is not as a sign but [considered like] a mole…when he is thirteen years old and one day and older he is termed a *gadol* and an *ish*.[10]

Elsewhere, though, Maimonides makes no distinction between boys and girls and the significance of physical maturity coinciding with their respective ages:

> A girl of twelve and a day and a boy of thirteen and a day who have brought forth two hairs are considered as adults with regard

---

[8] Mishha *Sanhedrin* 8:1.

[9] *Shulhan Arukh, Oreh Hayyim,* 55:1.

[10] Maimonides, *Mishneh Torah, Hilkhot ishut,* 2.9–10.

to all of the commandments and are obligated to complete [the fast on Yom Kippur]. But if they have not brought forth two hairs, they are still minors and their completion of the fast is rabbinical in status.[11]

The *Shulhan Arukh* follows Maimonides' position on this matter in *Hilkhot yom ha-kippurim* and echoes his formulation:

A girl of twelve and one day and a boy of thirteen and one day who have brought forth two hairs are considered adults with regard to all of the commandments and must complete [the fast] as an obligation from the Torah, but if they have not brought forth two hairs then they are regarded as minors and complete the fast as a rabbinical obligation only.[12]

At the time when a child shows physical signs of adulthood, he or she must begin to accept more adult responsibilities. Although a distinction might be made between girls and boys as to the significance of puberty for *mitzvah* observance, it is clear that maturity of mind and of body coincide regardless of gender, and that the Torah accords full adult status only to a person who begins to show physical signs of puberty. Boys and girls both move into adulthood physically; spiritually, though, the divergence begins.

The responsibilities that are assumed at this stage of development are relatively clear for males, from the wearing of *tefillin* to participation in daily synagogue prayer. For the female, according to Jewish law, the major rite of passage mentioned in the Talmud is fasting on *Yom Kippur*: "At the age of twelve, they must fast to the end of the day by biblical law, referring to girls."[13] The age of puberty, for the female, does not mark an added sense of outward communal responsibility or the acceptance of ritual, aside from the commandment just mentioned which is also incumbent upon the boy. "As far as religious responsibility is concerned, although a girl becomes so

---

[11] Maimonides, *Mishneh Torah, Shvitut Esor*, 2.11.

[12] *Shulhan Arukh, Oreh Hayyim*, 1216.2.

[13] *Yoma* 82a.

obligated at puberty, she never has the wide range of personal obligation that a male assumes. In addition, there are no central symbols, representing new roles, similar to the male's *tallit* and *tefillin*."[14] While the body of Jewish law does become incumbent upon the girl at this age, there are no public signs or an understood communal activity that represent rites of passage into adulthood. One cannot overstate the difference between the nature of *mitzvot* like the acceptance of personal prayer and fasting and *mitzvot* like *tefillin* and communal prayer, which the individual is expected to perform in the company of a community with outward symbols of maturity. Additionally, there are outward displays of acceptance into the community on the actual day of the *bar mitzvah* that are not permitted or demanded of the girl on her *bat mitzvah*. It is to these that we turn now.

The Blessing of the Parents

Even though the recitation of the *barukh sheptarani* blessing is the shortest part of the ceremony, it represents, as we saw in the midrash cited earlier, the beginning of the ritual of *bar mitzvah*. According to the *Magen Avraham*, the seventeenth-century Polish scholar, R. Avraham Gombiner, the blessing frees the father from punishment for the son's transgressions as the child assumes responsibility for his own actions.[15] Until that age, the father is responsible for the religious education of his son, and the child's misconduct can be attributed to poor training on the part of the father.[16] Consequently, the blessing is central because its meaning is seminal to what the *bar mitzvah* signifies – the assumption of adult responsibilities and the end of parental responsibility. The blessing recited is a dramatization, on a certain level, of an encounter between generations and a symbolic separa-

---

[14] Cherie Koller-Fox, "Women and Jewish Education: A New Look at Bat Mitzvah" in *The Jewish Woman: New Perspectives*, ed. Elizabeth Koltun, (New York: Schocken, 1976), p. 35.

[15] *Magen Avraham, Oreh Hayyim*, 225.5. See also, *Hokhmat Shelomo*, ad. loc.

[16] See also the *Pri Megadim* on the blessing as releasing the father from educational responsibilities toward his son. This has consequences regarding whether or not the blessing is recited over daughters: if the father has no responsibility to educate his daughter, the blessing would have no substantive meaning and would not, therefore, be recited. (For more on the issue of parental responsibility in education of daughters, see R. Aryeh Strikovsky's essay in this volume. [Editor's note])

tion. R. Yehuda Henkin in his work of *responsa, Benei Banim,* evokes Yitz-chak to explain the nature of the blessing. Yitzchak raised two sons, Yaacov and Esav, who took two very different life paths. This demonstrates that despite all that a parent can invest in a child, children have other influences and make life choices that go outside of the parental domain. It is for this that the parent makes the blessing, releasing himself of the culpability for choices that do not accord with his own will.[17]

The sixteenth century commentator, the *Levush,* R. Mordechai Yaffe, posits a novel interpretation for the blessing's meaning. He says that the child actually recites it to free himself of the father's sins, in accord with the biblical notion that the sins of the fathers are visited upon the children.[18] This is in contrast to one rabbinic authority who writes that the punish-ment of the son is in itself a punishment for the father, and that the blessing need not be read according to the *Levush's* interpretation.[19] The *Divrei Hamudot,* R. Yom Tov Lipman Heller, criticizes this interpretation as forced and brings the more traditional understanding of the verse.[20] The *Hokhmat Shlomo,* a later nineteenth-century commentary on the *Oreh Hayyim* of the *Shulhan Arukh,* R. Shlomo Kluger, adds that the concept of the child being punished for his father's sins, a complex idea with conditions, is operative during adulthood as well and would, therefore, serve no purpose at this juncture.[21] The language of the blessing also does not suggest that it is the son reciting this blessing over the father.[22]

The blessing, traditionally recited by the father, signals not only the pa-rental break of responsibility for commandment performance, but en-hances the child's sense of independence. Therefore, it would seem that

---

[17] R. Yehuda Herzl Henkin, *Benei Banim,* 18. For a lovely explanation of the blessing's meaning as the child transforming sin into merit and the father acknowledging this through recitation of the blessing, see R. Eliyahu Shlessinger, *She'elot uteshuvot sho'alin ve-dorshin* (Jerusalem, 1997) 1:70–74.

[18] *Levush,* Oreh Hayyim, 225.5.

[19] R. Henkin, 18.

[20] *Divrei Hamudot, Perush le-piskei ha-Rosh, Berakhot* 9.30.

[21] *Hokhmat Shlomo, Oreh Hayyim,* 225.5.

[22] R. Henkin, 18.

this blessing should equally be recited for the *bat mitzvah*, who is also under the guidance and training of her parents until she assumes responsibility for her actions. To this, *halakhic* authorities have generally followed one of two courses. The first assumes that the father is not essentially responsible for the education of his daughter and the second, in contradistinction, holds that the father is responsible for his daughter until marriage, and since the blessing is one of relinquishing responsibility, its recitation would be inappropriate. The *Magen Avraham, Pri Megadim* and *Kaf Ha-hayyim* concur that no blessing is involved for the daughter, following their ruling that the education of the daughter is in the mother's domain. Both the *Pri Megadim*, R. Yosef Te'omim in the eighteenth-century, and the *Kaf Ha-hayyim*, R. Yaakov Hayyim Sofer of the twentieth century, claim that as the father might give the girl in marriage while still a minor, he would not recite the blessing because she comes of age in her husband's home. The *Kaf Ha-Hayyim* adds that she is under her father's domain until she marries, minor or not, and he cannot relinquish responsibility for her.[23] He challenges the *Levush*'s novel interpretation that the child says this blessing and not the father. If the girl gets married as a minor, she carries, in his view, the fate of her husband and her father and should not be liable for the sins of both. Consequently, the father does not recite the blessing for her. His answer colludes with what might have been a modern day reality, that women were married or betrothed while still minors and that a shift in a father's responsibilities should occur for the girl when she marries, and not at the age of twelve. Should the modern reader find this alarming, the *Shulhan Arukh* states that even for boys, the optimal performance of the command to marry should take place when the boy assumes the performance of all *mitzvot,* at thirteen.[24]

The *Pri Megadim* adds that, "...even if we require a father to educate his young daughter, not many commandments apply to her anyway."[25] He implies that as she has few commandments to perform, the father's responsibility to educate her is minimal and he need not relinquish himself

---

[23] See *Oreh Hayyim*, 225.15 for the three commentaries mentioned on this issue.

[24] *Shulhan Arukh, Even ha-Ezer*, 1.3.

[25] *Oreh Hayyim* 225.5. See *Eshel Avraham,* ad loc.

from a responsibility so insignificant. Modern *posekim* and writers have questioned this traditional approach to the recitation of this blessing. R. Hanokh Grossberg challenges this interpretation, saying that women must observe all *mitzvot lo ta'aseh, mitzvot aseh* not bound by time, *as well as* many that are. He concludes with a question, "Why not recite a blessing for a daughter?"[26] R. Moshe Halevi Sternberg, citing R. Ovadiah Yosef[27] permits the recitation without *"shem umalkhut"* in his compilation, *Hilkhot Nashim*.[28] R. Yitzhak Nissim, former Sephardic Chief Rabbi of Israel, took this one step further and changed the text of the blessing to reflect a change of gender: *"Barukh shepatrani me'onshah shel zot."* His justification is that the daughter also requires an education and that while the traditional reading of the midrash from which the blessing was culled uses the word "son" [*ben*], this can connote children and not only sons. He concludes, therefore, that a blessing may be recited over a daughter, but without *shem umalkhut*, mention of God's Name and kingship.[29] While the blessing without *shem umalkhut* might be considered as less serious in status due to its omission of God's Name, there are in fact several *posekim* who suggested the same formulation for the boy, on the grounds that the Talmud itself makes no mention of this blessing.[30]

R. Getzel Ellinson, author of several contemporary works on women and Jewish law, in his appendix to *Ben Ha-ishah Le-yotzrah*, suggests that if the *Pri Megadim* did not obligate the father in the blessing because the mother educates her daughters,[31] then perhaps the mother could recite the

---

[26] R. Hanokh Grossberg, *Ha-Ma'ayan*, vol. 13, no. 2, p. 41.

[27] R. Ovadiah Yosef, *Yabiah Omer*, 6.29.

[28] R. Moshe Halevi Sternberg, *Hilkhot Nashim* (Jerusalem, 1986), p. 22. He mentions that there are *ahronim* who do not permit the recitation since it requires a quorum and women do not constitute one. See note 3 above.

[29] R. Yitzhak Nissim, *Noam*, 7:4. R. Nissim's rulings on this and related issues are discussed extensively in A. Ahrend, *"Hagigat ha-bat mitzvah be-piskei Rabbeinu Nissim,"* *Bat Mitzvah*, ed. S. Friedland Ben Arza (Jerusalem, 2002), pp. 109–116. [editor's note]

[30] See, for example, R. Shlessinger, #3.

[31] C.f., *Nazir* 29a in the name of Reish Lakish: "A man is obligated to train his son but not his daughter."

blessing. The same would apply to the thinking of the *Magen Avraham* and *Kaf Ha-hayyim*. This innovative ruling would depend on two factors. Firstly, the establishment of a responsibility for the mother to educate her daughters. Secondly, according to the *Levush's* reading, an affirmative answer to the question of whether the sins of the mother are transferable to her children, which would necessitate the recital of the blessing. Although the *Magen Avraham* rules that "perhaps all commandments are like *Yom Kippur* (with regard to a girl's obligation) and daughters must be trained in their performance, nevertheless the responsibility for this training does not devolve upon the mother."[32] R. Ellinson brings two points to challenge this view: 1) the mother is at home with the daughter and therefore, more likely to train her in the performance of commandments, and 2) a mother is closer to her daughter and can more readily influence her.[33] Here, too, generalizations that may not always hold true are made that lead their writer to certain *halakhic* conclusions. Is it true that a mother is home more with her daughter and that this ensures that the mother is educating her? Equally perplexing is the assumption that the daughter is closer to the mother and that this closeness will result in a stronger Jewish influence. Rather than showing that the mother is directly commanded to teach her daughters, R. Ellinson insists that because of certain factors – the mother's being at home and closer to her daughter than the father – Jewish education or transmission of values will occur naturally. This is not compelling enough proof to overturn the rulings of well-known *halakhists*, as sympathetic as we may be to R. Ellinsons' conclusion.

Regarding the issue of a mother being implicated in the suffering of her children for her own sins, R. Ellinson mentions several possibilities in the affirmative and concludes that, should the daughter recite this blessing, she is freed from her mother's sin. He even entertains the possibility of the mother reciting the blessing for the son as well.

---

[32] *Magen Avraham, Oreh Hayyim* 343.1.

[33] R. Getzel Ellinson, *Bein ha-iIshah le-yotzra* (Jerusalem: World Zionist Organization, 1987), p. 182. He supports this with the position mentioned by R. Hisda in *Ketubot* 102b, that when parents are divorced the daughter remains with the mother while the father gives financial support. In this instance, the mother must educate the daughter.

As we can see from this range of legal commentaries both classic and modern, the conclusions reached in regard to saying the blessing for a girl are based on assumptions about the girl's lifestyle and education. Today, when girls are assumed to require more educational background for active Jewish lives, and when the prospect of betrothal and marriage is in a future more remote than age twelve, serious rabbinical reassessment of the *halakhic* parameters of this blessing is necessary. Indeed, it has already begun.

The *Derashah*

As we mentioned earlier, the subject of a speech delivered by the *bar mitzvah* boy was raised by the *Maharshal*. Applying it to women broaches the broader question of a woman's participation in the public arena and in synagogue rites specifically. R. Moshe Feinstein forbids any synagogue involvement on the part of the *bat mitzvah*.[34] Some Orthodox synagogues attempting to be sensitive both to tradition and to the changing needs of Jewish women have tried to incorporate the *bat mitzvah* girl's remarks following the service, making her speech part of the synagogue service and yet not "officially" in the midst of the service. To circumvent this problem altogether, some rabbis address the *bat mitzvah* girl in the synagogue or she speaks off synagogue premises. The rabbi's comments to the *bar mitzvah* are an important acknowledgment of a future life in the public sphere and validates the young man's entry into the community of worshippers. Regardless of whether or not the girl herself speaks, the rabbi's comments would serve the same function for her as for the *bar mitzvah*. Rabbi J. David Bleich writes that the rabbinic notable, R. Jacob Ettlinger, "sanctioned the institution of such observances in Germany in order to combat the inroads of the early Reform movement, and himself delivered addresses on such occasions."[35] Today many twelve year-old girls' birthdays pass without mention in the synagogue sanctuary, without comments that are directed and focused on the *bat mitzvah* herself. The rabbi's address can convey

---

[34] R. Moshe Feinstein, *Iggerot Moshe, Oreh Hayyim* 1.104. For more on this subject, see essays by R. Benny Lau and Yardena Cope-Yossef in this volume. [editor's note]

[35] R. J. David Bleich, *Contemporary Halakhic Problems* (New York: Ktav, 1977) 1:77.

expectations for her in study, synagogue life and commitment to Jewish values and the community. Without public acknowledgment that these expectations are in place, she may not set them for herself or she may get the message implicitly that there are no such expectations. Saying nothing is not the same as doing nothing. The absence of addressing each child, boy or girl, as potential members of the Jewish community, conveys a message in its silence.

Today, an increasingly common practice is to make a *siyyum* marking the completion of a primary Jewish text in preparation for the occasion. While study is always a worthwhile endeavor and should be encouraged, the study, in itself, is not qualitatively different than any other the *bat mitzvah* may undertake before or after her twelfth birthday. Thus, once again the question arises as to whether or not rites related to this life passage exist. Here, too, uniformity becomes an issue since not every young woman will have the background or intellectual composition to embark on the same kind of task. Some ambitious young women may complete major works while others will use the same term "*siyyum*" to signify much more limited achievement. Nevertheless, the custom of making a *siyyum* has recently become more popular for two reasons. It is a substantive educational accomplishment for the *bat mitzvah* and, through explaining her choice and the meaning of the work she has studied, she has the opportunity for public discourse and recognition.

The *Seudat Mitzvah*

The *Magen Avraham* contends that parents should make a festive meal for the *bar mitzvah* of their son as they would on his wedding day.[36] The *Maharshal* illustrates the need to make a festive meal by referring to the story of R. Yosef, a blind scholar quoted in the Talmud. His blindness, according to *halakhah*, exempted him from the performance of several commandments. R. Yosef said he would have rejoiced and made a feast at the news that he had become obligated to perform all the commandments despite his disability.[37] The *Maharshal* writes that if R. Yosef would have

---

[36] *Magen Avraham, Oreh Hayyim* 225.2.

[37] *Kiddushin* 31a.

made a celebration on that occasion, one should certainly make a festive meal for a child's assumption of *mitzvot*.

R. Yitzhak Nissim, whose question we considered above concerning the recitation of the blessing for the *bat mitzvah*, also thought it significant to have a celebration in the form of a festive meal for a girl.

> ...it seems to me that a feast made on the day a girl becomes sub-ject to the *mitzvot*, on her twelfth birthday, is a *seudat mitzvah*, just as that of a *bar mitzvah* – what is the difference? It is a worthy cus-tom.... If invited to such an occasion, one is obligated to attend.[38]

R. Ovadiah Yosef, former Sephardic Chief Rabbi of Israel concurs with R. Nissim's opinion and cites the position of the *Ben Ish Hai* (R. Yosef Hayyim Ha-bavli), who lived in the nineteenth century, that such an occasion is significant:

> The day a girl assumes the obligation to observe the com-mandments, even in the absence of a festive meal, should be a fes-tive day for her. She should wear her Shabbat clothing, and if pos-sible put on a new dress and say the *shehechiyanu* blessing over it, bearing in mind when reciting the blessing that she is assuming the yoke of the commandments and it is a good sign. We do so in our family.[39]

Modesty

R. Grossberg states that although it is important to hold a festive meal, this should be done in the home rather than in public. R. Moshe Halevi Stern-berg writes that, "just as one organizes a commemorative meal for the *bar mitzvah*, so too are most accustomed to make a meal for the *bat mitzvah*, as it

---

[38] R. Nissim, p. 4. Regarding the obligation to attend a festive meal, see *Pesahim* 113b and the *Rashbam* loc. cit.

[39] R. Ovadiah Yosef, *Yehaveh da'at* 2.29 and *Ben Ish Hai, Re'eh*, 17.

marks her entrance into *mitzvah* observance and she is obligated in keeping all the commandments for women."[40]

R. Bleich assumes that R. Grossberg's insistence that the affair be celebrated at home is for "reasons of modesty."[41] R. Cohen also explains the distinction in the festivities for boys and girls as rooted in modesty.

> It has never been our way to put women in the forefront of public attention; this accounts for many instances in which we treat boys and girls or men and women in different ways. Having a girl be the center of attention in a synagogue celebration of her attaining maturity would be antithetical to our concept of *tzni'ut*, but one can readily appreciate that a celebration for her at home, with her family and friends, is more appropriate within the context of *tzni'ut*.[42]

R. Moshe Sternbuch in *Teshuvot Ve-hanhagot* uses the same rationale in forbidding the father to recite the blessing. His rationale is that it would require the girl to stand before him at the time, and "it is not in keeping with modesty to come with his daughter before the public and bless [her]."[43] The call for modesty is reflected in many *responsa* dealing with women and an enhanced role in Judaism. Modesty, though, is a quality not only for women, but to be encouraged in the Jewish community as a whole. Nor is modesty always in conflict with the promotion of genuine religious feeling. Ideally, the two operate in confluence. Dr. Joel Wolowelsky com-

---

[40] R. Sternberg, p. 22.

[41] R. Bleich, p. 78.

[42] R. Cohen, p. 11. Also see R. Sha'ul Yisraeli *Responsa Be-mareh ha-bazak* (Jerusalem, 1995) 2. 18–19 There he permits the celebration of a *bat mitzvah* within the synagogue, if the purpose is "for the increase of the fear of Heaven and the acceptance of the yoke of *mitzvot* for the girls and the families – this should be expressed through a Torah *derashah* (as it should be in all instances)." R. Yisraeli then adds in a footnote: "Consequently, this [the *bat mitzvah* celebration with words of Torah in the synagogue] is a real *mitzvah* and on par with a Torah study class *[sheharei zeh devar Torah mamash kmo shi'ur torani]*."

[43] R. Moshe Sternbuch, *Teshuvot Ve-hanhagot* (Jerusalem, 1992) 1.156.

ments on this phenomenon: "...honesty also requires avoiding simplistic answers to complex questions. For example, *tzni'ut* (modesty) is a core value in the *halakhic* community. But one cannot simply dismiss a suggestion by invoking the cry of modesty when our community regularly accepts analogous activities as modest and acceptable."[44] While we cannot readily dismiss the issue of modesty since it is a "core value," nor should we be quick to dismiss the views of those great scholars who see these practices as a breech of modesty, we can nevertheless question the use of the term. We generally use the term as a statement of humility or, in contradistinction, to physical exposure. Thus a person behaves immodestly if he or she speaks arrogantly or dresses in a revealing way. Naturally, the latter involves some degree of subjectivity. Generally, we also associate this term more with female behavior than with male. Even the *Oxford English Dictionary* has as one of its definitions of "modesty" the association with women: "Womanly propriety of behavior; scrupulous chastity of thought, speech and conduct." Yet, the way it is often used in current rabbinical literature is that even when the act is a religious one, the fact that it may involve a public appearance or performance deems it inappropriate. Is it immodest to give a *devar Torah* (Torah speech or discourse) in public? Is it immodest for a father to recite a blessing over his daughter when she turns *bat mitzvah*, even if it means that she will appear in public? To recall one example, the *Hatam Sofer*, in explaining why women did not light Hanukah candles, writes that since the custom in Israel was to light outside the home, and since this would lead to women being outside close to nightfall, women behaved modestly and refrained from lighting outside. In the Diaspora, although the custom was no longer to light outside, the behavior of women, nevertheless, did not change.[45] What this also means, however, is that according to this view, women were denied the privilege of participating in what Maimonides calls a "most beloved commandment."[46] The sacrifice required to behave modestly, according to the definition of modesty offered by some

---

[44] Joel B. Wolowelsky, *Women, Jewish Law and Modernity: New Opportunities in a Post-Feminist Age* (New York: Ktav, 1997), p. 5.

[45] R. Moshe Sofer, *Hiddushim, Shabbat* 21b.

[46] Maimonides, *Mishneh Torah, Hilkhot Hanukah* 4:12.

posekim – even in a different era – can, in some cases, contravene spiritual growth and active participation. Under the blanket clause of modesty, we can squelch many complicated issues without giving them the multifaceted consideration they deserve. And were we to pit the values of modesty against public performance and acknowledgment, would modesty always win out if our concern is to develop an inspired future generation of Jewish women?

Imitation of Reform and/or Gentile Practice

The other limitation on the festive meal, put forward most vigorously by R. Moshe Feinstein, is that the *bat mitzvah* is an imitation of practices performed by non-religious Jews, notably imitating the confirmation service.

> Concerning those who wish to conduct a formal celebration for a *bat mitzvah*, under no circumstances is it to be held in a synagogue, which is no place for an optional function. A *bat mitzvah* celebration is surely optional and even trivial, and cannot be permitted in a synagogue, especially since it was instituted by Reform and Conservative Jews. If, however, a father wishes to make some festivity in his home, he may do so, but there is no reason to consider it a *seudat mitzvah*.[47]

R. Moshe echoes the opinion of R. Aaron Walkin, a Lithuanian rabbi born in 1865, who saw that the ceremony smacked of reform.

> It is forbidden to arrange gatherings of men and women, young and old, to celebrate a daughter's reaching maturity, not only be-

---

[47] R. Feinstein, ibid. See R. Shlomo Aviner *Am Kelavi* (Jerusalem, 1983) 1:322–24 where he points out that it seems to him that the *halakhah* is "not in accordance with what [R. Moshe Feinstein] said" on this issue of *bat mitzvah*. This he shows by bringing some of the sources noted in this paper and concluding that "a *bat mitzvah* celebration is grounded in the holy foundations of the words of our Sages *(yesodah beharerei kodesh shel divrei hazal)*, and that the decided majority of the great Torah personalities of our time ruled that this is a *se'udat mitzvah*." R. Aviner also cites R. Amram Aburbi'ah who noted that having a *bat mitzvah* celebration was an ancient custom in Jerusalem *(minhag kadmon be-yerushalayim)*.

cause of the promiscuity involved, but also because anyone who arranges such gatherings is imitating Gentiles and irreligious Jews, and the Torah has warned us against following Gentile practices. Who will remove the dust from the eyes of such reformers? ...it is not right for men and women to mingle even when the Torah is read and everyone stands in awe; how much more so must this be avoided on more light-hearted occasions when no *mitzvah* is involved. We must not deviate from our forefather's customs even when no shadow of transgression is involved, and certainly when grave prohibitions are involved.[48]

R. Walkin cites a number of serious reservations about the *bat mitzvah* ceremony: 1) there will be a mingling of genders and the possibility of promiscuous behavior, 2) the imitation of Gentile practices, 3) the imitation of irreligious Jews, 4) the deviation from the customs of our fathers. Neither R. Walkin nor R. Moshe regard the *bat mitzvah* as a *mitzvah*, and, therefore do not obligate any acknowledgment of the occasion.

More recently, R. Moshe Sternbuch has followed the same mode of thinking.

It is well known that the Reformers celebrate a daughter's coming to *mitzvot* with a large festive meal as for a son. Such a party is completely forbidden *(issur gamur)*, and a deviation from the ways of our fathers. Any party motivated by the purpose of making women and men equal – as the nations of the world do – is completely forbidden. And in making a large celebration for the *bat mitzvah*, their intent is only to prove that women are like men. Although we ourselves do not have the practice of celebrating *bat mitzvah* at all, in places where it is customary to gather her friends and family together for a small meal – which bears no similarity to a festive meal for a *bar mitzvah,* as the meal is not large and is for women only – I do not find any prohibition against it. Since people are accustomed

---

[48] R. Aaron Walkin, *Zekan Aharon, Oreh Hayyim* 1.6.

to this, it need not be eliminated; it is not a public matter and is not like the *bar mitzvah*.[49]

In R. Sternbuch's *responsum*, we can detect that the underlying concern is against the in-roads of feminism and its adoption by more liberal segments of the Jewish community in imitation of the "nations of the world." Unlike R. Walkin who mentions the imitation of non-Jewish practice, R. Sternbuch concentrates on the women's movement as the main motivating factor to have a *bat mitzvah* and the aspect that should be of most consternation to the traditional Jew. Evident from R. Sternbuch's language is that his community does not have any form of celebration, even though he permits a small celebration within limitations.

It is difficult to understand R. Walkin's worry over imitating non-Jewish behavior. The Christian confirmation is not celebrated until age sixteen and does not involve any practice that the *bat mitzvah* simulates. More to the point is the contention that the *bat mitzvah* practiced in traditional communities was an imitation of the Reform confirmation for a girl which, depending on the community, can take place at various ages, even for middle-aged and elderly women.

The opinion of these authorities could be contrasted with the famous *responsum* of the *Seridei Esh*, R. Yehiel Weinberg (d. 1966), who had a very different response to the changes he witnessed:

> A [gentile] practice that is not a form of idolatry is prohibited only if done in order to imitate them. Some authorities oppose the *bat mitzvah* celebration on the grounds of "You shall not follow their ways" (Leviticus 18:3). However, the initiators of this practice claim that they intend thereby to inculcate in the girl's heart a feeling of love for the commandments and pride in her Jewishness. It does not matter that Gentiles also have celebrations on the maturing of their sons and daughters; they follow their traditions and we follow ours. They pray and kneel in their churches and we kneel and bow down and render thanks to the King of Kings, the Holy

---

[49] *Teshuvot ve-hanhagot*, 156.115.

One, blessed be He. Some oppose the *bat mitzvah* celebration because earlier generations did not practice this custom. Indeed this is no argument. In previous generations it was not necessary to give daughters a formal education since every Jew was full of Torah and piety; the very atmosphere of every Jewish settlement was thus infused with the spirit of Judaism. Girls who grew up in a Jewish home imbibed the Jewish spirit naturally, as if from their mother's breasts. Now, however, times have changed radically; the influence of the street destroys in our children any semblance of Judaism.

Sound pedagogic principles require that we celebrate a girl's reaching the age of obligation to fulfill commandments. Discrimination against girls in celebrating the attainment of maturity has an adverse effect upon the self-respect of the maturing girl who in other respects enjoys the privileges of the so-called women's liberation.[50]

R. Weinberg, in the continuation of this *responsum*, concurs with R. Feinstein's conclusion that the ceremony should not be held in a synagogue, although he does write persuasively of the ceremony's value. What is different here is not the conclusion of the *responsum* but its language. While it could be argued that the difference between the two positions is irrelevant if the conclusion is the same, R. Weinberg does sound more encouraging. Differences in language can eventually – although do not always – lead to differences in religious practice. They certainly lend credibility to the practitioners.

As text-oriented people, observant Jews should always be, and usually are, sensitive to the use of language. For example, in the heated controversy over women's prayer groups, R. J. David Bleich and the five rabbinical signatories of a *responsum* published in the *Beit Yitzhak* journal in 1985, both R. Bleich and the group were not permissive. The language of the *responsum*, though, was notably harsh. There was suspicion of the women's motives, questioning of the value of the endeavor, and a blanket statement that "we

---

[50] R. Yehiel Weinberg, *Seridei Esh* 3.93.

are not responsible for them" *ein anu ahra'im lahen.*[51] The behavior of these women, in their eyes, did not warrant rabbinic guidance, and the rabbis thus saw themselves as absolved of responsibility to them. In analyzing the *responsum*, R. Jonathan Sacks, Chief Rabbi of the British Commonwealth wrote of the main signatory:

> He accused women of wanting innovation for its own sake, of seeking publicity and of rebellion against Jewish tradition. What is more, such prayer groups never existed in the past; and when in doubt, we should follow only the existing customs. Besides which, if today we allow a significant change in Jewish custom, others will draw the conclusion that further changes are permitted, with tragic consequences for Jewish law.... The women's motives should also be examined. Undoubtedly, he argued, the move to create separate women's prayer groups was influenced by the general mood created by the women's liberation movement, which might therefore be forbidden as *hukkat hagoy.*[52]

The very same elements that were used in questioning the origin and practice of the *bat mitzvah* arise in the treatment of women's prayer groups. Contrast the skepticism with R. J. David Bleich's language on the same issue in his more recent *Contemporary Halakhic Problems*:

> For many women, the feminist movement has spawned reflection rather than rejection. Religious introspection and self-analysis with a view to seeking higher levels of spiritual awareness and enhanced observance are to be applauded. Thus, the newly awakened assertiveness of women in our society may well become a positive tool leading to their increased involvement in the religious life of the community. It is imperative that this singular opportunity be

---

[51] R. H. Schacter, *Tzei lakh be-ikvei ha-tzon, Beit Yitzhak* 17, 1985.

[52] R. Jonathan Sacks, "Three Approaches to Halakha" a paper given for the Fifth Immanuel Jacobovits Lecture, Jews' College, London, U.K., (March 10, 1987), p. 5.

seized and be utilized to maximum advantage in fostering the spiritual enrichment of all members of the community.[53]

Although both are skeptical of the value of women's prayer groups and neither permit them, R. Bleich did not cast aspersions on the spiritual animus of the women involved, and in direct opposition to the position *"ein anu ahra'im lahen,"* encouraged finding ways to use women's new roles as "tools" for enriching the community.

R. Weinberg also presents a challenge to R. Feinstein, R. Walkin and R. Sternbuch in his position on the changes of the female role in Judaism.[54] While R. Walkin in particular saw this advance as a challenge to the "customs of our fathers," R. Weinberg saw it as an opportunity to heighten self-respect and involvement in Judaism for the girl. He also acknowledges that the mimetic method of passing down tradition has been broken in our times and that this necessitates a more deliberate response to modernity.

R. Weinberg's language in his *responsum* highlights a critical distinction between intent to perform an action because it is a gentile practice and the desire to perform a religious act because it is inherently worthwhile. He notes that when Gentiles pray and Jews pray, their acts may resemble one another's, but are not for the sake of imitation. The *bat mitzvah* would not be imitative of gentile behavior, regardless of its possible non-Jewish origin, because it serves a legitimate need in Judaism – to inculcate a girl with a love of Judaism and observance of Jewish law. R. Weinberg, elsewhere in this *responsum*, writes that if the concern were only with its non-Jewish origins, then no distinction should be made between the *bat-* and *bar mitzvah*, and neither should be celebrated.

The *Bat Mitzvah* and Rabbinic Responses to Modernity

Two opposing approaches to modernity can be distinguished in this small, but significant area of Jewish law. It would be remiss to study rabbinical

---

[53] R. J. David Bleich, *Contemporary Halakhic Problems* (New York: Ktav, 1989), pp. 120–121.

[54] See also R. Weinberg's lengthy *responsum* on *kol ishah* in *Seridei Esh*, 2.8.

literature on the issue of *bat mitzvah* without putting it into the larger framework of concerns. The question of *bat mitzvah* involves the inter-relation of four separate questions, all of which have been noted, to a certain extent, by rabbinic authorities:

1) Has this celebration risen in popularity because of feminism and what should the Jewish response be to that phenomenon?

2) Is there any *halakhic* precedent for such an occasion and is one needed?

3) Will Orthodoxy be perceived as imitating Reform or Conservative practices by allowing or encouraging the *bat mitzvah* in particular and innovation in general?

4) To what extent must we be concerned with imitating non-Jewish be-havior when discussing Jewish ritual practices?

It is in no way the intent of this author to attempt to answer any of these questions. I would like merely to demonstrate that the issue became explosive because of these four sensitive questions. While some may be alarmed at the extreme positions recorded earlier, I believe they stem from the sense that, in treating any question, it is a rabbinical responsibility to offer an answer that colludes with the perceived future welfare of the Jewish community. Rabbis who sense that feminism, innovation, and imitation of gentile practices are the results of a modern culture, estranged from the values of Torah Judaism, will usually take a stringent view. Others, who view them as opportunities to invigorate Judaism and to incorporate more public female participation in Jewish life, tend to be more permissive. The creation of new customs has always aroused both excitement and cautious skepticism. A tradition thousands of years old cannot afford quick leaps to match societal norms at the expense of preserving its spirit. Time has always been the measure of whether or not *halakhic* "experiments" will work within a system of tradition.

In the camp that is skeptical of the *bat mitzvah*'s origins, the concern for imitation of liberal Jewish or gentile behavior, especially in the synagogue was the most significant factor in their stringent position. Perhaps that explains why, generally, the Sephardic *posekim* cited here were more suppor-tive of some form of *bat mitzvah*. Whether in predominantly Muslim countries or in the State of Israel, they did not have to contend with the larger societal issue of imitating Christian rites of passage. Currently, the influence of liberal Jewish behavior is more of a factor in the United States than elsewhere. Not under these shadows, they had more liberty to be permissive. Zvi Zohar, while not dealing with the issue of *bat mitzvah* per se, demonstrates this observation in his article, "*Halakhic* Responses of Syrian and Egyptian Rabbinical Authorities to Social and Technological Change."

> ...the rabbis had no need to define themselves as members of one camp or another and, paradoxically, their options in formulating halakhic responses to new situations evolving in the life of their congregations were, therefore, more open and diverse.[55]

In Ashkenaz, external factors usually succeeded in limiting the scope of this celebration. And that is part of the problem.[56] The one question that is not in our list is, in my view, the most important and the least discussed – with the exception of a few comments by R. Weinberg – in all of the rabbinic debate: What happens to the girl?

The *Bat Mitzvah* Girl

What happens to the girl in the absence of a meaningful, demanding, spiritually uplifting entry into the world of *mitzvot*? Should we be considering only the "political" concerns? Are we more worried about the statement that the ceremony makes to the non-Jewish world, liberal Jews, and our co-religionists, than we are to what it says to the twelve year old girl? For all of the broad concerns about what the *bat mitzvah* represents as a statement

---

[55] Zvi Zohar, "Halakhic Responses of Syrian and Egyptian Rabbinical Authorities to Social and Technological Change," *Studies in Contemporary Jewry*, vol. 2, Peter Y. Medding, ed. (Bloomington: Indiana University Press, 1986), p. 19.

[56] A different approach is presented by Solomon Freehof in his article, "Ceremonial Creativity among the Ashkenazim" in *Beauty in Holiness*, ed. Joseph Gutman, (New York: Ktav, 1970). He writes that the *bar mitzvah* is an example of Ashkenazi creativity: "...the ceremony itself as an entity and as a widespread regular observance was an original creation.... We see, therefore, that the Ashkenazim had developed a unique ability in ceremonial creativity. It was the power of visualizing. It can be called an artistic ability, to mold religious laws and doctrines into outward and enduring physical form."

about feminism, innovation, and modernity – and these are significant factors – we lose focus about what the *bat mitzvah* means to a young girl, who may have no clue about *hukkat hagoy,* feminism, or the *Seridei Esh.* Not infrequently, a middle-aged woman will recount the passing of her *bat mitzvah* to me as a non-event in her family. She may have received a new dress and there was a *kiddush* in her synagogue where her father said a few words. Some did not even get that. And whatever happened, it was a fraction of the attention that their brothers received on the very same occasion. Many say that that is when they turned their interests elsewhere. If Judaism was not interested in them, they weren't interested in Judaism. Intelligent women, who, on the cusp of adulthood, experienced indifference to their religious future, may still be observant of Jewish law, but received a clear message of silence about active participation that still influences them in their adult lives. That silence spoke loudly to them. While I cannot demonstrate the correlation between *bat mitzvah* and a meaningful Jewish future empirically, I can say, through intuition and countless conversations with adult women, that the *bat mitzvah* is a seminal experience in developing intellectual and spiritual curiosity about Judaism and the performance of its commandments.

On a broader note, more attention has been paid as of late to the psychological development of adolescents and specifically teen-age girls struggling with issues of self-esteem. In *Making Connections: The Relational Worlds of Adolescent Girls at Emma Willard School,* a group of educators and psychologists took a careful look at what girls of this age were thinking and doing in the context of one school. Carol Gilligan, one of the book's editors and a noted Harvard scholar who has written extensively on women and girl's educational development, had this to say:

> Adolescence poses problems of connection for girls coming of age in Western culture, and girls are tempted or encouraged to solve these problems by excluding themselves or excluding others – that is by being a good woman, or by being selfish. Many current books advocate one or the other of these solutions. Yet the problem girls face in adolescence is also a problem in the world at this time: the need to find ways of making connection in the face

of difference. Adolescence seems a watershed in female development, a time when girls are in danger of drowning or disappear-
ing.[57]

Although Gilligan's work reflects a case study in one school of girls
mostly well into their adolescent years, her observations, nevertheless,
should make us contemplate our own situation "back home," so to speak.
At this time of watershed, with introspection and sensitivity, we can make
sure that Judaism for the twelve year old girl does not "drown or disappear" but helps the young woman enter a time of increased study, *hesed*
activity, and communal awareness. Where the middle class white adolescent
female may be foundering for identity and increased connection to the
outside world, the Jewish equivalent must be anchored and nurtured and
welcomed into a world that is both spiritually meaningful and demanding.
We have to pay careful attention to what educators and psychologists are
alerting our attention to and see how, within the framework of *halakhah*, we
can address some of the pitfalls of female adolescence.

Where do these intuitive thoughts lead in terms of an actual celebration?
They emphatically do not lead to where we currently are. The attempt to
make a *bat mitzvah* more like a *bar mitzvah* in terms of the party, in my
opinion, is worse than the message of silence. R. Moshe Feinstein, although
no supporter of *bat mitzvah* innovation, showed no great support for
modern *bar mitzvah* celebrations either. Rather, he claimed that such occasions were responsible for a great deal of Shabbat desecration and that, "it
is well-known that they have brought no one, not even the *bar mitzvah*, any
closer to Torah and *mitzvot*."[58] Many think that by having the same lavish
affair, number of guests, and excess of gifts, we are helping the *bat mitzvah*
achieve equality with the *bar mitzvah*. Hopefully, the girl will produce a piece

---

[57] Carol Gilligan, "Teaching Shakespeare's Sister: Notes from the Underground of
Female Adolescence," *Making Connections: The Relational Worlds of Adolescent Girls at
Emma Willard School*, Carol Gilligan, Nona P. Lyons, and Trudy Hammer, eds. (Harvard UP: Cambridge, 1990), pp. 9–10. I am also grateful for my extensive conversations with Nona Lyons, a co-editor of the book, in making me aware of the urgency of
the matter and drawing my attention to recent literature on adolescent girls.

[58] R. Moshe Feinstein, *Oreh Hayyim* 1.104.

of Torah but, again, as is so common with the *bar-* and *bat mitzvah*, the speech is written by the parents and comprehensible only to them and their adult company. The celebration loses focus on the child's spiritual composition and becomes an occasion to impress others with words, food, and entertainment that hold little, or no Jewish, meaning for the child. And yet, because there has been no uniform celebration for the *bat mitzvah* put forward by the rabbinic establishment, people are left to their own devices.[59]

R. Eliezer Berkovits comments that:

> ...ignoring current developments in this way reflects a non-*halakhic* attitude. Instead of examining the basis of certain *takkanot* to see whether they still have meaning and purpose, the rabbinical establishment is afraid of any change and anything new. In certain areas, of course, life itself has taken over.[60]

Life has taken over and has left the laity to decide. In the absence of rabbinic guidance, the female equivalent to the male ceremony is sadly becoming the norm. In other periods of time where the position of women in society altered, rabbinic leaders and educators understood that Torah

---

[59] "Left to their own devices" presents the real danger for the *bat mitzvah* ceremony. Consider, for example, two suggestions for active rites of passage. Nina Freedman in, "When a Jewish Woman Comes of Age" (*Sh'ma*, 6, III, April 2, 1976) suggests that a girl should mark her coming of age with immersion in a *mikvah* following the onset of menstruation. This, she claims, would help her come to terms with her "physical womanhood" and would be a personal celebration of "self-awareness." This may have the opposite effect, signaling to the girl that this new stage in her life is marked by something physical or sexual rather than spiritual. In addition, it would change the traditional orientation of the *bat mitzvah* and differentiate it that much more from the *bar mitzvah,* which has no parallel rituals marking sexuality. One can well imagine the problems that may arise from this potential sanction of premarital intercourse.

Koller-Fox, in her article cited earlier, got together with her class of girls and "agreed upon the idea of designing a blue satin headband, with a meaningful verse from the Bible or prayer book embroidered on it" (p.40). In the absence of a uniform practice, Koller-Fox asked her twelve-year-olds what they wanted to do. They came up with a "religious" headband.

[60] R. Eliezer Berkovits, *Jewish Women in Time and Torah* (Ktav, 1990) pp. 80–81.

education for women had to magnify in its intensity in order to match the needs of secularly well-educated women. Whether we turn to R. Samson Raphael Hirsch, Sarah Shnierer, the *Hafetz Hayyim*, or the *Seridei Esh*, we see models of piety who also understood that Jewish women faced difficult transitions that required flexibility. Ignoring these developments or disparaging them, only alienated leaders from the very women who needed guidance, and possibly turned the women themselves away from Torah observance. Today we see, in areas of women's education, the fruits of their flexibility in all segments of the Orthodox community. In recent years, we have turned from the controversy over women's education to women's role in the public sphere and in ritual performance. Here, too, a strict adherence to Jewish law coupled with flexibility and sensitivity to language need to be the rubric under which we think about these issues.

In summation, R. Moshe Feinstein's words echo in their clarion call for spiritual authenticity. Perhaps that is why we read nothing of such a ceremony in talmudic times. Thirteen marked an age, only one of many, at which religious expectation became a reality. But the same was true for the five-year-old learning to read the weekly *sedrah* and the ten-year-old picking up his first copy of the Mishnah *Berakhot*. Only by ensuring that the early pieces and milestones are in place, i.e., a background of study and commitment, will the future dates have any meaning. And even with all of the background pieces in place, the *bat-* and *bar-mitzvah* ceremony must focus on the child and the implicit messages she or he receives from the adult world of Judaism.

Rabbinical leaders cannot cower in the face of modernity's challenges at the expense of a future generation of *halakhically* observant, knowledgeable young women and future Jewish mothers. A responsible rabbinate will work towards a more uniform practice that can effectively deliver the Jewish community's expectations to the young girl with active rites of passage. The components of that ceremony are, as of yet, unclear, but possibilities do exist. In the absence of responsible rabbinical guidance, life will take its own course and the laity will decide, much to the spiritual detriment of the Jewish future. More than any issue of feminism, innovation, and materialism, the planners of the modern day *bat mitzvah* — the parents, the rabbi, the educator — must put themselves in the mind of the twelve year old girl and think what will most enhance her chances of growing into an observant, spiritual, and humanitarian Jewish adult.

Responsa on Ways to Mark the *Bat Mitzvah* Day

HOW SHOULD *BAT MITZVAH* BE CELEBRATED?

RABBI YA'AKOV ARIEL

Chief Rabbi of Ramat Gan

Israeli parents and teachers are concerned with the question of appropriate ways of celebrating *bat mitzvah,* and so I thought it would be worthwhile to present the following thoughts to the wider public.

1. *Bat mitzvah* celebrations are a new thing; they were not the custom in earlier generations. In the past, young women did not feel there was anything special about the day. They had already begun to observe a number of *mitzvot* as a fundamental part of their education even before that time. At *bat mitzvah*, girls did not begin to lay *tefillin*; they did not become part of a *minyan*; they were not called to the Torah. As a result, girls did not feel that becoming *bat mitzvah* was a matter of special significance. Women were not given a formal education. Young girls carried on their family's tradition and felt no need to mark the point when they became obligated to abide by the *mitzvot.* Jewish law has, though, recognized the importance of marking the day on which a girl comes of age, and becomes required by the Torah to observe the *mitzvot.*[1]

2. Recent generations have felt a need to celebrate the entry of girls as well into the obligation to observe *mitzvot.* Girls started to learn and to be given a formal education, and self-awareness began to increase.

The conviction grew, on the one hand, that girls should be aided in developing a sense of personal responsibility for observing *mitzvot,* even when they lived in a partially non-observant environment. The girl's

---

* Translated by Judith Weil. This article originally appeared in the *Hatzofeh* daily on 13 Elul 5758/1998

[1] See *Kiddushin* 31a

personal realization of her obligation should thus be strengthened, and her joining the ranks of others similarly obligated should be celebrated.

3. On the other hand, the fear remained that *bat mitzvah* celebrations might be perceived as an imitation of the Reform movement, which followed various Christian customs in this connection. Some people therefore objected to holding *bat mitzvah* celebrations. However, bearing in mind the importance of a girl's education and of her holding her head high, many *posekim* permitted and even recommended the holding of *bat mitzvah* celebrations – within suitable dimensions as befitted a girl, and in a modest family atmosphere.[2]

4. Incidentally, the *bar mitzvahs* of the past were not celebrated the way they are today. When a boy reached the age of obligation in observing *mitzvot* there were no special ceremonies or lavish parties. The occasion was marked by the boy being called to the Torah, his laying *tefillin* and, at the most, a modest celebration attended by a small number of close individuals. Girls, therefore, did not feel they were missing out and discriminated against. Today, though, when a *bar mitzvah* boy is treated like a *hatan*, like a bridegroom, feted and feasted, wined and dined, when the family rent a hall, hire an orchestra, video the event, and so on and so on, a girl can feel that she is discriminated against by comparison. She is involved in a formal education system, undergoes professional or vocational training and feels she has her own position in society. In view of all that, she should be given equivalent treatment on reaching the age of obligation in observing *mitzvot*. And she should certainly not feel discriminated against.

I am not at all sure that the fuss on the occasion of a boy's *bar mitzvah* does much for his spiritual development. Worse than that, *bar mitzvah* parties sometimes even involve forbidden behavior. Even in the *shul* itself there are the proliferation of *aliyahs*, of *mi-sheberakhs*, of idle chat, women sometimes come dressed inappropriately, friends and relatives may travel by car to celebrations held on Shabbat – all this do nothing to raise the spiritual level of the occasion. There are other factors. The bread served at

---

[2]   See, for example, *Seridei Esh and Kol Mevaser*. [Precise references appear in essays by R. Benny Lau and Yardena Cope Yossef in this volume. – editor's note.]

the *kiddush* usually requires washing properly for *ha-motzi* and saying *birkhat ha-mazon* – but this is often not done. Then there is the Torah discourse that is not heard. For a long time now *bar mitzvah* boys have stopped bothering to prepare proper *derashot*, because they know that people will deliberately interrupt and prevent them from speaking. People hardly listen to the rabbi and to the various other speakers. This is especially the case when the occasion is a buffet-type affair. A "bar" there is – but where is the *mitzvah*?

Is this what the girls wish to imitate?

One the contrary, the girls should return to the wonderful ways of the past. They should be creative in thinking about new ways to celebrate their *bat mitzvah*. They should arrange an occasion that has content, at which the atmosphere is one of modesty befitting the occasion. It is to be hoped that boys would even want to copy the way the girls do things, and decide to celebrate their *bar mitzvahs* in a more suitable fashion.

5. In connection with a *derashah*, a discourse, given by the girl: In our day and age there is room for a girl to develop a nice ideal. She should prepare it by herself, as far as is possible, under adult guidance of course, and should present it to her close friends and relatives alone. A girl should be modest and should be educated to modesty. It is certainly not fitting for her to give a discourse in the *shul* after davening, and it would be quite wrong for her to give it during the davening.

There are places overseas where the shul president, who happens to be a woman, speaks in the shul after davening. But even then it is wrong that this should be done during davening.

I can personally testify that the late Professor Nechama Leibowitz refrained from giving discourses in *shul*. She told me this herself on a number of occasions. I attended her *shiurim* that she gave and I learned a lot from her, but not in *shul*.

6. As I suggested above, young girls should be encouraged to be creative. It is a good idea for them – with the help of their parents and teachers – to think out original ways to celebrate *bat mitzvahs*.

For example: A few months before her *bat mitzvah* a girl could adopt another girl of approximately her own age who is in hospital. She could visit the hospital once or twice a week, play with this girl and they could study together. A *bat mitzvah* celebration could be held for both of them in the hospital together.

7. *Hazal* viewed three *mitzvot* as exemplifying a woman's primary responsibilities. I think it would be worthwhile for a young woman approaching her *bat mitzvah* to contemplate ways she can observe the letter and spirit of these *mitzvot* in modern conditions. These three *mitzvot* are *niddah*, or family purity, *challah* and lighting Shabbat candles. They represent motherhood, *kashrut*, and the sanctified atmosphere of Shabbat and Yom Tov.

A girl's first indications that she is reaching adulthood are signs of potential motherhood. This situation provides an opportunity to help a young girl learn about a woman's primary role. In our modern conditions it is of highest importance to stress that although she is developing her abilities in various directions, she must not neglect her unique task, which is motherhood.

As a Jewish mother, she will be responsible for the *kashrut* of the home. This is true whether or not she does the actual cooking and baking herself. Nowadays many women do not personally prepare everything in the house, but that makes her no less responsible for the *kashrut* of the home.

The same holds true regarding the atmosphere in the home on Shabbat and holidays. In most cases, women are especially gifted at engendering and preserving the traditional atmosphere imbuing those around them with a Shabbat and yom tov spirit. I would be reluctant to rely on men in this area.

It might be beneficial, then, to provide *bat mitzvah* girls with some *kashrut*-related assignments. This could be done within the framework of *bat mitzvah* preparatory classes. Examples would be separating *challah* (and, in Israel taking *terumot* and *maasrot* as well), purchasing products and checking them for *kashrut*, learning to know the various *kashrut* symbols and ascertaining what they mean [e.g., the type of milk supervision, possibilities regarding meat, checking for insects, *shemmitah* provisions, etc.].

It may be worthwhile for the girls to visit food plants and see what *kashrut* supervision entails.

And in connection with Shabbat and holidays: One possibility would be for girls to adopt the recommendation of the late Lubavitcher Rebbe – to kindle Shabbat and Yom Tov candles themselves, and not only their mothers. Another possibility could be for an artistic girl or group of girls to make a handmade gift for the shul. She or they could embroider or weave their gift and present it at a special ceremony, at which community leaders would bless them in the name of the entire community.

These are but a few suggestions. I trust that *bat mitzvah* girls, their teachers, and their parents have other ideas that are more original and innovative than the ones I have proposed.

To sum up, no one can make the decision for you. Each rabbi must examine the situation of his individual community and, I hope in the spirit of these comments, offer his own guidance.

RABBANIT OSHRA KOREN – *RESPONSUM*

Rabbanit Oshra Koren

Director of MaTaN Hasharon in Ra'anana and MaTaN Chapters throughout Israel;
Founder of the MaTaN *Bat Mitzvah* Program

In my opinion, the process of preparation is more important than the *bat mitzvah* party. The party should be the culmination of the study preceding it.

In discussions held with parents before their daughter's *bat mitzvah,* I stress that the starting point needs to be the girl. First and foremost, her interests, inclinations and abilities need to be recognized. I've often met parents who put their own needs first, even though these do not correspond with their daughter's desires or social environment. Sometimes the mother seeks to make up for her own lack of a particular kind of *bat mitzvah* celebration by making such a celebration for her daughter, while the girl does not share this aspiration. Another example: I met a father who wanted to arrange a women's prayer group for his daughter's *bat mitzvah* so that she could read from the Torah. This was not what the girl wanted; moreover, the experience would not have fit into any sustainable framework, since there is no regular women's prayer group in our community. I therefore advised him to give up what he wanted and focus on his daughter's choices.

It's also important to find the right topic. To a girl drawn to ecology I suggested writing an essay on ecology and Judaism; a girl who was interested in animals wrote a sermon on animal imagery in rabbinical literature. A young woman who was a talented artist studied Judaism and the arts. Lately, I find that more and more girls are compiling booklets for their *bat mitzvah*. The girl's sermon and those of her parents are printed in these booklets, along with the relevant primary sources, and sometimes including songs and Grace after Meals.

Verbal-intellectual activities, though, are not appropriate for every girl; some girls do not want to give a sermon. These girls can express them-

---

* translated by Gershon Clymer

selves through a personal dance or an exhibition of drawings, by leading a tour or ceremony or by making a film.

I know of synagogues in which every *bat mitzvah* includes a ceremony. Before the weekly Torah portion is read on Shabbat, the girl who is entering into *mitzvot* gives a talk (in these congregations, women customarily also give sermons in synagogue on Shabbat). At the end of the prayer services, while the congregation remains seated, the girl approaches the Holy Ark, the mothers and grandmothers receive the honor of opening the Ark, and the girl says the special *bat mitzvah* prayer of the Jews of Italy. The congregation showers her with candies. After services, a *kiddush* is held in her honor. Of course, in addition to this ceremony, which is an integral part of the public prayer service in the synagogue, each young woman celebrates with a private party of her own choosing.

THE WAY TO REJOICE

RABBANIT RIVKA RAPPOPORT

Founder of the Ahavat Yisrael School, Jerusalem

Introduction – Getting Ready

As a child, when I said the *she'asani kirtzono* blessing ("Who made me according to His will") each morning, I felt I was expressing my gratitude for the fact that I would not have to celebrate a *bar mitzvah*. I would not need to read aloud from the Torah or deliver a long, complex sermon on a subject that was beyond the ability of most of my listeners to understand. I felt that the customary manner in which *bar mitzvahs* were celebrated placed a heavy burden on the young boys, and this disturbed me.

Today, thank God, we have taken a fresh look at the traditional way in which we mark Jewish life events. We have now become more aware of how important it is for the person at the center of the celebrations to feel an affinity to what is happening. People are becoming more flexible in their approach to these *simchahs*, and this has transformed the nature of the events. This applies to the *brit milah*, the *kiddush* that is held to celebrate the birth of a daughter, *bar* and *bat mitzvahs*, to weddings, to *sheva berakhot* and even to memorial services.

There has been a huge advance in recent generations in women's education, both in their Torah studies and in their general studies. The natural result has been a new awareness of the subject of the celebrations that are held on the occasion of a girl becoming obligated to observe the *mitzvot*. This awareness has manifested itself in many families in discussions on the subject of how the *bat mitzvah* should be celebrated. They concern both how the *bat mitzvah* year should be marked and how the schools should prepare a girl for the time when she becomes obligated to observe the *mitzvot*. Choirs, performances, *hesed* activities, class *shabbatons*, workshops attended by the girls together with their mothers, *bat mitzvah*

---

* translated by Judith Weil

outings, research into the lives of special women – all these activities have become integrated in religious schools throughout Israel and in other parts of the world.

It is certainly important that the day or week in which the twelfth birthday falls should be marked. Hardly anyone disagrees with that nowadays. Anything that can strengthen the Jewish commitment of the girl who is reaching adulthood is to be welcomed. The question is just how the event should be marked and how it should be celebrated. Five things should be borne in mind when answering these questions.

1. Involvement

First, it is important to involve the girl herself in all stages of the discussion concerning how that day, so meaningful for her, should be marked. It is a good idea for parents to sit down with their daughter shortly after her eleventh birthday and have a talk with her. What does being obligated to observe the *mitzvot* entail? What should she learn in preparation for entering into this obligation? What should be done? How should the day be marked? And how should the entire year be marked?

The parents must, of course, prepare themselves for this discussion. They should work out what they themselves wish to contribute, and are able to contribute, and how they should present their daughter with the various options that come into question. The discussion should be held in a pleasant atmosphere, and there should be no feeling of pressure.

The decisions that are made should be such that they are not burdensome for any of those involved and should be within the parameters of the girl's abilities. A girl who is too shy to give a *devar Torah* in front of outsiders, or even in front of the family, would perhaps agree to prepare written material on a relevant subject. She could then hand out copies to the members of her family or to her friends and they could then study them together. If a girl feels under pressure or that a task is too difficult for her, this might unfortunately detract from her joy in accepting the *mitzvot* upon herself and could even diminish her wish to observe them.

2. An Ongoing Obligation

Becoming obligated to observe the *mitzvot* is not something limited to a particular date. It means much more than that. It involves a preparatory process that continues for months or even years before that date, and it involves a consolidation process that lasts a lifetime. The path to this important day, and from this day on, should entail more than thinking about the celebration. It is preferable to invest thought, effort, time, money and creativity in preparing the girl for what lies ahead. She could study together with her parents, with her brothers and sisters, with grandparents, with a private teacher, or with anyone else in the family or in the area where she lives who is interested in being involved and who realizes that it is a privilege to be involved. If the situation lends itself to this, she can acquire "proficiency" in a particular *mitzvah* or in giving of her time and energy to others. To give just a few easy ideas: she could do *hesed* involving the elderly, the sick, or needy families; she could do volunteer activities in connection with Eretz Yisrael, the environment, or preventing cruelty to animals.

3. Modesty

A celebration based on big expenses for catering, music, entertainment or clothing may arouse envy. Emphasis on the material aspect of the celebration pushes aside Jewish values and messages that are so essential to invest our children with, especially now.

4. The Family

Preparations for the young woman's acceptance of *mitzvot* must include learning *halakhah* and Jewish thought not only within the framework of school but at home as well. It is essential to draw family members into the girl's celebration. On the birthday itself, a special meal should be held for close family members, or alternatively, a hike or trip, or any Jewish learning experience at which the entire family participates. This is a unique honor and joy for the family – seeing their daughters mature in the path of Hashem. On such an occasion, gratitude and thanks to God should be expressed at a family gathering. Other guests, such as friends, neighbors, teachers, relatives and acquaintances should only be invited if that does not create any hardship for the girl and the rest of her family. Through the attempt to minimize financial expenditure, the values of modesty will be applied in practice, and envy will be avoided.

5. **Atmosphere**

A pleasant atmosphere is essential at every stage of a child's education and development. It is all the more so in the case of *bat mitzvah*. The goal does not justify the means. On the contrary, here the path itself is the goal. A shared and calm preparation process alone is what will connect the girl to the gift of *mitzvot* and to their Giver, and what will grant her the strength to keep the *mitzvot* in joy all the days of her life.

RABBI SETH FARBER - *RESPONSUM*

RABBI SETH FARBER
Rabbi Seth Farber is the founding director of
ITIM: The Jewish-Life Information Center.

For the past thirty years, the religious and *halakhic* discourse relating to *bat mitzvah* ceremonies in the Orthodox community has taken place on two levels. On the one hand, *bat mitzvah* has been viewed as part of a global range of social and cultural innovations that generate discord because of their alien character, rebellious nature or synthetic (and transparent) form. All legal systems resist change, and *halakhah*, to the extent that one sees it as authoritative, is no exception.

Alternatively, the discussion of the logistics of *bat mitzvah* has been telescopic, focusing on particular ceremonies and rituals, debating their potential pitfalls, arguing for and against their legitimacy and questioning the intentions of those who seek to revise the tradition.

I believe that the question of the *bat mitzvah* ceremony for the *halakhic* community needs to be reformulated. Rather than asking "May we...?" I propose that we ask "How can we not...?" Given the precarious personal religious life and vulnerability of the Orthodox female adolescent (the "Orthodox Ophelia") who is maturing into the complexities of the contemporary world, we must rededicate ourselves to inspiration and education to the fullest extent possible.

A main point of contention regarding *bat mitzvah* in today's modern Orthodox world is the teaching of trop and educating of girls to read from the Torah for application in a women's prayer setting. The *halakhic* discourse has generally focused on the permissibility (vis-à-vis non-Jewish practice, or *hukkot hagoyim*) or the viability (lacking *tefillah be-tzibbur*) aspects of such an innovation. Respondents have raised earnest questions of a woman's public role and the restrictions on her touching a *sefer Torah*.

Have we, however, sufficiently weighed the religious ramifications of discouraging a young women from learning how to *lain*? The process of learning and utilizing the *taamei ha-mikra* (trope) has proven over and over again to boost the confidence and self-esteem of the young women who undertake this rigorous task. It increases their understanding and dedication to Torah itself, just as it does for the boys. In these times we must not casually dismiss a renaissance in *halakhic* observance and Talmud Torah, specifically among women, who play so critical a role in passing on the tradition to the next generation. What price will we pay by discouraging young girls from participating actively in organized *tefillah?*

Much of the negative reaction to innovative *bat mitzvah* ceremonies is generated by fear of the unknown. But a great deal of *halakhic* dialogue is motivated by immediate and imminent challenges. A ritualized *bat mitzvah* with a Torah-reading element may not be the choice of every girl in every generation, or even in this generation.

Indeed, this is not an easy decision for a young girl or her family in the face of peer pressure and previous rabbinical resistance. But the potential achievement deserves reconsideration from rabbinical authorities and the general community, given the vicissitudes of early twenty-first century Orthodoxy.

October, 2002

Derashot in Honor of the *Bat Mitzvah*

FOUR *BAT MITZVAH DERASHOT*

YAEL LEVINE, FELICE KAHN ZISKEN AND
SARA FRIEDLAND BEN ARZA#

Introduction

Girls celebrating their *bat mitzvah*, in recent years, are often interested in giving a *devar Torah*, or discourse. In many cases, it represents the culmination of an extended course of study and preparation. While a number of anthologies of *bar mitzvah* speeches – containing either authentic *derashot* that were actually given or essays written by Torah scholars to serve as guidelines for *bar mitzvah* speeches – have been published,[1] few *bat mitzvah* speeches have been printed, and no collections exist. Whether written solely by the *bat mitzvah* girl herself or with guidance, most *derashot* reflect, in one way or another, the revolution taking place today in the realm of Torah study for women of all ages. The following pages contain translations to English of the *bat mitzvah* discourses given by four girls in Israel. After each of them, we offer brief reflections on some of its aspects, and conclude with a few general comments concerning form and content.

The first discourse presented here was given by a *bat mitzvah* girl we will call "T" in 5752 (1991). The second was delivered by Ahava Friedland to a women's prayer group held at *Machon Pardes,* Jerusalem, in 5760 (2000), and

---

* translated by Miriam Weed

The following essay is based on an article originally published in Hebrew in *Bat Mitzvah,* ed. Sara Friedland Ben Arza (Jerusalem, 2002), pp. 155–174. The authors collected the four *bat mitzvah* speeches in it with permission from the girls who wrote and delivered them, and re-printed them with minimal stylistic alterations. They added an introduction, analysis of each *derashah* including a consideration of the preparation process, sources cited, and central values expressed in it, and an extensive conclusion. The following translation of that essay presents a full reproduction in English of the speeches themselves; the introduction, analyses, and conclusion are a condensed version of the original Hebrew discussion.

1 Some of these, in Hebrew, are: *Derashot le-bar mitzvah mi-geddolei Yisrael* (Bnei Brak, 5754); E.T. Melamed, *Derashot le-venei mitzvah* (Jerusalem, 5735); Yishayahu Heshin, *Divrei Yishayahu,* (Jerusalem, 5716).

is one of a series of *derashot* she gave. The third discourse was given by Chana Rosen in 5761 (2001) at a *kiddush* held at the *Yakar* synagogue, Jerusalem. The fourth, by "H" was given on *Hol ha-Moed* Sukkot 5761 (2000) in her family's *sukkah*.

1. *Derashah by T*

Heroines of the Megillot – A Discussion of the Characters and Actions of Esther and Ruth

Introduction

Two books of the Bible are named for women. Both are *megillot* – Esther and Ruth. I would like to discuss the personalities and actions of these two heroines.

At the beginning of both Esther's and Ruth's story, we are told of a break in their relationships with their families and the support they then receive from a substitute parent. Esther's father and mother have died, and she is adopted by her uncle Mordechai, while Ruth leaves her parents to join Naomi.

During the course of these stories both heroines undergo a change of identity. Ruth, with the proclamation, "Your people are my people and your God is my God" leaves her birthplace, moves to the Land of Israel and converts to Judaism. Esther does not "reveal her kindred or her people, as Mordechai had instructed her" and lives as a non-Jew – at least until the moment of revelation.

At the end of each story the heroine disappears from center stage and leaves room for the supporting character. Esther makes way for Mordechai, viceroy to the King, and Naomi rather than Ruth is considered to be the mother of baby Oved, at least in the eyes of the neighbors.

Keeping this in mind, I would like to compare these two heroines, Esther and Ruth.

Esther

What is Esther's character and how does she act?

Esther is an orphan, and her uncle Mordechai has taken her in as his daughter. She is "shapely and beautiful" and wins "the admiration of all who behold her." At the beginning of her story, Esther is not portrayed as an initiator. She consistently carries out the orders given her and carefully makes sure to obey Mordechai's every word. This is Esther at the time she is chosen to become Queen of Persia.

After Haman's decree to destroy the Jews is sent out, the Jews of Shushan are confused and depressed, but in the palace, Queen Esther knows nothing of the matter. Mordechai informs Esther of the dangerous situation and asks her to appear before the king and plead for her people.

At this moment, Esther refuses to obey Mordechai's command. Fearing for her life, she is reluctant to go to the king and plead for her people. Her will to live overcomes her lifelong habit of obeying Mordechai. When Esther does finally agree to approach the king, what motivates her is not Mordechai's definitive authority, but her own conviction that her status in the king's household will not protect her from the fate of the Jews. Moreover, perhaps she was put in this position of power for this very purpose. And she does not simply approach the king as Mordechai commanded. She initiates a plan of her own that includes three days of fasting and two parties before she pleads for her people before the king.

The development of Esther's personality reaches its peak here – at the moment she moves from Mordechai's domain to her own. Her decision to endanger her life to save the Jewish people is not a blind reaction to Mordechai's order but a deliberate act of courage based on recognizing the danger involved and deciding to risk her own life for the sake of her nation. Thus, Esther is an example of a true heroine ready to sacrifice her soul for a higher ideal, the salvation of the Nation of Israel.

Ruth

What is Ruth's character and how does she act?

As the story begins, we already see in Ruth the developed personality of an initiator. Adamant in her refusal to desert Naomi, her mother-in-law who has lost her two sons and husband, Ruth does not give in to Naomi's urging. Instead, she returns with Naomi to the Land of Israel and converts to Judaism.

Once they have settled in Beit Lehem, Ruth suggests that she collect the gleanings of the harvesters to provide food for herself and Naomi. When she is invited to share the meal of Boaz, owner of the field, she puts some of the food aside for Naomi.

To ensure that the name of her husband not be erased from the people of Israel, Ruth accepts Naomi's bold plan to confront Boaz, Elimelekh's relative, and ask him to redeem her. This is despite his advanced age and her opportunities to find someone much younger and wealthy.

Thus, Ruth is portrayed as a kind individual who loses no opportunity to benefit the living and the dead alike. At times she initiates; at others, she acts on someone else's advice, but she consistently persists in giving to others.

Although Ruth commits no dramatic act of heroism, her daily acts of self-sacrifice for the sake of others are indeed heroic. In the second blessing of the *Amidah*, the silent prayer of devotion, the "heroism" of God is described. In this *berakhah*, God is portrayed not as a warrior, the One who split the sea or the One who brought about the ten plagues, but rather as the One who sustains life with kindness, raises up the fallen, heals the sick and releases those who are imprisoned. Thus, with respect to God, basic acts of kindness are considered heroism.

Comparing the Heroism of Esther and of Ruth

The acts of Esther and Ruth represent two different kinds of heroism: the bold single act of heroism – Esther's willingness to risk life itself to save the Jewish people; and the day-to-day heroism of Ruth's constant acts of kindness to others.

In this regard, the opening words of the *midrash* in *Lamentations Rabba* are particularly interesting. As God was about to destroy the Temple, the great leaders of the nation came before Him to beseech Him to have mercy on his people, but God remained unmoved. Then Rachel stepped forward.

"Lord of the universe, You know that Jacob toiled for my father Lavan for seven years so that he would be allowed to marry me, but when the time came my father determined to substitute my sister for me. When I learned of this plan I devised a signal by which my husband would be able to identify me. Afterwards, though, I took pity on my sister, and couldn't see her publicly shamed. As she was to be led [to the *huppah*], I revealed the signal to her so that he would think she was Rachel. And if I, flesh and blood, dust and ashes was not jealous of my rival and did not allow her to be shamed, You Living King, epitome of mercy, how could You be jealous of idols that have no substance, that You have exiled my sons, allowed them to be slaughtered by the sword and gave their enemies free reign over them?" At once, God's mercy was aroused and He proclaimed, "For your sake, Rachel, I shall return Israel to her place."

The question is asked why Rachel had greater merit than Avraham, Moshe, and all the other great leaders of Israel? Rav Yosef Dov Soloveitchic, in his book *On Repentance* explains that it was this act of compassion towards her unfortunate sister that carried weight and stood the test of time more than extreme acts of valor like the binding of Isaac and all the many other heroic deeds of our ancestors. All of this shows how highly Judaism values deeds. Sometimes a small, modest, and seemingly insignificant deed goes unnoticed; although hardly discernible, it may be that very deed that reaches a place higher than great and renowned heroism.

Rachel's act of kindness is similar to the deeds of Ruth. Although they may seem unimportant, they may have greater significance than other, more dramatic acts. Rachel's act ensured the return of her sons to their land, and Ruth's kindness led ultimately to the birth of David, King of Israel.

We have spoken of different types of deeds – the bold heroism of Esther and the less obvious heroism of Ruth's acts of kindness. One saves the nation and the other gives birth to the dynasty of *Mashiah*. Both are necessary, and we must learn to discern which path is dictated by any given circumstances. In the words of Kohelet, or King Solomon, David's son, at the end of his *megillah*: "The sum of the matter, when all is said and done, revere God and observe His commandments; for this applies to all of humankind."

Some Comments on T's Speech

The central value that comes to the fore in T's *derashah* is kindness, with the message that constant small acts of kindness do not pale in comparison with a one-time dramatic act of heroism. Other values expressed are: independence and initiative – the importance of Esther's transformation as she moves from Mordechai's domain to her own; self-sacrifice in order to save the Jewish people; and flexibility in choosing the type of action mandated by a given situation.

2. *Derashah by Ahava*

(Shabbat *parashat Nitzavim-Vayelekh* 5760)

Shabbat Shalom.

In the weekly Torah portion I read the following verses:

> For this *mitzvah* that I command you this day, it is not hidden from
> you, neither is it far off. It is not in heaven, that you should say, Who
> shall go for us to heaven and bring it down to us, that we may hear it
> and do it? Nor is it beyond the sea, that you should say, Who shall go

over the sea for us, and bring it to us, that we may hear it and do it? No, the word is very near to you, in your mouth and in your heart, that you may do it. [Deuteronomy 30:11–14]

These verses tell of a *mitzvah* that is close. It's not clear from the verses which *mitzvah* it is. We could interpret these words in several ways.

One possibility is that they don't refer to any particular *mitzvah* but instead use *"mitzvah"* in the collective sense of the entire body of *mitzvot*. A second possibility is that it refers to the *mitzvah* of *teshuvah*, or repentance. A third interpretation identifies the *mitzvah* that is close to all people as the study of Torah. I will adopt this interpretation as the starting point for my discussion.

To look for insight into what this closeness implies, I studied the *midrash Deuteronomy Rabba* on our Torah portion as well as a parallel discussion in tractate *Eruvin*.

The *Gemara* emphasizes that Torah is near to us in that it is not intangible or cut off from us, but rather actually bound to our physical body. At first glance this does not seem to make sense. In what way is Torah study related to our body – isn't it a more intellectual matter?

In the Talmud, *Eruvin* 54, several tales are told about scholars who discuss the connection between the Torah and the body.

a) Beruriah, wife of Rabbi Meir enters the study hall and sees a student studying silently. She kicks him, exclaiming, "That is not what is written. The Torah says 'Ordered in all things and sure....'" This verse [from 2 Samuel 23:5] means that only if Torah is there in all 248 of your limbs is it preserved. Only if the Torah is expressed by your entire body while you study will you be protected from forgetting what you have learned. I think that she wanted to make clear to him that Torah is not to be studied silently but in a loud voice and with the entire body, and thus she used her body and kicked him.

b) The *Gemara* then tells of a student of Rabbi Eliezer who studied Torah silently and after three years forgot all that he had learned. This student forgot his Torah learning because he had not studied out loud and with all parts of his body. Only if the words of Torah come out of our mouths will they endure within us.

c) The next story also revolves around someone who studied silently. Rabbi Yehudah was studying quietly. Shmuel said to him *"shinnena"* which in Aramaic means having teeth – that is, one who can talk. It was also meant as a reprimand. In

Hebrew, it means open your mouth and read, open your mouth and learn, thus shall Torah endure in you and lengthen your life, as it says, "For they are life to all who find them, and a cure to all flesh." [Proverbs 4:22] Shmuel reads the verse with a play on words, "Don't read it as saying 'all who find them' *(motzeihem)* but as 'all who bring them out' *(motzi'eihem)*, all who draw words of Torah out of their mouths. If all the body and senses participate in Torah, your Torah will be connected to your body and will actually lengthen the life of that body.

Shmuel's comment to Rabbi Yehudah is similar to what Beruria said, or did, to the student studying quietly. The reprimand *"shinnena"* parallels Bruria's kick, and each story interprets a verse: "For they are life to all who find them..." and "Ordered in all things and sure...."

In conclusion, the closeness of Torah to a person is expressed in physicality. This does not refer to the actions of performing *mitzvot* (such as winding *tefillin* around one's arm) but to the physical aspect of Torah study, even though that appears to be a purely intellectual matter. The *Gemara* and *midrash* emphasize that even the experience of study is connected to the body, influences the body, and must involve participation of the body.

A somewhat different aspect of the connection between Torah and the one who studies it is related to the question of who is doing the studying as well as the question of what exactly is Torah. The section in *Eruvin* 53b opens with a personal comment of Rabbi Yehoshua ben Hanina. "In all of my days, no one triumphed over me, except for one woman, young boy, and young girl." The scholar, Rabbi Yehoshua then tells three stories illustrating the wisdom of a woman, boy and girl that surpassed his own wisdom. Due to their age or gender the people he mentions do not normally frequent the *beit midrash*. These stories show that the wisdom such people have may sometimes be greater than that of people who spend all of their time immersed in Torah study. These people acquire Torah not from books (they may not even be able to read), but from life itself. The lesson Rabbi Yehoshua learned in each case was gained outside the four walls of the study hall. Two of the three encounters took place "along the way," and the subject of the discussion each time was related to "the way."

The *Gemara* goes on to tell of yet another meeting "along the way" between a woman and a sage. Rabbi Yossi the Galilean met Beruria along the way. He asked her, "Which is the road to Lud?" She responded, "Foolish Galilean, have the Sages not taught, 'Do not speak excessively with women'? You should have said, 'Which to Lud.'" This story, too, concerns those who do not study in the *beit midrash*, yet defeat the scholar. It, too, takes place along the way, but here the woman is exceptional in that she is able to utilize the language and concepts of the *beit midrash*: This is not what the Sages have taught. I know their teaching and you don't?

The story just after this one is the incident I mentioned earlier in which Beruriah kicks the student. Here the setting shifts, and Beruriah does enter the *beit midrash*. There, too, she is not silent.

Some aspects of Torah cannot be found in books or in the *beit midrash*. Only by meeting a child or a woman can the scholar acquire this living Torah. In the *Gemara* a process unfolds that begins with encounters with simple people outside the *beit midrash* and progresses to an encounter with a learned woman, still outside the *beit midrash*. At the end of this process she enters the *beit midrash* and she, like all of the other scholars, quotes Scripture. But she brings an additional element into the *beit midrash* with her, something from the sensory physical nature of the living Torah outside, the kick.

Where do I fit into all of this? As I assume the obligation of *mitzvot* I begin to enter the *beit midrash*. In the days of Rabbi Yehoshua ben Hanina, the child represented someone outside of the *beit midrash* until he grew up, became obligated in *mitzvot* and began to delve into Torah study. During that time period girls, other than Beruriah, did not cross the threshold of the *beit midrash* even when they grew up.

I thank God that I was born at a time when I don't need to be a Beruriah in order to enter the *beit midrash*. Torah study that was unattainable for my female ancestors in earlier generations has become in my generation something close indeed in my mouth and heart to do.

When children enter the world of adults, they can remind adults of things that have long ago been forgotten and lost. So, too, when women engage in Torah study they bring to the *beit midrash* a perspective of Torah that is more personal. The Torah of women is the Torah of the physical and of life itself.

May it be Your will that the Torah learned from life shall blend with the Torah of books of all the generations.

Some Comments on Ahava's Discourse

Ahava's speech relates to the Torah portion of the week, *Nitzavim/Va-yelekh*. It centers on the verse, "For this *mitzvah* that I command you this day, it is not hidden from you, neither is it far off." The speaker and her mother, who helped her prepare the speech, chose the interpretation that identifies "this *mitzvah*" with Torah study, and developed the connection between "this *mitzvah*" and people with rabbinical sources. Throughout the year before her *bat mitzvah*, Ahava and her mother studied a section from the tractate *Sukkah* (the daughter's choice). This was Ahava's first experience learning *Gemara*. As her *bat mitzvah* drew near, they learned, with commentaries, the Torah portion Ahava would read herself, at a women's prayer group, from the Torah on the Shabbat of her *bat mitzvah*. They then studied the *midrash Deuteronomy Rabba* on those portions, as well as a parallel text in *Eruvin*. Ahava wrote the first draft of her speech; her mother then helped the speech reach its final form.

Evident in her conclusion is Ahava's awareness not only of the novelty of her reading from the Torah but also of new opportunity inherent in the opening of the doors of the *beit midrash* and the Talmud to women. She notes some characteristics intrinsic, in her eyes, to women's Torah study. "Feminine Torah" is bound up in the limbs and in vocalization, intimately connected to the body of the person studying. In contrast to "masculine Torah," based primarily on books and authority of the generations, "feminine Torah" springs from natural intuition and from life itself. It is Ahava's hope that this feminine Torah will ultimately influence the masculine *beit midrash*. Conscious that her schoolmates and teachers might not feel comfortable with some of these innovative ideas led her to chose to express them during a women's prayer service. Ahava prepared a more conventional speech for the *bat mitzvah* celebration held during the week, to which she invited all of her classmates and extended family.

3. Chana Rosen's *Derashah*

Rain and Dew

He'azinu hashamayim li'devar Torah sheli, Listen, O Heavens, to my *devar Torah*, *Ve-tishma ha'aretz imrei fi* – And may the earth hear the words I utter. *Ya'arof ke-matar li'kkhi tizal ke-tal imrati.* May my discourse beat down as drops of rain, my speech sprinkle like the dew [after Deuteronomy 32:1–2].

I have two questions: Why is the Torah compared to dew and rain, and what is the difference between the two?

Some say that the Torah is compared to water because everyone needs it and it's impossible to live without it. Both dew and rain are made of water. The difference between them is that, for example, newly planted seedlings need both rain and dew. Some plants need only dew and not rain. That is how I see the Torah. With regard to the Torah, people who are only beginning need a lot more help just to understand the simple meaning of the verses. Others, who are more advanced, do not need help any more and can study alone and even add commentaries.

The *Seforno* brings another idea. He says that rain comes in a stream and may be strong, like those who are advanced in Torah and can accept it in a strong stream. Likewise, the Torah can come in a strong stream for those who are able to take it in that way. The Torah also comes in the form of dew, more gently, good for everyone, especially beginners.

The *Sifra* says, "Just as dew comes down upon the trees and helps them to bring forth delicacies, each according to its nature – the vine according to its nature, the olive according to its nature, the fig according to its nature – so, too, though the words of Torah are all one, they include Scripture, *Mishna*, laws, and stories." Each person receives something different from the Torah – what *that person* needs at that time.

I think the Torah is compared to dew and rain in another way. In the winter, when there is always rain, why do we need dew? In the same sense, there is always Torah, so why do we read the Torah on Shabbat and recite *Shema* each day? My answer is that, indeed, the Torah is always there but it comes each day to recall its presence to us, and to remind us to do *teshuvah*, to come closer to Hashem. So too dew comes each day.

To conclude, I hope that everyone here will find their way in the Torah and the path on which God wants to lead them, whether it is like dew or rain or both.

Some Comments on the Speech

Chana Rosen gave this *derashah* on *Shabbat Haazinu* 5761 (2000), *Shabbat Shuva*. During the six months before her twelfth birthday, Chana and her mother studied Mishnah *Shabbat*, and with her mother's help, wrote a discourse on the topic of witchcraft, including some *halakhic* aspects, discussed there (*Mishnah Shabbat* 6.10). She gave that talk both at a family gathering and at a *siyyum* with invited friends, and decided to prepare a new one, appearing here, for the *kiddush* held in *shul* on Shabbat. Chana's mother suggested some sources for this *derashah*, which mother and daughter learned together. After writing the first speech with her mother's guidance, Chana was now ready to write on her own. Her mother noted that this *derashah*, in her daughter's own words, and was delivered more freely than the one written with her mother's help.

Torah study is her central topic; using the images of rain and dew, she relates to the manifold paths in Torah study, and the manifold rewards of Torah study that are granted to each student individually. She also addresses the question of the relationship between the ongoing *mitzvah* to study Torah day and night and the set readings of Torah at particular times. Chana begins with a paraphrase of the opening verse of her Torah portion, which serves as a sort of personal prayer, and ends with the hope that each person present will find a personal message in Torah.

4. H's *derashah*

"Ve-hayyita akh sameakh – And be simply joyous"

Today is my delayed *bat mitzvah* celebration. Since it is Sukkot, the holiday about which it is said, "Be joyous on your festival" [Deuteronomy 16:14], I'd like to talk about the subject of joy. For us, it became mixed with great sadness and much longing when my grandmother, Savta Ronnie, was taken from us two-and-a-half months ago.

For me, Sukkot is particularly associated with my grandmother. She would present herself even before we were ready, urging us to trim the ivy, wash away the year's dust and iron the white cloths. And then, no matter how she was feeling, she wouldn't leave the *sukkah* until the wee hours of the morning – until she had hung the last cloth. The next morning she would travel to her other *sukkah* in the Golan, parting with some difficulty from the *sukkah* in which she had invested her whole self. She would come back, though, in the middle of the holiday to admire it again, because my *Savta* loved to celebrate.

Each year, my father says that the white cloths remind him of the clouds of glory that hovered over the Camp of Israel and calmed them, and that this is one of the things a *sukkah* is meant to remind us of. Each year, as I hang the *sukkah* cloths, I'll remember *Savta* and miss her all over again.

With all of this happening, and with the difficult situation in Israel, it's not easy to rejoice. How can the *Torah* command happiness? And why does the *mitzvah* of joy relate specifically to *Sukkot?* This is written three times: "And you shall rejoice on your holiday"; "And rejoice before the Lord your God for seven days"; "And be simply joyous."

Our *sukkah* has one very strange wall that I never really understood – the wall of the seven beggars. Every year, in our *sukkah* we read excerpts from Reb Nahman of Breslav's "Tale of the Seven Beggars." I never paid much attention. At the top of the wall it says, "I will tell you how they were happy." It's not clear how this is connected to the story of the Seven Beggars.

I'd like to read the introduction to the story. This year we learned it together in the hope of understanding something about the nature of that joy.

> Once there was a king and he had one son. The king wished to pass the crown to his son during his lifetime, and so he made a great feast. Now, whenever a king makes a feast, it is a joyous occasion. And now especially, as he is passing the rule of the kingdom down to his son while he is still alive, there was surely much rejoicing. The entire kingdom celebrated, for it was a great honor for the king.
>
> In the midst of the rejoicing the king said to his son, I can read the stars and I see that one day you will have to relinquish your power. See that you will not be sad when you give up your rule, but will be happy. And when you are happy, I too will be happy. But if you are sad, I will be happy nevertheless – happy that you are no longer king, since you are not fit to rule if you cannot maintain your joy when you relinquish power. If you are happy, though, I will be happier still.

That's the introduction to Reb Nahman's "Tale of the Seven Beggars." In this story the king represents God and we are the son. The king tells his son that without joy he cannot rule. So, too, when we are sad we distance ourselves from God and lose faith. We cannot be sons of the King, then, if we lack joy.

We know, too, that the *sukkah* is called *tzeila de-mehemnuta* – a canopy of faith.

Reb Nahman also told about a person who makes a feast. Everyone is happy except for one, who stands apart and doesn't join the merrymakers and dancers. The joy of the occasion is spoiled. The host, or happiness itself, tries to convince him to enter the circle of dancers. He refuses and runs away, and joy chases after him. This is what is meant by the verse, *Sasson ve-simkha yasigu ve-nasu yagon ve-anakha*

[Isaiah 35:10] – "Joy and happiness shall triumph and sorrow and sighing shall flee away." In these troubled times, I'd like to wish all of Israel and my family, that joy shall be our portion. *Sasson ve-simkha yasigu ve-nasu yagon ve-anakha.*

Some Comments on the Speech

H's *derashah*, given on *Hol ha-Moed Sukkot* 5761 (2000), revolves around the concept of joy. She speaks of the tension between the communal season of Sukkot, "the time of our rejoicing," and the family's experience of mourning the recent passing of H's grandmother. The mourning period was in fact the reason the celebration had been postponed until *Hol ha-Moed.* H's feelings are further affected by the precarious situation overall in Israel. Due to these difficult circumstances, the *derashah* was less the result of an intellectual process than of an existential search for the significance of the threefold command to rejoice during their painful moment. In reading the introduction to Reb Nahman's "Tale of the Seven Beggars," she underlines the connection between joy and the ability to rule. Joy can be a power that can "grab" a person standing in sadness into a circle of dancers.

Conclusion

These four discourses, though very different, are enlightening in the possibilities they illustrate. In terms of form, they often introduce ideas with a question or challenge – a comparison between characters, between elements (dew and rain), the interpretation of a verse, or an attempt to understand something unclear (how to be joyous). They then proceed to suggest an answer or answers. In many cases, they end with some kind of lesson or wish for the future based on the sources they have presented.

These *derashot*, "oral Torah" in essence, are enmeshed in the specific life context of the speaker. Some signs of the interconnections between the *bat mitzvah* girl and her subject present in them are mention of the relevant Torah portion or holiday, contemporary personal and national events, life cycle events (her becoming obligated in *mitzvot)*, and social context. Due to their personal nature, we have omitted the final words of good wishes and thanks.

In terms of content, the subject each speaker chose is clearly central to her life. Ahava's *derashah* focuses on a girl's joining the circle of Torah scholars. H speaks of happiness and rejoicing on the festival in the shadow of events in her family circle and on the broader national scale. T emphasizes the great value of small acts of kindness in her world. The individualistic aspect of Torah learning Chana discusses is clearly an important value for the maturing young woman.

Most of these speeches show an awareness of differences between people. Ahava speaks of variances between methods of Torah study – book learning as opposed to life experience. T's *derashah* distinguishes between types of heroism appropriate in different life situations, and Chana focuses on the personal messages people seek in learning Torah.

While it's difficult to generalize on the basis of these few examples, we could note some ways that these *bat mitzvah derashot* differ from most *bar mitzvah derashot*. First, the focus of *bar mitzvah* speeches is nearly always an *halakhic* topic. The *derashot* presented here do not include any (although Chana's first speech, not reprinted here, did); the passages from the Talmud and *midrash halakhah* they discuss are *aggadic* rather than *halakhic* in nature. All four *derashot* presented here use classical texts (*Tanakh*, rabbinical commentary, medieval sources, hasidic texts), but do not directly deal with *halakhic* sources or topics. Second, *bar mitzvah* speeches often address issues of religious obligation and new responsibilities. Questions of personal identity as a maturing Jewish woman, similarly, are intrinsic to these *bat mitzvah* speeches, but with a vital difference in context. The *bat mitzvah* girls here consider essential aspects of self by evoking female characters who serve as role models, and by speaking of Torah study itself. In many cases they express a sense of involvement in the movement in recent years toward expanding learning opportunities for girls and women of all ages.

We hope that the *bat mitzvah* discourses presented here will help guide more *bat mitzvah* girls, their teachers, and families in learning and preparing for that special event. In addition, we believe it is essential to collect *bat mitzvah derashot* of all kinds and make them available to a wider public.[2]

We are truly grateful and fortunate to witness the development of these creative and inspired treasures in Torah learning in our generation.

---

[2] All contributions of such speeches are welcome. If you have one to submit or can put us in touch with others who may be of assistance in this, please contact us at Felice@netvision.net.il or ylkpk@netvision.net.il.

BAT MITZVAH AS I EXPLAINED IT TO MY DAUGHTER

MANUEL WEILL

One father wrote the following discourse on the occasion of his daughter's *bat mitzvah*. In preparation for her *bat mitzvah*, the daughter learned together with her mother within the framework of Matan's Jerusalem *Bat Mitzvah* program;[#] she and her father studied the material summarized in this address, which her father delivered. The more personal introduction and conclusion of the sermon have been omitted.

"You are twelve years old. You're about to become an independent individual. I want to prepare you for this transition.

Over the years, I've told you much of what I am about to express, either directly or indirectly. Still, though, part of the transition to adulthood involves developing an ability to clarify our innermost feelings verbally. The basis of all social life may really be no more than an unending attempt at such clarification.

As you stand upon the threshold of this transitional period, it was only natural for me to choose to teach you the *halakhah* concerning the *mezuzah* – the laws proscribed in the *mezuzah* are placed on the doorpost, at the threshold marking the passageway between the inside and outside.

Rather than studying abstract principles, I decided to convey my message to you by teaching you about a tangible *mitzvah*. I hoped, in that way, to help you form a bond with our manifold tradition and the many possibilities it contains. In facing the future you are not alone: your mother and

---

[*] translated by Etka Liebowitz

[#] This program is described in this anthology, by O. Koren and T. Kelman (Garber), "Towards a *Bat Mitzvah*, the Jewish Woman throughout the Ages – MaTaN's *Bat Mitzvah* Program."

I, and all our family accompany you; generations of experience, tradition, and sources escort you as well.

We studied the talmudic discussion in *Sanhedrin* 71a. There we considered R. Eliezer's opinion that a town "led astray" (in which the majority of the inhabitants had turned to idolatry, and which was thus condemned to be burned) can be saved if a single house in it has a *mezuzah*.

This is indeed a strange law. A town "led astray" is a sick society. Such a town is inherently corrupt, since one condition for defining it thus is that the person responsible for leading the inhabitants astray must live in the town itself. Neither outside influences nor evil spirits from abroad produced the town's moral bankruptcy. Being "led astray" came from within the town itself. The town had no defense mechanisms. Its foundation was not healthy enough to subdue the streams polluting it. A radical change transpired. The minority overpowered the majority. Perhaps they waited silently for too long; perhaps they hoped the evil would disappear by itself. In any case, the outcome was that the town became a stranger to itself. It lost its identity.

In effect, an actual physical burning was almost unnecessary. The internal conflagration already existed. Burning is disappearance, obliteration of what existed. The town that was is no more. It lost its stability and sways upon its ruined self. This is the significance of the law (*Sukkah* 28b) that the obligation of waving the *lulav* is not fulfilled if the *lulav* used comes from a town "led astray" – that which is on the verge of being burned is as good as burned already [unfit for a *mitzvah*]. And yet, R. Eliezer (*Sanhedrin* 71a) maintains that if one house with a *mezuzah* stands in such a town, it is not deemed a town "led astray" even if all the inhabitants are idol worshippers. The Sages apparently believed that a city containing one house with a *mezuzah* still had a healthy enough foundation to make rehabilitation possible. The question, of course, is how a *mezuzah* can provide the basis for a city's recovery.

To gain a better understanding of its significance, let's consider the *mezuzah*'s location – at the threshold. The threshold marks the transitional point between the inside and outside. According to the Talmud, the prospect of a society's rehabilitation depends upon the separation between the public and private domain. Only when a person is able to cross the threshold, go inside, calm down from the hustle and bustle of the street can she return to herself. A basic requirement for remaining true to oneself is freedom from the influence of fads and societal pressure.

Entering the house, though, may not solve all the problems. Inside the house there is always the danger of being alienated from what happens in the outside world; a person can confine himself to the house and ignore everything outside of narrow personal interests, believing he is unique. A narcissistic person's world is as small as that of an ant.

I think that where you are standing today – at the end of your childhood and the beginning of adolescence – is a place where one wavers between the inside and the outside. You forge your own identity by examining both the inside and the outside world. How much will you be alone and how much with others? To what extent will you see yourself as the center, and to what extent will you see others as existing by their own right?

We're familiar with questions like these from the laws concerning prayer (*Shulhan Arukh, Oreh Hayyim* 90.20). A Jew stands in the doorway of the synagogue and prays. He hasn't decided yet where he belongs. He isn't all the way outside but he isn't completely inside either. He hesitates, wavering between inside and outside. The ruling is that he should enter the synagogue "the distance of two doorways and then pray."

Nonetheless, in choosing the door post as the location for the *mezuzah*, the Torah probably meant to do more than merely set boundaries between inside and outside as part of identity formation. The threshold is more than a transitional point; it exists in and of itself. We recall that the religious court was always situated at the city gate. "You shall appoint judges and officers in all your gates, which the Lord your God gives you, throughout your tribes, and they shall judge the people with due justice" (Deuteronomy 16:18). Having the seat of justice at the city gate is not accidental. Justice and law can only exist if objective examination is possible. The judge is associated with the city but is not entrenched in it. He can take a critical view. He can understand the position of someone who does not belong to the city, a stranger, someone whose lifestyle is different. Examining things from a broad perspective is a prerequisite for enacting justice.

The location of the door itself is closely linked to the idea and contents of the *mezuzah*. As you know, the *mezuzah* contains the first and second paragraph of the *Shema*, beginning "Hear, O Israel! The Lord our God, the Lord is one." Realizing God's unity is crucial to understanding the *mezuzah*. The perpetual tension between inside and outside will never be resolved. The search for equilibrium is a journey towards unity. The point of balance is not and cannot be fixed once and for all. In every age and every generation it changes, and for that reason it stands on the door's threshold.

Another theme in the *Shema* is this: "And these words, which I command you this day, shall be in your heart. Teach them to your children. Talk of them when you sit in your house and when you walk by the way, when you lie down and when you get up" (Deuteronomy 6:6–8). What is the meaning of this continual demand to be immersed in such matters? When you ride on a bus in Jerusalem you sometimes see people absorbed in saying *tehillim* (Psalms). They take advantage of every moment. Is this what is demanded?

My thinking is a little different. I see the injunction to be occupied continually with Torah as part of an approach. True and authentic Torah learning is possible only if one takes it "to heart," only if it is connected to your life, or more precisely, if it is connected to the things that interest and concern you.

I'll give you another example from the laws concerning *mezuzah*. The *mezuzah*, as you know, is attached to the doorpost diagonally. We talked about the dispute between Rashi, who holds that the *mezuzah* should be placed vertically, and Rabbenu Tam, who holds it should be placed horizontally. The *halakhah* found an interim solution: it was decided that the *mezuzah* should be on a diagonal, ostensibly to satisfy both opinions. On the face of it, though, this seems to be a poor solution: neither view is really satisfied, since a diagonal is neither horizontal nor vertical. This is one instance of the kind of problem that may, in my opinion, bother us – what is Rashi's intention when he says the *mezuzah* should be placed vertically? Does he want to emphasize the relationship between a person and higher powers? What is Rabbenu Tam's intention when he says the *mezuzah* should be placed horizontally? Does he want to emphasize the interpersonal relationship?

And what is the meaning of the solution, which proposes acting in accordance with no method at all, placing the *mezuzah* on a diagonal? Is this the way to resolve a dispute? Should we always seek the meeting point between two methods?

Maybe you're thinking this is all exaggerated – why invest so much thought in a technical dispute over the way to affix a *mezuzah*? When you visit a museum, though, and examine the paintings you'll soon realize that the tension between horizontal and vertical finds expression in lines and their direction. The up-and-down movement of the paintbrush very often suggests a wavering or tension in the search for place and direction.

I'll tell you something else – the entire discussion concerning how a town "led astray" is saved due to a *mezuzah*, which we have just studied, relates to R. Eleizer's methodology in *Sanhedrin* 71a. This issue reveals R. Eleizer's great optimism. In his opinion, there is no town without a *mezuzah*. The whole discussion of a town "led astray" is consequently transformed into something hypothetical.

The well-known saying, "There never was and never will be 'a town led astray.' Why, then, was this written? Study the matter and earn your reward" appears in this context. This teaches us that the question of a *mezuzah* in a town "led astray" is not a pragmatic issue or a *halakhah* that must be fulfilled. Its purpose is to spark a theoretical discussion.

Do issues limited to the abstract realm have any importance? In a world that judges everything by the "end products," does study for its own sake have any place? The Talmud apparently feels that practical necessity is not the highest value; a discussion of abstract principles also has validity. Its underlying assumption that a town without a *mezuzah* cannot exist is not based on any survey or field study, but on an understanding of the tension inherent in human existence. This, too, is important for me to say to you as you set out on your path.

We find ourselves in a strange situation. We started with a town "led astray," in danger, a sick society, and we searched for stability. We found it in the most unexpected place: the transitional point. The threshold represents the geometric point where one can find a temporary equilibrium between pressures of inside and outside, between the individual and the group. The threshold is a sort of membrane permitting osmosis between the inside and outside. Standing at this threshold, we found the demand for perpetual study, and the tension between the vertical and horizontal.

Finally, we saw that certain forms of study do not produce any practical results.

How does all of this relate to your *bat mitzvah*? Adolescence, we know, is a time of upheavals. What I wanted to do was give you some tools in facing the unknown future, to prepare you as much as possible for things to come. But parents are always either too over-protective or indifferent; it's sometimes hard for us too to know when to be at your side and when to keep our distance.

You are now approaching the Torah, but coming close to Torah is possible only if you see it as a source and environment for deliberation, not a book with ready-made answers. Only that way will you fulfill the commandment "which one should do, and live by them" (Ezekiel 20:11).

As you draw away, setting off on your own path, your mother and I stay here, in our natural place. We watch you leaving us, but we wait here as well, hoping to see you come back to us from time to time – on the threshold."

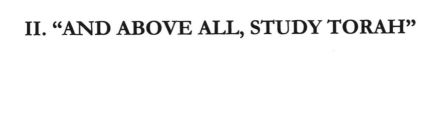

II. "AND ABOVE ALL, STUDY TORAH"

On Women and the Feminine

RE-CREATING EVE

Rachel Adelman

Prelude

This *drash* was inspired by studies with my daughter, Ariella, in the context of MaTaN's *Bat Mitzvah* program. As the teacher of the program I couldn't be Ariella's *hevruta*, so her grandmother, Sandy, assumed "the mother's role" during class times. For our final project we decided to do a play on "Eve in the Garden of Eden": Ariella was the snake (played with a proper British accent), her grandmother was the Tree of Good and Evil (replete with plastic fruit), and I was Hava (or the "naïve Eve"). We played out Rashi's interpretation: the serpent was able to trick Eve because she "added a fence to the Torah," changed God's words, in saying that one couldn't eat *or even* touch the Tree in the center of the garden. Whereupon the snake pushed her, she fell against the tree with no fatal consequences, and the snake exclaimed, "See, you didn't die," and invited her to eat the fruit which, in turn, would prove to be harmless. She eats, and then gives the fruit to Adam to eat, and the rest is history. Eve, at least in Rashi's rendition, is at fault because she had "added to the truth and thereby diminished it," in her caution or over-zealousness with regard to touching the tree.

Yet Eve never heard the original command, "From the Tree of Knowledge of Good and Evil, do not eat because on that day you will surely die" (Gen. 2:17). She hadn't yet been created! It could have been Adam who set Eve up for failure in reporting God's original command with a tone of protective paternalism, "By the way dear, there's a tree in the middle of the garden that you shouldn't go near...." When the snake "trips her up" literally and figuratively, she feels betrayed by Adam – for the words proved false. She touched the tree and she didn't die. She was compelled to listen to the snake *because* she had never heard the words directly from God. Her husband had been the mediator, the arbiter of the Torah for her. Now, Ariella somehow understood all this on a profound level, for when I turned to her and asked a very simple question, "Why did Eve listen to the serpent, after all he was 'the most cunning of all the beasts of the field'? Wouldn't she sense that?" Ariella answered very simply, "Well, she didn't have a mother!" Floored and flattered, I was. "You mean if Eve had had a mother [like me, I thought] she would have known better?" "Yes. The snake was her teacher. She didn't have anyone else to talk to in order to know what to do."

Somehow my daughter felt a mother was a better, wiser resource than a serpent; that a girl "not of woman born" was more vulnerable to the wily ways of the cold-blooded reptile world than one brought up in loving maternal arms. Perhaps I am flattering myself, reading into Ariella's statement, but I don't think so. And it wasn't just her feelings about me that were so striking. Here we were, grandmother, mother and daughter, learning Torah together directly from God's words. There was no mediator. "Adam" was conspicuously absent. Though we drew on the resources of Rashi, and the midrashim (*Avot de Rabbi Natan* in particular), father figures so to speak, it was just us women grappling directly with the text, coming up with our own creative responses. No one was there in a paternalistic capacity to tell us what the sources meant. Through our *bat mitzvah* studies, we had created a link to the Torah, a very deep link through mother and daughter. This was truly "*Torat imekha*" – mother's Torah – or really my daughter's Torah, what she taught me about what I meant to her.[1]

I myself was not raised with Torah learning in the home; nevertheless, I have had many "mothers" teaching me, most notably Dr. Avivah Zornberg, Dr. Bryna Levy, and Osnat Braverman-Shiloh – all of them wise and wonderful teachers. This drash draws on insights from a lecture Bryna gave during Tishrei of 1997 (תשנ"ח) and a graduate seminar with Osnat Braveman on the garden of Eden story, at MaTan, in the Spring of 2000 – תש"ס. I still remember Osnat's opening question, "And what if you had been born without parents, no educational or cultural context, who would you be?" When she heard Ariella's insight, she commented, "It's a very deep idea – that Eve had no mother." We, as mothers and as teachers, as daughters and as students engaged in Torah learning together, are

---

[1] After the verse in Proverbs 1:8, "Hear, my child, the instruction of your father and forsake not the Torah of your mother."

re-creating Eve, an Eve who has a heritage, who has the deep waters of Torah to draw from. As all mothers want to protect their daughters against their own mistakes, against the folly of listening to wily snakes, we all hope this source of truth, learning Torah together, will inoculate the next generation against a fall.

The Origin of Eve's Folly

The third chapter of Genesis opens with a description of the serpent, "And the serpent was the most cunning (ערום) of all beasts of the field that God had made…" (Gen. 3:1). We are well primed for his future manipulations in his conversation with Eve. Yet the term "cunning" is loaded – echoing the last description of man and woman, "And they were both naked (ערומים), the man and his wife, but they were not ashamed" (2:25). Nakedness/cunning are somehow related, and somehow not – the first ערום seems positive, the latter negative.[2] The first ערום suggests unselfconscious nudity, the way children are with their bodies, unfettered and playful. Yet this "innocence" is lost immediately after they eat from the fruit, "And their eyes were opened, and they knew that they were naked – וידעו כי ערומים הם…" (3:6). It is Adam's newborn awareness of his own nakedness, more than any confession, that betrays his deed, "I was afraid because I was naked (ערום) and so I hid." And so God responds, "Who told you were naked (כי ערים אתה)? Did you eat of the tree…" (Gen.3:11). If, as I would like to contend, the two terms "cunning" with reference to the snake, and "naked" with respect to man, are *related*, wherein lies the overlap, wherein the difference?

The first state of nakedness is one of *not knowing*; they have not yet eaten of the Tree of Knowledge of Good and Evil; unfettered, free, and blissfully ignorant. The second nakedness, is one of *knowing*. They have eaten the fruit, and are suddenly boundaried beings who hear the voice of God

---

[2] According to *The Brown-Drivers-Briggs Lexicon of the Hebrew Bible*, the first ערום is related to the root ע.ר.ה., "to be naked or bare," from whence the term ערוה, nakedness comes (implying shameful exposure as in Gen. 9:22, Ex. 20:23, and Lev. 18:10) (see p. 788, entry 6168 and 6172). The two terms ערום and עריח are used synonymously in Ezek. 16:7, 22, 39, and 23:29. The term ערום as "cunning," is derived from the root ע.ר.מ., "to be shrewd or crafty," as in I Sam. 23:22, Prov. 12:23 (B.D.B. p. 791, entry 6191 and 6175). However it is not incidental that *the same sounding word* is used in this context to mean two seemingly diametrically opposite states of being.

wandering through the garden even before He has addressed them. When they realized they were naked, "they sewed together fig leaves, and made themselves loincloths (חגורות)" (3:7). Knowing one is naked compels one to cover up.[3] Fear. Conscience. The desire to hide. All this comes with self-conscious knowledge. So how is the snake "naked," ערום? According to R. Hezekiah ben Manoah (*Hizkuni*), a mid-thirteenth century commentary on the *Humash*, the serpent, along with all the other beasts in the garden, heard the command not to eat of the Tree of Knowledge. Yet he decided to abrogate the command and ate, and became *knowingly naked*, more na-ked/cunning than all the beasts of the field (ערום מכל חיית השדה) *because he knew he was so*. His awareness of his nakedness compelled him to "dress up" just as Adam would. The snake's "clothing," however, takes the form not of fig leaves or loin-cloths, but of the *manipulation of language*. When he turns to Eve in conversation, he is looking for company, for someone who could join him in his unique status as the knowingly naked/cunning animal in the garden.

Poor Eve. She is an open book, a *tabula rasa*, waiting to be written upon. The snake first wields the pen over her pages, and "re-writes" God's word. He broaches the subject thus: "Did God indeed say, 'You shall not eat of *all* (כל) of the trees of the garden?'" (Genesis 3:2). The serpent, the "knowingly naked/cunning one," gives the original command a "dressing." In effect, he is either lying or manipulating the truth. In either case, he evidently heard the original command, which did not open as a *negative* prohibition at all, "And the Lord God commanded man, saying, 'Of all כל the trees of the garden you may surely eat. But of the Tree of Knowledge of good and evil you shall not eat of it, for on the day that you eat thereof, you shall surely die'" (Gen. 2:16–17). God was a liberal father and believed his children would fare better in a permissive atmosphere, with a limited number of rules, than in a world composed of too many "thou-shalt-nots,"

---

[3] The term חגורת, translated as "loincloth" in the NJPS, actually means "belt" and is most commonly used in a military context, referring to the protective covering used by soldiers to defend the area of the groin and to carry the sword (II Kings 3:21, Isaiah 3:24, II Sam. 18:11). The connotations of חגורה suggest Adam and Eve live tenuously, as *embattled*, in the garden of Eden even before God has rebuked them. (I owe this insight to Osnat Braverman who taught us the significance of "clothing" – in both the figurative and literal sense).

which would have invited rebellion. So "all" trees are available for the pleasures of their palate, except one. Yet the snake's statement is true as well, at least on the level of surface grammar, "You cannot eat from *all* the trees…" because one is forbidden. So, in order to have that "all," the first part of God's command, one must eat of that one, the forbidden one, "the tree of Knowledge of Good and Evil." Now, I will not claim that Eve was sophisticated enough to compare the surface grammar of God's original statement with that of the serpent's. In a way, she "didn't get it"; she was not yet on his level of "cunning," knowing one is naked and trying to "dress it up," for she hadn't yet eaten of the tree. The snake might have succeeded, otherwise, by pointing out the contradiction between "having it all" and "not being allowed to have one," but she proved thicker than he thought. She simply insinuates that he is a liar, and corrects him, but she *too* misrepresents God's word.

"Of the fruit of the trees of the garden we may eat. But of the fruit of the tree that is in the midst of the garden, God said, 'You shall not eat of it, and *you shall not touch it*, lest you die'" (Gen. 3:2-3). She distorts the original command in two ways: 1) she doesn't refer to the tree *specifically* as "the tree of Knowledge of Good and Evil;" it is only the tree "in the midst of the garden," and 2) she *adds* the command "you shall not touch it." The classical commentators take her to task for the second mistake, but very few take note of the first one. *Or HaHaim*, the interpretation of the *Humash* by the kabbalist R. Hayyim ibn Attar of the eighteenth century, presents an exception. He suggests that Adam had not told his woman what the tree was. Instead he had called it "the tree that kills" in order to exaggerate the danger and distance her from it. He didn't say, "If you eat of the tree of Knowledge of Good and Evil you will have committed a sin punishable by death."[4] I would offer the following analogy. One parent says to his child, "Don't open the cookie jar and eat cookies whenever you want because then it will spoil your appetite for supper, and you will develop bad eating habits and you won't grow up to be a strong, fit adult." Adam, rather, is like

---

[4] This would explain the conflict between God's warning ביום אכלך ממנו מות תמות "on *that day* you will surely die" (Gen. 2:17), and the facts on the ground – on the very day of eating they did not die. Instead they were punishable by death, or in the existentialist sense they began *living unto death* now that they understood they would one day die.

another parent. This one says, "Don't open *that* jar [he doesn't even say what it contains] because if you do, all the Demons will jump out at you." Now the mischievous of mind would be tempted to do precisely that, not *knowing* what was in the jar, as Eve wasn't told what the tree was. (Curiosity killed the cat.) Furthermore, the cookie-jar-raider has never met a Demon, just as Eve didn't understand the meaning of her own mortality. Death presented no real threat to her. Adam's paternalism does not protect her from the tree; instead, it sets her up for failure.

The analogy of the jar is appropriate for it reminds us of the Greek myth of Pandora's box. Here, the first Woman is sent to Prometheus and his brother Epimetheus, by the gods "to punish them for their presumption in stealing fire from heaven."

> Epimetheus had in his house a jar, in which were kept certain noxious articles for which, in fitting man for his new abode, he had had no occasion. Pandora was seized with an eager curiosity to know what this jar contained; and one day she slipped off the cover and looked in. Forthwith there escaped a multitude of plagues for hapless man – such as gout, rheumatism, and colic for his body, and envy, spite and revenge for his mind – and scattered themselves far and wide. Pandora hastened to replace the lid! But, alas! The whole contents of the jar had escaped, one thing only remained, which lay at the bottom, and that was *hope.*[5]

Here again the woman, not the owner of jar, is at fault for bringing these evils into the world on account of her curiosity.

The second problem lies in the added words – "you shall not touch it." Rashi blames Eve, "She added to the command; therefore, she came to diminish it גרעון. As it is said (Proverbs 30:6): 'Do not add to His words.'"[6] Rashi's source, the talmudic tractate *Sanhedrin* 29a suggests *this* passage in

---

[5] Thomas Bulfinch, *Bulfinch's Mythology*, The Modern Library, Random House, Inc. 1867, p. 16–17.

[6] רש״י בראשית פרק ג

(ג) ולא תגעו בו - הוסיפה על הצווי, לפיכך באה לידי גרעון, הוא שנאמר (משלי ל ו) אל תוסף על
דבריו :

Genesis is a proof text for the principle, כל המוסיף גורע "all those who add [to the truth] diminish the truth." Yet we have the equally famous adage, "Make a protective fence around the Torah (עשו סייג לתורה)" [i.e., add restrictions, or preventive measures].[7]

When is a fence protective and when is it set up to be pulled down? In conversation with a serpent, whether the fence was intended as *defence* becomes a moot point as he maneuvers her into knocking it over. Rashi, comments on the serpent's words, "You will surely not die": "He pushed her until she touched it. He said to her, 'Just as there is no death in touching, so is there no death in eating.'"[8] The homiletical message is spelled out clearly in Rashi's second source, *Genesis Rabbah* 19:3. Here the metaphor of the "fence" prevails. "R. Hiyya taught: That means that you must not make the fence *more than* the principal thing, lest it fall and destroy the plants." Which is to say, one should not let the added stricture obscure the principal prohibition – the touching should be clearly *secondary* to the eating of the tree. Did the problem then lie with Hava's learning? Did she confuse a "first degree" prohibition from the Torah (*de'oraita*) with a "second degree," rabbinic ordinance (*derabbanan*)? If so, who was her rabbi? The midrash quotes from Proverbs (30:6) as its proof text, and herein lies the crux of the problem. "Add not to His words, lest He *test you* and prove you wrong and you be found a liar."[9] Who is testing God's words here? The serpent.[10] And who is proved the liar? Apparently Eve, for *she* said, "God said, "Do not eat of it, and do not touch it...."[11]

---

[7] *Pirkei Avot* 1:1.

[8] (ד) לא מות תמתון - דחפה עד שנגעה בו, אמר לה כשם שאין מיתה בנגיעה כך אין מיתה באכילה:

[9] אל תוסף על דבריו פן יוכיח בך ונכזבת.

[10] Hizkuni suggests the serpent is the extension of God in that He opens the mouth of the snake just as He opens the mouth of Bilam's donkey (Numbers 22:28).

[11] בראשית רבה (וילנא) פרשה יט.

ומפרי העץ אשר בתוך הגן וגו' ולא תגעו בו הה"ד (משלי ל) אל תוסף על דבריו פן יוכיח בך ונכזבת, תני ר' חייא שלא תעשה את הגדר יותר מן העיקר שלא יפול ויקצץ הנטיעות, כך אמר הקב"ה כי ביום אכלך ממנו וגו', והיא לא אמרה כן, אלא אמר אלהים לא תאכלו ממנו ולא תגעו בו כיון שראה אותה עוברת לפני העץ נטלה ודחפה עליו, אמר לה הא לא מיתת, כמה דלא מיתת במקרביה, כן לא מיתת במיכליה, אלא כי יודע אלהים כי ביום וגו'.

Yet who heard the original command? Adam. Must we assume he reported the command accurately to his wife? Not necessarily. Perhaps *he* was the one to add to God's words. This is *Avot de Rabbi Natan's* version of the story:

> What fence did Adam make to God's words? For it says, "God commanded Adam saying, 'From all the trees in the garden you may freely eat. But of the Tree of Knowledge of Good and Evil you shall not eat, for on the day you eat thereof, you shall surely die'" (Gen. 2:16–17). Adam didn't want to tell Eve what the Holy One Blessed be He had told him. Instead he told her, "But from the fruit of which is in the midst of the garden don't eat, and *don't touch it,* lest you die." (Gen. 3:3). So the evil serpent conceived a plan. "Because I probably can't outwit Adam, I'll try my luck with Eve." So he went to sit with her and spoke with her at length. "You say The Holy One Blessed be He commanded us with regard to *touching* [the Tree of Good and Evil]. Well look, I'll touch it and I won't die, yet you say that if you touch it you'll die!." What did that evil serpent do? He stood up and touched the tree with his hands and feet and shook the tree till its fruit fell to the ground. When that tree saw him, it cried out against him, "You wicked man! You wicked man! Don't touch me!" As it is said, "Let not the foot of pride come against me, and let not the hand of the wicked drive me away." (Psalm 36:11).[12]

According to this midrash, Adam felt it incumbent upon himself to add to God's words – perhaps he did not trust her with the truth. The serpent, in turn, presumed he couldn't trick Adam (since he had the command directly from God), and instead thought he'd try his luck with Eve. "Frailty, thy name is woman!"[13] – only because men presume women to be so. Poor naive Eve, caught between a rock (the law-giving husband/father) and a

---

[12] *Avot de Rabbi Natan*, 1:1, my translations.

אבות דרבי נתן, מהדורת ש״ז שכטר, וינא תרמ״ז, נוסח א, פרק א.

[13] Hamlet, I.ii.

hard-place (the snake). She doesn't know where to turn. She listens to the snake *because* she had never heard the words directly from God. Her husband had been the mediator, the arbiter of the Torah, *for her*. The midrash explains the dynamic by way of an allegory:

> R. Shimon ben Elazar said, "I'll tell you a story to illustrate what Adam was like. A man married a convert to Judaism, and he sat her down and instructed her, "*My daughter*. Don't eat bread when your hands are ritually impure, and don't eat fruit unless they have been tithed, and don't violate the Sabbath, and don't break any fences, and don't go with any other man (אל תלכי עם איש אחר). For if you transgress any of these commandments you will die." What did *that man* (האיש ההוא) do? He proceeded to eat a piece of bread with ritually impure hands, ate fruit that hadn't been tithed, and violated the Sabbath, and broke down fences, and took her by the hand. What did that convert say to herself, "All that my husband had been so strict about initially was a lie." She then proceeded to transgress, doing everything he had forbidden her to do.[14]

The analogy is fascinating in its portrayal of the three protagonists of our drama: Adam is like a strictly law-abiding husband, a *frum* Jew, who has married a convert, Eve. She, apparently, has no access to the law, being "newly born" ("derivative of the rib," created after Adam and therefore not privy to God's original command "not to eat..."). In fact, he calls her, either endearingly or condescendingly, "my daughter" but the term may very well be intentional, for only here does man actually "give birth" to woman. Not only is he father and husband, but he is also the arbiter of the law for her, her rabbi, though not a very good one at that, since he tells her the *halakhot* as if they are all on the same level of stricture. The first three laws he reveiws indeed have the same degree of severity, but what of "breaking fences" – does he mean it in the metaphorical sense or the literal sense? And "don't go/walk with any other man"? Certainly, the woman's reputation is at stake; if she is found alone with another man (*yihud*) she

---

[14] *Avot deRabbi Natan* 1:1

may be accused of adultery. Walking with another man in public is not worthy of a death sentence. The phrase is really a clever prelude to the introduction of the serpent as האיש ההוא *the other man*, or *the-self-same-man*. The pronominal reference is deliberately ambiguous. The man who flagrantly demonstrates the breaking of the law is merely the flip-side of the first man, the pious husband. Both as snake and as husband, man is "the keeper of the keys" – he locks the doors and unlocks the doors. She is removed from the gates of the law, with no direct access, like a Kafkaesque character wandering the stairwells, knocking on doors.

When she witnesses *that man* breaking the law with impunity she feels betrayed. The original strictures were a lie. She then immediately begins to break all the rules her husband had commanded her to observe. Yet if we take the ambiguity in the midrash seriously, it is the pious husband who plays both roles, who *wants* her to break the law. By setting too many strictures, he sets her up for a fall. Likewise Adam, who misrepresents God's word, invites disaster. The serpent is the "other side" of Adam as arbiter of "the word," and is able to take advantage of Eve *through* Adam's misrepresentation when he demonstrates his own immunity to consequence in touching the tree.[15] He actually shakes it until its fruits fall. In the first rendition, the tree cries out. This is the cry Eve cannot utter. She is mute witness to the shaking of the trunk, leaves, branches, falling fruit. The fence totters, the fence mistaken as the *ikar*, as the prohibition itself. Once that is down, she has already tasted the forbidden *with her eyes*, has already ingested the sense of "You shall not" transformed into "but I will." "And the woman *saw* that the tree was good for food and that it was a delight to the *eyes*..." (Genesis 3:6). Her eyes led to her hand, and then to her mouth. And she enjoins Adam in the dance towards "knowing good and evil,"

---

[15] Osnat Braverman, in our MaTaN seminar on "the garden of Eden," pointed out that the term *nahash*, serpent in Hebrew, is inextricably related to the verb לנחש, to divine, to practice divination (cf. Lev. 19:26, and Deut. 18:10), a sin punishable by death. The problem with divination, or necromancy, lies in the use of signs or rituals to read the future. One sets up arbitrary or irrational means of determining the truth – "if the stars are aligned with Jupiter east of the Milky Way, then you will encounter a strange man...." The *nahash* is the ultimate diviner in that he *distorts* God's words by setting up these signs. "If you touch it, you won't die...." He plays God to Eve in mediating between action and future consequences. "You will surely not die. For God knows that on the day that you eat thereof, your eyes will be opened, and you will be like God, knowing good and evil" (Gen. 3:4–5).

aware of their own nakedness, עֲרוּמִים הֵם conscious of the immanence of death.

In shifting the onus onto Adam, I am not thereby absolving Eve of responsibility. When God rebukes them, they commit yet another abrogation in not owning up to their part in the drama. "God says, 'Who told you that you were naked? Did you eat of the tree, which I commanded you not to eat from?' And the man said, 'The woman whom you gave me, she gave me from the tree and I ate.' And God said to the woman, 'What have you done!' And the woman answered, 'The serpent tricked me, and I ate'" (Gen. 3:11–13). Each one "passes the buck" – she did it; he did it. It's not my fault. Evie started it! No, it was Snakie who tricked me! The barrage of displacements is familiar to any parent. No one owns up. It is like the original distortion of the word – a broken telephone from God to Adam and the serpent, and then to Eve. No one accounts for the original words; no one is accountable for the original sin. With whom does the responsibility lie?

Now I turn to you: mother and daughter, teacher and student alike. How do we assume responsibility for Eve's folly? We open the book, and we read the original words, God's words, which Eve should have heard all along, "Of every tree of the garden you may surely eat. But of the Tree of Knowledge of Good and Evil you shall not eat…." Yet in opening the book, and *reading* for ourselves, are we not partaking of that Tree of Knowledge? The problem was and still remains how to reconcile "having it all" (i.e., eating from all the trees), and "not having *that one*." It seems that there is a way in which we *can* eat of the Tree, making the "all" inclusive of the "one." According to hasidic teaching, most notably the *Mei HaShiloah*, there is a way of partaking of the "Tree of Knowledge of Good" while excluding "Evil." "There will come a time when the original sin will be repaired and the verse will read, 'From all the trees of the garden you will surely eat, as well as from the Tree of Knowledge of Good, but from Evil you will not.' Which is to say, the Good of the Tree you will eat; but of the Evil you won't eat."[16] The difference lies not in how we parse the verse, but in how we view knowledge.

---

[16] *Mei HaShiloah* on Gen. 2:17.

For Jewish women today, only one or two generations removed from a *real* exile from the word, we are just beginning to understand what the knowledge of Torah entails. For us, to eat of the *Tree of Good* is to read the words directly. We need to know for ourselves both God's ordinance and the "fences" around it. And we need to guard against disappointment, the sense of betrayal, if the strictures imposed under false pretexts prove to be untrue or present rules we cannot live with. When I turned to my daughter, Ariella, and asked her simply, "But why did Eve listen to the snake? Didn't she sense that he was 'the most cunning of all the beasts of the field'?" She answered me simply, "She listened to him because she didn't have a mother." Eve's vulnerability stemmed from not being "of woman born."[17] As a teacher and a mother, I feel that the only way we can correct Eve's error is to give her the mother she never had, "re-create Eve" in God's image, in our image, as women learning Torah together. "She is a tree of life to those who grasp her, And whoever holds on to her is happy" (Proverbs 3:18).[18]

‏"עץ חיים היא למחזיקים בה ותמכיה מאושר."

---

[17] For MacDuff, in Shakespeare's "Macbeth," his ceasarean birth granted him *invulnerability,* enabling him to conquer the king. Here I claim the opposite for Eve. Because she was created from Adam, his "daughter" so to speak, she was "once removed" from the source and therefore *more* vulnerable. He became the arbiter of truth for her and laid her open to the snake's wily ways.

[18] There is a kabbalistic tradition that in the ideal world, "The Days to Come," the Tree of Life (also in the midst of the garden) merges with the Tree of Knowledge of Good and Evil. *Etz ha-Hayyim* (‏עץ החיים) becomes *Etz ha-Da'at* (‏עץ הדעת) when we cleave to the Torah, *the source of life,* as a source of truth, knowledge.

HANNAH'S TIMELESS PRAYER

Gabriel H. Cohn

1.

In biblical times women performed almost all of the governmental tasks –
prophets, judges, queens, and so on; only the religious roles were the
exclusive domain of men.[1] It is interesting to note that all of the women
mentioned were very successful in their roles. Only Queen Atalyah failed
and caused others to do so; it is uncertain, though, whether she was actually
Jewish.

Women, then, took on central roles in national life, and succeeded in
them. They had a tremendous influence both on social conditions in their
time and on historical trends in the ongoing life of the nation.

Despite all of this, it is clear that the biblical woman's activity was centered in the family as a spouse and mother. She is called "his fitting
helper"(Genesis 2:2), "covenanted spouse" (Malakhi 2:14), and "capable
wife" (Proverbs 31:10); in many passages of the Bible she appears as a
partner in the formation of the family, wielding a critical influence on her
husband and on her children's education. The familial context of the
women in the Bible is so significant that even in the case of public figures,
we are informed of their interpersonal relationships: Miriam is "Aharon's
sister" (Exodus 15:20) and Devorah is "the wife of Lappidot" (Judges 4:4).
There were many more women who, although they had no official task,
hold, in their dedication to the family, a unique place in Jewish history. One
individual biblical figure who left a special mark on the Jewish people
through personal initiative in her family life is Chana, the wife of Elkanah.

---

* translated by Gershon Clymer

[1] There was even a female *mohel*: Tzipporah, Moshe's wife (Exodus 4:25). Concerning
women in public offices, see my essay, "*Ha-isha u-mekoma be-gibbush ha-hevrah ve-
hahistoria be-tekufat ha-mikra,*" *Hevra ve-historia* (Jerusalem, 1980), pp. 397–407.

Chana's great contribution to the spiritual world of the Jewish people was as a prototype of a woman at prayer.

2.

We will investigate the background of her prayer, and then take a closer look at the words of the prayer she said at the Tabernacle of Shilo, in the hope of revealing the secret of the power of this prayer.

Elkanah, from Mount Ephraim, seems to have married Chana early in his life, and she bore him no children. The detailed account of his lineage – "Elkanah, son of Jeroham, son of Elihu, son of Tohu, son of Tzuf, an Ephraimite" (I Samuel 1:1) could suggest the depth of Chana's frustration: with the generations of Ephraim's family before her eyes, she doubtless understood this family was about to come to an end because of her infertility.

As the years passed, Elkanah took a second wife, Peninah, in order to raise a family, as was customary in those days.

We should point out here that the Bible favors monogamous marriage. That seems to be the intent of the phrase, appearing early in the Torah, that "Hence a man leaves his father and mother and clings to his *wife*," (Genesis 2:24) and not "his wives." This same idea can be found in the words of Psalms: "Your *wife* shall be like a fruitful vine" (Psalms 128:3), and not "your wives." Exceptions to the monogamous practice were that a man would take a second wife when the first was infertile, and a king could take more than one wife due to his station. Even so, the Torah does warn him, "And he shall not have many wives" (Deuteronomy 18:18).

Tensions rise in Elkanah's house when the second wife, Peninah, bears children while Chana remains childless. Yet Elkanah reaffirms to Chana the depth of his love for her. Both his words, "Am I not more devoted to you than ten sons?" (I Samuel 1:8) and his actions, "but to Chana he gave a double portion" (1:5) express this emotion. Chana, though, remained deeply frustrated and suffered greatly. The dynamic in Elkanah's home was comparable to that of Ya'akov's house: Rachel/Chana is the beloved wife, but Leah/Peninah is the mother of the children.

Life in Elkanah's house continued this way. Chana's surroundings – society as a whole and her family as well – apparently grew accustomed to her infertility, and saw it as an expression of God's will, which she should simply accept – "…the Lord had closed her womb…for the Lord had closed her womb" (1:5–6). The Bible also notes that religious life in Elkanah's home continued to follow the regular cycle. At set times, Elkanah would go up to Shilo with his family to pray and worship: "The man used to go up from his town *every year*…. This happened *year after year*" (1:3; 1:7).

In the context of these visits to Shilo, the text notes that, "Hofni and Phinhas, the two sons of Eli, were priests of the Lord there" (1:3). A clear correspondence is drawn between the centrality of Eli's sons and Chana's helplessness. She, it seems, will remain barren while Eli's sons will inherit his position.

Chana, however, does not resign herself to the situation, or to the routine that has been set for her. "Chana rose." Chana gets up and abandons the routine: with her initiative and creativity, she will confront that bitter fate. Out of her suffering, she comes to utter the prayer that will win her acclaim for all times.

3.

> And Chana rose, after they had eaten and drunk at Shiloh. The priest Eli was sitting on the seat near the doorpost of the temple of the Lord. In her wretchedness, she prayed onto the Lord, weeping all the while. And she vowed this vow: "O Lord of Hosts, if you will look upon the suffering of your maidservant and will remember me and not forget your maidservant, and if you will grant your maidservant a male child, I will dedicate him to the Lord for all the days of his life; and no razor shall ever touch his head" (1:9–11).

"Chana rose…"

The word "rose" (*vatakom*) is perhaps the most important one in the text. Chana accepts the situation no longer and shatters the routine. She rises to fight in any way she can to have a family of her own.

Thus, after the other family members have finished eating and drinking – deep depression prevents her from doing so ["…she wept and would not eat" (1:7)] – she approaches the temple, where the priest Eli, who is in charge of worship in the temple, is sitting. Eli, as later verses indicate, does not comprehend the nature of Chana's prayer; this underscores the distinctiveness and innovation of her prayer.

"In her wretchedness…"

The text describes the depth of Chana's pain and despair with clear expressions like "wretchedness (*marat nefesh*)" and "sorrowful spirit (*keshat ruah*)" (1:10; 1:15). The starting point of Chana's prayer, then, is real heartache.

"…she prayed onto the Lord…"

On this phrase, the Talmud comments: "Rabbi Elazar said, Chana hurled her words at God, as it says, 'She prayed *onto* the Lord.' This teaches us that she spoke to God with audacity."[2]

According to the Rabbis, Chana argues with God, and makes her case to Him. The unusual biblical turn of phrase "to pray onto *(lehitpallel al)*" becomes more significant when we look at it alongside the other ways this verb appears in our text:

"she prayed onto *(al)* the Lord" (1:10)

"to pray before *(lifnei)* the Lord" (1:12)

"to pray to *(el)* the Lord." (1:26).

With a bitter heart, Chana raised her voice *onto (al)* God; but after she has relieved her heart of its pain, she grows calm and her prayer is characterized as being *before (lifnei)* God. We find a similar phenomenon in interactions between people: after expressing intense feeling, we are usually able to relate to others with greater self-possession.

After weaning the child, Chana returns to Shiloh. Looking back, she tells Eli that in his day she had prayed *to (el)* God.

Through careful analysis of the text, the Rabbis thus determine that Chana, a model of prayer for all future generations, stated her claims before God in a forceful way. The audacity of "challenging" God may seem surprising, but this has been the way of Jewish prayer since the days of early biblical figures. Moshe ardently inquired, "Why, Lord, should your wrath

---

[2] *Berakhot* 31b. [The phrase R. Elazar uses is *hetikha devarim klapei ma'alah*, which suggests an inappropriate verbal "attack" on God, hence the accusation of audacity – translator's note.]

burn against your people!?" (Exodus 32:11) Jeremiah exclaimed, bewildered, "Why are the wicked so successful in their ways!?" (Jeremiah 12:1). Job certainly makes harsh claims against God. The Jewish worldview evidently sanctions, within the authentic relationship between the individual praying and God, an open prayer-conversation – which may well have a distinct aspect of "daring" towards God.[3]

"...weeping all the while."

The Rabbis take note of the double form of Hebrew verb for weeping *(bakho tivkeh)* used here:

"she vowed a vow *(vatidor neder)*" – all of her actions are double. Her anger is double: "Moreover, her rival, to make her miserable, would taunt and taunt her." Her portion is double: "one double portion." Her weeping is double: "weeping and weeping" *(bakho tivkeh)*. Her seeing is double: "look, only look" *(ra'oh tireh)*. Her vows are double: "she vowed a vow *(vatidor neder)*.[4]

We could add one more example: "[if] you will remember me and not forget your maidservant" – although the verb itself is not double, the same concept is repeated.

These formulations, which use doubling for emphasis, indicate the intensity with which Chana was praying. Her words are not the rote fulfillment of a commandment; they are real and vital.

"O Lord of Hosts..."

The Rabbis find special significance in Chana's use of the term "Lord of Hosts":

---

[3] Consider, in this context, the following from the introduction to Isaac Bashevis Singer's *The Pentinent* (Middlesex, 1986), p. 126: "To me, a belief in God and a protest against the laws of life are not contradictory. There is a great element of protest in all religion. Those who dedicate their lives to serving God have often dared to question His justice and to rebel against His seeming neutrality in man's struggle between good and evil. I feel therefore that there is no basic difference between rebellion and prayer."

[4] *Yalkut Shimoni* 78, apparently based on *Midrash Shmuel* 1:9.

Rabbi Elazar said, Since the day God created the world no one called God "Lord of Hosts" until Chana came and called him "Hosts." She said before God, "Master of the Universe, with all the myriad hosts you have created in Your world, is it so difficult for you to give me one son?!" To what can this be compared? To a human king who was hosting a feast for his servants. A poor man came, stood in the doorway and said to them, "Just give me one slice of bread!" and they paid no attention to him. He pushed his way in and approached the king. He said to him, "My master, the King, from this entire feast you have made, is it so hard for you to give me one slice of bread?"[5]

For the first time in the Bible, then, a person addresses God by the name "Lord of Hosts," alluding to His awesome greatness on high. Chana feels God's infinite authority and power.

The text describes Chana's consciousness using a reverse tactic as well, emphasizing her perception of herself as a maidservant before God. The Rabbis take notice:

"…the suffering of Your maidservant"…"do not forget Your maidservant"… "and grant Your maidservant"… R. Yossi, son of R. Haninah, said, "What do these three 'maidservants' mean?"[6]

The word "maidservant"(ama), repeated three times in a single verse (1:11), becomes the key word of the entire prayer.

Various midrashim have their own way of explaining this repetition. I would say it is an obvious literary device opening a window onto Chana's feelings: she senses her nothingness before the Creator, and nullifies herself completely before Him. Extraordinarily, though, her sincere modesty does not diminish the power of her plea and prayer. On the contrary, her awareness of her own vulnerability and recognition of her dependence on God are what give her prayer its vitality. We see something similar in the

---

[5] *Berakhot* 31b.

[6] Ibid.

Avraham's forceful prayer on behalf of Sodom: "Shall the Judge of all the earth not deal justly?" (Genesis 18:25). Was he really relating to himself as "dust and ashes" (Genesis 18:27)?

Self-nullification before the Creator, it seems, does not preclude spirited debate; rather, it serves as a firm basis from which the individual can turn to God, without whom nothing could happen in the world.[7]

"...and if you will grant your maidservant a male child, I will dedicate him to the Lord all the days of his life..."

This, perhaps, is the heart of the prayer. Chana does not settle for self-pity, and she does not seek assistance and redemption from God alone. She prays in the full sense of the word. It is not enough for her to turn to God with her request: she also seeks more from herself. According to most scholars, the verb *"lehitpallel"* (to pray) comes from the root *pey-lamed-lamed* and connotates judgement. *Tefillah* (prayer), then, means self-judgment.[8] The Jew at prayer, then, is evaluating and judging him or herself.

Chana judges herself: she assesses what she should ask from God, and what she should expect from herself. Her repetition of the root for "give" (*nun-tav-nun*) suggests her expectation for reciprocity: *v'natata* (and if You will grant) – *u'netativ* (then I will dedicate him). You, God, *give* me a son, and I will *give* him to You, to serve You.

4.

Chana's prayer has guided us to some elements that form the basis of true prayer. All the points we outlined above – the sincerity that makes trench-

---

[7] This unique combination of self-abnegation and assertiveness finds expression in the religious world after the biblical period as well. Consider, for instance, what is said of the Hasidic rebbe, R. Levi Yitzhak of Berdichev – though exceedingly humble in his religiosity, he aggressively beseeched God on behalf of the Jewish people.

[8] Compare this with R. Shimshon Rafael Hirsch, *Horev*, in the first of the Chapters of Service. It should be noted that in most languages the word for prayer comes from a word for request. Thus, in English and French, prayer and *prier* come from the Latin *precare,* and in German *Gebet* comes from *bitten,* which means "to request." The unique approach of our tradition to prayer is apparent already in the Bible, where prayer is seen as an act of self-disputation in the presence of God. Compare G.H. Cohen, *Prayer in Judaism – Continuity and Change,* ed. G. Cohn, H. Fish (Northvale/London, 1996), Introduction. See also *"Defusim meyesodo shel beit hamishpat batefillah"* in Y. Heineman, *Hatefillah betekufat haTannaim veha Amoraim,* (Jerusalem, 5726).

ant discourse with God possible, the intensity of the prayer, the self-abnegation of the supplicant before the Creator while preserving the demand that the needs of the individual and the society be met, the need for reciprocity in a relationship with God – all are drawn from the biblical text itself through literary-midrashic exegesis. Without a doubt, all of them express the deeper literal meaning of the biblical text.

Beyond these comments on the innate quality of Chana's prayer, the Talmud in *Berakhot* 31a–b derives a number of *halakhot* from the verses in Samuel 1. These laws, technical in nature, compliment the introspective prayer we discussed earlier.

> Rav Hamnunah said, "So many important laws can be learned from the verses concerning Chana: 'Now Chana was praying in her heart' – from here we learn that the heart must be directed in prayer. 'Only her lips moved' – from here we learn that one must form the words of prayer with one's lips; 'but her voice could not be heard' – from here we learn that it is forbidden to raise one's voice in prayer. 'So Eli thought she was drunk.' – from here we learn that a drunk person may not pray. 'Eli said to her: How long will you make a drunken spectacle of yourself?' – R. Elazar said, "From here we learn that one who sees something improper in his friend must reprimand him." "And Chana replied, 'Oh no, my lord!'" – Ulla, or R. Yossi, son of R. Haninah said, "She meant, 'You are not my master in this matter.'" Others say, "She was saying to him, 'You are not my master in this matter, and you do not have divine inspiration, since you suspect me of this.'" Others say, "She was saying to him, 'You are not my master, and neither God's presence nor divine inspiration are upon you, for you judged me unfavorably and not favorably; did you not know that I am a very unhappy woman?' "I have drunk no wine or other strong drink" – R. Elazar said, "From here we learn that one who is falsely suspected must let his fellow know the truth." "Do not take your maidservant for a worthless woman" – R. Elazar said, "From here we learn to pray when drunk is like idolatry; here it says 'a worthless woman' and in another context it says 'worthless men went out

from among you'; in both instances, the issue is idolatry." "'Then go in peace,' said Eli." – R. Elazar said, "From here we learn that one who falsely suspects his fellow must appease him, and what is more, he must even bless him, as it is written, 'and may the God of Israel grant what you have asked of him.'"

Later in the story, after the birth of Shmuel, Chana prays again, a prayer of thanksgiving (I Samuel 2:1–9). Prayers of supplication, in the Bible, tend to describe the supplicant's current existential state with an explicit statement of a specified request; prayers of thanksgiving, in contrast, reflect the inner experience undergone by the person praying.[9]

In Chana's case, too, her prayer is well phrased and expresses her personal state. In her prayer of thanksgiving, Chana's poetic language depicts the power of her experience, a transformation from a lowly person to a woman of stature. She does not mention the birth of Shmuel in her prayer, focusing, rather, on the emotions of a barren woman who has become the mother of many children.[10] Chana expresses her pain in prayer, through which she seeks to merit a divine remedy, and it is through prayer that she gives thanks to God for her recovery and the new life she has been granted.

Here we will not discuss the prayer of thanksgiving; let's just note the important lesson that comes to light when we realize that prayers of request and of thanksgiving came into the world together. Both originate in the same root, *pay-lamed-lamed*. The circumstances of one's life change: there are days of suffering and pain and days of joy and thanksgiving. In all situations, we should turn to God in intimate conversation.

---

[9] Yehudah Kiel analyzed Chana's story in his article *"Haftarah leyom rishon shel Rosh Hashanah," Mayanot,* vol. 9 (Jerusalem, 5728), pp. 96–144. Some of those comments were included in his commentary on Samuel in the *Da'at Mikrah* series. More recently, Uriel Simone related to the birth and consecration of Shmuel in his book *Reading Prophetic Narrative* (Indiana, 1997), pp. 1–50.

[10] This phenomenon occurs repeatedly in the Bible. Similarly, Yonah's prayer of supplication depicts his state of being (Jonah 4:2–3), while his prayer of thanksgiving reveals the feelings he had as a result of the experience he went through (Jonah 2). Other prayers of supplication in the book also depict the circumstances that gave rise to them (Jonah 1:14). Compare Y. Kaufman, *Toledot haemunah haisraelit,* vol. 2 (Tel Aviv, 5723), p. 504. Torah commentators nevertheless detected an allusion to the birth of a son in Chana's prayer of thanksgiving. "While the barren woman bears seven," Chana declares. The numerical value of "seven" (377) is equal to that of "Shmuel."

5.

Chana's prayer has won a unique place in Jewish tradition: it stands at the center of the *haftarah* of the first day of Rosh Hashanah. Why were these particular verses chosen to be read at the beginning of the Days of Awe? The usual response to this question recalls the talmudic statement that "On Rosh Hashanah, Sarah, Rachel and Chana conceived."[11] The synagogue readings thus contain passages that deal with the foremothers Sarah, Rachel and Chana. But perhaps another, more profound message could be found as well connecting Chana's prayer to Rosh Hashanah. Her story, read at the beginning of the Days of Awe, days of spiritual self-examination, tells us what true prayer really is. On Rosh Hashanah in particular, we must break out of our routine and carefully reassess our place in the world. Each of us must ask, "Where are you?" We must summon ourselves to understand what we can do to fill our live with meaning and substance. Eli's sons were destined for greatness, and presented at the chapter's outset as priests of the Lord in Shilo. Yet they left the stage of history before their time, while the son of Chana, who had been a barren and wretched woman, took their place. This turn of events teaches us that everything is subject to change, and one must never succumb to despair and passivity. Chana's prayer, read at the beginning of a new year and a new chapter in the life of a Jew, clearly shows that when one summons up the strength to give one's life a new and meaningful direction through real prayer-conversation with God, truly and authentic change is possible.

Chana's name is mentioned in the *haftarah* of Rosh Hashanah twelve times.[12] This underscores Chana's centrality. Although our lives are fully dependent on God's mercy, a great deal is also determined by our beliefs, initiatives and actions. The two verbs, "give" *(natan)* and "loan/borrow" *(sha'al)*, appear seven times. This emphasizes the reciprocity of the story: God gives, or loans a child to Chana, and Chana gives, or loans that child to God.

---

[11] *Rosh Hashanah* 11a.

[12] Twice Chana is called "woman" (I Samuel 1:18, 23) and the desire seems to have been to mention the name "Chana" exactly twelve times, the number of the twelve tribes and the symbol of Israel's completeness.

Some have the custom that when a girl reaches her *bat mitzvah*, and stands before her personal "New Year" with the wish to formulate the direction her life should take, she recites Chana's prayer on the day of her celebration. This is to be encouraged.[13] Like Chana, whose ancestry is completely unknown from biblical sources, every *bat mitzvah* girl, regardless of her abilities or family connections, can offer her prayers to heaven, and ask with all her heart for God's help in succeeding in her path in life. This request must be coupled with a personal readiness to dedicate all of her internal strengths to the fulfillment of the destiny that she established for herself, together with God, through her prayers.

---

[13] In one of his *responsa,* R. Yitzhak Nissim, former Chief Rabbi of Israel, writes: "A day of celebration for a *bat mitzvah* should be made just as it is for a *bar mitzvah*. Friends, relatives, and acquaintances should be invited to take part in the celebration. On that occasion, the *bat mitzvah* girl should make the *Shehechiyanu* blessing on a new garment; if she is able, she should say something in public about the day, and read the Song of Devorah and the first two verses of Chana's Prayer. The father of the *bat mitzvah* girl should recite, "Blessed is He, Who freed me of this one's punishment." All bless her, saying, "O sister! May you grow into thousands of myriads" (Genesis 24:60). Cited in A. Ahrend, "*Hagigat habat mitzvah bepiskei haRav Yitzhak Nissim*" in *Bat Mitzvah*, ed. S. Friendland Ben Arza (Jerusalem, 2002), p. 113.

A TENT OF HER OWN

RABBANIT MALKE BINA

Sarah lived 127 years, the Torah tells us, "and she died in Kiryat Arba which is Hebron, in the land of Canaan, and Abraham came to mourn for Sarah and to weep for her" (Genesis 23:1).

Read literally, the text implies that Abraham arrived in Hebron to mourn his wife and bury her, and nearly all the classical commentaries ask where Abraham came from. The most perceptive answer, perhaps, is offered by the great medieval commentator Nahmanides (Ramban). Had Abraham arrived in Hebron from elsewhere, the text would have stated this explicitly, he argues. The emphasis, rather, is on Abraham's destination. In life, Sarah enjoyed the privacy of her own tent in Hebron; it was there that she died; and it is into that personal domain of hers that Abraham entered to mourn her. Nahmanides shifts the focus away from Abraham's route and to the distinctive realm inhabited physically and spiritually by Sarah.

Rachel and Leah are also described as having their own tents (Genesis 31:33). And Deborah the prophetess, in extolling the virtues of Jael, who rescued the Jewish people by killing the Canaanite general, Sisera, states: "Blessed is she more than women in the tent" (Judges 5:24).

Who are these women in the tent? In the midrash *Yalkut Shimoni* (Judges 5.55), R. Nahman identified them as the matriarchs. Both the Bible and the midrash, then, stress that the matriarchs had tents of their own. No doubt, the phrase "women in the tent" is ambiguous; it may carry connotations of meekness and seclusion – even taboo. But I would suggest another reading, based on an emphasis on the definite article "*the* tent" – the implication being that the women who occupy it are women of stature, possessing qualities of leadership and creativity, who inhabit their own independent realm.

---

* First published, in slightly different form, in *The Jerusalem Report* (Nov. 7, 1991).

Virginia Woolf, in *A Room of One's Own*, writes that for a woman "to have a room of her own, let alone a quiet room or a sound-proof room, was out of the question...even up to the beginning of the nineteenth century."

Woolf speaks for women throughout the ages who were unable to develop their gifts for want of privacy. A woman who lacks a room of her own, argues the novelist, lacks the freedom, independence and awareness of self that one needs to become a creative, productive and thinking person.

Over 3,500 years ago, Sarah had her own tent. We find an indication of the high value set on Sarah's privacy and independence in the early rabbinic commentary *Genesis Rabbah* (39.16), where it is noted that on their journeys, Abraham would pitch her tent before his own. But what precisely did Sarah accomplish within her tent? Based on biblical and midrashic accounts, it is possible to reconstruct our matriarch's life. She gained the spirituality and wisdom that enabled her to assume a role of leadership alongside Abraham. In partnership with her husband, she taught the belief in one God to the idolatrous Canaanites, with Abraham teaching the men and Sarah the women. She attained the level of receiving God's work in prophecy. In fact, Abraham was instructed on occasion to listen to Sarah's words because her level of prophecy was greater than his.

We are given further, moving insight into Sarah's special sphere after her death, in the account in *Genesis Rabbah* (60.15) of Isaac bringing his betrothed wife Rebecca into his beloved mother's tent. The tent, we are told, once again became the vibrant domain it had been during Sarah's lifetime. Once again the cloud of God hovered above the tent, the tent doors were hospitably open, there was a blessing in the bread dough, and the candle remained burning. When Abraham came to eulogize Sarah and weep for her, he entered her tent, her special realm, and wept for all he had lost.

NEHAMA ON WOMEN AND WOMANHOOD*

RABBI ARYEH STRIKOVSKY

Nehama Leibowitz, whose students have always called simply "Nehama," numbers among those eminent persons who established a methodology for learning *Tanakh* in general, and for learning Torah and Torah commentaries in particular.

Just as R. Hayyim Soleveichik of Brisk established a conceptual method for learning Talmud that transformed the *yeshiva* world, just as Prof. Gershom Sholem created a scientific approach to learning Jewish mysticism, so Nehama paved an innovative pathway toward understanding Torah through *midrash*, commentaries, and translations into the vernaculars as well.

Nehama knew how to unearth the sparks of *peshat* (the "simple" meaning) concealed in the *midrashim* and integrate them within a textual context. She bequeathed this unique way of learning to two generations of teachers and students. Her success stemmed from her unique intellectual and pedagogical abilities as well as her radiant and refined character. Over the years, her exemplary students went on to become well-known teachers and educators, and continued to develop and innovate within the context of her methodology.

Our generation and her students in particular had the privilege of drawing from her wealth of Torah knowledge until two months before her passing. In this aspect, Nehama may be compared to R. Yosef Karo and R. Hayyim Heller, who encompassed generations and bore fruits until a ripe old age.

---

* Translated by Zipporah and Jonathan Price.

My thanks to Shoshanna Rabin, Adaya Greenstein, Yitshak Reiner and Prof. Moshe Arendt, who reviewed this essay and offered their comments. [The present essay is adapted from a longer piece in Hebrew first published in *Bat Mitzvah*, ed. S. Friendland ben Arza (Jerusalem, 2002), pp. 302–316. –editor's note]

Nehama respected her students and was always willing to hear their *hiddushim*, their Torah innovations. She listened to them with the sensitive awareness that "Who is wise? One who learns from every individual." She was open to hearing rational arguments, questions, and novel insights into Torah not only from scholars but from the layperson as well. Personally, by telephone, by mail – Nehama was always accessible. She would add to and refine these conversations, and even include them in her lectures and in her writings in the name of the person who first raised the issue. She was patient and gentle with non-professionals, but demanding and exacting with teachers. She wouldn't tolerate mediocrity. Once she remarked: "How could a person teach *Tanakh* in a university without knowing the entire *Tanakh* by heart? Would a person teach English literature without knowing Shakespeare by heart?"

As long as she remained alive, she was the address for clarifying questions and receiving answers in *Tanakh*. With her death, the address was orphaned.

Nehama, as the teacher of the generation, was a unique phenomenon in the history of the Jewish people. It is said of Hulda the prophetess that "She would teach the Oral Torah to the scholars of the generation" (note in Rashi to II Kings 22:14). Nehama merited the same praise. She would travel far and wide to ensure her lectures were accessible to scholars and lay people alike. On the trip home, by the light of a small flashlight, she would correct her student's papers.

Happy is she who reaches the World to Come with her learning in hand! (Translated from A. Strikovsky, *"Nehama z"l,"* *Daf le-tarbut yehudit* 228, Jerusalem, Iyyar 5757 (1997), pp. 5–6.)

Nehama Leibowitz was the greatest Jewish woman of the twentieth century, or at the very least, the woman recognized as having the largest influence on the religious Zionist world.

Her brother, Professor Yeshayahu Leibowitz, considered her the leading expert of the generation in Scripture.

Nehama would frequently quote her brother as saying "the greatest revolution of the twentieth century is the entrance of women into the world of learning." Nehama's contribution to this revolution was undeniable. It was in her footsteps that Jewish men and women walked as they began to learn Torah. For Nehama, there was no doubt that all the gates of Torah had to be opened wide to receive women, including the gates of *Gemara*. In the course of her lectures, her references to legal matters demonstrated excellence in understanding *Gemara* and highly developed analytical reasoning.

Nehama practiced what she preached. In addition to her considerable talents in Torah learning, Nehama excelled at performing acts of *hesed*. The stories of her acts of kindness rival the tales told of *tzaddikim*. Her personal combination of scholarship, modesty, and righteousness make her an outstanding role model for a Jewish girl entering adulthood.

Nehama hated feminism. Once, when asked if she wanted to put on *tefillin*, Nehama jumped up, stamped her foot, and exclaimed "Have I fulfilled all the *mitzvot* to my fellow person? Have I fulfilled my allotment of *hesed*? Am I lacking in *mitzvot* (that I am obligated in) that I need to lay *tefillin*?"

One who examines Nehama's writings will not find the traits characteristic of feminist writings. Nevertheless, it is possible to glean, from her writings and lectures, indications of Nehama's views on women and femininity.

Nehama utilized every available opportunity to discuss the personalities of women in the *Tanakh*, and to learn from their ways. The topics she discussed included the exile of Hagar, Rachel's suffering, Rikvah's exemplary *hesed*, and her role as Yaakov and Esav's mother, as well as the role of the Jewish midwives during the Egyptian exile.

We can learn about Nehama's views on women both from what she wrote and taught regarding women in the *Tanakh* and from what she chose to ignore. Her great desire to have her students identify with her subject matter led her at times to chose to not teach certain topics, and even books of *Tanakh*.

She did not teach the issue of the *sotah* (suspected adulteress), or the punishment described as "chop off her hand and do not have mercy on her." She did not teach the Book of Ruth, because she was not comfortable with Naomi's advice to Ruth to go to Boaz and lie with him.[1] Similarly, she refrained from teaching the Book of Proverbs. This book, which opens with the topic of an incestuous woman, and closes with a description of the ideal woman, did not appeal to Nehama. She said, rather, that the book's treatment of womanhood missed the most essential aspect – a woman's role as mother and guide to her children.[2]

Nehama also published nothing on the Book of Esther or the Song of Songs. She was uncomfortable with the book's emphasis on Esther's physical beauty. The Shulamite woman in the Song of Songs, even if the book is taken entirely on a metaphorical level, is still described sensually and erotically, and Nehama was careful to refrain from discussing such matters in her lectures and conversations.

Prof. Moshe Ahrend theorizes that Nehama did not want to deal with topics concerning women that did not correlate with the type of woman she herself strove to become.

Nehama did not always state her opinion explicitly. However, it is possible to learn of her views by considering the topics she chose to treat extensively as well as the topics she refrained from teaching. It is clear that her selected curriculum represents the inclinations of her heart.[3]

I would like to investigate those topics she did discuss explicitly, whether orally or in writing. In the course of my discussion, I will permit myself to draw connections and read between the lines.

The Dignity of Women

In Nehama's understanding, Scripture accords the same respect to women as it does to men. Regarding the verse, "It is not good that man should be alone; I will make a help meet for him" (Genesis 2:18), Nehama wrote:

---

[1] I was told this by Shoshanna Rabin.

[2] In the name of Shoshanna Rabin.

[3] Ariella Yadger distinguished a similar phenomenon in the domains of ethics and Jewish thought as well. See her Hebrew essay, *"Aharayut ishit u-ven ishit be-khetaveha shel Nehama Leibowitz – Iyyun bemegamata ha-erkit-hinukhit,"* *Pirkei Nehama* (ed. Cohen, et.al.), Jerusalem, 5761, pp. 377–406. This phenomenon seems to me to be particularly noticeable concerning women and femininity, realms that Yadger did not discuss in her essay.

The text is not stating a subjective fact that "it is not good for man to be alone" – man's feelings on the subject are not referred to, but rather "it is not good – that man should be alone" an objective statement, that the fact of man being alone is not good – in God's eyes.[4]

Woman's worth does not consist in her preventing man's loneliness. The existence of man alone, without a wife, is established objectively as not "good." Nehama proceeds to elaborate on this point.[5] She quotes the Maharal of Prague in his commentary to Rashi, *Gur Aryeh*, "If he is worthy – a help; if he does not show himself worthy – against him."[6]

The Maharal writes:

This explanation contains a profound truth. The male and female respectively represent two opposites. If man is worthy they merge into a single whole. In all cases two opposites merge to form a single whole when they are worthy, i.e., when the Almighty who makes peace between opposites links and joins them. But when they are not worthy the fact that they are opposites causes her to be "against him."

Nehama comments, "In other words, the good effected by the introduction of woman and the 'not good' dissipated by her separate creation is conditional on man's choice of the good…. Only if they combine harmoniously in conformity with the will of God will these two opposites merge into a single whole."[7] In her evaluation of marriage, Nehama chooses to express her thoughts symmetrically and to emphasize the unity of the marital bond.[8]

---

[4] Nehama Leibovitz, *Studies in Bereshit* (Jerusalem, 1972), p. 12.

[5] *Studies in Bereshit*, p. 13.

[6] Rashi on Gen. 2:18, quoting *Yevamot* 63a.

[7] R. Judah Loew ben Bezalel, the Maharal of Prague, *Gur Aryeh on the Torah*, Genesis 2:18. Cited in *Studies in Bereshit*, pp. 13–14.

[8] In her Questions for Further Study at the end of that chapter (*Studies in Bereshit*, p. 14), Nehama adds the words of the *Akedat Yitzhak*: "His Divine wisdom ensured that the mating of man and woman should not be just sexual on a par with the beasts. He introduced a special personal relationship strengthening their love and social bonds, to help one another in all their affairs with a complete and perfect helpfulness, as is meant for them…." Here too the egalitarian note is audible, with stress on the spiritual bond uniting man and woman.

Nehama was vehemently opposed to abusive treatment of women. This is apparent in her discussion of Genesis 6:1–4, describing "the sons of God – i.e., the sons of the judges" who "took for themselves wives whomsoever they chose." It was on account of this sin, Nehama believed, that the decree of destroying the world by flood was ultimately sealed.[9] Brutal treatment of a woman is also explicit in the treatment of Dina by the sons of *Shekhem*. In her discussion, Nehama expresses repulsion over this incident as well.[10]

The Merits of Righteous Women

Nehama concerned herself with the great female figures in Scripture. Rivkah, Tamar, the Hebrew midwives, the daughters of Tzelofhad, and the women with their offerings of mirrors, all merited her commentary and illuminating insights.

As a woman of *hesed* in her own right, outstanding in her acts of charity and kindness, she admired the charitable acts of the forefathers and foremothers. Rivkah merited a comprehensive analysis of her ability to withstand the test of *hesed* she underwent with Avraham's servant. Nehama compared the repetitive and seemingly contradictory biblical accounts, and demonstrated how Rivkah's righteousness is an integral part of these differences. Her personality was an eternal symbol of *hesed*. From her analysis of the verses, Nehama highlighted Rivkah's tremendous effort in providing sufficient water for ten camels "until they had done drinking" (Gen. 24:22).[11]

At the sight of all this, the man stood "wondering at her" and "held his peace." He and the men that were with him looked on at the way Rebecca discharged her self-appointed task, industriously, unquestioningly and

---

[9] *Studies in Bereshit*, pp. 57–8. On the question where an allusion to monogamy can be found in the Torah, Nehama is said to have answered, "It is written, 'He shall cleave to his wife' and not 'his wives.'" Regarding the attitude of the Torah towards polygamy she is said to have replied, "The Torah usually speaks about what is permitted, even though this may not be the ideal, like eating meat which was permitted to Noah.... But as Rav Kook explained...the ideal is not to eat meat...and similarly a man is permitted to have many wives with the hope that he will ultimately reach monogamy." (Heard from Yitzhak Reiner.)

[10] *Studies in Bereshit*, pp. 380–388.

[11] *Studies in Bereshit*, pp. 226–227.

without murmur. "And she drew for all his camels." Those realists and practical folk who might be drawn to pity the simplicity of the maiden, who went to all this trouble to quench the thirst of a total stranger and his camels, would do well to remember Akavia ben Mahallel's (Sage distinguished for his "fear of sin" and "wisdom") maxim in the Mishnah: "מוטב לי להיקרא שוטה כל ימי ולא ליעשות שעה אחת רשע לפני המקום."

"Better that I should be dubbed a fool for the rest of my days, rather than become a wicked man for one hour before the Omnipotent!" (*Eduyot* 5,6)

Similarly, Rebecca entered into no calculations of profit and loss, when she gave man and beast to drink. It is just such "fools" who have always succeeded in becoming benefactors of mankind.

Central to a discussion of Tamar[12] is the fearlessness of that heroine, ready to be burned alive rather than disgrace her father-in-law. Tamar was guided by a tremendous desire to be part of this family/nation and its divine Creator, a desire that remained unshaken by the significant personal obstacles set before her by certain individuals in the family. In her radio program, Nehama said:[13]

> Nothing is said about Tamar's lineage and her people. This led Yaakov's son to realize that she was a unique individual. She understood how to differentiate between the idea and the people [Er and Onan] who represented that idea. She wished to cleave to this family. She saw it as her role to bear children stemming from this house. Thomas Mann portrays the aging Yaakov as recounting to Tamar the tradition, beginning with Avraham, of a benevolent God who hates licentiousness and iniquity. And she – her soul longs for this new world of purity and innocence taking form before her own eyes. She wants to be a part of building it.
>
> As opposed to the Book of Ruth, which divides its action between Naomi who plans and Ruth who acts, Tamar both plans her actions and carries them out. When Tamar said to Yehudah, "Recognize these!" (Genesis 38:25) she recalled his own utterance

---

[12] *Study sheets, parashat Vayeshev*, 1961.

[13] Contributed by Prof. Mirah Ofran.

of the very same words to his father upon bringing him Joseph's torn coat. In that manner, she compelled Yehudah to confront his dark past, and acknowledge it as well to the people of Adullam who had gathered to see her be burnt – "She has been more righteous than I" (Genesis 38:26).

The Hebrew midwives represent a spark of light in the spiritual darkness of Egypt. Nehama placed special emphasis on the opinion that identifies the midwives as righteous Egyptians who uplifted themselves:[14]

> If we accept that the midwives were Egyptian, another and very vital message becomes apparent. The Torah indicates how the individual can resist evil. He need not shirk his moral responsibility under cover of "superior orders." The text contrasts the brutal decrees of enslavement and massacre initiated by Pharaoh and supported by government and people with the God-fearing "civil disobedience" of the midwives. Neither moral courage nor sheer wickedness are ethnically or nationally determined qualities. Moab and Amnon produced a Ruth and Naamah respectively, Egypt two righteous midwives.

Nehama, who protested that relatively few trees had been planted at *Yad Vashem* to commemorate righteous gentiles,[15] never lost her faith in mankind's ability to choose to do good.

The daughters of Tzelofhad, whose story is told in Numbers 27:1–11 won themselves a blessing for their wisdom and love of the Land of Israel. Part of Yaakov's blessing for Yosef, "Yosef is a fruitful bough…whose branches run over the wall [*benot tza'adah alai shur*]" was praise for those women who loved the land, and who settled on both sides of the Jordan.[16] The midrashic sources Nehama chooses to quote on the subject are quite

---

[14] *Studies in Shemot*, Page 33.

[15] Heard from Judy Klitsner.

[16] *Study sheet*, 1946, question 2; N. Leibovitz and M. Arnad, *Perush Rashi le-Torah*, The Open University (Tel Aviv, 1990), pp. 364-365. Based on Rashi's explanation of Onkelos interpreting this verse as referring to the daughters of Zelofhad.

deliberate. For example, "'The daughters of Tzelofhad speak correctly' (27:7) – that is the law…the law that you don't know, the women know it!'"[17]

In the same vein, "R. Nathan taught: The women are superior to the men. The men said, 'Let's appoint a leader and return to Egypt.' The women said, 'Give us a portion from among our father's brothers.'"[18]

Women were active participants in the spiritual and religious life of the nation. Nehama learned this from words uttered by the husband of the "great woman" of Shunam. When she requested to go to the prophet, he responded, "Why are you going to him today, when it is neither *Rosh hodesh* nor Shabbat…?"(II Kings 4:23)

The man's words suggest that women had the practice of going to the prophet on Shabbat…. Her husband, in his naivete, thought she was going to greet the Messiah. Who takes the role of welcoming him, in spiritual exaltation? – the woman![19]

The Bible portrays two women of the generation as wise women: Avigail and Bathsheva. Avigail is said to be *tovat sekhet* – very intelligent. Nehama describes her words to David as comprising one of the most beautiful speeches in the *Tanakh*. Beautiful from a literary perspective, in phrasing, and in content.[20]

Scripture describes Bathsheva's clever actions behind the scenes to establish her son's kingship. By dividing the words of the verses into four parallel columns, Nehama shows how scrupulously Bathsheva chose her words. She selects what to stress and what to omit from the message the prophet conveyed to her, and in that way demonstrates real-life experience and a profound comprehension of God's ways and mankind's responsibilities.[21]

Neither Nathan nor Batsheva relied on miracles, that the prophecy would be fulfilled by itself. They did not regard prophecy as freeing them

---

[17] *Midrash Bemidbar Rabbah*, 21.

[18] *Study sheet, parashat Pinhas*, 1963.

[19] From a radio talk; contributed by Prof. Myra Ofran.

[20] Prof. Arnad told me this. Nehama did not publish the article on Avigail.

[21] *Studies in Bereshit*, p. 251.

from action, absolving them of responsibility for their destiny. On the contrary, they accepted the promise of God as obliging them to work and strive to the best of their ability and understanding towards its fulfillment.[22]

When Nehama was asked about the meaning of the expression "an extra measure of understanding" – *bina yeterah* – the Sages used to characterize women, she replied: "Perhaps [it means] intuitive understanding."[23]

Here, then, are some ideas and motives concerning women in the world of Scripture gleaned from Nehama's teachings. May her words illuminate the path of young women in their acceptance of *mitzvot*, and may they burn as a candle to her memory.

---

[22] *Studies in Bereshit*, p. 255. This corresponds with the rabbinical comment in *Sanhedrin* 70b that Batsheva served as a sort of spiritual and ethical guide for King Shlomo.

[23] Heard from Yitshak Reiner. She poses the same question herself to her readers in *Studies in Bereshit*, p. 15, question 3.

FROM FEMININITY TO HOLINESS

Chana Ross Friedman

"In the merit of righteous women, the Israelites were redeemed from Egypt."

This statement is very flattering to women, essentially giving credit for the entire redemption story to womankind. From a very young age, I heard it often, most likely because I studied in girls' schools and was always among girls. In my naivete, I imagined that those "righteous women" were just like the heavy-set ladies with their heads wrapped in scarves I encountered on the bus in Jerusalem, where they sat and murmured ceaselessly, reading from the miniature editions of Psalms they held in their hands, somehow knowing exactly when to look up just as they reached their bus stop. These women, I would tell myself, are the incarnations of those righteous women in our generation, and in the merit of women just like them we were redeemed from Egypt. As I got older and matured a bit, I realized how great was the discrepancy between the righteous women in my imagination and the righteous deed the Rabbis attribute to the Israelite women in Egypt – enticing their husbands to have marital relations and bearing children despite their enslavement and the harsh decrees of Pharaoh. The Rabbis spare no words in their detailed account of their feminine techniques of seduction:

> R. Avirah taught: In the merit of righteous women of that generation, the Israelites were redeemed from Egypt. When they would go to draw water, God would summon little fish into their pails. They would draw out half water and half fish, and then go home and boil two pots, one of water and one of fish. They would

* translated by Gershon Clymer and Ora Wiskind Elper

bring them out to their husbands in the fields, where they would bathe them, anoint them, feed them, and make love with them....[1]

In another context, *Midrash Tanhuma* (*Pikudei* 9) offers further details:

> They would eat and drink and the women would take the mirrors and gaze into them with their husbands. She would say, "I am better-looking than you," and he would say, "I am better-looking than you." Thus, they would arouse themselves and have relations, and God would immediately cause the women to conceive.

These tales of seduction surprised me. After the initial shock over the stark contrast between these women and "my" righteous women, the ones on the bus, I also wondered from what source the Rabbis drew these stories.

If there is a catalyst, besides God himself, to whom we can attribute the redemption from Egypt, it is certainly Moshe. His amazing biography, unlike those of other biblical heroes, is recounted in great detail. We follow his story step by step, from the moment he is born – and even before then – until he stands his ground before Pharaoh, King of Egypt, before the Israelite nation, and, at times, even before God, who has sent him on his mission. While Moshe labors relentlessly to redeem the Israelites, they do not respond enthusiastically to the idea of redemption. The backbreaking burdens of slavery have left them too weary to cast a glance towards a better future. In moments of crisis, they even blame Moshe and Aharon for the deterioration in their living conditions in Egypt:

> May the Lord look upon you and punish you for making us loathsome to Pharaoh and his courtiers – putting a sword in their hands to slay us. (Exodus 5:21)

Why, then, do the Rabbis take the crowning glory of the redemption from Moshe and place it upon the women of that generation?

---

[1] *Sotah* 11a.

A second look at the redemption story, with an emphasis on uncovering clues about the unnamed "righteous women" whom the Rabbis praised, reveals that women played crucial supporting roles at every stage in the process. The Hebrew midwives, Shifrah and Puah defied Pharaoh's decree and spared the male newborns (perhaps they even participated in Moshe's birth). Moshe's mother, Yocheved hid him for three months, until it was no longer possible to conceal him (where was his father in this?); his sister, Miriam, watched over him from a distance "to know what would befall him' (where was Aharon, his brother?). Pharaoh's daughter drew him out of the water and had mercy upon him; although she knew that "this is a Jewish baby," she acted in direct defiance of her father's decree. The daughters of the High Priest of Midian brought Moshe into their father's house, and Moshe's wife, Tzipporah, saved his life (according to most commentators) by circumcising their son during their journey back to Egypt.

All of these instances led the Rabbis to conclude that there was a wide-spread phenomenon taking place, and not just a succession of exceptional individual women. The women were struggling with great determination to continue bearing children, raising them and nurturing them, even when it put their own lives in danger. With this in mind, it is easy to understand the midrashic identification of Shifrah and Puah as Yocheved and Miriam, and the depiction of Moshe's parents' wedding as a remarriage brought about by Miriam:

> Shifrah – [was named so] because she smoothed over (me-shaperet) her daughter's words and appeased [Pharaoh] on her be-half. Puah – [was so called] because she stood up (hofia) to her fa-ther [Amram]. For Amram was the head of the Sanhedrin at the time, and when Pharaoh decreed "every male child who is born [shall be cast into the river]" Amram said, "Are the Jews having babies for naught?" He immediately removed Yocheved from his house, ceased having marital relations, and divorced his wife who was three months pregnant. All of the Jews then divorced their wives. His daughter said to him, "Your edict is harsher than Phar-aoh's. Pharaoh decreed only against the males, and your decree is

against the males as well as the females. Pharaoh is an evil person; his decree may be fulfilled and it may not, while you are a righteous person, and your decree will surely be fulfilled." And so Amram had his wife return, and all the Jews reunited with their wives as well.[2]

According to this *midrash*, Yocheved and Miriam's struggle for Moshe to be born served as an example for all the women of that generation. While the men succumbed to the despair and distress of Amram, the head of the Sanhedrin and divorced their wives, the women persevered with a quiet hope, one that led in the end to the redemption of the nation.

The Rabbis continue this midrashic idea in their commentary on another verse. The description of the construction of the various vessels for the Tabernacle by the craftsman Bezalel ben Uri as God commanded includes this sentence:

> And he made the laver of brass, and its pedestal of brass, *where it would be seen by* [or of] *mirrors donated by* the assembling women, who assembled at the door of the Tent of Meeting.[3]

The meaning of the Hebrew phrase *"bemarot hatzovot"* is unclear. R. Hezekiah ben Manoah, or Hizkuni, says the phrase explains the strategic placement of the laver in this spot "so that the women who assembled here would see it and remember that women accused of adultery by their husbands are given water from here to drink." Ibn Ezra and others understood this phrase as a description of the raw materials that were used to make the laver:

> It is the practice of all women to beautify themselves by looking at their reflection in copper or glass mirrors each morning.... There were women who were servants of God, who had aban-

---

[2] *Shemot Rabba* 1. 13; compare *Sotah* 12a.

[3] Exodus 38:8. The first variant in the translation of this verse follows the understanding of Hizkuni; the second variant follows Ibn Ezra, et. al., as explained below.

doned all worldly desires and donated their mirrors, since they no longer needed them to beautify themselves. Rather, they came each day to the opening of the Tent of Meeting to pray and hear about the *mitzvot*.

Midrash Tanhuma, followed by Rashi, takes the approach that the phrase in question describes the raw materials used to make the laver, but with one important difference from ibn Ezra's view. The mirrors being donated are not just any mirrors; they are the very same mirrors the women had used to entice their husbands in Egypt. Their gift to the Tabernacle stems not from their abstention from beautification, but just the opposite. It is a symbol of the sexual desire that brought them to employ the mirrors in the first place.

When God told Moshe to build the Tabernacle, all the Jews offered contributions. Some brought silver, some gold or copper or onyx or jewels; they brought everything quickly. The women said, "What do we have that we can contribute to the Tabernacle?" Then they took the mirrors and brought them before Moshe. When he saw them, he became enraged and said to the Israelites, "Take sticks and break their legs! What do we need these mirrors for?" God said to Moshe, "Moshe, are you deriding them over these mirrors? It was they who gave rise to all the legions in Egypt! Take them and make a brass basin with a pedestal for the priests, so that the priests may sanctify themselves with it. This is what the verse means when it says, "And he made the laver of brass, and its pedestal of brass, *be-marot ha-tzovot asher tzavu*" – of the mirrors that gave rise to all those legions *(tzevaot)* in Egypt.

At first glance, nothing in this midrash seems to go beyond what we have already found: the libidinal activity by the righteous women in Egypt won great praise. However, I think that by projecting their action forward in time to the construction of the Tabernacle, *Midrash Tanhuma* succeeds in clarifying the underlying message of the story. The women's choice of life and desire was not a fleeting moment in history; it was the memory they chose to preserve in their donation to the Tabernacle. Perhaps this represents the feminine way to connect to holiness. It is precisely the radical nature of this idea that brings the author of the midrash to record Moshe's initial resistance to their donation: "Take sticks and break their legs!" From his point of view, while such conduct by the women was desirable while they were slaves in Egypt, it is completely inappropriate to involve elements of desire and sexuality in the construction of the Tabernacle. When God responds to him by insisting on accepting their gift and using it to make the laver, their behavior is defined as a model for sanctification – "so that the priests may sanctify themselves with it."

This was not the only time in Jewish history that great suffering caused the generation to give up on childbirth. Rabbinical literature contains references to two other periods in which a sense of devastation and loss overwhelmed the will to create new life: the first was in the time of Adam and the second in the time just after the destruction of the Second Temple. One such reference is made in a *halakhic petihta* found in the midrash *Devarim Rabba.*

A *petihta*, or introduction to a midrashic commentary, may be *halakhic* or *aggadic* in content. This sort of introduction was commonly made as part of public sermons given in synagogues in Israel during the first two centuries C.E., apparently before the reading of the Torah on Shabbat. The orators who gave these sermons would pique the congregation's interest by fielding *halakhic* questions posed by listeners, taking into account their fields of interest and level of knowledge. From that starting point, they would launch into an exegetical discourse on the weekly Torah portion. When we study such a sermon, we need to pay close attention not only to the response given by the orator, but also to the question. Together they reveal a unique dialogue between an ordinary congregation in Israel in the beginning of the era of the Talmud, and the orator, a representative of the *beit midrash,* the bastion of Torah study.[4]

---

[4] For more on the genre of the *petihta* see Yosef Heinemann, *"Hapetikhtaot be-midrashei ha-aggadah – mekorn vetafkidan,"* Fourth World Congress in Jewish Studies, vol. 2 (5729), pp. 43–47; Y. Heinemann, *"Petihtaot shel tannaim vetekhunoteihen hatzuraniot,"* Fifth World Congress in Jewish Studies, vol. 3 (5732), pp. 121–134; Y. Heinemann, *"Derashot be-tzibbur be-tekufat ha-talmud,* Jerusalem 5731; Avigdor Shinan, *"Le-torat ha-petihta,"* Mehkerei Yerushalayim be-sifrut ivrit, vol. 1 (5741) pp. 133–145. On the *halakhic petikhta* in particular, see Levi Ginzburg, *"Maamar al yelamdeinu"* in *Ginzei Schechter,* vol. 1, New York (5685), pp. 449–513, and Hannah Friedman, *Hapetihta be-she'elah: le-olamah shel derashah be-tzibbur,* M.A. Thesis, Hebrew University, 5758.

"The Lord, your God, has caused you to multiply." (Deuteronomy 1:10)

How many children must one have in order to desist from the *mitzvah* of procreation?

Our Rabbis taught: One should not desist from the *mitzvah* of procreation.

But how many children may one have to be permitted to stop?

Beit Shammai [the school of Shammai] says: Two boys.

R. Elazar ben Azariah said in the name of *beit* Hillel: A boy and a girl.

What was the precedent for *beit* Shammai's requirement of two boys? The model of Cain and Abel. What was the precedent for *beit* Hillel's requirement of a boy and a girl? The model of Adam and Eve.

R. Elazar said: To abstain from procreation is as if to diminish the image of God in the world, as it is written, "In the Lord's image was the human being formed" (Genesis 9:6). One should therefore not abstain from procreation.

R. Shimon said, Adam abstained from marital relations for 130 years. Why? He fathered Cain and Abel, and then Cain killed Abel. It wasn't enough that Abel was murdered; Cain, his killer, was cursed and devastated, as the Torah says, "You shall become a ceaseless wanderer on earth" (Genesis 4:12). Both of them were lost. Once Adam saw this, he said, "When I bear children, they are destroyed." What did he do? He ceased having marital relations for 130 years, as it is written, "Adam lived 130 years…" (Genesis 5:3), and then, "He fathered children in his likeness and in his image." What did God do about this? He renewed [Adam's] desire, and he had relations with Havvah and fathered Shet. God said, "I created my world solely for the sake of procreation." As it says, "He did not create it to be a void, [but to be populated]" (Isaiah 45:18) and "God said to them, Be fruitful and multiply" (Genesis 1:22, 28). Thus, God created Adam and Havvah in the first place so they would be fruitful and multiply and bear children. Why? That is God's true honor and glory.

As a result, when the Jews left Egypt, they numbered 600,000, as it says, "The children of Israel traveled from Ramses..." (Exodus 12:37). They reached the desert and continued to multiply without cease; they gathered together and were full of pride, as it says, "And the Children of Israel were fruitful and prolific" (Exodus 1:7). [Moshe] said to them, "What am I to do with you? God Himself has caused you to be this way." How do we learn this? From the words, "The Lord, God of your fathers has caused you to multiply" (Deuteronomy 1:10).[5]

The orator first responds to the question from the audience ("How many children must one have in order to desist from the *mitzvah* of procreation?") by citing the opinions of *beit* Hillel and *beit* Shammai recorded in the Mishnah.[6] He then introduces R. Shimon's depiction of Adam's response to Cain's act of murder: Adam chose abstinence in the wake of his son's patricide. According to R. Shimon, Adam understands that not only Abel, the murdered son, but also Cain, the son who committed the murder, will be lost forever, and he is filled with despair – what is the point of having children and raising them, if nothing good comes out of it? Thanks only to God's direct personal intervention by renewing Adam's sexual desire can Adam have relations with Eve once again. The fruit of this intervention is the birth of Shet. The orator proceeds to mention another difficult period we discussed earlier – the years of slavery in Egypt,[7] and notes that the children of Israel continued to procreate prolifically even then, despite the hardships of slavery. They ultimately left Egypt numbering sixty myriad and during their wanderings in the desert they continued to multiply greatly.

---

[5] *Devarim Rabba* (ed. Lieberman), Jerusalem 5700, pp. 9–11. In the conclusion of this passage, the midrash alters the verse; the phrase "of your fathers" does not appear in the biblical text (Deuteronomy 1:10).

[6] *Mishnah Yevamot* 6.6.

[7] In the sermon, the verse "And the children of Israel were fruitful and increased abundantly" (Exodus 1:7) is applied not to the time of the Egyptian enslavement but the later period in the desert. The orator's desire to conclude with the opening verse of the weekly Torah portion, which concerns Moshe's words in the desert, was apparently what caused him to remove the verse from its literal meaning and context. See Heinemann, *Derashot be-tzibbur*, p. 97.

Professor Heinemann points out that beyond teaching of Adam's "historical" choice of abstinence, this speech teaches us of a similar tendency in the orator's own day, among those very Jews he is addressing. The question itself posed at the beginning of the sermon alerts us to a problematic societal context: why do the listeners want to know when they can stop doing a *mitzvah*?[8] Furthermore, the orator chooses to respond not only with a clear *halakhic* answer, but also to sing the praises of procreation without limitations, particularly in times of strife, suggesting that audible "between the lines" of the question was a tone of despair and hopelessness. His words respond to this. Heinemann posits, then, that the sermon was delivered during oppressive times, when tens of thousands of Jews were perishing in wars and rebellions against the Romans. The same sort of attitude, Heinemann suggests, was prevalent at the time of the destruction of the Temple, as we can see in descriptions of "the mourners of Zion":

> After the Temple was destroyed, the *perushim* [ascetics] among the Jews were many, abstaining from eating meat and from drinking wine.
>
> R. Yehoshua approached them, saying: My sons, why do you not eat meat?
>
> They answered, How can we eat meat when the sacrifices that were offered daily on the altar have now ceased?
>
> He said, We will not eat. … And why do you not drink wine?
>
> They said, Shall we drink wine, which was poured in libations each day over the altar, and now is no more?
>
> He said to them, Should we also not eat figs or grapes – they were brought as first-fruit offerings on Shavuot? Should we not eat bread – it was brought in the two-loaf offering and the showbread

---

[8] Interestingly, the Mishnah itself, which the orator uses in his answer, is formulated in the negative: "One should not desist from the *mitzvah* of procreation unless one has chidren." It may be that this text also teaches of the same dialectic. In any case, the *halakhic* context of the Mishnah differs from that of our orator. It brings the dispute between the schools of Shammai and Hillel in relation to laws concerning *yibbum*, marrying an *ilanit* [infertile woman], and other issues of infertility. In that framework, it relates to the need for an *halakhic* obligation to strive for conditions of fertility, precisely in abnormal situations of infertility – unlike our orator.

offering? Shall we not drink water – it was poured as a libation on the festival of Sukkot?

They were silent.

He said to them, Not to mourn at all – that is impossible, since the decree has already been passed; to mourn excessively is also wrong. And so the Rabbis have taught:

When one paints one's house, a patch should be left unpainted in memory of [the Temple in] Jerusalem.

One prepares a feast and omits something, in memory of Jerusalem

A woman adorns herself with jewelry, but leaves out some piece, in memory of Jerusalem. As it is written, "If I forget you, O Jerusalem, let my right hand wither, let my tongue stick to my palate, if I cease to think of you, if I do not keep Jerusalem in memory, even at my happiest hour (Psalms 137:5)."[9]

In contrast to the midrashim detailing the response of the Israelite women in Egypt to their husbands' choice of abstinence, we find no similar records of women's responses in the case of Adam or in the generation after the destruction of the Temple. We might then conclude that women and men both chose celibacy in these situations. A closer reading, however, suggests that the same gender distinction can be made here as well. Indeed, R. Shimon's depiction of Adam's decision not to have children makes no mention of Havvah at all. The very fact that God intervenes by increasing Adam's desire would suggest that Havvah did not share his problematic attitude. Celibacy, then, was forced on her by her husband. Even more definitively, R. Yehoshua himself, speaking in another context, provides us with insight into the attitude of women in the generation of the destruction of the Temple towards the prevailing tendency toward celibacy:

R. Yehoshua taught: A woman prefers one measure [a meager livelihood] and sexual license over nine measures and abstinence.[10]

---

[9] *Tosefta Sotah* 15.11. A similar version appears in *Bava Batra* 60b.

[10] *Mishnah Sotah* 3.4.

R. Yehoshua's words suggest that women are not receptive by nature to celibacy, and that every woman, if given the choice, would prefer to have minimal nourishment and available sexual relations[11] over abundant possessions and infrequent intimacy. And if anyone objected to R. Yehoshua that some women are different, and that some do prefer abstinence, he would say, "An overly pious man, a clever schemer, a celibate woman, and those who practice asceticism to impress others – all of them destroy the world."[12]

Understanding the meaning of everything listed here is no simple matter, but there does seem to be a common denominator. As Maimonides writes in his commentary on the Mishnah, "All of these people go beyond what is required of them and make a big show of it to deceive others." If so, that would imply that R. Yehoshua would not consider a woman who appears to be abstinent to be genuine. Instead, he would suspect her of deception or false piety, since celibacy contradicts her real nature, and, even worse, ruins the world.

An isolated reading of R. Yehoshua's opinion in the Mishnah in *Sotah* could leave the impression that he derides women's libidinous nature. His response to "the mourners of Zion," however, teaches us that he is far more troubled by ascetic trends in behavior, and actually looks favorably upon the female sex drive, which promotes childbirth and continuity.

To sum up what we have seen until this point, the Rabbis repeatedly indicated a distinctive female personality trait – the avoidance of abstinence and steadfast resolve to bear children and give life, even in difficult times. At times, this attribute is viewed in a positive light, as in the case of the Israelite women in Egypt and the women's contribution to the Temple. At other times, it is portrayed simply as an aspect of their nature, as R. Yehoshua would hold. It both instances, it is seen as a major factor in the existence and continuity of the world. If a woman tries to deny her nature and to be celibate, she becomes a destructive force in the world.

What, then, is the source of this attribute among women? Ostensibly, it could be attributed to a woman's physiological makeup: it is the woman

---

[11] As the commentator R. E. Bartenura explains, loc. cit.

[12] *Mishnah Sotah* 3.4.

who bears children. Her entire body is designed to enable her to carry a fetus in her womb and to perform the act of childbirth. It could be that this function, biologically imprinted upon her, has a decisive impact in her moral decision-making process. It causes her to reject any reality of ideological abstinence, no matter how difficult the circumstances.

My purpose is not to deny this assertion. It does seem to me, though, that loading the entire explanation onto the woman's womb and the act of childbirth reduces the greatness of the phenomenon and distorts the truth. At the most basic level, I believe, there is a more fundamental difference in the nature and style of the value systems constructed by each gender. This difference permeates to a variety of issues: the relationship between ideology and reality, between nature, society, and ethics, as well as the desired mutual balance or hierarchical relationship between them.

I'd like to exemplify this with a story that anyone involved with gender studies and women's issue has probably encountered.[13]

In the early 1930s the famous developmental psychologist Jean Piaget published some research concerning the influence of childhood games in the formation of children's self-image and social identity. His contention was that through games, the child learns to take on the role of "other" and see himself through his playmate's eyes. Janet Laver, one of Piaget's followers, studied the play modes of boys and girls, and discovered significant differences in the ways each gender plays. While girls tend to play non-competitive games inside in small groups, boys' games tend to go beyond the bounds of the home; they play competitive games in large groups of mixed ages, and their games tend to continue over a longer period of time. In both cases, she observed that disagreements frequently arose during the game. The boys usually succeeded in settling the dispute, while disagreements between the girls usually led to the game ending. The boys seemed to be pleased with the judicial sophistication of their game rules and their developing of fair guidelines to resolve disputes. The girls, in contrast, related more pragmatically to the rules and were more willing to tolerate "exceptions to the rule" and improvise as the situation demanded or,

---

[13] The following is a condensed version of the story appearing in Carol Gilligan's book, *In a Different Voice: Psychological Theory and Women's Development* (Harvard: Cambridge, 1982), chapters 1-2.

alternatively, to stop the game if an argument between the players began. These findings let Piaget to claim that the "legal sense" – an essential component in human ethical development – is much less developed in young girls than in boys of the same age. In light of the theory formulated by Piaget, Lawrence Kohlberg constructed a six-stage model of human moral development, and made a series of studies of children faced with ethical dilemmas they were asked to resolve. One such dilemma, posed to eleven-year-old children, was "Heinz's dilemma."

Heinz's wife has a serious disease. A new medicine has recently been developed for this illness. It is available at pharmacies and is very expensive. Heinz wants to save his wife's life, but he's unable to get enough money together to buy the medicine. Despite Heinz's request, the pharmacist refuses to lower the price. In order to save his wife's life, should Heinz steal the medicine?

Comparison of the answers given by two different children cited in Kohlberg's research, a boy and a girl reveals significant differences in their analysis and resolution of the dilemma. The boy, Jack, identified two fundamental values underlying it – ownership and life – and decided that life had precedence. He then immediately concluded that Heinz should steal the medicine. The girl, Amy, was much more hesitant. She looked for alternate solutions to the problem – (Heinz could try to get a loan, or talk again to the pharmacist); she considered the potential damage that might result from the theft – (if he steals it, he might go to jail and then if his wife gets sick again he won't be able to help her at all). In the end, she decided he shouldn't steal. Evaluation of their answers according to Kohlberg's scale of moral development put Jack's answers at a higher level than Amy's. Since this example represents the answers of additional boys and girls even in the case of other dilemmas, Kohlberg remarked, as children's logical thought develops, human moral development becomes far less advanced in little girls than in boys of the same age. Kohlberg's student, Carol Gilligan, who reexamined his findings, focused on that comment and claimed that Kohlberg ignored the alternative method of moral judgement expressed in the girls' thinking. That is, while Jack analyzed the dilemma posed to him as a conflict between two pure values, which could be solved by drawing logical conclusions, Amy saw it as a web of intertwined human relations to be resolved with great care. From Kohlberg's perspective, Gilligan remarked, Amy's answers really don't belong to the realm of ethics. In making that distinction, Gilligan effectively broke the path, for herself and other researchers after her, toward analysis and characterization of the variant of ethical thinking between men and women. This trend, it seems to me, continues until today.[14]

The increasing awareness of gender-based differences in ethical thinking, especially in the ways men and women approach resolution of problems and dilemmas, finds expression in many contexts within Israeli society. One example is the liaison system, which seeks to provide an alternative to the overloaded courts by referring citizens involved in monetary or legal disputes to find a compromise with the help of an arbitrator. While an appointed judge's decision is made, in most cases, by putting the full weight of the law and moral truth with one of the sides, the liaison process will attempt to find, through dialogue, a compromise acceptable to both sides while ignoring questions of absolute truth and justice involved in the matter. There are those, not accidentally, who attribute the relative flourishing, in recent years, of the numbers of liaison institutions and training programs for licensed arbitrators to the entrance of women in the judicial arena, and to the feminine perspective they contribute to problem solving. If this association is indeed correct, women's contribution to the judicial system is in that initial willingness, at the root of every act of liaison, to renounce any abstract value judgement, regardless of the logical truth it might contain, for that might harm the fragile web of social relationships. Here, too, to a certain extent, we find a preference for life and its natural, dynamic flow over disembodied ideologies.

A second example, a good deal more complex and loaded, is the partially obscured connection between the opposition to the war in Lebanon and the battle for withdrawal from Lebanon, and women. Disregarding, for a moment, the various security considerations for and against the war and the necessity of protecting Jews living in northern Israel, it is no

---

[14] My intent here is not to present a comprehensive review of the research that has been done either in psychology or in feminism. Aside from Gilligan's book itself and the reactions it aroused, it is enough to cite the popular literature on the best seller lists, such as *Men are from Mars, Women are from Venus,* etc.

coincidence that the banner in favor of withdrawal was borne by an organization that called itself "Four Mothers," run by mothers of soldiers serving in Lebanon and bereaved mothers. In an exceedingly bitter article that appeared in the paper *Nekudah*, entitled "One-parent withdrawal," Hanokh Daum wrote: "What is even stranger in this dispute is the feminist issue. Whenever something bad happens in Lebanon, the 'Four Mothers' come out of their closet and assault army officers with all sorts of not particularly intelligent things, sending a pretty clear message about the macho aspirations of the fighters. There's something very insulting and unfair about that wild accusation. The concerned mothers object that we men take their dear children to battle. They, unlike us, love their sons…. In any case, no matter how feminist the 'Four Mothers' will be, the best goal in honor of men was scored by their opponents in calling their organization the 'Three Fathers' – in that, they essentially verified the thesis connecting the masculine drive to the occupation in Lebanon."[15]

Even if Daum's sense of insult (in the name of all men) from the veiled feminine accusation of deficient paternal love is justified, we can still wonder why in that war, like other wars throughout human history, the revolt (or defeatism) against its very existence was incited by women.[16] It's hard to imagine that the entire sphere of security or national considerations leading to a going to war are concealed from women's eyes or, to the same extent, that all desire for love of life and peace are hidden from men's eyes. It seems that here, too, we find a manifestation of differences in value judgement – the one choosing life and its preservation over every other possibility, regardless of its value.

Returning to the teachings of the Rabbis, we see that the world of midrash also alludes to a recognition of this broader moral quality we have suggested. In portraying Sarah's reaction to the *akedah*, to her son's being bound upon the altar (something the Bible itself passes over in silence), the

---

[15] Hanoch Daum, "One-parent Withdrawal," *Nekudah* 220, Kislev 5759, p. 63.

[16] There is a Greek myth that describes original battle tactics used by the women of Athens against a war fought by their husbands: they threatened to abstain from having sexual relations with them until the men ended their war. Ironically, that is the only precedent I have found so far of female abstinence. Its object in this case, however, is ultimately to serve the purpose of perpetuating life and birth.

event is moved from its original context to the sidra of *Hayyei Sarah*, which recounts her death.

"And Avraham came to mourn for Sarah" (Genesis 23:2).

Where did he come from? R. Levi said, He came from burying [his father] Terah. R. Yose responded, Wasn't Terah's burial two years before Sarah's?! Rather, he came from Mount Moriah, and Sarah died of that same sorrow. For that reason, [the account of] the *akedah* comes right before the account of Sarah's death.[17]

Sarah passed away, according to R. Yose, in reaction to the *akedah* itself – or, as he says, "of that same sorrow." From his statement, though, it is hard to know what that sorrow really was. Did Sarah know that Avraham had gone to offer up their son, but was unaware the angel of God had saved him (as Avraham hadn't yet returned from Mt. Moriah when Sarah died)? Or perhaps it was all the psychic suffering expended in Avraham's test despite the happy ending?

Both possibilities are voiced in the midrash. Some views link her death to Satan's crafty meddling, coming to tell Sarah about the *akedah* while Avraham was still away:

> When Avraham returned from Mt. Moriah, Satan was furious that he had not succeeded in attaining his heart's desire – to impede Avraham in offering his sacrifice. What did he do? He went and said Sarah: Hey, Sarah, haven't you heard what's happened? She answered, No. He said, Your old husband took young Yitzhak and offered him up as a sacrifice, and the boy is crying and wailing that he can't escape. Sarah started to cry and wail herself. She uttered three cries, corresponding to the three *tekiyot* [of the shofar], three wails, corresponding to the three *yebavot* [of the shofar]. Then her soul departed from her and she passed away.[18]

Others put the tidings of the *akedah* in the mouth of Yitzhak himself, and say that Sarah died despite her awareness of the happy ending.

---

[17] *Genesis Rabba*, 68.5.

[18] *Pirkei de-Rabbi Eliezer*, ch. 32.

> When Yitzhak returned to his mother, she asked him, Where have you been, my son? He told her, Father seized me, took me up mountains and down valleys. And she said, Woe to this son of a miserable woman! If not for an angel from heaven, you would have been slaughtered? He answered, Yes. At that moment, she uttered six screams, corresponding with the six *tekiyot*. And it was said that she didn't manage to finish before she passed away....[19]

One way or another, the result is that Sarah was unable to accept Avraham's choice (or his undergoing the test as he understood it), and died from the ordeal. What is interesting, as Yehudah Gellman remarks in his essay on the subject, is that Sarah's cries became the model for the shofar blasts on Rosh Hashanah that are now part of Jewish tradition. Their role in the Rosh Hashanah service would imply that Sarah died not in a display of weakness or a moment of irresponsibility. "In truth, her cries express the recognition of a religious imperative of which Avraham had no part, for Avraham and Sarah represent two different types of the religious personality."[20]

The various types of the religious personality could be characterized and defined in a number of ways.[21] It seems to me, in any case, that emphasis would be on the distinction between religious life in the spirit of Avraham, seeking totality and devotion, and attaining transcendence and connection with God through acts of renunciation and sacrifice, and religious life in Sarah's way, searching in the whole of human experience for that divine point of connection and meaning, driven by the conviction that life itself, ultimately, is God's will, and that people cannot make the decision to annul one value for the sake of another.

The tremendous awakening now taking place in the religious community to the issue of the status of women, their involvement in religious life in general and in the world of Torah learning in particular mandates, I believe,

---

[19] *Vayikra Rabba*, 20. 2.

[20] Yehudah Gellman, "'*Ve-tamot Sarah*' – *Bein Sarah le-Avraham be-sippur ha-akedah*," *Akdamot* 3, Jerusalem 5757, p. 85.

[21] See Gellman, loc. cit., pp. 85–90.

some consideration of this issue. Possible differences in religious types characteristic of each sex would clearly dictate variations in approaches to learning and worship. I'm not talking about the traditional distinction made between the "soft," sensitive woman and the "hard," brainy man, a division that actually served to prevent women from entering fields thought to be "masculine" – *Gemara, halakhah,* leadership roles, etc. What I'm suggesting, rather, is awareness that when women enter these fields, they are not trying to imitate the accepted way things have been studied and done until now. The opposite – it would be better for them to make their own contribution. I'd like to cite Hanoch Daum once again, this time in relation to the developing world of women's learning:

> When I told a certain young woman, who learns in a certain *midrashah*, about a certain event that was going to take place, she said that she and her friends would really have liked to come, but the event was set for 8:30 p.m. That was right in the middle of their evening *seder* [set learning block], and they were reluctant to neglect their Torah. What a laugh…could anyone have imagined the scenario that women, who carry the so-modern banner of feminine learning, would in the end of the process turn into simple, old-fashioned scholars who can't comprehend that attending that creative event would not be *bitul Torah,* "neglecting Torah" – if Torah is perceived in the broad sense it deserves.[22]

I don't know what sort of event it was that Daum invited the woman and her friends to, and whether, as he said, it would have been worthwhile for them to cancel their learning schedule for that evening. There is, however, truth to his claim that a broader and more encompassing perception of the world of Torah, and especially a "feminine" perspective as we have defined it – one that finds God's will not in totality, renunciation, and sacrifice, but in gathering together all life forces – will de-emphasize values like "neglecting Torah" or "annulment" [*bitul*] as a whole in defining religious experience.

---

[22] See Hanoch Daum, "*Bezekhut nashim lamdaniot,*" *Nekudah* 231, Adar 2, 5760, pp. 42–44.

The Holy One, blessed be He taught Moshe, in the midrash from *Tan-huma (Pikudei)* we saw above, not to disdain the unusual contribution of mirrors offered by the Israelite women. He instructed him, instead, to make a brass laver of them, in which the priests would purify themselves. May it be His will that, in our own generation as well, women will understand how to offer their own unique contribution to the world of holiness, and will merit the same approval and esteem to which the midrash testifies.

Halakhic Issues Concerning Women

ROSH HODESH – THE WOMEN'S HOLIDAY

Rabbanit Malka Puterkovsky

Introduction

Many years ago, as a young student, I first became acquainted with the practice of women's celebrating *Rosh Hodesh* as a festive day. This celebration commemorates the refusal of the Jewish women in the wilderness to participate in making the golden calf. As I had the privilege of growing up in a Torah-observant household, I was surprised to discover a women's custom that was not kept in our house. My mother, whose faith in God was deeply rooted, and who strove to observe the more lenient *mitzvot* as carefully as the stricter ones, treated *Rosh Hodesh* as a normal weekday, working ceaselessly in keeping the house and taking care of the children. Around me as well – in my extended family, the neighborhood I grew up in, in my friend's houses – I did not notice women relating to *Rosh Hodesh* as a special day.

After a little research on the subject, I discovered to my amazement that this is not a forgotten custom of unknown origin, neglected for generations. On the contrary, the practice women have to refrain from work on *Rosh Hodesh* stems from an explicit *halakhah* in the *Shulhan Arukh* and other mainstream *halakhic* works. Similarly, many testimonies throughout history record that women were careful to refrain from performing any (or some) tasks on *Rosh Hodesh*, as we will see later.

I then set a double goal for myself. First, I would learn as much as I possibly could about this custom. This would include thorough examination and research of all the *tannaic, amoraic* and *halakhic* sources in order to trace the origin of the custom, its development and its *halakhic* authority and breadth. Mine would be a scrupulous search for verbal and written testimonies concerning its actual practice: where and when were women zealous in refraining from doing work on *Rosh Hodesh* in one form or

---

* translated by Zipporah and Jonathan Price

another? This part of the goal I set for myself, was, thank God, completed over a period of several years. I present it to you here.

Secondly, I wanted to understand how it is possible that this Jewish custom is so little observed by women, both in our generation and in the one before it. Why have women given up the God-given privilege of abstaining from work on *Rosh Hodesh,* especially considering that by observing this custom we commemorate the depth of faith, spiritual power and attachment to Hashem that characterized the women in the generation of the Exodus from Egypt? And why has this custom, which falls among the *halakhic* obligations that are not actually observed, not been encouraged and reinforced by *halakhic* authorities of the last generations?

My examination and research of the various sources has not unearthed a satisfying explanation in answer to these questions. In the last section of this essay, I will thus present some of my own suggestions based on what I have learned.

This essay has one purpose – to increase women's awareness of the custom of abstaining from work on *Rosh Hodesh*, its sources, *halakhic* authority and breadth, and to awaken women's interest in renewing its observance. May the *roshei hodashim*, with God's help, be crowned once more with the faithfulness and cleaving of women to God.

1. *"Roshei Hodashim…* when women do not do work"[1] – For what reason?

In the fourth chapter of the tractate *Pesahim*, the *Mishnah, Tosefta* and both the Bablyonian and Jerusalem *Talmudim* discuss the status of a custom practiced in a community, and its obligatory powers. Within the framework of a wide overview of customs not universally observed by the Jewish people, this principle appears in the Jerusalem Talmud: "They made everything dependent on custom." Immediately following is a list of festivals on which Jewish women were accustomed to refrain from

---

[1] Rashi on *Megillah* 22b, ד״ה ראשי חודשים. *Rashi* is the acronym for R. Shlomo Yitzchaki, the great commentator on the Torah and the Babylonian Talmud, who lived in France in the eleventh century. In addition to his commentaries, he also wrote responsa to various questions he was asked, and *halakhic* rulings.

working.[2] Concerning each festival, the Talmud indicates whether the women's abstention from work is a proper custom or not – "proper" implying that it is anchored in the tradition and should therefore continue to be observed. When the custom is not rooted in tradition, however, it should be abolished. Within the list, *Rosh Hodesh* appears as a day women refrain from working, and the following principle is laid down:

"Women who customarily abstain from work... on *Rosh Hodesh*, it is a [proper] custom."

According to two of the commentators on the Jerusalem Talmud[3] these words would indicate that, already at the time of the Talmud itself, it was a given, recognized and commonly known occurrence that women refrained from work on *Rosh Hodesh*. And since the abstention from work on this day merits the title "*custom*," we may conclude that at issue is not merely an extant custom; rather, the intent of the Talmud is to encourage its continuation.[4]

This description of the situation is also supported by what we find in the Babylonian Talmud. In *Megillah*, in the discussion of the number of men who ascend to the reading of the Torah on days that are not usual weekdays, a *beraita* appears with the following ruling:[5]

"This is the rule: Any day on which work would be delayed, for example a public fast day or Tisha be-Av, three people read [the Torah]. Any day on which work would not be delayed, for example *Rosh Hodesh and Hol HaMoed*, four people read."

This would imply that any day on which work is intrinsically permitted, a minimal number of people ascend to read the Torah to avoid delaying the congregation in the synagogue longer than necessary, so they should be free to go to work at the earliest opportunity. Thus, on those fast days on which work is permitted, only three people ascend to read the Torah. On every

---

[2] JT *Pesahim* 4:1

[3] See *Penei Moshe* and *Korban HaAidah, ad loc.* ד"ה יומא דירחא

[4] R. Moshe ben R. Yitzchak me-Vinah (who will be discussed at length later) establishes the following in reference to the Jerusalem Talmud: "The custom of women to refrain from work on *Rosh Hodesh* is a legitimate and upright custom" (*Or Zarua*, vol. 2, s. 454).

[5] *Megillah* 22b

festival, however, when work is forbidden for everyone, more people ascend to read the Torah, as the public has no workday to begin. One example given for a day on which it is forbidden to work is *Rosh Hodesh*; on that day four people ascend to read the Torah. From this *beraita* we could possibly conclude that the entire nation was forbidden to work on *Rosh Hodesh*.

In the tractate *Hagigah*, however, *Rosh Hodesh* is described as a day when it is permissible to do work:[6]

"*Rosh Hodesh* is a proof, for an additional sacrifice is offered and work is permissible."

The question is raised by the *Tosafot*.[7] They offer the following answer:[8]

"Men are certainly permitted to do work; women, however, must refrain, because they did not remove their earrings [refusing to contribute them] for the golden calf."

To understand the answer the *Tosafot* propose, we must relate to Rashi's words:[9]

"[On] *Roshei Hodashim* – abstention from work is minimal, for [it is only the] women who refrain from labor... and I heard from my honored teacher [*mori hazaken*], of blessed memory, that they were given this *mitzvah* because they did not take off their earrings to make the golden calf."

As an explanation for the source of women abstaining from work on *Rosh Hodesh*, Rashi brings the midrash *Pirkei deRabbi Eliezer*.[10] The original midrash reads:[11]

---

[6] *Hagigah* 18a

[7] *Baalei ha-Tosafot* is the collective name for a group of French and German scholars who lived in the twelfth to thirteenth centuries in the generations after Rashi (initially composed of his sons-in-law and grandsons). Their work is essentially an expansion on Rashi's commentary, coupled with their own comments, questions and answers and *halakhic* rulings.

[8] *Tosafot* to *Megillah* ad loc. ד"ה ושאין בו ביטול מלאכה

[9] Rashi ad loc. ד"ה ראשי חדשים

[10] *Pirkei deRabbi Eliezer* is a collection of midrashim concerning the Creation, the period of the forefathers and the generation of the wilderness, and ascribed to R. Eliezer ben Horkanus. This collection, in many cases, provides the sole source for certain Jewish customs.

[11] Chapter 45 (ed. R. David Luria).

"Aaron reasoned as follows. He said to himself: If I say to them, Give me silver and gold – they will bring it immediately. Instead, I will say to them: Give me the earrings of your wives and sons and daughters, and the plan will be nullified immediately. Indeed, the verse says, "And Aaron said, Remove…" (Exodus 32:2). The women heard but were not willing; they refused to give their earrings to their husbands, saying: To make something detestable and abominable that has no power of salvation – no, we will not listen to you! God gave them their reward in this world: that they observe the *Roshei Hodashim* more than the men. And He gave them their reward in the world to come – in the future they will be renewed like the new months…. The men saw that their wives would not heed them and surrender their earrings to them. What did they do? Until that time they had earrings like the Egyptians and Arabs, [and now] the men removed their own earrings and gave them to Aaron, as the verse says "And all the people took out the golden rings that were in their ears" (ibid. 33:3). The verse does not say "in their wives' ears" but "in their ears."

Close examination of this midrashic account reveals the source of the women's custom, and enables us to appreciate its *halakhic* power and its breadth. Let us dwell on some central points the midrash raises.

Aaron the Priest, beloved by the nation because he "pursued peace and engendered love,"[12] feared for his life. He was afraid that the Jews would kill him if he refused to cede to their desperate request to "arise [and] make for us a god"[13] – a request born out of the alarm created by Moshe's "delay" in descending from Mt. Sinai. According to the passage in the midrash prior to the one quoted, Aaron's fear seems to have been based on what he had seen with his own eyes.

Hur, a member of the tribe of Judah and one of the generation's leaders began to rebuke the Jews harshly. Lowly ones from among the Jews arose

---

[12] See Rashi on Numbers 20:29 ד"ה כל בית ישראל. There he explains that the entire nation wept at the death of their beloved leader Aaron, as he was the epitome of a lover of peace.

[13] Exodus 32:1

and killed him. When Aaron saw that Hur had been killed, he built an altar, as the verse says, "And Aaron saw…" (Exodus 32:5). What did he see? That his nephew Hur had been killed; thus he built an altar.

At the same time, though, an individual of Aaron's stature would surely not contribute to actions that would lead to the entire nation hysterically worshipping idols. Based on his calculation that Moses had been temporarily delayed and would certainly soon reappear before the people, Aaron opted for a "delaying tactic." He would ask the men to provide the raw material to build the golden calf specifically from their wives' jewelry, rather from their own, in the deliberate hope that the plan would be aborted. Now it could be argued, as Rashi indeed does,[14] that Aaron's true motivation in employing this "tactic" to delay the building of the calf was the expectation that the women would refuse to give over their jewelry because they are possessive about their wealth. In the continuation of the midrash quoted above, however, the women are portrayed with a different rationale for their refusal. We might suggest, then, that in effect, Aaron knew the women would refuse to hand over their jewelry, not out of possessiveness, but due to more deeply rooted moral qualities. He recognized well the special behavior the Jewish women had shown during the exile in Egypt and in the wilderness. These women's actions welled from strong faith and spiritual awareness that everything God does is right. Their long-term perspective enabled them to remain patient and dedicated to their goal. Aaron was well aware of the nature of these women, about whom it is said, "In the merit of the righteous women the Jews were redeemed from Egypt."[15] The midrash that opens with these words relates the efforts of the Jewish women in Egypt to continue to give birth and raise children despite the tremendous difficulties entailed in doing so, both because of the Egyptian captivity and because of the despair and hopelessness of their husbands.

Pregnancy, birth and raising children are inarguably very complex and difficult processes, even during calm and comfortable days. They become

---

[14] See Rashi on Exodus 32:2 ד"ה באזני נשיכם

[15] *Sotah* 11b. The midrash describes at length the faithful conduct of the Jewish women in the Egyptian exile. For a fuller understanding of the continuation of this essay, please see the midrash in the original.

even more trying in times of enslavement and decrees forbidding reproduction. The most natural feeling in such periods would be unwillingness to continue the process of bringing forth the next generations of the Jewish people. In truth, according to the midrash,[16] this was the reaction of Amram, the Jewish leader of his generation. Father of Miriam the prophetess, Amram opted to divorce his wife to avoid the injunction to procreate. All the Jewish men followed in his stead, until Miriam came and pointed out her father's error to him: "Father, your decree is harsher than that of Pharaoh...." The young Miriam realized what her father, despite his prominence, had not understood: To join forces with Pharaoh and his decrees, whether actively (as the midwives were commanded to do) or passively (as Amram had done) was wrong. Everyone must continue to fulfill a unique purpose in the world. We must do our part, and God will help us. And not Miriam alone was infused with this faith; it was shared by all the Jewish women in Egypt, for whom it would certainly have been easier to not conceive, give birth and raise children at a time of enslavement and pain. They acted intuitively even though there seemed to be no hope. With the power of their faith the Jewish women caused their husbands to desire them, and so they conceived and bore children.

The impossibility of giving birth in their homes under normal conditions forced the women to give birth in the fields, despite their fear that the Jewish babies would be discovered and killed. The midrash describes how God participated, as it were, in this complicated process. He Himself assisted them in labor, and provided the needs of the tender newborn. This further highlights the women's merits – their faith and role in the nation's exodus from Egypt.[17]

---

[16] *Sotah* 12a; *Exodus Rabbah* 1:14, 18, 19.

[17] See *Iyyun Yaakov* (by R. Yaakov Ryser) to *Sotah* 11b, who links the willingness of the women to continue reproducinging with the advancement of the date of the exodus from Egypt: "In the merit of the righteous women... the explanation is [they were redeemed] before the set time, because the flocks of children that were born enabled them to complete the hard work [earlier than had there been fewer of them] as the commentators say." This midrash is significant from a *halakhic* perspective as well, because it provides a basis for the rabbinic obligation of women to participate in the *mitzvot* of the *Seder* night, despite the general exemption of women from time-bound *mitzvot*.

We could, then, reasonably propose that Aaron was well aware of the faithful spirit of the Jewish women in Egypt and their conduct there, given that the women's leaders were his mother and sister.[18] It would be logical to conclude that Aaron sent the men to ask their wives with the clear knowledge that this action would delay the building of the golden calf. He was convinced, apparently, that they would never agree to help or take part in a process that would lead, directly or indirectly, to worshipping alien gods.

Now Aaron was not mistaken. The women flatly refused to give over their jewelry to make the calf:

The women heard but were not willing; they refused to give their earrings to their husbands, saying: To make something detestable and abominable that has no power of salvation – no, we will not listen to you!

I think we may understand this principled refusal on two levels. First, these women had a profound belief in the intangible Creator of the world. They wouldn't lend their contribution to making something "detestable and abominable." Even when their human leader, God's agent, was late in arriving, this did not alarm them so profoundly as to undermine their faith, and cause them to yearn for a tangible replacement in which they could trust. At the same time, the reason the women give for refusing contains an implicit double rebuke – of all who desired the golden calf (e.g., their husbands) and of the one seemed to have overlooked the absurdity in their demand to make the golden calf (Aaron). Beyond their opposition to the abomination of making the golden calf to be worshipped, they stressed that it has no power to save. Exposing the paradox of human beings creating an object they will instill with the power of salvation, the women effectively confronted their husbands with a challenge: You are asking for raw materials to create a tangible object. Your hysteria alone deludes you into imagining it can save you. Nothing is more absurd...[19]

---

[18] See the midrash mentioned in note 15, which quotes the tradition identifying Yocheved, mother of Aaron, and Miriam, with the midwives Shifrah and Puah.

[19] Compare the sequence of midrashim in *Tanna deBei Eliyahu*, chapter 6, and in *Genesis Rabbah* 38, which describe Abraham's attempts to prove to his father illogic of idol worship. Abraham leads his father to admit that since idols cannot possibly speak or strike, more complicated actions can surely not be ascribed to them.

Furthermore, as we have seen, Aaron, the beloved leader, hesitated in refusing to heed the nation's request, for fear they would kill him. Each woman who unhesitatingly opposed her husband's request for her jewelry, in contrast, courageously refused with truthful, elemental faith, to join her husband in making the golden calf. And hence their recompense:

"God gave them their reward in this world, that they observe *Rosh Hodesh* more than the men. And he gave them reward in the next world, that in the future they will be renewed like the new moon…."

Presently we will examine the nature of this "split reward" between this world and the world to come that God granted the women. To enable a deeper understanding, though, it is important to understand the concepts of "this world" and "the world to come" in our context. The intention is not that women received a certain reward during their lifetimes and a different one after their death. In our context the expression "this world" implies present, imperfect human existence, while "the next world" is the ideal, complete reality that will exist in the end of days. In this world, the women merit "that they observe the *Roshei Hodashim* more than the men." This statement can be understood in many ways; in effect, the midrash proceeds to bring a wide range of views concerning its practical implications. In any case, comments by various *halakhic* authorities suggest that the words "they observe" indicate the abstention from work on *Rosh Hodesh*.[20] In the coming, ideal world, however, their reward is "that they will be renewed like the new moon [*roshei hodashim*]."

Valuable light could be shed on the meaning of this reward by turning to an extraordinary explanation offered by the author of *Or Zarua*[21] in the laws of *Rosh Hodesh*:[22]

"I saw in *Pirkei deRabbi Eliezer* that God rewarded the women with the observance of *Rosh Hodesh* for not sinning with the golden calf, and in the world to come God will renew them like the renewal of the moon, as it is

---

[20] For the views of the *halakhic* authorities concerning the practical *halakhic* implication of this reward, see the following section of our discussion.

[21] *Or Zarua*, a *halakhic* work in four parts, is one of the earliest sources used in establishing the *halakhah* in Ashkenazic communities. Its author was R. Yitzhak ben R. Moshe me-Vinah, who lived in southern Germany in the late-twelfth to early-thirteenth century.

[22] *Or Zarua,* vol. 2, Laws of *Rosh Hodesh*, s. 454.

written: "When the heavens and the earth will be renewed" and "Your youth shall be renewed as the eagle." Know that each and every month a woman is renewed by immersing, and returns to her husband, and she is as beloved to him as on the day of their marriage. Just as the moon is renewed each month and all yearn to see it – so, too, when a woman becomes renewed each month, her husband desires her and she is as dear to him as a new woman. Thus *Rosh Hodesh* is a *yom tov* for women."

From the midrash itself, it is unclear why the women's reward was fixed specifically on *Rosh Hodesh*. The author of *Or Zarua*, in explaining the reward in the next world, focuses on an intrinsic point of connection between the life cycle of women and the special time of *Rosh Hodesh*. The uniqueness of the woman is her ability to conceive and give birth to children. The process of birth is tied to monthly cycles. In our present world each woman becomes ritually impure and purified at her own special time. In the ideal world, as I understand the *Or Zarua* to be explaining, not only will all women have the same monthly cycle and all of them will become purified on one day, but this cycle will also coincide with the cosmic cycle. The woman will be renewed each month and she will be beloved to her husband as she was on the wedding day, at exactly the same time as the moon is renewed, at a time when a new cycle of natural life will take place. What we have, then, is an incredible correlation between the process of human procreation and the process of the creation's renewal; between the joint actions of mankind – men and women – in creation through giving birth to future generations and populating the earth,[23] and the cycle of renewal of nature and Creation, beginning with the moon's re-birth, and sensed throughout the month as it waxes and wanes.

In addition to this explanation, there is a tradition that connects the abstention of women with their reward of refraining from work specifically on *Rosh Hodesh*.

---

[23] The commandment "Be fruitful and multiply and fill the earth and conquer it" (Genesis 1:25) is part of the description of mankind's creation, and it includes the purpose God designated for mankind in the process of creation. In *Niddah* 31a, we learn: "The Rabbis taught that there are three partners in [the creation of] a person: God, the father and the mother...."

In the laws of *Rosh Hodesh*, after presenting sources concerning women's abstaining from work, "*Baal haTurim*," R. Ya'akov ben HaRosh[24] brings an explanation heard from his brother, R. Yehudah,[25] of the special connection between women and *Rosh Hodesh*:[26]

"The festivals were instituted corresponding to the Patriarchs, *Pesach* corresponding to Avraham… *Shavout* corresponding to Yitzhak… *Sukkot* corresponding to Yaakov… And the *Roshei Hodashim*, which are also called festivals, corresponding to the twelve tribes. Now, when they sinned concerning golden calf, these were taken away from them and given to their wives, to commemorate that they did not take part in the sin."

What R. Yehudah teaches is that *Rosh Hodesh* was meant to be a national holiday for the nation as a whole, but when the men sinned with the golden calf they lost these festive days. As a result *Rosh Hodesh* remained a festive day only for the women. According to this understanding, however, the language of the midrash, "God gave them their reward" is problematic. In effect, the issue is not reward but simple justice. If God had been "planning" to grant a festival to the whole nation and part of the nation sinned, the festival would justifiably be taken away from those who sinned and would remain as a festival for the group that did not sin. R. Yosef Karo, author of *Beit Yosef*, raises this question against the explanation quoted by R. Yaakov, author of the *Tur*:[27]

"We could ask: If so, how could R. Eliezer say, 'Therefore God gave them their reward'? *Rosh Hodesh* had already been given to the Jews; thus, although the sin of the men caused it to be taken away from them, it would

---

[24] R. Yaakov ben HaRosh, who lived in the fourteenth century, was born in Germany and moved to Spain with his father. He authored the *Tur*, a comprehensive *halakhic* compendium on the *mitzvot* that are presently applicable. It is divided into four parts: *Oreh Hayyim, Yoreh Deah, Even ha-Ezer* and *Hoshen Mishpat*.

[25] R. Yehudah ben HaRosh took over the post of dean of the academy and head of the judicial court in Spain following his father's death. He is mentioned by the government as "head of the Spanish Rabbis." He authored the *responsum Zikharon Yehudah*.

[26] *Tur, Oreh Hayyim, Rosh Hodesh*, s. 417

[27] *Beit Yosef* is a work written by R. Yosef Karo, author of the *Shulhan Arukh*, designating sources for, explanations of, and expansions on the *Tur*. The *Beit Yosef* served as a foundation for the *Shulhan Arukh*. The author was an exile from Spain following the Inquisition, and lived in Turkey and Safed in the sixteenth century.

not be reasonable to deprive the women of it, as they did not sin. What is not taken away cannot be called a reward."

R. Yosef Karo proposes two solutions. The first is as follows:

"The answer could be that the prohibition against doing work on *Rosh Hodesh* had not yet been given to the Jews but was ready to be given. Due to the sin of the golden calf, this benefit was denied them. Since women, by nature, are drawn after their husbands and are secondary to them, it would have been appropriate to deny it to them [the women] as well – what is secondary in status should not be more important than what is primary in status. God, however, did not want to deprive the women of their rightful reward."

The description here is *not* of two separate elements – men and women – composing the nation, and when one element sins, privileges initially intended for them are denied and preserved for the group that did not sin. Rather, it bespeaks a profound interrelationship between the two groups. In this case, the group that did not sin is dependent on and subservient to the group that sinned; logically speaking, if the privilege is taken away from the primary group, or the dominant sector, it should be taken away from the secondary group subservient to it as well. The reason: "so that what is secondary in status should not be more important than what is primary in status." The reward, then, is that God preserved *Rosh Hodesh* for the women as a festive day, despite their secondary status relative to the men, to whom it was denied. In doing so, God actively transformed them in this context from secondary to primary in status. This essential shift in the women's position, achieved through giving them, and them alone, the central obligation of refraining from work on *Rosh Hodesh* – this is their true reward.

The second solution the *Beit Yosef* offers is as follows:

"Furthermore, we might say that *Rosh Hodesh* was originally given to the men and not to the women; when the men sinned with the golden calf it was taken away from them and given to the women. This is the precise intent of the midrash in saying, "It was taken away from them and given to the women." And now it can really be called giving reward, for now they merited something for which they had previously been unfit."

According to this, *Rosh Hodesh* was originally intended to be a festive day for men alone. The privilege to abstain from work on that day was meant only for them. Their sin caused this privilege to be transferred from them to the women. In other words, the reward consists in the women being given a festive day not originally intended for them at all.

This answer is somewhat surprising, for the Jewish calendar does not include any holiday given to only part of the Jewish people. Each holiday has its unique characteristics, but the common denominator of all of them is that the entire Jewish people inherited them, hence their unifying power. It seems strange to me that God would have planned to give such a festive and frequently recurrent holiday to one sector of the nation alone.

Our puzzlement deepens with closer examination of the comments voiced by *Baal haTurim*; as he wrote, *Rosh Hodesh* was supposed to be a festival for all the twelve tribes. There is no hint in his words of an inner division amongst the twelve tribes. On the contrary, he stresses the common denominator linking *Rosh Hodesh* with the other festivals mentioned: *Pesach, Shavout* and *Succot* – festivals in which the entire nation is forbidden to do work. This highlights an additional problem with the argument that *Rosh Hodesh* was intended to be a holy day whose character would be essentially different than these festivals.

Abudraham[28] offers yet another explanation why *Rosh Hodesh* was designated as a festive day for women:[29]

"Grounds have been cited for women refraining from work on *Rosh Hodesh*.... And the midrash says it is because the women were zealous in bringing voluntary donations for the tabernacle (*Mishkan*), as the verse says "And the men brought, along with the women," and it was erected on the first of *Nissan*. And because they were not willing to donate their earrings for the golden calf, they were given the reward of observing the *Roshei Hodashim*."

According to the *Abudraham*, women were specially designated to observe *Rosh Hodesh* not only because of their "passive" refusal to take part in

---

[28] *Abudraham* is a collection of laws and explanations concerning prayers and blessings, written by R. David Abudraham, who lived in Spain in the fourteenth century. Some hold he was a student of R. Yaakov, the author of the *Tur*.

[29] *Abudraham, Rosh Hodesh* ד״ה למנחה מתפללין

making the golden calf. God granted them that honor on account of the active role they had taken in initiating voluntary donations towards the building of the *Mishkan*. And since the *Mishkan* was erected on *Rosh Hodesh Nissan* the women received the reward of abstaining from work on *Rosh Hodesh* – this connected the two events.

R. Shimon ben Tzemah Doran, the Rashbatz,[30] also points out the connection between the stance of the women at the time of the making of the golden calf and their immediate mobilization in building the *Mishkan*:[31]

"It appears to me that the reason women customarily refrain from spinning [on *Rosh Hodesh*], but do other forms of work such as sewing, etc., is that during the process of building the *Mishkan,* the women were more zealous than the men. It is written, "And the men brought, along with the women [who brought spun items]; and it is said, "And every wise-hearted women spun with her hands and brought ..." also, "They spun goats' wool," an act requiring great wisdom. And because the men were more enthusiastic than the women in making the golden calf, the prohibition of doing work on *Rosh Hodesh* was deprived them, on account of their alacrity in making the golden calf and their sluggishness in making the *Mishkan.* And it was given to the women, due to their passivity in making the golden calf and alacrity in making the *Mishkan.*"

With the aid of verses from the Torah, the Rashbatz highlights the significant part the women played in making the *Mishkan* and their exalted motivations in donating everything they could for the creation of a house for God to accompany the Jewish people in the wilderness. It is only natural that when God commands and shows the most fitting way to serve Him, the women, with their faith throughout the Egyptian exile and in the wilderness, would be the first to offer themselves and their skills in building, cultivating, and developing this way of serving Him.

---

[30] The Rashbatz, R. Shimon ben Tzemah Doran, author of Responsa *HaTashbatz,* was one of the great scholars of North Africa. He lived in Morocco, Spain and Algiers at the end of the fourteenth and beginning of the fifteenth century.

[31] Responsa *HaTashbatz,* vol. 3, par. 254

2. "...That they observe *Rosh Hodesh* more than the men" – In what manner?[32]

Having clarified the source for women abstaining from work specifically on *Rosh Hodesh*, and having understood the promised reward for women in the world to come, let us consider now the women's reward in this world. In other words, what practical *halakhic* ramifications should be deduced from the words "that they observe *Rosh Hodesh* more than the men"? Is all work forbidden them – that is, are they to abstain from doing any form of work, or are some types of work permitted and others forbidden? If the *halakhic* authorities do in fact make such a distinction, we must understand the *halakhic* basis for it, and whether that distinction is universal and constant in all times and places. And maybe women are not really forbidden to do work at all; their reward would then be that on *Rosh Hodesh* no one, their husbands included, can force them to do work. If they wish, then, they are permitted to abstain from all the domestic tasks normally required of them,[33] an event that occurs at no other time.[34]

Halakhic authorities, in effect, disagree over the practical implication of the women's reward. There is a spectrum of opinions, on one extreme forbidding all women from doing any form of work, and on the other advocating that each woman can choose the work she wants to do as well as the tasks she wishes to refrain from doing.

In this section, we will cite the various *halakhic* authorities, and present the main opinions in the *halakhic* process of deciding the *halakhah* concerning the question at hand. In addition to assembling the different opinions and arranging them in a *halakhic spectrum* and in a chronological

---

[32] *Pirkei deRabbi Eliezer*, ch. 45, cited above.

[33] According to *Mishnah Ketubbot* 5.5 women are required to perform certain household tasks. Which ones – that depends on her financial status, but in any case she is obligated to do a minimal amount of work. The Talmud ad loc (59b ff.) discusses this issue at length. Rambam summarizes the matter in *Hilkhot Ishut,* ch. 21.

[34] The Rambam rules (ibid., 21.10): "If she refuses to do any of the tasks incumbent upon her, she may even be forced to do so...." The Raavad, however, takes issue on that point, arguing: "I have never heard of physically forcing women; rather, provision for her material needs may be constricted until she consents." According to both authorities, though, it is clear that her husband can force her to do the tasks that are incumbent upon her.

order, I will try to center on understanding the *halakhic* considerations that form the basis for the decision of each *halakhic* authority.

The Rif[35] connects the custom of women not working on *Rosh Hodesh* to the general obligation incumbent on a community of continuing to observe an established custom of forbidding something that is generally permitted. He makes this connection by linking a discussion found in the Jerusalem Talmud of the custom to abstain from work on *Rosh Hodesh* with a discussion found in the Babylonian Talmud about the obligatory power of a local custom:[36]

"R. Elazar ben R. Bun taught: Anything that one does not know is permitted, and mistakenly considers it to be forbidden – if he asks [what its *halakhic* status is] we permit it to him. Anything that one knows is permitted, but acts as if it were forbidden – if he asks, we do not permit it to him. Everything has been made dependent on custom. Women who are accustomed to refrain from work on *Rosh Hodesh* – [it is a] custom."

From the flow of his argument, we can see that the Rif sees the source of the women's obligation to refrain from work on *Rosh Hodesh* as a custom that they actively observed. Even if work had *a priori* been permitted to them, over the course of numerous generations they customarily considered work to be forbidden to them on *Rosh Hodesh* – therefore, all women are now obligated to observe the practice, since it has acquired the status of an ancient and founded custom. This, however, does not fit with the language of the midrash: "God gave them their reward." Where is the divine commandment from God, which engendered the women's practice to abstain from work on *Rosh Hodesh*?

R. Tzidkiyahu HaRofe[37] integrates the two perspectives: commandment and actual practice:[38]

---

[35] The Rif, R. Yitzhak Alfasi, an eminent teacher of the Spanish sages along with the Rambam and Ramban, lived in North Africa and Spain in the eleventh century. He authored *Hilkhot Rav Alfas,* a work that essentially condenses the *halakhic* discussions of the Talmud with the aim of extracting the definitive *halakhah.*

[36] *Hilkhot Rav Alfas* to tractate *Pesahim* 17a.

[37] R. Tzidkiyahu ben Avraham haRofe lived in Rome in the thirteenth century. His work *Shibbolei ha-leket* is a collection of *halakhot* from the great sages of Babylon and the earlier scholars from Italy, France and Germany.

[38] *Shibbolei ha-leket,* par. 169.

"Everything has been made dependent on custom" – This is a proof that since they customarily acted as if it were forbidden [to work], they are not permitted to abolish their custom. To do so would be a case of "[essentially] permitted things that are treated by some people as if they were prohibited cannot become permitted to them." Furthermore, it was instituted as a statute from the time of Moshe.

R. Tzidkiyahu identifies two reasons women should continue to observe their custom: first, a practiced custom, particularly one that has been observed for many generations, cannot be nullified. Second, it is a statute fixed (the agent is unclear) during the time of Moshe.

To understand the *halakhic* approach taken by the author of *Shibbolei ha-leket* and the two reasons he cites, we must consider the sources on which he bases his ruling. In the context of the talmudic discussion[39] of the possibilities open to a woman to revoke a vow she has made, we find a *beraita* containing a ruling drawn from this verse. "If a man takes a vow to God or swears an oath to establish a prohibition upon himself, he shall not desecrate his word; according to whatever comes from his mouth he shall do."[40] The verse speaks of a man's obligation to keep any vow he utters; the Sages, though, learn from the phrase "he shall not desecrate his words" that an additional form of obligatory behavior may also be considered like a vow. That is, namely, a practice that has been scrupulously observed for a long period of time by an individual or community: observance of it must be preserved just as if a vow had been made to continue the practice until a specified time. The obligatory force involved is equivalent to that of an actual vow – it cannot be nullified or desecrated (except under certain conditions laid down by the *halakhah*):

[Essentially] permitted things that have been treated by some as if they were prohibited – you cannot permit them to yourself and thereby annul them. As the verse says, "He shall not desecrate his word."

---

[39] *Nedarim* 15a

[40] Numbers 30:3

The rule is that when an individual or a community chose, in practice, to consider something they know is essentially permitted as if it were prohibited, they must continue active preservation of that practice. Their consistent behavior over the course of time expresses a personal sort of commitment to a "vow" of deliberate stringency, forbidding themselves what is essentially permitted. There is an important condition, however: their stringency must not stem from a mistaken premise that what they wish to prohibit is essentially forbidden. Rather, it must be a conscious decision to prohibit a permitted action. This is how this law is presented in the *Tur*:[41]

"Permitted things, if people know that they are permitted but treat them as if they were forbidden – it is as if they accepted [that practice] upon themselves with a vow, and those things cannot become permitted to them…. However, permitted things that people consider forbidden under the erroneous assumption that they are indeed forbidden – in that case, their practice does not constitute a vow."

The *Shulhan Arukh*[42] states clearly that prolonged observance obligates not only the community itself who took the stringency upon themselves, but also anyone who comes to dwell in that place, as well as all future generations who dwell there:[43]

"Acceptance by the community binds them as well as their descendants. [This also holds true in matters] to which all the inhabitants of the city did not actively agree to accept, but which they willingly practice in order to make a fence and boundary for the Torah. Similarly, anyone who comes from outside to dwell in that town is considered like all its inhabitants, and is obligated by their established practice…."

Returning to the ruling of the *Shibbolei ha-leket*, his opening statements indicate that the determining factor in fixing the *halakhah* relevant for his times was the custom, observed by all the generations of women before him, to abstain from work on *Rosh Hodesh*. In citing the rule set out in the Talmud, however, concerning "those things that are permitted," he creates

---

[41] *Tur, Yoreh Deah* 214

[42] *Shulhan Arukh*, ibid. par. 2

[43] These rules are based on the Talmudim in the tractate *Pesahim*, chap. 4, which deals with the obligatory powers of a community practice or any practice observed by only a minority of the Jewish community.

an internal contradiction between that opening and the second part of his comments.

His opening statement would suggest that originally, women were allowed to work on *Rosh Hodesh* – "permitted things" – but chose, from their own initiative, to forbid themselves from doing work on *Rosh Hodesh*. This, though, is at odds with the description in the midrash, especially the words, "God gave them the reward of observing the *roshei hodashim*...."

In the second part of his comments, he states: "Furthermore it was instituted as a statute in the days of Moshe." In other words, the women of old began to observe the custom as "an externally given directive" (as opposed to something internally motivated), a statute instituted in Mosaic times.

Other unclear elements are: who it was who instituted it; why it is called a "statute" (*hok*)[44] rather than a commandment (*mitzvah*);[45] and why it does not appear, in sources written up until the end of the first millenium, as an obligatory practical teaching (rather than a description of an action women practiced, thus warranting continued observance as the Jerusalem Talmud prescribes). Finally, the *Shibbolei ha-leket* lacks a detailed explanation of the practical scope of the obligation to rest on *Rosh Hodesh*. What exactly are women permitted to do on this holy day and what is forbidden to them?

Rabbeinu Yeruham[46] presents the practical implications of the custom in his description of how women observe it:[47]

"In my opinion, those women who are accustomed to refrain from

---

[44] The expression "statute" usually describes God's command whose reason is not known and which we have to do by virtue of it being a decree. See, for example, Rashi on the opening verse concerning the red heifer (*parah adumah*) – "This is the Torah's decree [*hok*]" (Numbers 19:2). In the light of the midrashic explanation for the source of the custom to abstain from work on *Rosh Hodesh*, it seems problematic to call this custom a "statute."

[45] The sole legal authority who terms the custom a "commandment" is R. Mordekhai ben Hillel, who lived in Germany at the end of the thirteenth century and authored *Piskei Hamordekhai*, a collection of comments on the *halakhic* decisions of the Rif according to the German custom. In his comments to *Megillah*, s. 806 he writes "this commandment was given only to women because they did not take off their earrings at the time of the sin of the golden calf."

[46] Rabbeinu Yeruham ben R. Meshulam, a student of the Rosh, lived in Provence, France and Spain in the fourteenth century.

[47] Rabbeinu Yeruham, *netiv* 11, vol. 1, 52

work should do no work whatsoever. I have witnessed many women mistakenly saying, "We cannot spin, but we will do other forms of work." In accordance with their custom, work of all kinds should be either uniformly forbidden or permitted."

This statement is the earliest testimony we have found that some women did not practice abstaining from doing all types of work on *Rosh Hodesh*. Note that Rabbeinu Yeruham does not distinguish between the types of work that are permitted and those that are prohibited. Rather, he speaks of women who are accustomed to abstain from work on *Rosh Hodesh* – and their practice, he holds, obligates them to abstain from all kinds of work – and women who do not keep such a custom. The latter, he says, are permitted to do any kind of work on *Rosh Hodesh*.

From the statements of the *halakhic* authorities we have presented, it would appear that most women did have the custom of abstaining from work on *Rosh Hodesh*, and treated the day exactly as a holy day which work is universally forbidden.[48] Since women have accustomed themselves to do so over the course of numerous generations, Jewish women must continue to abstain from doing work on *Rosh Hodesh*.

Not all the legal authorities, however, share that *halakhic* standpoint. Some rule that the prohobition of doing work is not widespread; others distinguish between forbidden and permitted types of work. The distinction each authority does make concerning the various kinds of work is based on actual observation of women's practices in the time and place they themselves lived. When *halakhah* is formulated in this manner, the deciding factor is "go and see how people act, and follow them," in the talmudic formula. We find, in a variety of talmudic discussions,[49] that when doubt

---

[48] A comment in the *Tosafot* to *Megillah* 22b ד"ה ושאין בו ביטול מלאכה seems to point to a universal and widespread prohibition: "The answer is that men are certainly allowed to do work, while women are prohibited from doing so, because they did not remove their earrings at the sin of the golden calf." The authority initiating this prohibition is unidentified, but its existence is clear. It should be stressed that in the case of rulings integrated by Rashi or the Tosafot into their commentary to the Talmud, their status – solely as explications of the words of the Talmud, or as a *halakhic* ruling – is unclear. This question is treated in the responsum *Taalumot Lev* by R. Eliyahu ben R. Avraham Hazan (who lived in Egypt in the nineteenth century), vol. 3, p. 115. There he cites other works dealing with the same question.

[49] Following are two examples of *halakhic* uncertainties that were clarified by observing common practice: In *Berakhot* 45a the question arises: What is the correct blessing if

arises over how to resolve a *halakhic* question due to lack of a clear tradition, the solution is reached by observing how the community is accustomed to act concerning the issue. The principle underlying this tactic of determining the *halakhah* is that community practices are no coincidence; rather, they are based on ancient traditions whose origin have been somehow lost. Their roots go so deep, however, that they have become entrenched in communal life.

The legal authorities whose comments we have cited make clear that women had differing customs concerning the types of work that were forbidden or permitted them on *Rosh Hodesh*. Some authorities fixed the *halakhah* according to actually observed custom, while others sought to change it.

When asked the *halakhah* concerning women's obligations on *Rosh Hodesh* and how to determine them, the Rashbatz wrote:[50]

"And this is the women's *Torah* [or "teaching"] – we will ask them what their custom is, and we have nothing other than their custom [with which to guide us]."

This would suggest that the women in the Rashbatz's time and place customarily refrained only from spinning on *Rosh Hodesh*, as a commemoration of the special donations women made to the building of the *Mishkan* (as the Torah describes); other forms of work were permitted. By refraining from spinning alone, and only on *Rosh Hodesh*, those women actively perpetuated two sources of merit: the refusal to assist or abet in the sin of the golden calf, and the immediate participation in building the *Mishkan*. If this is the custom practiced by women in his generation, the Rashbatz holds, it has obligatory status; all other women are even required to act as they do. His assumption is that the custom is no coincidence, and its source is deeply rooted, apparently, in ancient tradition.

---

someone drinks water to quench his thirst? In *Shulhan Arukh, Oreh Hayyim* 204. 7 the law is formulated based on popular custom. Before drinking water, one says "*shehakol*"; afterwards, one says, "*borei nefashot*." In *Menahot* 35a the question arises: Is it permissible to tie together torn *tefillin* straps? In *Shulhan Arukh, Oreh Hayyim* 33.5 the law is also formulated based on the commonly held custom not to tie together the straps but to exchange them for other ones, unless there are pressing circumstances.

[50] *Responsa Ha-Tashbatz* 3.244.

In his work *Beit Yosef* on the *Tur*, R. Yosef Karo quotes Rabbeinu Yeru-ham's opinion that women who are accustomed to refrain from working on *Rosh Hodesh* should abstain from all forms of work. He then deliberates whether to endorse the custom practiced by women in his own era, or whether to seek to change it:[51]

"I have seen women whose practice it is to abstain from tasks done for financial profit, but who do sew/mend household clothing. But this, it seems, should also not be done; as it is the practice of women to abstain from work, they should take care not to do any form of work whatsoever. It may indeed be that this is really what they initially accepted upon them-selves – to make a differentiation from normal workdays, and because of that – they are refraining from work done for profit."

The *Beit Yosef* himelf seems to favor prohibiting women on *Rosh Hodesh* from doing any form of work that women originally forbid themselves on that day. A major factor in the equation, however, is the types of work that women initially accepted upon themselves. Since women may initially have abstained only from work done for their livelihood and not from other tasks (the custom he himself observed among women of his generation), the *halakhah* would rightly be fixed according to that custom. Accordingly, all women from then on would have to perpetuate the practice of their foremothers.[52]

Interestingly, in the *Shulhan Arukh*, R. Yosef Karo's later work, the *ha-lakhah* is presented as follows:[53]

"Work is permitted on *Rosh Hodesh*, and those women who refrain from doing any work – it is a good custom. *Note by the Rema*: And if it is the custom to do some forms of work but not others, we follow that custom (actively practiced in our days – *Beit Yosef*)."[54]

---

[51] *Beit Yosef* to *Tur*, *Oreh Hayyim* 417.

[52] The "permitted things" mentioned in the Talmud would imply, in this context, work done by a woman on *Rosh Hodesh* for her livelihood; "and other [things]" were those tasks from which women "customarily abstained – these cannot become permitted to them."

[53] *Shulhan Arukh*, *Oreh Hayyim* 417.1.

[54] See *Mishnah Berurah* 417.4. He expands on the Rema by quoting the main ideas of the *Beit Yosef*.

R. Yosef Karo's comments in the *Shulhan Arukh* contain no mention of the uncertainty he raised in his work on the *Tur*. In the *Shulhan Arukh*, all forms of work are forbidden to women who practice that custom. Here the distinction he makes is not between various forms of work, but between women – those who customarily abstain from work on *Rosh Hodesh* and those who do not. In this, he follows Rabbeinu Yeruham whom he quoted in the *Beit Yosef*.[55]

The Rema,[56] in his commentary on the *Shulhan Arukh*, includes what R. Yosef Karo himself had written in the *Beit Yosef*.

The Magen Avraham[57] found it necessary to stress the Rema's comment, "We follow the custom" by adding the distinction raised by the Beit Yosef:[58]

"Initially, this is what they accepted upon themselves *(Beit Yosef)* – that is, when they made the explicit condition; if it was not made explicit, however, there is no room for leniency."

I would like to conclude the survey of *halakhic* authorities who distinguish between forms of work based on the customs practiced by women themselves with comments voiced by R. Yehiel Michael HaLevi Epstein,[59]

---

[55] See *Mishnah Berurah* 417 in *Biur Halakhah*. The *Hafetz Hayyim*, R. Yisrael Meir HaCohen, who lived in the early twentieth century, presents the central ideas raised by the *halakhic* authorities. He then states: In truth, though, although we could say that Rabbeinu Yeruham intends to be lenient here; even so, we should not be lenient. Most of the earlier *halakhic* authorities [*ha-poskim ha-rishonim*] seem to hold that the issue does not depend on contemporary women [of any particular generation]; rather, their obligation is perpetuated from their foremothers in generations passed. See *Shibbolei ha-leket*, who says it was established it as a statute in the time of Moshe; this is the opinion of the *Rokeah* and the *Or Zarua* as well. They simply wrote that women are forbidden to work. The same can be understood from the *Eshkol*, and it is also the view of *Avudraham, Sefer ha-manhig;* the opinion of Rashi and the Tosafot in *Megillah* and other places is definitely consistent with it…."

[56] The Rema, R. Moshe Isserles, wrote comments to the *Shulhan Arukh* based on the *Ashkenazic* custom. He lived in sixteenth century Poland, and Ashkenazic customs are fixed according to his notes.

[57] *Magen Avraham* – a commentary with *halakhic* additions to the *Shulhan Arukh, Oreh Hayyim*, written by R. Avraham Evli Gumbiner, who lived in Poland in the seventeenth century.

[58] *Magen Avraham, Shulhan Arukh*, loc. cit.

[59] R. Yechiel Michael HaLevi Epstein, one of the great rabbis of nineteenth century White Russia (who passed away at the beginning of the twentieth century) authored

author of *Arukh Hashulhan*. He summarizes the sources concerning women's abstaining from work on *Rosh Hodesh* (*Pirkei deRabbi Eliezer*, the discussions in the Babylonian and Jerusalem Talmud) and the opinions of *halakhic* authorities before him. In his own decision, the author of *Arukh Hashulhan* follows the ruling of the *Shulhan Arukh* in principle, but his decision is different in practice:[60]

"If there is a custom to do some forms of work but not others, we follow the custom, as long as it is known there is already such a custom. But without this women are forbidden to do any form of work. In our community, the wives of working men abstain from work, but women who have a trade do work; we must say that they did not take it upon themselves to damage their livelihood."

Nineteenth century reality was quite different from that of the sixteenth century. The testimony of the Beit Yosef leads us to understand that in his times, women took care to abstain, on *Rosh Hodesh*, from work done for their livelihood, but they did permit themselves to do other tasks. The reason: that was the practice they had taken upon themselves from the very beginning, and the *halakhah* was thus fixed in accordance. In the nineteenth century, in contrast, the complete opposite was true. Women abstained from all work on *Rosh Hodesh* except for work in which they specialized and earned their living. The reason: out of fear that if they abstained from working on *Roshei Hodashim* they would lose their source of income. Hence, we see that the *Arukh Hashulhan* ruled, in principle, like most of the *halakhic* authorities that a distinction should be made between forms of work that are forbidden and those permitted to women on *Rosh Hodesh*. The distinction is made in practice by observing the prevailing customs actually held among women on *Rosh Hodesh*.

This approach, in sum, seems to me to provide a wonderful example of "go with the *halakhah*" or, in other words, "*halakhic* development." It draws its strength from the principle that guided *halakhic* authorities throughout the generations when questions arose over the correct ruling: "Go out and see what people do" and act accordingly.

Arukh Hashulhan. It addresses most of the *Shulhan Arukh*, explaining the sources cited by the *Shulhan Arukh* and notes by the Rema.

[60] *Arukh Hashulhan, Oreh Hayyim* 417.

On one hand, *halakhic* authorities are careful to preserve observance of an age-old women's tradition, and hold *Rosh Hodesh* as a *yom tov* – that is, a festive day on which some or all work is prohibited. On the other hand, their sensitivity and responsiveness to changing needs and conditions is highly evident in their endorsement of change in actual custom in accordance with what women do in each historical context.

3. "God gave them their reward – to observe *Roshei Ho-daoshim…*"[61] – But do they really?

All the *halakhic* authorities we have cited consider women's abstaining from some or all forms of work on *Rosh Hodesh* to be a custom women took upon themselves in ancient times (perhaps even in the wilderness) as a tangible expression of their reward for refusing to help in making the golden calf and for contributing gladly in building the *Mishkan*.

R. Yoel Sirkas,[62] in his work on the *Tur* entitled *Bayit Hadash*, makes an interesting *halakhic* innovation concerning the practical implication of the words, cited in the title of this section, from the midrash:[63]

"Thus, there is certainly no prohibition on women if they chose to work…. Rather, the reward God gave them was to observe *Rosh Hodesh* – in that the husband cannot force his wife to do work. As it says in the Jerusalem Talmud: Women who customarily refrain from work on *Rosh Hodesh* – it is a custom, in other words, her husband cannot compel her…. This was apparently decided to instruct the men and to warn them not to force their wives to work on *Rosh Hodesh*. It is no transgression, however, if she does work. When a few women are seen to work, then, and we do not impede them, we can be sure no transgression is involved, as I explained [above]."

Thus, although it is termed a "prohibition" [*issur*], it applies only to the head of the household and constrains him from forcing his wife to work…. But if either he or she wants to do work – no prohibition would be trans-

---

[61] *Pirkei deRabbi Eliezer*, ch. 45.

[62] R. Yoel Sirkas, lived in Poland in the seventeenth century. In his work *Bayit Hadash* (*Bach*) on the *Tur*, he explains and expands on the contents of the *Tur*. At times he challenges the *Beit Yosef* and often concurs with the *Maharshal*.

[63] *Bayit Hadash* on the *Tur*, *Oreh Hayyim* 417 ד"ה ולפי זה נראה

gressed, not even a rabbinical prohibition. This is the practice followed by everyone. The *halakhah* we follow, then, is to avoid forcing women to work. If they wish to, however – even difficult labor is permitted.

The Bach holds that women are not prohibited from any form of work whatsoever on *Rosh Hodesh*. The reward God gave them is that in those days, around twelve times a year, their husbands are not allowed to force them to do work of any kind, unlike all other days on which their husbands can force them to do perform their household duties.[64]

R. Yoel Sirkas was and remains the only *halakhic* authority who considers this to be the practical *halakhic* interpretation of the statement, "God gave them the reward of observing *Rosh Hodesh* more than the men."

Halakhic authorities after the Bach disagree with him. R. Yisrael Meir HaCohen writes in the *Mishnah Berurah*:[65]

"The Bach's view is different. He holds that the custom is not meant to exert stringency on women by preventing them from doing work on this day. Rather, it expresses leniency: if they themselves wish to work, even difficult labor, they can surely do so, but their husbands cannot force them to work. (Excluding housework such as cooking and baking, etc.)… But none of the *halakhic* authorities I have presented above concur with this; in their view, women themselves have a *mitzvah* to abstain from work on *Rosh Hodesh* [and as a result the husband can surely not force her to work]."

The *Mishnah Berurah* quotes the Bach while constricting him somewhat. He suggests the Bach himself held that a husband can force his wife to do housework – an idea I do not see in the Bach's words.[66] After close examination of all the halakhic opinions he mentions, however, R. Yisrael Meir HaCohen rules in principle not in accordance with the opinion of the Bach.

Although the novel suggestion, with its interpretative and practical ramifications, raised by the Bach was not formally adopted as *halakhah*, I think it's very important to try and understand what led an authority of the

---

[64] See notes 33, 34.

[65] See note 55 for the source.

[66] Please note that the minimization of the *Bach* suggested in the *Mishnah Berurah*, i.e., that the husband can force his wife to do housework, is not only absent from the *Bach*'s actual words, but that the *Bach* actually stresses the fact that a husband cannot force his wife to do any kind of work on *Rosh Hodesh* because of her privilege that described in the *Pirkei deRabbi Eliezer*, ch. 45.

stature of R. Yoel Sirkas to raise it. The question is intensified when we see that it is somewhat at odds with the language of the midrash. There, the reward the women received is that "they observe the *Roshei Hodashim*." I would like to introduce some possibilities in understanding his *halakhic* decision based on our discussion.

1. As we have seen, actual observance of the custom by women throughout the generations is quite varied. In some times and places women do not seem to have kept the custom to abstain from work on *Rosh Hodesh* at all (as Rabbeinu Yeruham suggested), while others did observe the custom. The forms of work that women prohibited or permitted to themselves varied and were even reversed (the *Beit Yosef* versus the *Arukh Hashulhan*). Thus, in the course of no era was there a custom observed in a coherent, uniform and obligatory manner, passed from mother to daughter, concerning the forms of work that are permitted or forbidden (if at all) to women on *Rosh Hodesh*. The Bach may have observed a variety of ways in which women kept the custom; perhaps he thought that if some women do work (of various kinds) on *Rosh Hodesh*, then work itself is not forbidden. The issue, then, would be that others cannot force them to work.

2. Contemplating more deeply on the nature of the reward God gave the women, it seems very strange that their recompense for such outstanding behavior would be the compulsion not to work on a particular day (recurring throughout the year) when no one else abstains from working. Another obvious problem is in partaking of this reward, for the work that women do centers on taking care for their husbands and children and tending to household needs – tasks that require constant vigilance. Resting from it one day each month is no easy endeavor. Beyond that, we could easily imagine that if a woman rests from work while her spouse and others around her continue to function as usual, she might well feel somewhat uncomfortable. This is not a festive day for the entire Jewish people, but for a part of it.

This practical difficulty and the discomfort involved may be one reason for the deterioration of the custom of women's abstaining from work on

Rosh Hodesh in commemoration of their great merits, and its constriction to certain times and specific communities.[67]

3. Perhaps the Bach's unique interpretation stems from the idea that the greatest reward a person can receive is full independence to "be one's own boss" – to set one's own schedule and activities, plan one's free time, etc. Such a reward is especially great for women, who (certainly until recent generations) were subservient to their husbands. Maybe that is why the Bach innovates as he does. The reward given women for all generations, in memory of the heroism of their foremothers in the wilderness, as he sees it, is no subjugation or prohibition. It is liberation, the total freedom to do whatever work each woman wishes, and a corresponding prohibition on her husband, like anyone else to whom she is subservient, from obligating her to do anything. And it may be that the conception underlying R. Yoel Sirkas's novel explanation was something like this: On *Rosh Hodesh* the woman is subservient to no one other than God Himself. Hence her freedom to act in accordance with her own thoughts, emotions and will. Through his novel explanation, the Bach draws a deep, inner connection between the women's refusal to give their jewelry to make the golden calf (an object of idolatry) and the reward God gave them. God, as it were, said to the women: By refusing to take part in idolatry, a refusal that required determination and courage, you have expressed your faith in Me and your loyalty to Me alone. As a reward, I will give you a special day that occurs twelve times a year on which you will be free from subjugation to any other human being. When you abstain from work on *Rosh Hodesh*, and when subsequent generation of women continue to observe this custom vigilantly, all women will remember, and the Jewish people as a whole, in each generation will remember, month by month, the precious, inner faith in God that was instilled in the hearts of Jewish women throughout the exile in Egypt and in the wilderness.

---

[67] For more on this, see the conclusion of my discussion, in which I focus on this women's custom in its varied forms.

Conclusion

The source of the custom for women to abstain from work on *Rosh Hodesh*, as we have seen, is the midrash *Pirkei deRabbi Eliezer*, a work attributed to R. Eliezer ben Horkanous[68] — one of the great *tannaic* Sages.

Aside from this midrashic passage describing the event that led to the women's reward, treated extensively in our discussion, there is no testimony from the *tannaic* period mentioning women actually observing this custom. This includes the six orders of the *Mishnah*, the *beraitot*, *Tosefta*, as well as *halakhic* and *aggadic* midrashim compiled in the period of the *tannaim*.

The only indirect testimony is a *beraita* that appears in the Babylonian Talmud: *Rosh Hodesh* is brought as an example of a day on which it is permissible for more people to ascend to the reading of the *Torah*, because on this day work is prohibited. Rashi and the authors of the *Tosafot* resolve the contradiction between this *beraita* and the rule in the Talmud in *Hagigah* that work on *Rosh Hodesh* is permitted by saying that on *Rosh Hodesh* work is not prohibited, but women do not work.

Rosh Hodesh was probably mentioned in the *beraita* as an example of a day on which work is prohibited due to the custom, apparently common during *tannaic* times, for women to abstain from work on *Rosh Hodesh*. We can conclude indirectly, then, from these comments in the Babylonian Talmud that the custom was kept by women in practice as early as the times of the *tannaim*.[69]

The first direct testimony we have that women were accustomed to abstain from work on *Rosh Hodesh* dates from the period of the *amoraim*.[70] In the Jerusalem Talmud, we find the statement: "*Rosh Hodesh* — is a custom." This would imply that the custom women have to refrain from work on *Rosh Hodesh* is proper and correct, and should be perpetuated.

[68] R. Eliezer ha-Gadol clearly did not write, collect, or edit the entire contents of *Pirkei deRabbi Eliezer*, for that collection includes midrashim quoting *Tannaim* who lived after R. Eliezer. The title is due to chapters describing the life of R. Eliezer ha-Gadol and traditions preserved in his name.

[69] The period of the *tannaim* extended from the days of the second Temple until the conclusion of the *Mishnah* by R. Yehudah ha-Nasi in 220 C.E.

[70] The period of the *Amoraim* began with the conclusion of the *Mishnah* and lasted until about 400 C.E. in Israel and until about 500 C.E. in Babylon.

From the *rishonim* and *ahronim* who relate to the women's custom, we obtain the following picture:[71]

All the *halakhic* authorities recognized clearly the women's custom to refrain completely from doing work on *Rosh Hodesh*, both from sources that preceded them and from observing women in their close environment. The majority of those women were stringent in active observance of the custom to abstain from work on *Rosh Hodesh*. Some *halakhic* authorities distinguished between women who observe the custom and are thus obligated to continue observing it, and those who did not observe it and are therefore not obligated to do so. Some *halakhic* authorities made a distinction between different forms of work – tasks that women are permitted to do on *Rosh Hodesh* and tasks they are prohibited from doing.

The common denominator shared by all the *halakhic* authorities is that their *halakhic* decision concerning the practical consequences of the midrashic source is based on the behavior of women around them. This follows the principle to "go out and see what people do." We can conclude, then, that the custom was actually observed and hence was recognized well by all the *halakhic* authorities.

We find testimony already in the writings of Rabbeinu Yeruham (from the period of the *rishonim*) that some women were not stringent in keeping this custom. Most of the *halakhic* authorities presented in this essay, though, describe a custom that was observed in their time, albeit in a variety of ways and with varying emphases. For example:

In some generations, women were very careful to refrain from spinning on *Rosh Hodesh*, in commemoration of their involvement and donations of spun items in the building of the *Mishkan* – but allowed themselves to do other forms of work on *Rosh Hodesh* (as the Rashbatz describes).

In other generations, women customarily did all forms of work within the home but did not work on *Rosh Hodesh* for their livelihood (as the *Beis Yosef* testifies).

---

[71] The period of the *rishonim* dates from the first *halakhic* authorities after the period of the *geonim* (from the ninth century) until the expulsion from Spain at the end of the fifteenth century. The period of the *ahronim* is considered to be from the end of the period of the *rishonim* until about the nineteenth century, when the period of the *ahronei ahronim* began.

In different periods, women practiced the opposite: they permitted themselves to work on *Rosh Hodesh* for their livelihood so they should not lose the source of their income, but abstained from doing housework (as described in *Arukh Hashulhan*).

The urgent question, then, is why women have not observed this custom for the last hundred years. After all, it is a continual recollection of the uniqueness of Jewish women, and serves as a remembrance for generations of the significant part they played in the redemption of the Jews from Egypt. Observance of this custom bears witness to a heritage of profound, authentic faith in God. It has been kept by women throughout history (at least from the times of the *Tannaim* and until the end of the nineteenth century), and won honor, appreciation and encouragement by *halakhic* authorities. All this makes it extremely difficult to understand why women have largely abandoned this custom, particularly in our age of striving for equality between the sexes and recognition of unique qualities of women.

I have no clear or unequivocal answer to this question. But I would like to raise some possibilities:

In our days especially, new developments are taking place in the status of women. They are called upon to perform two complicated and difficult tasks: on one hand, to fulfill their Jewish purpose of (it seems to me) bearing and raising children while maintaining responsibility for the continual upkeep of the home.[72] On the other hand, they are overtly or covertly expected to help financially.

Particularly in times such as these, when women are weighed down with obligations, it is only natural and logical that the custom would be eroded until it is effectively nullified in practice. If women would abstain from working a whole day each month they would face a two-fold danger:

1. Fulfillment of all their household tasks, neglected on *Rosh Hodesh,* would be even more difficult; on the morning after *Rosh Hodesh* women would awaken to a new day tightly filled with tasks. Life, as we know, continues with all its demands.

---

[72] This does not mean that the husband cannot help his wife in certain tasks such as child-care and housework. Yet despite the significant changes that have occurred over the last few decades in the status of women, these functions are still unfortunately viewed as "unmanly," and consciously or unconsciously placed upon women — something I hope will change in the future with God's help.

2. In our modern world, few jobs exist that would be attainable to a woman who demanded being absent for a whole day each month. Keeping this custom would threaten women with losing the source of their livelihood.

It seems to me that this is the process that has led to fewer and fewer women abstaining from work on *Rosh Hodesh*.[73] Now in only a very small number of Jewish communities in the world do women observe this incredible custom zealously guarded by generations of Jewish women.

As we have seen, in every era *halakhah* has been shaped according to actual practice. The writings of the *halakhic* authorities preserve the inner core of the custom of women abstaining from work on *Rosh Hodesh* in accordance with what the women in each time could prohibit and permit themselves to do. Precisely for this reason, women of our generation should not abandon the custom of their foremothers totally. Its perpetuation throughout history should remind us and the entire Jewish nation of the merits instilled in Jewish women throughout times of exile, enslavement, decrees and wandering. These merits stemmed from the sincere, autonomous faith they had in the Creator, their self-determination and their total recognition that He created everything.

May it be God's will to enlighten our eyes, and may He show us how to continue observing the essential custom of refraining from work on *Rosh Hodesh*. May that day be formed so that the entire community and the women within it can experience *Rosh Hodesh* as a festive day, the women's festival with all its implications. And, at the same time, may God grant us the strength to continue fulfilling the obligations women have set for themselves.

---

[73] At the end of presentations that I give on this topic, I usually address the audience with the request to tell me of any encounters they may have had, however minimal, with actual observance of *Rosh Hodesh*. Occasionally, a women (usually older) will come and tell me that her mother would refrain only from sewing on *Rosh Hodesh* (perhaps to commemorate the prohibition of spinning on *Rosh Hodesh*). Or someone might say that in her family the women would not cook on *Rosh Hodesh*. Each time, though, I am surprised and saddened at how few testimonies there are. Nearly each time I present this topic, listeners have been recognizably surprised to hear that an explicit *halakhah* deeply rooted in midrashic tradition is hardly kept nowadays.

It is our hope that in our time and in the future we will merit that *ha-lakhic* authorities can enact the injunction to "Go out and see what the people do, and act accordingly."

CANDLELIGHTING

Leora Bednarsh

There is a general principle regarding blessings said on *mitzvot*, called *over le-asiyatan* (עובר לעשייתן), which requires that the blessing precede the performance of the *mitzvah*. The source for this principle is found in the tractate *Pesahim* 7b. While discussing the proper formulation of the blessing on the burning of the leftover *hametz* on the day before Pesach, Shmuel states, "On all *mitzvot*, the blessing is recited before the performance of the *mitzvah, over le-asiyatan*."

This requirement of precedence of the blessing may be understood in a number of ways, each of them perhaps reflecting a different understanding of the nature of the blessings over *mitzvot*. One way may be to see the blessings as praise of God for giving us the *mitzvot*, or for granting us the ability to fulfill the commandments. This fits very nicely with the phraseology of the blessings: "Blessed are You, our God, King of the universe, Who has sanctified us with His commandments and has commanded us...." In this understanding, however, the relevance of the requirement that the blessing precede the action is not completely obvious. Perhaps it is the anticipation of performing the *mitzvah* that inspires this expression of praise. Alternatively, the blessing may be an expression of praise for the command itself (*hiyyuv*) as opposed to the performance of the *mitzvah*, and that command only exists prior to the performance of the *mitzvah*.

R. Joseph B. Soloveitchik *z"l* has a different understanding of the blessings of the *mitzvot*. He compares them to *berakhot ha-nehenim*, blessings said over "enjoyment" or "pleasures" such as eating and drinking. Just as these blessings serve to grant us "permission" (*heter*) to partake in the pleasures of the world, so too the blessings on the *mitzvot* allow us to come closer to God through the performance of His commandments. This understanding, of course, stems from the requirement of preceding the performance with the blessing. One asks for permission before one does something.

A third understanding of the purpose of blessings over *mitzvot,* and in turn the requirement of having recitation of the blessing precede performance of the *mitzvah* (עובר לעשייתן) is brought by R. Yom Tov ibn Asevilli (the Ritva) on *Pesahim.* He suggests that the blessing serves to "set the mood" of the *mitzvah.* Before performing the act, a person reminds him or herself and announces that the reason for the act about to be done is God's commandment and the purpose is to fulfill the *mitzvah.*

There are some noted exceptions to the requirement of reciting the blessing before performance of the *mitzvah,* generally in situations in which there is a conflicting requirement. The classic exception discussed in the Talmud is the ritual immersion of a convert. Before the convert dips in the *mikvah* he or she is not a Jew, and is thus not required to say blessings or do *mitzvot;* for that reason, he or she cannot say the blessing before the action of immersion in the *mikvah.* Once the immersion is completed, the convert is now a Jew and can say the blessing, and does. Another exception is the blessing over the washing of the hands before eating bread. Since one cannot say *berakhot* when one's hands are not clean, the blessing is said after the washing of the hands. Interestingly, the *halakhah* is that one should say the blessing before one dries one's hands. To eat bread with wet hands is considered to be distasteful; drying one's hands, then, is still part of the *mitzvah* of washing before eating bread, and saying the blessing at that point, before drying the hands, preserves the requirement of preceding performance with recitation of the blessing.

Another exception, well known nowadays, is the blessing over candle lighting on Shabbat eve. R. Moshe Isserles, the Rema, in his gloss on the *Shulhan Arukh* brings two opinions about when the blessing should be said. One opinion is that it should be said before the lighting of the candles, just like all other *mitzvot,* in order to fulfill the requirement of precedence. The other opinion is that the blessing should be said after the lighting of the candles. Similar to the compromise we saw in hand washing, in order to fulfill the requirement of preceding the act with the blessing one should light, then cover one's eyes while saying the blessing, and then uncover one's eyes and look at the candles. To understand this second opinion, which is in effect our custom, we need to understand what the conflicting requirement is that necessitates saying the blessing after the performance of the *mitzvah*. This requires an excursion into the laws of *kabbalat Shabbat*, the acceptance of the Shabbat.

Observance of Shabbat involves the concept of "adding on from the profane to the holy" (להוסיף מחול על הקודש) and, specifically, *tosefet Shabbat*, which requires adding some time considered to belong to the weekday onto Shabbat. Most of the *Rishonim* see this as a positive commandment to start the Shabbat earlier than is literally necessary (sunset) and ending it slightly later than absolutely required (nightfall). When performing this *mitzvah*, by blurring the demarcations of the Shabbat day and allowing it to spill over on both ends into the "profane" week, one is effectively infusing the holiness of Shabbat into one's everyday life. The amount of time that should be added seems to be variable, as long as one accepts Shabbat at least a few minutes before sunset, the time preceding nightfall, yet no longer definitively daylight. The widespread custom in most of the world nowadays is to accept Shabbat eighteen minutes before sunset. (In Jerusalem, the *minhag* is to accept Shabbat forty minutes before sunset).

In order to fulfill this *mitzvah* of *tosefet Shabbat*, adding from the weekday to Shabbat, one must actively accept Shabbat at a time when the prohibitions that so characterize Shabbat do not necessarily apply. It is an active acceptance of the holiness and beauty of Shabbat, not a passive imposition of the prohibitions of Shabbat. How does one signify or enact this acceptance of Shabbat? The general custom is that the community accepts Shabbat together in prayer, with the recitation of *Kabbalat Shabbat* in the synagogue.

The *mitzvah* of candle lighting has come to signify for many the accepting of Shabbat. This is certainly true among women, who customarily are the ones who light the candles (although the *mitzvah* is obligatory upon men as well as women).

The *mitzvah* of candle lighting, while not of biblical origin, has had great significance attached to it in the course of *halakhic* history. A few indications of the importance attached to this *mitzvah*: Even a poor person who has trouble finding food to eat must beg on doorsteps for oil with which to light a candle for Shabbat. A women who once forgets to light candles must, every subsequent Shabbat, light an additional candle as a "fine" – this *halakhah* is brought by the Rema. There are several themes or reasons for candle lighting. One of the themes is *kavod Shabbat*, honoring the Shabbat by preparing for it properly. Connected with this theme is the obligation to light candles soon enough before Shabbat so that it is recognizable that they are being lit for the sake of Shabbat. This has been determined to mean no earlier that an hour and a quarter before sunset. The most prominent reason is *oneg Shabbat*, the enjoyment of Shabbat. This is connected with the theme of *shalom bayit*, peace in the home. One must ensure a pleasurable atmosphere is one's home on Shabbat, an atmosphere that will lead to enjoyment and comfort. The prohibitions that accompany Shabbat, such as the inability to cook and to kindle a flame, have the danger of making Shabbat seem too restrictive and, if not prepared for properly, uncomfortable and unpleasant. In reality, Shabbat is meant to be a time of rest, of relaxation, of enjoyment. If one takes the proper precautions, by preparing tasty food in advance, and insuring that it will remain warm for the meals, and by making sure that the house is well lit by lighting candles where they are needed, then one sets up an environment of peace, tranquility, and comfort. I believe it is for this reason that the *mitzvah* of candle lighting has taken on such significance, because it represents a theme that is so crucial to the way one observes Shabbat overall. It can transform Shabbat from a potentially oppressive and uncomfortable day to a day of warmth and peace.

This also might be why candle lighting has come to be so integrally linked with the active acceptance of Shabbat upon oneself, *kabbalat Shabbat*. Ensuring an atmosphere of enjoyment by providing enough light in the home and welcoming Shabbat early through an overt act both emphasize the positive and liberating aspects of Shabbat as opposed to the restrictive ones.

There are two opinions in the *Shulhan Arukh* concerning the connection between accepting Shabbat (*kabbalat Shabbat*) and candle lighting; these opinions have an impact on the matter with which we began – the timing of the blessing. The first opinions says that the two, acceptance of Shabbat and the lighting of the candles, have nothing to do with each other, and that Shabbat is accepted with the actual *Kabbalat Shabbat* prayer in *shul*. The blessing over the candles should therefore be recited before the lighting of the candles, like all other *mitzvot*, so that it will precede the action. The second opinion says that one accepts Shabbat through recitation of the blessing. The blessing must therefore be recited only after the candles are lit, since with the blessing all of the prohibitions take effect, making the kindling of a flame prohibited. The Rema states that the custom follows the second opinion, and therefore we light the candles, cover our eyes, recite the blessing, and uncover our eyes immediately and gaze at the candles, as explained above.

What if a person states explicitly that he or she is not accepting the Shabbat with the lighting of the candles? The need to do this comes up in certain situations – for example, if one still needs to do tasks or acts that are prohibited on Shabbat (*melakhah*) after one lights the candles, such as driving in a car to *shul* when planning to return home for dinner. According to the first opinion brought in the *Shulḥan Arukh* (in the name of the Bahag – *Baal Halakhot Gedolot*) that Shabbat is accepted with the blessing over the lighting of the candles, there seems to be no possibility of doing *melakhah* after candle lighting. What would happen if the person lights candles with the explicit condition in mind that he or she is *not* accepting Shabbat with the lighting of those candles? Those who follow the opinion of the Bahag disagree. Some say that the condition is effective; others argue that it is ineffective – once the candles are lit, Shabbat has come, and *melakhah* is prohibited. According to the second opinion, however, which holds that the acceptance of the Shabbat has nothing to do with candle lighting, actions that are prohibited on Shabbat can be done even after the candles have been lit – up to the time that the community accepts Shabbat. That is at the recitation of *Kabbalat Shabbat* in *shul*.

The Rema adds that the custom is that when a *woman* lights candles without making the explicit condition that she is *not* accepting Shabbat with this lighting, she automatically accepts Shabbat when she says the blessing over the kindling. If she does make such a condition, however, then she is not considered to have accepted Shabbat yet. (This condition need not be spoken; having it in mind is sufficient). This applies specifically to women because the custom of accepting Shabbat with the lighting of the candles (as the Bahag holds) has always been much more prevalent among women than among men. The *Mishnah Berurah*, though, notes that if a man is lighting and intends to do work afterwards, it is preferable for him to make the condition as well. The *Mishnah Berurah* also states that since some opinions hold that this condition is ineffective, and that Shabbat begins once the candles are lit, one should use this condition only in a time of dire need.

An interesting *halakhic* custom was put into practice by a woman named Beila, the wife of R. Yehoshua Falk Katz, famous for his commentaries on the *Tur* (*Derishah U-Perishah*) and the *Shulhan Arukh* (the Sma, an acronym for *Sefer Meirat Enayim*), and the daughter of R. Yisrael Eidels, a communal leader of the Jewish community in Lemberg during the sixteenth century. She was noted for her piety, charity and erudition, and her son in his preface to the *Derishah U-Perishah* cites several *halakhic* customs she initiated. In light of the tension, described above, between *kabbalat Shabbat* through candle lighting and the requirement that the blessings over *mitzvot* precede their performance, she innovated the following custom. She reasoned that since on festivals (unlike Shabbat) it is permissible to transfer (although not to ignite or extinguish) a flame, no conflict exists between accepting the sanctity of *Yom Tov* with its prohibitions and reciting the blessing over candle lighting, and then lighting the candles after that acceptance. For that reason, she held, on *Yom Tov* a woman should reverse the order practiced on Shabbat: first she should say the blessing and then light the candles.

With the exception of the Magen Avraham, one of the great commentators on the *Shulhan Arukh*, this innovation was accepted. The Magen Avraham's objection to this practice was based on the principle that no distinction should be made between such similar actions – לא פלוג. The principle means that in similar situations, a minimal number of distinctions should be made in order to limit confusion. Once it is decided that the blessings should be said at a particular time on Shabbat, this should apply to all occasions on which candles are lit. He brings other instances in which the principle applies. For example, the *Tosafot* conclude, based on the exception presented above of the case of the convert's immersion, that one should always, in all circumstances, immerse in the *mikvah* first and recite the blessing for immersion only afterwards. R. Yehezkel Landau, in his gloss on the *Shulhan Arukh*, defends the *minhag* practiced by Beila, the wife of the Derishah. He argues that the case of candle lighting on Shabbat and Yom Tov is not one in which the principle of minimizing the number of distinctions (לא פלוג) need apply: since the text of the blessing is different in each case, reversing the order will not lead to confusion. In addition, he responds to the Magen Avraham that if the Rabbis applied the principle of *lo plug* to all *mitzvot* involving candle lighting irrespective of the wording of the blessing, then the blessing over Hanukah candles should also be said after they are lit. That, however, is not our practice. R. Landau thus favors the innovation of the wife of the Derishah, and concludes by praising her as a "...woman whose heart was elevated in wisdom" (after Exodus 36:2).

WOMEN AND *ZIMMUN*

RABBI JOEL B. WOLOWELSKY

The *Zimmun*

One of the formal ways of expressing the idea that those eating together have transcended their individual identities is the *zimmun*, the "call" (*"Haverai nevarekh...berishut..."*) that precedes the Grace after Meals, *birkhat hamazon*. "Three who ate as one," says the Mishnah, "are required [to say] the *zimmun*."[1] The Mishnah seems to be referring to any three people who ate together, but most people associate the *zimmun* only with men, so much so that many *birkonim* introduce it with the instruction, "If three or more men ate together, the following is added before *birkat hamazon*." The *zimmun*, however, involves women as well, and their obligation has an interesting development that is worth examining in some detail.

The Classic Sources

The original talmudic source in *Arakhin* seems straightforward enough: "All [including women, presumably] are obligated in *zimmun*."[2] The subsequent *halakhic* development over the ages, however, has led us in a slightly different direction. Let's review this interesting process briefly, leaving out some of the subtle digressions that various authorities have taken over the centuries.

The *Arakhin* text quotes the *baraita* from *Berakhot* 45b:

> Women recite the *zimmun* among themselves and slaves recite the *zimmun* among themselves. But if a group of women, slaves and minors want to recite the *zimmun*, they may not.

---

[1] Mishnah *Berakhot* 7:1; *Berakhot* 45a.

[2] *Arakhin* 3a.

Rashi interprets this to mean that women are not obligated to recite *birkat hazimmun,* but may do so if they wish;[3] Tosafot agree with this reasoning.[4] Tur, quoting Rosh, notes that this goes against the face reading of the text in *Arakhin,* which seems to obligate women; yet he accepts Rashi's interpretation in order to reconcile the text with the accepted custom in Ashkenaz that women do not have this obligation in *zimmun.*[5] Semag, quoted by the Bet Yosef, attempts to avoid violence to the literal meaning of the text by interpreting the *Gemara* in *Arakhin* as referring to a case in which the women ate with three or more men, while the *Gemara* in *Berakhot* refers to a situation in which three or more women ate together without any men present. In the former case they are obligated to recite *birkhat ha-zimmun,* while in the latter case it is optional.[6] (Tur contends that this was a practical way of reconciling the talmudic texts that seem to suggest that they have an obligation to do so with the then-current practice of women not reciting the *zimmun.*)

The Current Halakhic Position

The *Shulhan Arukh* codifies the current *halakhic* position: when three or more women eat without men being present, they are exempt from the obligation in *zimmun,* but may recite it if they wish. Women who eat with three or men become obligated in the *zimmun* required of the men.[7] (The Vilna Gaon is among the later authorities who side with Rosh in obligating three women to say *birkat hazimmun* even if they ate together without any men present. All agree, however, that ten women eating together would not add the word "*Elokeinu,*" as that requires a quorum of ten adult men.[8]) Ben Ish Hai suggests that the women in a household should recite the *zimmun* when they eat together.[9] That current practice in many homes is the

---

[3] *Berakhat* 45b, s.v., *shani.*

[4] *Berakhot* 45b, s.v., *shani.*

[5] *Tur Shulhan Arukh, Oreh Hayyim* 199.

[6] Ibid., s.v. *she-yesh mefarshim lekayem.*

[7] *Shulhan Arukh, Oreh Hayyim* 199.7.

[8] Ibid., *Beurei Ha-Gra.* This was anticipated by *Sefer ha-Rokeah,* no. 333; Rambam, *Mishneh Torah, Hilkot Berakhot* 5.7; *Shulhan Arukh, Oreh Hayyim* 199.6.

[9] *Parashat Korah,* par. 13.

opposite should cause us to ponder. The fact that many women do not regularly say the *zimmun* may actually not reflect any particular ideal but rather an accommodation to an unfortunate situation. The *Mishnah Berurah* suggests that the Rabbis exempted women from the obligation in *birkhat hazimmun* if fewer than three men ate with them simply because they felt that most women could not recite *birkhat hazimmun* and hence it would be unfair to obligate them.[10] (Tosafot take for granted that women do not understand *birkhat hazimmun* when they hear it.[11])

It is surprising, then, that any contemporary woman would want to take advantage of the exemption *Hazal* provided based on the social reality of their day. Unquestionably, women are permitted to say the *zimmun*. Declining to do so simply perpetuates, in many ways, the presumption that contemporary women are too ignorant to be able to recite the *zimmun* or that they could not understand a *berakhah* as men could. Women reciting the *zimmun* when they eat together is nothing more than a natural consequence of a woman's new high standard of Torah education.

Whether or not three women are *halakhically* obligated to say the *zimmun*, there is no doubt that they may if they wish. As we saw, *Shulhan Arukh* takes specific note of this,[12] as do contemporary *halakhic* guides for women.[13] If three or more men were present, the women would have to defer to them in forming the *zimmun*; within *halakhah*, obligation takes precedence over volunteerism, and the three men are obligated. R. Shelomo Zalman Auerbach ruled that the presence of one or two men eating with three women presents no impediment to saying *birkhat hazimmun*; in such a case one of the women rather than one of the men should lead the *zimmun*, but the men should answer.[14]

We can thus understand why a women's *zimmun* is a regular

---

[10] *Mishnah Berurah* to *Shulhan Arukh, Oreh Hayyim* (M.B.) 199, n. 16.

[11] *Berakhot* 45b., s.v. *shani*.

[12] *Shulhan Arukh, Oreh Hayyim* 199.7.

[13] For example, R. David Auerbach, *Halikhot beita* (Jerusalem, 5743 [1983]), 12.6, p. 93ff; and R. Yitzhak Yaakov Fuchs, *Halikhot bat yisrael* (Jerusalem, 1983), 3.14, p. 62.

[14] Quoted in Rabbi David Auerbach, *Halikhot beita*, 12.6, n. 14. R. Yehuda Herzl Henkin (*Benei banim* 3:1) notes that in such coed situations, the *zimmun* may be led by one of the two men who are present with the three or more women.

phenomenon in modern religious homes when, say, parents eat with their son and two daughters. Young girls look forward to their reaching the age of *bat mitzvah*, when they too may be counted for the family *zimmun*. (In Sephardic custom, two men can include an older minor boy in order to say *birkhat hazimmun*. Similarly, two Sephardic women may include an older minor girl to form the quorum required for saying the *zimmun*.[15]) Certainly students in a girl's yeshiva high school or junior high school should introduce lunchtime *birkhat hamazon* with the *zimmun*, as should those in a coed yeshiva in which the *zimmun* is said in small groups of people who ate together.

The Coed *Zimmun*

The permissibility of three women or three men joining together to form a *zimmun* is uncontested. However, that is not the case for two men and one women, or for two women and one man. This ruling has an interesting development, and we will, once again quickly review the classic sources.

The Mishnah rules that "women, slaves and children – one may not recite the *zimmun* with them."[16] The Gemara states that women, slaves and minors may not join together to say *birkhat hazimmun*.[17] Rashi explains that slaves were sexually promiscuous and suspected of homosexuality; allowing them to mingle freely with either women or minors would lead to immorality.[18] Despite that, Tur quotes a ruling of R. Yehudah HaCohen that a woman may join two men to complete the quorum necessary for reciting *birkhat hazimmun*.[19] As R. Yehudah was not a radical who would cavalierly disregard a Mishnah, some argue that he interprets the Mishnah to exclude two women joining a man but allows one woman to join two men.[20] Others maintain that he surely limits this ruling to the quorum of ten required to add the word *"Elokeinu"* to *birkhat hazimmun*, but would allow a woman to

---

[15] R. Hayyim David Halevi, *Mayim Hayyim* (Tel Aviv, 5751 [1991]), *responsum* 10, p. 49ff.

[16] *Mishnah Berakhot* 6.1; *Berakhot* 45a.

[17] *Berakhot* 45b.

[18] Ibid., s.v. *im ratzu ein mezamnim*.

[19] *Tur Shulhan Arukh, Oreh Hayyim* 199.

[20] Ibid., *Hiddushei hagahot*, n. 2.

complete the quorum of three necessary for reciting the *zimmun* proper.[21]

These attempts at reconciliation, however, appear to be somewhat forced. A more plausible interpretation would be that of the Taz. He explains that R. Yehudah understood the Mishnah to mean that a woman may not lead the *zimmun* but may participate in it.[22] (We shall soon turn to the logic of such a position.) Perisha to Tur cleverly justifies R. Yehudah's ruling by having him interpret the Mishnah to be a stronger version of the Gemara's prohibition: even with free men present, a mixed group of women, slaves and minors cannot be put together for the purpose of creating an eating fellowship.[23] If the slaves are absent, it would follow, there is no reason to exclude the women.

R. Eliezer Berkovits argues that although it is not the current custom, in our contemporary situation "there is every justification" for accepting as a practical matter the interpretation that allows a woman to join two men to form a *zimmun*.[24] In any event, we should note that there is nothing inherently offensive in not allowing a woman to join two men to form the *zimmun* quorum. The rule is fully reciprocal in that a man may not join two women to effect such a quorum. *Halakhah*, as we have seen, has no objection to men and women eating together; in fact, when they do in large numbers, all present – men and women – are obligated in the *zimmun*.

Here, *halakhah* is expressing a concern that is well established and accepted within every religious Jewish community: sexual modesty. *Halakhah* insists that, while coed situations are not inherently promiscuous, one must be aware that they have the potential to deteriorate to that state. It therefore recommends a subtle hesitation in forming the quorum, insisting that a coed situation in and of itself not effect a change in the liturgy in this case, to allow *birkhat hazimmun* to be said. (Once the principle is laid down, the argument would go: *lo plug* – we do not define the real nature, and therefore rule that a woman may not join her husband and son – hardly a promiscuous situation – to say the *zimmun*.)

---

[21] Bah, *Tur Shulhan Arukh* 199, s.v. *verabi yehudah hacohen.*

[22] Taz, *Shulhan Arukh, Oreh Hayyim* 199, n. 2.

[23] Perisha, *Tur Shulhan Arukh* 199, n. 5.

[24] R. Eliezer Berkovits, *Jewish Women in Time and Torah* (Hoboken, New Jersey: Ktav, 1990), p. 92.

After the existence of a single-sex quorum has effected the change (i.e., the addition of *birkat hazimmun*), the presence of members of the other sex is not objectionable in the least. Thus, when women join a situation in which the *zimmun* is obligatory, they too become full members of the fellowship and share in the obligation in the *zimmun* (and, according to the Bah's reading, would be allowed by *Ba'al halakhot gedolot* to lead the *zimmun*).[25] When one or two men join a voluntary *zimmun* established by three women, they too may participate, as we saw in the name of R. Shelomo Zalman Auerbach above.

Mishnah Berurah ruled that "it is not pleasant" for a woman to join two men in forming the quorum.[26] It is unclear here whether *halakhah* is describing perceptions or prescribing attitudes. In past times, one might argue, a man might have been offended by the thought of a woman joining him to complete a formal religious sub-community. Such an argument does not maintain that *halakhah* must adapt itself to the values of contemporary society. It simply states that since *halakhah* itself originally intended only to reflect the frame of mind of the participants, then, in this case, when those attitudes have legitimately changed, the ruling would change automatically. In the past, when women were assumed to be uneducated and illiterate, it would not have been pleasant to associate with them. Such assumptions might therefore be unwarranted in our religious community. The question of how changed attitudes should influence normative *halakhah*, however, is beyond our present discussion.

The *Zimmun* Leader

We turn now to the logic of why a woman who eats with three or more men may not lead the *zimmun* even though she too is obligated in the *zimmun* itself. An original component of *birkhat hazimmun* was to have everyone present fulfill his or her obligation to say *birkhat hamazon* by answering "*amen*" to the leader's *berakhah*. This is possible only if the leader has at least the same degree of obligation as the participants. For reasons that do not concern us here, doubt was raised as to whether women share

---

[25] Bah to Tur Shulhan Arukh 689, s.v. *u-Ba'al.*

[26] *Mishnah Berurah* to *Shulhan Arukh, Oreh Hayyim* 199, n. 12.

men's Torah obligation in *birkhat hamazon*. (They inarguably have a rabbinical obligation.) Indeed, *Shulhan Arukh* refuses to adjudicate the issue, ruling that it is matter of doubt whether women are obligated from the Torah or from the Rabbis in *birkat hamazon*, thereby creating doubt whether a man could fulfill his obligation through a woman's *berakhah*.[27] This would preclude a woman leading the *zimmun* when a man is included. Hence Taz's interpretation of the Mishnah: All may participate in forming the quorum; but because women, slaves and minors do not have the same degree of obligation as the men, none of them may serve as leader.[28] Of course, nowadays those present usually say *birkhat hamazon* on their own, finishing each section before the leader does and are thus able to answer "*amen*" to the *berakhot* of the *mezamein* (leader).

The function of *birkat hazimmun* is simply to acknowledge the existence of the eating fellowship. Thus, if everyone present is saying *birkat hamazon* individually, the only objection to women leading would be the traditional reluctance to allow (or encourage) women to assume public roles, especially in coed situations. This is not a negligible point, but although leading the *zimmun* is rather minor in comparison to the public roles now regularly assumed by women with general consent, the original rule remains in place.

Women's Participation in *Sheva Berakhot*

The final ancillary issue regarding *zimmun* that we will consider is the question of women's participation in *sheva berakhot*, the series of seven special blessings added after each meal held in honor of the bride and groom during the week long period of festivities.

The Mishnah records the basic limitation on saying these blessings: "One does not say *birkat aveilim* (the mourners' blessing) ...or *birkat hatanim* (the grooms' blessing)[29] ...with fewer than ten [adult free men present]." This, of course, is not the only parallel between the religious laws associated with the life-cycle events of marriage and of death. The marriage

---

[27] *Shulhan Arukh, Oreh Hayyim* 186.1.

[28] *Shulhan Arukh, Oreh Hayyim* 183.7.

[29] In various sources, *birkat hatanim* refers to all *sheva berakhot* (the blessing for wine plus the six specific blessings in honor of the bride and groom) or, alternately, to only the last and longest of them ("*asher bara…*").

celebration lasts seven days, as does the period of mourning. Both *birkat aveilim* and *birkat hatanim* are repeated throughout the week in the presence of a *minyan*, provided someone who has not previously heard them recited (*panim hadashot*) is present along with, respectively, the mourner and the bride and groom.[30] While *birkat aveilim* has fallen into disuse, the laws of *birkat hatanim* have evolved considerably.

The Talmud records the dictum of R. Helbo in the name of Rav Huna: "Anyone who takes pleasure from a marriage feast (*seudat hatan*) and does not cheer him [the groom] has made a fivefold violation."[31] Maharsha notes that *Hazal* enacted the seven *birkot hatanim* in this regard; that is, although there are many ways of cheering the bride and groom, the Sages decreed that it be done by reciting the *sheva berakhot*.[32] In the course of time the *halakhah* evolved that the obligation of *sheva berakhot* was linked to the obligation in *zimmun*.[33] Thus, in response to the question of whether one may leave a wedding meal before *sheva berakhot* are said, R. Moshe Feinstein ruled that those obligated to hear *birkhat hazimmun* must hear the *sheva berakhot*. The way to free oneself from the obligation of the latter is to exempt oneself from the obligation of the former.[34] Women who eat with men at the wedding feast share with them the obligation for *zimmun*, as we have seen. It therefore follows that they share the men's obligation in *sheva berakhot* and prima facie should be able to recite them on behalf of those assembled.

This is not analogous to the issue of women leading the *zimmun* in a coed situation. As we saw, the problem there is that the person leading the

---

[30] At least with regard to the wedding feast, the *panim hadashot* must be "important" people. *Hiddushei HaRitva* (*Ketubbot* 7b) postulates that part of the definition of "important" is the ability to make up the quorum required for the recitation of the *sheva berakhot*. Thus he rules that a woman cannot qualify for *panim hadashot*, although she may be "important" in other senses. On the other hand, *Hiddushei Hatam Sofer* (*Ketubbot* 7a, s.v., *bemakhelot*) allowed women to be *panim hadashot*. [R. Menashe Klein (*Mishne Halakhot*, 2:27–48 and 7:246), though, held that this approval was only theoretical.]

[31] *Berakhot* 6a.

[32] To *Berakhot* 6a, s.v. *oveRabbi*.

[33] I discuss this evolution in detail in my book *Women, Jewish Law and Modernity: New Opportunities in a Post-feminist Age*, pp. 56–69.

[34] R. Moshe Feinstein, *Iggerot Moshe, Oreh Hayyim* 1:56, pp. 129 ff.

zimmun might also have to share an equal obligation in *birkat hamazon*, which may not be the case for women. In the case of *sheva berakhot*, on the other hand, women share the same obligation as men because of their identical obligation both in the general *mitzvah* of "gladdening the groom and bride" [*lesameah hatan vekalla*] and in the *zimmun*. (The latter *mitzvah* evolved on them by virtue of their having eaten with the men.) The use of a separate cup of wine for the *sheva berakhot* shows that we are dealing with concerns separate from those of *birkat hamazon*.

Indeed, Rambam notes that "Neither slaves nor minors recite this blessing." Notably, his not excluding women is a meaningful departure from his usual triad of "women, slaves and minors."[35] Similarly, *Shulhan Arukh* rules that *birkat hatanim* is not to be recited by slaves and minors, and also does not exclude women.[36] *Helkat Mehokek* explains there that the slaves and minors are excluded because they cannot be counted among the three required for the *zimmun*. Women, though, are obligated in *birkat hazimmun* if they eat with the men, and have the option of doing so if they eat alone. For that reason, it seems, they are not excluded from saying *birkat hatanim*.

Opposition to Women's Participation

When a *zimmun* takes place at a wedding meal but there is no *minyan* of ten men and *panim hadashot*, only the last of the *sheva berakhot* ("*asher bara*") is said. There seems to be general agreement that if two women eat with the bride and groom, they may add *asher bara* after the meal as a result of their having created a *zimmun*.[37]

However, there is disagreement with regard to a woman saying one of the *sheva berakhot* that may be said in the presence of a *minyan*. In my opinion, these objections are not compelling. R. Moshe Halevi Steinberg objects to women saying *sheva berakhot* because of *kol isha* (the provocative

35 Rambam, *MishnehTorah, Hilkhot Berakhot* 2.9.

36 *Shulhan Arukh, Even Ha-ezer* 62.4-7.

37 R. David Auerbach (author of *Halikhot beita*), in a letter to Joel B. Wolowelsky, 18 Heshvan 5747 [20 November 1987]. Similarly, see R. Yehuda Herzl Henkin, *Benei banim* 3.27, p. 100; and R. Zalman Nehemia Goldberg, "*Ha-im mutar le-isha levarekh berakhah misheva berakhot*," *Hameir la-aretz*, no. 36, Av 5760 (2000), p. 33.

power of a woman's voice), comparing it to a woman saying *Kaddish*.[38] But while there were authorities who objected to women saying *Kaddish*, it was not usually on the basis of *kol isha*. Indeed, a woman saying one of the *sheva berakhot* seems more closely related to a woman saying *birkat hagomel* in *shul* in the presence of the men. Some might feel that this is immodest behavior, remarked R. Ovadiah Yosef, *Rishon LeTzion* and former Chief Rabbi of Israel, "But I say that the evil inclination is not to be found for such a brief matter... especially nowadays when women regularly go out to public places among men.... [Similarly, under these circumstances] one need not be concerned about the issue of *kol zemer shel isha erva* [the melody of a woman's voice being arousing]."[39]

This ruling should not be applied haphazardly, but it does certainly seem to be relevant to the case at hand. Indeed, R. Steinberg himself goes on to express his real concern: "If we allow women to say the *sheva berakhot*, it will be used as a precedent for other demands, including mixed seating in public prayer, as is done by Reform and Conservative [congregations]." This, logic, however, could be argued for the opposite conclusion, and R. Aharon Soloveitchik's comments regarding *Kaddish* might thus well apply to *sheva berakhot*. "Nowadays, when there are Jews fighting for equality for men and women in matters such as *aliyot*, if Orthodox rabbis prevent women from saying *Kaddish* when the possibility exists to allow it, this will strengthen the influence of Reform and Conservative rabbis. It is therefore forbidden to prevent daughters from saying *Kaddish*."[40]

Another objection emerges from the statement interpolated into *Kessef Mishneh*'s commentary on Rambam's discussion of *sheva berakhot*. Marked in square brackets and missing from the first printed edition, it reads: "It seems to be obvious [that slaves and minors cannot say this blessing, as they may not join to make up the necessary quorum of ten adult free men] and a fortiori cannot say the blessing."[41] This reasoning would, of course, exclude women as well. But in addition to the fact, noted above, that

---

[38] R. Moshe Halevi Steinberg, *Mishberei yam* (5752 [1992]), no. 85, p. 96. See my discussion in *Women, Jewish Law and Modernity*, pp. 84–94.

[39] R. Ovadiah Yosef, *Yehave da-at*, 4.15, n. **, pp. 77 ff.

[40] R. Aaron Soloveitchik, *Od Yisrael Yosef beni hai* (Yeshivas Brisk, 1993), no. 32, p. 100.

[41] On Rambam, *Mishneh Torah, Hilkhot berakhot* 2.10.

Rambam deliberately changed his traditional phrasing in specifically not excluding women, he made this ruling in *halakhah* 9, which refers to an individual's additional blessing, not requiring the presence of any quorum. Moreover, the a fortiori argument itself is invalid. There is no principle that individuals who do not qualify to establish a *minyan* are excluded from saying prayers that depend on the existence of that *minyan*. The Mishnah that sets out the requirement of ten adult free men to say *birkat hatanim* requires the same *minyan* for the public reading of the Torah and Haftorah. Today, though, minors regularly read from the Torah and say the Haftorah, and women were originally permitted *aliyot* to the Torah. Similarly, women and minors say Mourner's *Kaddish*, which also requires the presence of a male *minyan*.

R. Shaul Yisraeli argues that women are exempt from the general obligation to cheer the groom – and it is the groom exclusively who must be cheered, he writes, and not the bride and groom. The reason he cites is that one of the main ways of cheering him is to dance before him and it would violate all laws of modesty for women to do so publicly.[42] Rambam, in contrast, clearly states that the *mitzvah* to cheer the bride and groom is part of the *mitzvah* to "love your neighbor as yourself." There is no reason, he argues, to exempt women from this general obligation or from any of the other specific ones he mentions there (to visit the sick, console mourners, bury the dead, marry off brides, etc.).[43] More important, this reasoning ignores the fact that whatever the origins of the *mitzvah*, current *halakhah* ties the obligation to say *sheva berakhot* to the obligation in *zimmun*, and the women who eat with the men are clearly obligated in the latter.

R. Zalman Nehemia Goldberg writes that Rambam did not explicitly exclude women here from saying the *sheva berakhot* because he already excluded them from public reading of the Torah [*betzibbur*] on the grounds that it is not comely for the congregation [*kavvod ha-tzibbur*], and *sheva berakhot* is likewise said in a public forum. Here, however, I would argue that reading from a text is not comparable to reciting a *berakhah betzibbur*, as we see from the general agreement that women may say *birkat hagomel* in

---

[42] R. Shaul Yisraeli, "*Be-inyan birkat hatanim ve-shituf isha bahen,*" *Barka-i*, Summer 5743 [1983], no.1, pp. 163–166.

[43] *Mishneh Torah, Hilkhot tefillah* 13.17.

shul in a public forum.

A Contemporary Permissive View

All in all, we could conclude with the ruling of R. Moshe Ehrenreich and R. Yosef Carmel, the *Roshei ha-Kollel* of Machon Eretz Hemda. They note that authorities disagree on the issue and that in such cases the general policy is to refrain from reciting *berakhot*. Their conclusion, however, is that those who wish to permit women to say any of the *sheva berakhot* have authorities on whom they can rely. "It is inappropriate for those present to cause a dispute, thereby bringing anguish to the bride and groom, and preventing them from honoring the people they would please. This is especially true in our times, when this might offend those women who wish to participate for pure reasons in God's worship, and every effort should be made to accommodate them when the *halakhah* permits it."[44]

---

[44] *Responsa Be-mareh ha-bazak*, no. 5575, Heshvan 5760 (1999).

"AND YOU SHALL TEACH THEM TO YOUR DAUGHTERS"*

RABBI ARYEH STRIKOVSKY

1. Is Teaching Torah to Women Permitted?

R. Eliezer taught, "Whoever teaches his daughter Torah, [it is as if] he has taught her lewdness."[1] Maimonides cites this statement; upon closer study, however, we see that his approach is more complex:

> A woman who learns Torah has a reward, but hers is not commensurate with a man's, for she has not been commanded....[2] And although she is rewarded, the Sages taught that a man should not teach his daughter because the minds of most women are not inclined to learning; words of Torah thus become, for them, words of emptiness due to the deficiency of their capacities [da'atan]. The Sages said: Whoever teaches Torah to his daughter, it is as if he has taught her lewdness. To what does this refer? To Oral Torah. In

---

* This essay was first published in 1983, and re-printed in expanded form in the Hebrew anthology *Hapeninah: Ha-ishah ha-yehudit be-hevrah, be-mishpahah, u-vehinukh*, ed. D. Rafel (Jerusalem, 1989), pp. 215–243.

The present essay is a translation by Ora Wiskind Elper of the abridged Hebrew version that appeared in *Bat Mitzvah*, ed. S. Friendland ben Arza (Jerusalem, 2002), pp. 374–384.

[1] *Mishna Sotah* 3.4.

[2] Rambam rules following the view of R. Hanina that "greater is he who is commanded and performs than he who is not commanded and performs" (*Avodah zara* 7a). R. Yosef, though, held that "greater is he who is not commanded" (*Kiddushin* 31a), and that is the approach voiced in the Yerushami as well (*Shevi'it* 6.1). C.f. R. Shlomo Sirilleo ad loc. In this spirit, R. Kalonymus Kalmish Shapira of Piasezna compares the "Torah" of Miriam the prophetess with the Torah of Moshe. Precisely because she is not commanded to learn yet does so of her own initiative, her status is in a sense preferential. See *Sacred Fire*, trans. J. Hershy Worth, ed. Deborah Miller (Jason Aronson: New York, 2000), p. 329.

the case of Written Torah, though, he should not teach her *a priori*, but if he has taught her, it is not as if he has taught her lewdness.[3]

In writing "she is rewarded," Rambam asserts that the Sages did not exclude women from the *mitzvah* of learning Torah, and in delimiting the reservation to "most women" he effectively creates an opening for teaching Torah to a small category of women. What was a minority in one era may well become a majority in another.[4]

In analyzing Rambam's discussion of the laws related to Torah learning [*hilkhot talmud Torah*], we realize that the prohibition against teaching Torah to most women is but an outgrowth of the prohibition against teaching an unfit student [*talmid she-aino hagun*].[5] This prohibition applies to men and women equally. Most of the people who sought to learn in Rabban Gamliel's *beit midrash* were turned away until they were able to prove that "they were as respectable in mind as they outwardly appeared" [*tokham ke-baram*].[6] In Yavne, though, the approach followed the view of R. Elazar ben Azariyah – as long as the student is not commonly held to be "unfit", he cannot be barred from the *beit midrash*. In light of this ruling, Rambam's *halakhic* approach, now normative, is that an unknown male student who wishes to learn is considered "fit" until the opposite is proven; an unknown female student, however, is considered "unfit" until the opposite becomes clear.

---

[3] Rambam, *Mishneh Torah, Hilkhot Talmud Torah* 1.13.

[4] I heard this hypothesis from R. Yonah Ben-Sasson. In effect, Maimonides here combines the views of R. Eliezer and Ben Azai; see *Mishneh Torah, Hilkhot Sotah* 3.20.

[5] Lack of seriousness or a demeaning attitude toward Torah would put a student in the category of "unfit." See Maimonides, *Mishneh Torah, Talmud Torah* 4. 1. In the *Shulhan Arukh, Yoreh Deah* 246.6–7 the injunction against teaching Torah to women is similarly drawn from the case of the unfit student. Including women in the *mitzvah* of learning Torah comes from the ruling that a woman can be called up for an *aliyah* to the Torah on Shabbat (*Megillah* 223a). Many *halakhic* authorities have cited this point. Interestingly, even the prohibition against teaching Torah to non-Jews was limited, in the Rambam's ruling, to the case of an unfit gentile. Christians were thus excluded from the prohibition (c.f., *Teshuvot ha-Rambam*, ed. Blau, *responsa* 149.) This principle can help us in understanding how the presidential house [*beit ha-nasi*] could take the liberty of teaching Torah to slaves and maidservants despite the explicit prohibition involved (*T.Y. Megillah* 4.3). The same applies to the instance in *Moed Katan* 17a, in which the Sages refused to absolve a *niddui* imposed by a maidservant from the house of Rabi.

[6] *Berakhot* 28a.

When her "fitness" is proven, she can be taught and "she has a reward." This is R. Yosef Karo's interpretation as well, which we can draw from the arrangement of the *halakhot* on the issue in the *Shulhan Arukh*.[7]

2. "And You Shall Teach Them to Your Children – These Are Your Students"

Here is one other aspect to the issue of Torah learning raised by Maimonides:

> Just as a man is required to teach his son, so is he required to teach his grandson, as it is written, "And you shall inform your son and the sons of your son" (Deuteronomy 4:9).... It is a *mitzvah* upon every wise man to teach any student, even though he is not his own son, as the Sages taught, "'And you shall teach them to your children' – they are your students."[8]

Implicit in the commandment to pass on Torah knowledge are two other complementary *mitzvot*:

1. *The mitzvah to educate*, which encompasses teaching Torah in the widest possible sense, including guidance in keeping the *mitzvot* and in ethical behavior.[9]
2. *The mitzvah to remember the revelation at Mount Sinai*. According to Nahmanides, this includes, among other things, "that we let it be known to

---

[7] *Shulhan Arukh, Yoreh Deah* 246.

[8] *Mishneh Torah, Talmud Torah* 1.2.

[9] Regarding the sources of the *mitzvah* to educate, opinions are divided. Rambam, Rashba, Ritba, Meiri, Hashla, and *Menorat ha-meor* (R. Abuhav) all link it to the verse "Educate the youth according to his ways" (Proverbs 22:6), which R. Avraham Danzig interprets as a positive commandment originating in received tradition [*divrei kabbalah*]. C.f. *Hayyei Adam, kellal* 66. Yitzhak Lange cited a variety of sources from *halakhic* midrashim linking the *mitzvah* to verses from the Torah; this would indicate the contention it is actually *de'oraita* – originating in Torah itself. (See note 23 below.) R. Meir Simhah Hacohen links the *mitzvah* to Genesis 18:19 in his commentary on that verse in *Meshekh Hokhmah*. It is doubtful, though, that his intent in doing so was to grant it the status of "*de'oraita*." For more on this subject, see the entry on *Hinukh* in *Ha-encyclopedia ha-talmudit*, vol. 16.

all our descendents, from generation to generation, all that happened
there – all that was seen and heard."[10]

These two additional *mitzvot* supplement the injunction to impart the Torah
in thought and deed; they accompany it in the faithful tradition, spanning
generations, that "it shall not be forgotten out of the mouths of their seed"
(Deuteronomy 31:21). R. Shimon bar Yohai understands that verse as an
assurance from Above, embracing the Jewish people eternally, and promis-
ing that the labors of all the generations will never be lost.[11]

Historians of the future will testify that in the twentieth century, the
traditional imparting of the Torah was perpetuated through the active
participation of thousands of women teachers, and hundreds of thousands
of mothers and daughters. Such a scenario was probably not foreseen by
those rabbinic scholars who, in their time, excluded women from teaching
Torah.[12] But now that the reality exists, we cannot entrust female teachers
with teaching *halakhah*, prayer, and Mishna and impede them from learning
Talmud. The Gemara called the teaching profession "labor for God's sake"
[*malekhet ha-Shem*] and cautioned against doing it half-hearted or
deceivingly.[13]

The situation is more serious, however, when we speak of the mother's
role as educator. Although *halakhic* tradition put the responsibility of
imparting Torah in the hands of the father, freeing the mother of it,[14] times
have changed and nowadays it is usually the mother who takes charge of

---

[10] Ramban, commentary on Deuteronomy 4:9–10.

[11] *Shabbat* 138b.

[12] The injunction against women teaching children includes girls, and is founded on
the fear that they might find themselves in a situation alone with the pupils' fathers
[*yihud*] (*Shulhan Arukh, Even Ha-ezer*, 22.20). The only *posek* who tends to permit it is R.
Yaakov Pardo, author of *Apei zutrei* on *Shulhan Arukh* (*loc. cit.*, 32). See *Otzar haposekim*,
vol. 9, p. 158. In a *responsum*, Rambam permits a woman who had been teaching
children to continue in her profession. (*Teshuvot ha-Rambam*, ed. Blau, 34, p. 58.
Compare, however, *Teshuvot ha-Rambam* 42, p. 67.) There were also women in Italy who
taught. See S. Assaf, *Mekorot le-toledot ha-hinukh be-Yisrael*, vol. 2, pp. 174–175; 197–199.

[13] *Bava Batra* 21b. Here the statement is applied to the failings of Yoav ben Tzaruyah's
master. Many prominent authorities have stressed the importance of examining the
sources for *halakhic* rulings rather than merely reviewing the final decisions. This
subject, though, lies beyond the bounds of our discussion.

[14] Rambam, *Talmud Torah* 1.1.

overseeing her children's homework. In most cases, however,[15] her own education enables her to follow her children's progress only in their general studies, yet her tools remain deficient when it comes to Torah subjects.[16]

It could be argued that Rambam's contention that most women make "words of Torah to become words of emptiness" can be explained against the background of his own era, in which women as a whole were excluded from general and religious education alike. That is the situation described by the authors of the *Tosafot* as well:

> ... An illiterate [*bur*] understands the Holy Tongue and knows a bit of Torah, but does not know the blessings.... But women, who know nothing at all...[17]

Maimonides, similarly, writes: "Conversation with one's wife usually only concerns intimate matters [*inyanei tashmish*]; for that reason, it is forbidden to speak too much with her."[18] When the vast majority of women were in such a situation, there was a danger that Torah might turn into empty words. This is not true, though, in our age. *Hazal* did not create the situation of ignorance among women; rather, they examined their reality and then took their stance accordingly.[19] Let's elaborate on the two complementary *mitzvot* cited above.

---

[15] This essay was originally written in 1983. In the intervening nearly twenty years, the situation has improved dramatically in the national-religious community. In order to realize with what rapidity this revolution has taken place, and its impact and dimensions, I have chosen not to update this sentence. (editor's note).

[16] R. Radnitzsky described the following situation. In his Orthodox community in Charleston are some "mixed" couples – either husband or wife is not observant. He found that Torah tradition continued to be preserved only in those families in which the observant parent was the mother. See also R. Aharon Lichtenstein, "*Beayot yesod be-hinukhah she ha-ishah*," *Ha-ishah ve-hinukhah*, 5740, p. 149.

[17] *Tosafot, Berakhot* 45b, d.h. *Shani.*

[18] Rambam, *Commentary on the Mishnah, Avot* 1.5. This statement stems from the rabbinical injunction (*Avot* 1.5), "Do not speak excessively to women."

[19] For further comments on this subject, see section 4 below. R. B. Feurer discussed the necessity of Torah education for women as a component of teacher-training in *Noam*, vol. 3, p. 131, quoted by R. E.G. Elinson, *Ha-ishah ve-hamitzvot*, (W.Z.O.: Jerusalem, 1975), pp. 169–171.

The *Mitzvah* to Educate [*Hinukh*]

Many *halakhic* authorities hold that the *mitzvah* to educate applies to mothers as well as fathers, and to daughters as well as sons.[20] The *mitzvah*, in principle, was split: the father was given exclusive responsibility for teaching the Torah, while the mother was made a partner in her children's general religious education and guidance in keeping the *mitzvot*. If family conditions changed, however, the mother became obliged to try to compensate for deficiencies in the intellectual realm as well.

Even those *posekim* who absolve the mother from the *mitzvah* of educating, rule that if the father is absent, his place is taken by the *beit din* [religious court] and the mother. Some hold that the mother and the *beit din* have equal status;[21] others hold that "if [the child] has no father, the mother is obligated; if there is no mother, the *beit din* is responsible."[22] In such a case, the mother and the court fill the role of the father to the best of their ability. In effect, just as the court is not to content itself with technical instruction in keeping the *mitzvot*, so the mother should not settle for a minimum if she has the possibility of educating in the most complete sense of the word.

The concept "he has no father" certainly includes the case in which the father does not devote his energies to his child's education and leaves the *mitzvah* of educating in the hands of the mother. Situations like this are common enough to warrant arming our daughters with the Torah knowledge they will need.[23]

---

[20] A condensed discussion of this subject may be found in the *Encyclopedia talmudit*, vol. 20, "*Ha-ishah*" adjacent to n. 209, 210; vol. 16, "*Hinukh*", between notes 49–69. On the problematic nature of rulings and interpretation concerning this subject, see R. Shmuel Halevi Kalin, *Mahatzit ha-shekel*, *Oreh Hayyim* 343, 1. See also R. A. Lichtenstein, "*Ha-mishpaha be-halakhah*," *Mishpahot beit Yisrael*, Jerusalem 5744, n. 39; Y.S. Lange, "*Le-inyan shoresh mitzvat hinukh*" in the collection *Mikhtam le-David*, 5738, pp. 47–54; R. Y. Shaviv, "*Mehalkhot hinukh*," *Noam*, 5737, pp. 154–155.

[21] *Terumat ha-deshen*, quoted in *Hagahot beit meir* on *Oreh Hayyim* 640.

[22] *Eliyahu Rabba*, quoted by R. Eliya Shapira in *Hagahot beit meir* on *Oreh Hayyim* 640.4 (Jerusalem, 5759), p. 739.

[23] Such situations are indeed recorded in various sources; *halakhic* authorities determined that the mother is required, to a greater extent that the father, to reprimand her children, as she is more available and present in the home than the husband. See *Shnei luhot ha-brit*, *Sha'ar ha-otiot*, *ot Derekh eretz*; *Menorat ha-Meor*, s. 168; R. Yaakov Emden, *Migdat oz*, *ta'alah* 3,25.

The *Mitzvah* to Remember the Revelation at Sinai

Both the author of *Halakhot gedolot* and the Ramban numbered this *mitzvah* among the negative commandments, equally incumbent upon women and men.[24] Women's responsibility for it is interwoven in the *midrashim* reconstructing the part women originally played in receiving the Torah and in the chain of Jewish tradition. The Bible itself sees the mother as a link in transmitting the Torah from one generation to the next: "… And do not abandon the Torah of your mother." (Proverbs 1:8; 6:20)[25]

3. Torah Learning as Preparation for Prophecy

There is an additional, meta-*halakhic* factor mandating Torah study:

> Each man in obligated to give new life to his own being by modeling his personality upon the image of the prophet; he must carry through his own self-creation until he actualizes the idea of prophecy – until he is worthy and fit to receive the divine overflow…every man should make a supreme effort to scale the mountain of the Lord, until he reaches the pinnacle of the revelation of the Divine Presence…. For the image of the prophet and the structure of his consciousness…serve…as the ideal of ethical perfection, as posited by Halakhah.[26]

---

[24] In his commentary to Deuteronomy 4:9-10, Ramban also defines it as a positive, time-dependent commandment. This subject is summarized in the *Encyclopedia talmudit*, "*Zekhirat ma'amad har sinai,*" vol. 12, pp. 212-213. I heard about women's responsibility regarding this *mitzvah* from R. Hayyim Zimmerman, who said that women are included in the *mitzvot* incumbent upon the entire Jewish people as a national entity. On the basis of that assumption, R. Eliyahu David Rabinovitz-Teumim (Ha-aderet) included women in the *mitzvah* of *hakhel* (c.f. Deuteronomy 31:10–13). In his monumental Hebrew essay, "*U-bikashtem mi-sham*" in *Ish ha-halakhah – Galui ve-nistar*, Jerusalem 5739, pp. 115–235, R. Yosef Dov Soloveitchik places this *mitzvah* at the center of the Jew's religious-*halakhic* existence.

[25] See: R. Soloveitchik's eulogy of his mother-in-law, the Rabbanit Rivka Twersky, *z"l*, in *Tradition* 1968; also, the commentary by Dr. Z. Harvey, *Tradition* 1982; R. A. Lichtenstein, "*Be'ayot yesod behinukhah shel ishah,*" *Ha-ishah ve-hinukhah*, 5740, p. 159.

[26] R. Soloveitchik, *Halakhic Man*, trans. from Hebrew by Lawrence Kaplan (Philadelphia, 1983), pp. 128–129.

Most Jewish religious thinkers would agree with this statement, but they vary on the nature of this preparation for receiving prophecy and divine inspiration. Does one make oneself fit via an intellectual-moral process, founded on Torah learning, or does it depend on an emotional awakening? Rambam[27] and R. Hayyim of Volozhin[28] speak of intellectual preparation for receiving prophecy, and the great *yeshivah* thinkers of recent generations follow in their footsteps. Perhaps most prominent among them is R. Yosef Dov Soloveitchik, *z"l*, who bestowed the crown of prophecy upon the "*halakhic* man."[29]

Jewish tradition tells not only of prophets but of seven prophetesses – even of 600,000 of them.[30] And indeed, when Rambam discusses the

---

[27] Rambam, *Mishneh Torah, Yesodei ha-Torah*, chapters 2–4. In effect, Rambam considers the *mitzvah* to learn Torah in two places. In his discussion of the laws of *Talmud Torah* he speaks of it as an obligation applying to everyone, while in the laws of *Yesodei ha-Torah* he speaks of it as preparation for prophecy. In *Hilkhot Talmud Torah*, the study of the four hermeneutical levels implicit in the Torah, known as *PaRDeS*, are mentioned as part of Talmud study. At the end of *Hilkhot yesodei ha-Torah*, however, study of "the opinions of Abaye and Rava" [*havvayot Abaye ve-Rava*] is presented as the appropriate introduction to learning on the four hermeneutical levels of *PaRDeS*. That sort of learning empowers a person to fulfill the *mitzvah* of loving God and knowing God; from there, one can reach the stage of preparation for prophecy. In *Hilkhot Talmud Torah* Rambam also discusses unfit students and teachers, and women in general, stating that the person who teaches them ostensibly instructs in lewdness. In *Hilkhot yesodei ha-Torah*, however, he raises the question of Torah learning for its own sake, and in purity. It goes without saying that anyone interested in that sort of learning, women and men alike, engage in it out of love for God and the Torah.

[28] See his introduction to the Gaon of Vilna's *Perush le-sifra de-tzniuta*.

[29] See *Halakhic Man*, end of part two, pp. 128–137. In Rambam's view, the Torah learning that prepares a person for prophecy is composed of study of Talmud and *halakhah*, as well as study of physics [*ma'aseh bereishit*] and metaphysics [*ma'aseh merkavah*]. R. Hayyim of Volozhin replaces the metaphysical premises the Rambam suggests. In his view, both *ma'aseh bereshit* and *ma'aseh merkavah* are contained in the *Zohar* and mystical tradition of R. Yitzhak Luria, but because authentic kabbalistic teaching is beyond our understanding, we should restrict our Torah learning to study of 'revealed' Torah – that is, Talmud and its commentaries. These, too, are containers of Divine essence. For R. Soloveichic's "*halakhic* man", in contrast, there are "the four *amot* of *halakhah*" alone. While a Rambamistic prophet could fulfill his obligation by reviewing the *Mishneh Torah*, R. Soloveitchik's prophetic "*halakhic* man" must master the entire range of Oral Torah.

[30] We find the list of seven prophetesses in the commentary of Rabbeinu Hannanel to *Megillah* 14b. The total equality between those people worthy of prophecy is stressed in the midrash *Tanna de-bei Eliyahu rabba* 8: "Whether Jew or non-Jew, man or woman – the divine Spirit will rest on a person solely dependent on one's actions." Equality of another type is expressed by R. Berekhiyah in the name of R. Halbo (*Midrash Shir ha-*

obligation to learn *halakhah* and the disputes of Abaye and Rava as preparation for delving into more esoteric matters [*iyyun be-ma'aseh ha-merkavah*], he specifies: "And everyone may know them – great and small, *man and woman,* broad and narrow of heart."[31]

Shirim Rabba 4.22): "Just as 600,000 prophets of Israel came to be, so were 600,000 prophetesses engendered. King Shelomo made this evident in the verse, 'Thy lips, O my bride, drop as the honeycomb...' (Song of Songs 4:11)." The number 600,000 is not an exaggeration, according to Rambam's method set out in *Guide to the Perplexed* 2.45 of the twelve levels of prophecy. The lower levels are limited neither in time nor space. See Avraham Yehoshua Heschel, "*Ha-he'emin ha-Rambam shezakha lenevuah?*" *Sefer ha-zikaron le-Levi Ginzburg.* See also Yonah be-Sasson, "*Torat ha-nevuah shel ha-Rambam,*" *Hagut u-mikra,* Jerusalem 5737, pp. 27–73.

[31] *Hilkhot yesodei ha-Torah,* end of chapter 4. Although Rambam does draw the parallel between "woman" and "small" and "narrow of heart," the thrust of the contention remains the same. It could be argued that women are included in this list merely as a rhetorical gesture, with the intent of being all-inclusive. My understanding of Rambam's view on Torah study for women, though, finds further support elsewhere in his writings. In *Hilkhot Sotah* 3.20 and in his *Commentary on the Mishnah,* Rambam choses to interpret the words of the Mishnah concerning the woman's merit differently that what appears in the Talmud (*Sotah* 21a). The contention in the Talmud is that they are rewarded for fulfilling the *mitzvot* they are obligated to do, or for taking their children to school and awaiting their husbands' return from the *beit midrash.* In the former contexts, in contrast, Rambam recognizes her merit in her own act of learning Torah. His sources seems to be the Yerushalmi Talmud, cited above.

On Torah learning for women as part of preparation for prophecy in general, see R. Yosef Kapah, "*Hinukh ha-bat le-limmud Torah*" *Ha-ishah ve-hinukhah,* pp. 33–34. See also Dr. Zeev Harvey on his essay on the Rambam's approach in *Tradition,* Winter 1982. This appears to have been Rambam's intent in leaving an opening for the minority of women who were an exception to the rule in his time. Needless to say, women are included in the *mitzvah* of loving God and knowing God, including all its relevant intellectual components.

R. Yitzhak Arama's suggestion in *Akedat Yitzhak, sha'ar 9,* should also be mentioned in this context, concerning spiritual improvement as a way of life for childless women. "The two names 'woman' [*ishah*] and '*Havvah*' indicate two purposes. The first teaches that woman was taken from man, stressing that, like him, she can understand and develop in the intellectual and moral realms, as the matriarchs did, and as righteous women and prophetesses have done – this is clear in a simple reading of "*Eshet hayil*" (Proverbs 31). The second alludes to the power of childbearing and raising children, as we learn from the name *Havvah,* mother of all life. And so, a woman who bears no children is prevented from fulfilling the smaller purpose [i.e., the second], and is left to do evil or good just like a man who is unable to bear. Of both [the barren man and woman] Isaiah (56:5) says, 'I have given them in my house and in my walls a name that is better than sons and daughters' – for the offspring of the righteous is surely their good deeds...." These convictions underlie R. Yitzhak Arama's reading of the interchange between Yaakov and Rachel.

4. Torah Learning as the Source of a Jewish World View

R. Yisrael Meir Hacohen, the *Hafetz Hayyim*, writes about the women of his generation:

> Particularly women who customarily learn the language and writing of the gentiles – surely it is a very great *mitzvah* to teach them *humash* as well as *nevi'im* and *ketuvim* [that is, all three parts of the *Tanakh*] and the moral teachings of the Sages...so that our holy faith will be proven true in their eyes. Otherwise, they may stray completely from the path of God and violate the very foundations of our religion, Heaven forbid.[32]

In his age, "enlightened" Jewish women had reached the stage of literacy. Today,[33] when the gates of the university are open before women, and we are offering our daughters the fruits of the Tree of academic Knowledge without boundaries, the Tree of Life, the Torah itself, is still given them in a partial and limited way. This intrinsically unbalanced pedagogical method is oriented to women whose internal cultural world is sophisticated, while their Jewish world remains constricted and naive.[34] One result might be doubt in their minds that the Torah could be a source of real knowledge, commensurate with secular intellectual achievements.[35] For women like these, the anachronistic prohibitions against women learning Oral Torah

---

[32] *Likkutei halakhot, Sotah*, p. 22. For other references on this subject in the writings of the Hafetz Hayyim and other thinkers, see Y. Ben-Arza, *Yosef Daat* 18, *Sotah*, Jerusalem 5761, p. 83.

[33] This refers, as we noted above, to the prevalent reality when this essay was first published in 1983.

[34] R. Hayyim Zimmerman used to say that anyone who could complete the first year of university study and remain observant was either a genius or an idiot. A genius – for managing to resolve the theological and religious problems involved, or an idiot – for remaining oblivious to them.

[35] Opinions among Jewish thinkers through the ages have been divided on whether or not a Jew must develop a worldview loyal to the Torah. All, however, agree that it is forbidden to have a worldview that is opposed to the Torah. Thus, without a doubt, every Jew – man or woman – who founds his or her uniqueness in the formulation of a worldview must do so in light of the Torah. That may be Rambam's intention in defining the Creation [*ma'aseh bereishit*] by combining physics, metaphysics, and the fundamentals of Jewish belief.

might actually engender a situation of desecration of God and the Torah itself. Those who bear the responsibility for religious education must take this seriously into consideration. We must aid our daughters in confronting these challenges by offering them a balanced education, in which Talmud and *halakhah* are taught at a high level, equal to their secular pursuits.[36]

Conclusion

We have discussed four factors that mandate Torah learning for women:

1. Torah study for its own sake.
2. Learning Torah in preparation for prophecy.
3. Learning Torah to enable transmission to children and students.
4. The necessity of balancing the internal world of an intellectual woman with the more profound aspects of Torah and Jewish thought.

While the first two of these factors present Torah study for women as a purely optional *mitzvah*, the last two consider it an absolute responsibility incumbent upon the contemporary educated woman.

On the other hand, we have seen that, in Rambam's eyes,[37] Torah law itself [*de'oraita*] holds that, ideally, all women should occupy themselves with Torah for its own sake at all times and circumstances, but that certain social reasons necessitated a *halakhic* ruling which prevented most women from doing that *mitzvah*. That ruling evolved in the wake of a historical-social anomaly; it reflects not an ideal but the demands of reality.[38] In our own days, then, our changed reality renders that ruling obsolete, making the *mitzvah* to learn Torah incumbent upon women comprehensively, including all of its elements.

Even when Torah sages opposed teaching Torah to women, they did not exclude them from the *mitzvah* of learning Torah, nor did they exempt

---

[36] See also, R. Eliezer Berkovits, *Jewish Women in Time and Torah* (Ktav, 1990).

[37] *Hilkhot talmud Torah* 1.2.

[38] Compare the statement by R. Soloveitchik: "In other words, the present time is only a historical anomaly in the ongoing process of the actualization of the ideal Halakhah in the real world, and there is no need to elaborate about a period which is but a temporary aberration that has seized hold of our historical existence. The Halakhah remains in full force, and we hope for and eagerly await the day of Israel's redemption when the ideal world will triumph over the profane reality." *Halakhic Man*, p. 28.

them from the *mitzvot* connected to the latter: education, remembering the revelation at Sinai, and preparation for prophecy.

Both the *mitzvah* of teaching Torah and the *mitzvah* of education include *halakhic* recognition of someone who might substitute for the father. Just as, in the *mitzvah* to educate, the mother can fully substitute for the father, in the *mitzvah* of teaching Torah the mother and female teacher can take on the role of the father and male teacher. In modern times, as a woman's educative roles as parent and teacher continue to expand, she must be trained in taking on these roles in the realm of Torah as well – not only because reality demands it, but as a *mitzvah* and a mission.

I would like to end with the words of R. David ben Zimrah (Radbaz). In response to the question whether one is obligated in *keriyah* [tearing one's clothing as a sign of mourning] when a woman passes away, Radbaz considers the possibility that a woman could be compared to a *sefer Torah* due to her Torah learning. He first cites the Talmud, *Moed katan,* chapter "*Elu megalhin*" [25a]. "R. Shimon ben Elazar taught: Whoever is at the deathbed when the soul departs from the body is required to tear. To what can this be compared? To a *sefer Torah* that is being burnt – one must tear one's clothing [in mourning]." He then quotes Rashi on Rif (R. Yitzhak Alfasi) that the case of a woman's death may also be comparable to a *sefer Torah* being burnt. Likewise, *Shulhan Arukh, Yoreh Deah* 340.5 rules that if one is present at the moment the soul departs from the body – whether the deceased is a Jewish man or woman – one is indeed obligated to tear one's garment. Thus, R. David ben Zimra explains, "a woman, although she is not commanded to learn Torah, if she did learn she will be rewarded. Hence, a woman, too, can learn, and she too is comparable to a *sefer Torah*. And thus one tears one's clothing for a woman as well as for a man.[39]

---

[39] *Responsa HaRadbaz*, vol. 3, 988.

WOMEN'S *MEGILLA* READING[1]

RABBI ARYEH A. FRIMER[2]

I. Talmudic sources

Jewish law generally frees women from those positive biblical commandments which, like *sukka*, *shofar* and *lulav*, are not continual obligations but,
rather, time-determined. Such commandments are known in the halakhic
literature as *mitsvot asei she-ha-zeman geramman*.[3] There are exceptions to this
rule, such as the obligations of *Shabbat*,[4] *hak'hel*, *simha* (rejoicing on the
holidays) and eating *matsa* - which are binding on women like men.[5] Each
exception, however, is based on a specific verse or derived via exegesis.

The consensus of authorities from the period of the *rishonim*[6] is that this
exemption from time-determined commandments applies not only to

---

[1] For recent reviews on the question of women's *Megilla* readings, see: R. Alfred S.
Cohen, "Women and the Reading of the *Megilla*," *Journal of Halacha and Contemporary
Society*, 30 (*Sukkot* 5756, Fall 1995), pp. 25–41; R. Ariel Pikar, "*Keri'at ha-Megilla Al Yedei
Isha Lifnei Nashim*," *Tehumin* "Women and the Reading of the *Megilla*," XVIII (5758),
pp. 361–368; R. Avraham Weiss, "Women and the Reading of the *Megilla*," *The Torah
u-Madda Journal*, VIII (1998–1999), pp. 295–317; R. Aaron Cohen, "Women Reading
the *Megilla*h for Men: A Rejoinder," *The Torah u-Madda Journal*, IX (2000), pp. 248–263;
R. Chaim Jachter, *Gray Matter* (2000), "May Women Read the *Megilla*," pp. 224–233.
The subject was first treated by us in: Aryeh A. Frimer and Dov I. Frimer, "Women's
Prayer Services: Theory and Practice. Part 1 – Theory," *Tradition*, **32:2**, pp. 5–118
(Winter 1998). Avilable online through http://mail-jewish.org.

[2] My heartfelt thanks to Prof. Dov I. Frimer for reviewing the manuscript and for his
many valuable and insightful comments. This paper is dedicated to the memory of our
son Yaakov Yehudah Frimer *z"l*.

[3] See *Mishna, Kiddushin* 1:7; Tosefta *Kiddushin* 1:10; BT *Kiddushin* 34a; *Encyclopedia
Talmudit*, II, "*Isha*," pp. 244–246.

[4] *Berakhot* 20b.

[5] *Kiddushin* 34a.

[6] The period of the *rishonim* (the "earlier" scholars) is generally viewed as beginning
from the middle of the eleventh century (the time of R. Isaac Alfasi) until the sixteenth
century (just prior to the time of R. Joseph Caro and R. Moses Isserles). The period of
aharonim (the "later" scholars) is today generally considered to start from the time of R.
Joseph Caro and R. Moses Isserles and to continue down to the modern period. The

biblically ordained *mitsvot*, but to those of rabbinic origin, as well.[7] The rationale for this position is that, in establishing and defining the character of new ordinances, the Rabbis generally followed the Torah's lead (*kol de-takun rabbanan, ke-ein de-oraita takun*).[8] Nevertheless, there are several instances of time-determined rabbinic innovations where the Rabbis felt it important to obligate women. Thus, women are rabbinically commanded in private prayer because it is "a request for mercy,"[9] which women require from the Almighty no less than men. Similarly, they are required to light Hanukka candles (*neirot Hanukka*)[10] and drink the four cups of wine at the Passover *seder* (*arba kosot*),[11] because "they [women], too, were involved in the same miracle [of salvation] (*she-af hen hayu be-oto ha-nes*)." Consequently, women must thank and praise the Lord as do their male counterparts.

The question of women's rabbinic obligation of reading *Megillat Esther* appears four times in the Talmudic literature:

(1) Said R. Joshua ben Levi: Women are obligated in reading the Book of Esther on Purim (*mikra Megilla*) for they, too, were involved in the miracle.[12]

(2) Bar Kappara said: One must read the *Megilla* before women and minors, for they, too, were involved in the doubt [i.e., danger] (*she-af otam hayu ba-safek*). R. Joshua ben Levi acted accordingly – he gathered his sons and the members of his household and read [the *Megilla*] before them.[13]

---

nineteenth and twentieth century scholars are often referred to as the *aharonei ha-ahronim*.

[7] *Inter alia*: *Tosefot, Berakhot* 20b, *s.v.* "*beTefilla*;" *Tosefot, Pesahim* 108b, *s.v.* "*sheaf*." R. Solomon ben Isaac (Rashi), *Berakhot* 20b *s.v.* "*veHayyavin beTefilla*" seems to dissent. See: *Encyclopedia Talmudit*, II, "*Isha*," p. 247; R. Isaac Arieli, *Einayyim laMishpat, Berakhot* 20b, *s.v.* "*de-Rahamei ninhu*."

[8] *Pesahim* 30b and 116b; *Yoma* 31a; *Yevamot* 11a; *Gittin* 64b and 65a; *Avoda Zara* 34a.

[9] *Berakhot* 20b and *Tosefot ad loc. s.v.* "*beTefilla*."

[10] *Shabbat* 23a.

[11] *Pesahim* 108a.

[12] *Megilla* 4a.

[13] *Jerusalem Talmud, Megilla* 2:4 (73b). See *Tosafot, Pesahim* 108b, *s.v.* "*Af hen*" who maintains that the Babylonian Talmud's formulation "*she-af hen hayu be-oto ha-nes*" is equivalent to the Jerusalem Talmud's statement "*she-af otam hayu ba-safek*."

(3) 'All are obligated in the reading of the *Megilla*;'[14] 'All are empowered (*kesheirin*) to read the *Megilla*'[15] – ['All'] to include what? To include women. And this is in accordance with the opinion of R. Joshua ben Levi – for R. Joshua ben Levi said: Women are obligated in the reading of the *Megilla*.[16]

(4) All are obligated in the reading of the *Megilla*: Priests, Levites, Israelites…All are obligated and can assist the masses (*ha-rabim*, to be understood as "others" or "the community") in fulfilling their obligation. A *tumtum* (one whose sex is undetermined because the genitalia are covered) and an *androgonus* (hermaphrodite) are obligated, but cannot assist the masses in fulfilling their obligation.… Women…are exempt and cannot assist the masses in fulfilling their obligation.[17]

II. Rishonim

In their attempt to apply the above sources to the question of women and *mikra Megilla*, the *rishonim* divide themselves into three schools:

(1) **The "Equal Obligation" School:** Most *rishonim*[18] maintain that the first three sources, particularly that from *Arakhin* (source #3), establish that women are obligated to read *Megillat Esther* and, therefore, should also be empowered to read it for others. The connection between obligation and the ability to assist others in fulfilling their obligation is based on the

---

[14] Based on *Tosefta* (Lieberman), *Megilla* 2:7; see source #4 below.

[15] Based on *Mishna, Megilla* 2:4; *Megilla* 19b.

[16] *Arakhin* 2b-3a.

[17] *Tosefta* (Lieberman), *Megilla* 2:7.

[18] See, for example: Rashi, *Arakhin* 3a, *s.v. "leAtuyei nashim;"* R. Moses ben Maimon (Rambam), *Mishnah Torah, Hilkhot Megilla* 1:1 (see *Magid Mishne* and *Haggahot Maimoniyot ad loc.* and *Shiltei Gibborim* to Rif *Megilla* 4a); R. Isaac of Vienna, *Or Zarua*, II, sec. 368; R. Solomon ben Aderet (Rashba), *Megilla* 4a; R. Menahem haMeiri, *Bet haBehira, Berakhot* 47b and *Megilla* 4a; R. David ben Levi, *Sefer haMikhtam, Megilla Nikret;* R. Nissim (Ran), on Rif *Megilla* 4a; R. Isaiah ben Eliah the later, *Piskei Riaz (Machon haTalmud haYerushalmi*, Jerusalem, 5731) *Megilla* Chap. 2, 3:2 - cited in *Shiltei Gibborim*, to Rif *Megilla* 4a; R. Joseph Haviva, *Nimukei Yosef, Megilla* 4a, *s.v "she-Af.* See also R. Ovadiah Yosef, *Resp. Yehave Da'at*, III, sec 51; *Sha'ar haTsiyyun*, O.H., sec. 689, sec. 2, note 16. The following cite both the views of Rashi and Behag without taking a stand themselves: *Hiddushei haRan* (authorship unclear), *Megilla* 4a; R. Asher ben Jehiel (Rosh), *Megilla* (4a), Chap. 1, sec 4; R. Eliezer ben Samuel of Metz, *Sefer Yereim, "Amud Vav, Issurim Na'asim veAdam Na'ase Ra laShamyim veLo laBeriyot."*

mishnaic dictum: "Anyone who is *not* obligated, *cannot* assist the masses in fulfilling their obligation."[19] This latter ruling readily leads to the converse conclusion, namely, that "one who *is* obligated *can* assist others in fulfilling their obligation."[20] Indeed, Rashi in his commentary to *Arakhin* 3a writes "[All]…to include women – that they are obligated in reading the *Megilla* and can assist the men in fulfilling their obligation."[21]

We note, of course, that this conclusion would appear to be contradicted by the last sentence of the *Tosefta* in *Megilla* (source #4), which exempts women from the obligation of *mikra Megilla*, and further indicates that they *cannot* assist the masses in fulfilling their obligation. This first "equal obligation" school of *rishonim* maintains that since the Talmud in *Arakhin*[22] rejects the conclusion of the *Tosefta* in *Megilla*, the latter source is to be set aside as being neither authoritative nor normative *halakha*.

(2) **The "*Kavod haTsibbur*" School:** The second school of *rishonim* maintain that fundamentally women share equal obligation with men and should, therefore, also be empowered to read it for them. However, for external considerations, they are enjoined from doing so.[23] The external

---

[19] "*Kol she-eino mehuyav ba-davar, eino motsi et ha-rabim yedei hovatam.*" *Mishna, Rosh haShana* 3:8.

[20] "*Kol ha-mehuyav* [or *ha-hayav*] *ba-davar, motsi et ha-rabim yedei hovatam.*" This implication can be derived from the talmudic statement in *Berakhot* 20b that if women are biblically obligated in *birkat ha-mazon*, they can assist the masses in fulfilling their obligation ["*le-afukei rabim yedei hovatam*"]. It is, however, clearly delineated in the Jerusalem Talmud, *Berakhot* 3:3 ["*Im haya hayyav afilu im yatsa motsi*"] and various *rishonim* and *aharonim*; see, for example: R. Joseph ben Meir ibn Migash, *Resp. R"i mi-Gash*, sec. 86; *Sefer haOra*, I, sec. 44, *Din Pat haTsenuma be-Ke'ara*; Rosh, *Berakhot*, Chap. 7, sec. 21 and *Rosh haShana*, Chap. 3, sec. 12; R. Isaac ben Aba Mari, *Sefer haIttur, Aseret haDibrot, Hilkhot Shofar*, p. 99a; R. Abraham ben Isaac of Narbonne, *Sefer haEshkol* (Albeck), *Hilkhot Seuda*, p. 24b, *s.v. "veKhol ha-berakhot;"* R. Simeon ben Tsemah Duran, *Resp Tashbets*, I, sec. 131; R. Yeruham, *Toldot haAdam, Netiv* 13, part 1, p. 103, column 2, *s.v. "haHelek haRishon;"* R. Hayyim Joseph David Azulai, *Birkei Yosef*, O.H. sec. 124, no. 2; R. Yihye ben Joseph Tsalah (Maharits), *Resp. Peulat Tsaddik*, III, sec. 184, *s.v. "u-miKol makom;"* R. Eliezer Waldenberg, *Resp. Tsits Eliezer*, VII, sec. 1, *"Kuntres Katan le-Maftir,"* Chap. 1, *s.v. "u-beSefer haManhig,"* Chap. 2, *s.v. "ve-Davar ze,"* and Chap. 5 *s.v. "veHitbonanti ve-ra'iti."*

[21] Rashi, *Arakhin* 3a, *s.v. "leAtuyei nashim – she-hayyavot be-mikra Megilla u-kesheirot likrota u-le-hotsi zekharim yedei hovatam.*

[22] *Supra* at note 16.

[23] Behag according to *Tosafot, Sukka* 38a, *s.v. "be-Emet Amru;"* R. Moses of Coucy, *Sefer Mitsvot Gadol (Semag), Divrei Soferim, Aseh*, no. 4; Meiri, *Megilla* 4a, *s.v. "Nashim;"* R. Yom

reason most commonly cited by this school is *kevod ha-tsibbur*[24] (maintenance of the honor/dignity of the community) or *zila milta*[25] (maintenance of propriety/modesty within the community), based on the analogy to *keriat haTorah*.[26] Thus, Tosafot[27] write:

…because were are dealing with a community, it would be a breach of propriety (*zila be-hu milta*) were a women to assist the masses in fulfilling their obligation. Thus, women are obligated in *Megilla* reading; yet, *Ba'al Halakhot Gedolot* (Behag) rules that women cannot assist the masses in fulfilling their *Megilla* obligation.

Some *rishonim* cite as an external factor *kol be-isha erva* (that the singing voice of a woman is sexually distracting).[28] As far as the *Tosefta* is

---

Tov ben Abraham Ashvilli (Ritva), *Megilla* 4a, *s.v* "*she-Af hen*;" *Tur*, O.H. 689; R. Isaac of Corbeil, *Sefer Mitsvot Katan* (*Semak*), *Yom Shlishi*, no. 299.

[24] R. Moses of Coucy, *Sefer Mitsvot Gadol* (*Semag*), *Divrei Soferim, Aseh*, no. 4; Ritva, *Megilla* 4a, *s.v* "*she-Af hen.*"

[25] Behag according to *Tosafot, Sukka* 38a, *s.v.* "*be-Emet Amru.*" It has yet to be determined whether or not *kevod ha-tsibbur* and *zila milta* are synonymous terms. R. Hayyim Zalman Dimitrovsky in his comments to Rashba, *Megilla* 4a, note 431 suggests that they are. See also the related comments of R. Joseph B. Soloveitchik in R. Zvi Joseph Reichman, *Reshimot Shiurim* [New York: 5749], *Sukka* 38a, p. 184, *s.v.* "*Beram le-fi haTosafot*"; *Otsar Mefarshei haTalmud, Sukka*, II, 38a, p. 345, *s.v.* "*I nami mishum*" and note 56. On the other hand, from *Mishnah Berura*, sec. 271, no. 4, it would seem that *zila milta* is a propriety/modesty issue.

[26] The invocation of the term "*kavod ha-tsibbur*" presumes a valid comparison between public *Megilla* reading and public Torah reading - in which women's participation has been ruled out because of *kavod ha-tsibbur*; see *Megilla* 23a. Clearly, the *rishonim* of the first school reject this suggestion. Indeed, this comparison is not at all self-evident, particularly since women are obligated in *mikra Megilla*, but exempted from *keriat haTorah*. In addition, *keriat ha-Megilla* is essentially a private obligation which can be preformed in private, in the absence of a *minyan*; *keriat haTorah*, on the other hand, is a communal obligation requiring a *minyan*. See: R. Moses ben Nahman (Ramban, Nahmanides) *Milhamot haShem, Megilla* 5a; Ran *ad. loc.* Further analysis of *kevod ha-tsibbur* is beyond the scope of this paper.

[27] *Tosafot, supra,* note 25.

[28] Based on *Berakhot* 24a. This reason is attributed to R. Isaac ben Aba Mari, *Asseret haDibrot*, cited by: R. Meir haMe'ili of Narvonna, *Sefer haMe'orot, Megilla* 19b; R. Aaron ben Jacob of Lunel, *Orhot Hayyim, Hilkhot Megilla uPurim*, sec. 2; *Kol Bo, Megilla* 103; R. David ben Levi of Narvonna, *Sefer haMikhtam, Megilla* 4a. This reason is also given in Auerbach's edition of R. Abraham Av Bet-Din, *Sefer haEshkol, Hilkhot Hanukka u-Purim*, sec. 9. Various *aharonim* concur with the stringent view of *Asseret haDibrot*, invoking "*kol be-isha erva*" in regard to the question of women chanting the Torah or *Megilla*; see: R. Hayyim Palagi, *Ruah Hayyim*, O.H., sec. 75, no. 2; R. Hayyim Palagi, *Yefeh Lev*, VI, O.H., sec. 282; *Resp. Atsei Hayyim*, I, sec. 7 (cited in R. Abraham Yaffe Schlesinger, *Resp. Be'er Sarim*, sec. 55); R. Shlomo Yosef Elyashiv, cited in R. Abraham-

concerned, this school maintains that the text is corrupted. The last sentence which reads "Women…are exempt and cannot assist the masses in fulfilling their obligation" should either be deleted[29] or emended to read: "Women are obligated but cannot assist the masses in fulfilling their obligation."[30]

(3) **The "Lesser Obligation" School:** The third school, also attributed primarily to Behag,[31] makes a distinction in the nature of a woman's

---

Sofer Abraham, *Nishmat Avraham*, V, *Y.D.*, sec. 195, p. 76–77; R. Shlomo Zalman Auerbach, cited in R. Abraham-Sofer Abraham, *Nishmat Avraham*, V, *Y.D.*, sec. 195, p. 76–77 – see also *Halikhot Shlomo*, I, *Hilkhot Tefilla*, Chap. 20, sec. 11, note 20; R. Eliezer Waldenberg, *Resp. Tsits Eliezer*, sec. 36, nos. 2 and 3; R. Nathan Gestetner, *Resp. leHorot Natan*, I, *E.H.*, sec. 60 and V, *O.H.*, sec 5; R. Efraim Greenblatt, *Resp. Rivevot Efrayyim*, I, sec. 449. See also R. *Azriel Hildesheimer, Resp. R. Azriel*, *O.H.*, sec. 128.

On the other hand, many *posekim* maintain that the position of the *Asseret haDibrot* (*Ba'al haIttur*) does not reflect normative halakha. More specifically, women chanting the Torah or *Megilla* with the appropriate notes (*ta'amei ha-mikra*) is not included in the prohibition of *kol be-isha erva*. See: R. Jacob Hayyim Sofer, *Kaf haHayyim*, sec. 689, no. 2; *Resp. Divrei Heifets*, cited by *Sdei Hemed, Klalim, Ma'arekhet kuf, klal* 42; R. Jehiel Jacob Weinberg, *Resp. Seridei Eish*, II, sec. 8; R. Nahum Tsvi Kornmehl, *Resp. Tiferet Tsvi*, II, sec. 7; R. Samuel haLevi Wosner, *Resp. Shevet haLevi*, III, sec. 14 – who indicates that most *rishonim* are lenient by *keriah de-mitzvah*; R. Ovadiah Yosef, *Yehave Da'at*, III, sec. 51, note, and IV, sec. 15, end of note; R. Ovadiah Yosef, *Resp. Yabia Omer*, VIII, *O.H.*, sec. 22, no. 10 and IX, *O.H.*, sec. 98, no. 9, and sec. 108, no. 74; R. Ovadiah Yosef, *Me'or Yisrael*, I, *Megilla* 4a, *s.v.* "*beTosfot d"h Nashim*," p. 251, and *Megilla* 23a, *s.v.* "*Tanu Rabbanan, haKol*," p. 279; R. Ovadiah Yosef, *Halikhot Olam*, II, *Ekev*, sec. 2, note 2, p. 74; R. Ovadiah Yosef, *MeShiurei Maran haRishon leTsiyyon, Rabbeinu Ovadiah Yosef Shelita*, I, *Gilyon* 19, *va-Yeira* 5756, sec. 2, p. 73. R. Isaac Yosef, *Yalkut Yosef*, V, *Dinei Keriat Megilla*, sec. 12 and notes 19 and 22, and VII, sec. 23, no. 11, end of note 16; R. Isaac Yosef, *Yalkut Yosef, Otsar Dinim la-Isha ve-laBat*, sec. 24, no. 6; R. Simeon Hirari, "*Kol be-Isha Erva ve-Nashim bi-Keriat Megilla*," *Or Torah*, *Adar* 5731, sec 123, pp. 289–292 and *Nisan* 5731, sec. 148, pp. 339–343 – see especially p. 341 *s.v.* "*u-le-Or*," and R. Yehuda Herzl Henkin, *Resp. Bnai Vanim*, II, sec. 10 and III, sec. 1; Yehuda Herzl Henkin, unpublished responsum to R. Abraham-Sofer Abraham, 24 Menahem Av 5761 (regarding *Nishmat Avraham*, V, *Y.D.*, sec. 195, p. 76–77).

[29] Semag, *supra*, note 24. This is also clear from *Rosh, Megilla*, Chap. 1, sec. 4, where he brings proof to the status of women from the *Tosefta's* ruling on *tumtum* and *androgonus*.

[30] See: Meiri, Rashba and Ran (R. Nissim ben Reuben) to *Megilla* 4a.

[31] Behag, *Halakhot Gedolot, Hilkhot Megilla, s.v.* "*haKol hayyavin.*" Cited by: *Tosafot, Arakhin* 3a, *s.v.* "*leAtuyei*;" Rosh and Ran, *supra*, note 18; R. Eliezer ben R. Yoel haLevi (Ra'avya), *Megilla*, sec. 569; R. Mordechai ben Hillel (Mordechai), *Megilla* 4a. (See: R. Hayyim Zalman Dimitrovsky in his comments to Rashba, *Megilla* 4a, note 431 who indicates that there were two distinct formulations of the position of the Behag.) A similar view is maintained by other *rishonim*: R. Hananel ben Hushiel, *Megilla* 4a *s.v.* "*ve-Amar*"; R. Elazar of Worms, *Rokei'ah, Hilkhot Purim*, no. 36; *Ba'al haIttur, Asseret haDibrot, Hilkhot Megilla, s.v.* "*Mi kore*," p. 226; R. Simha of Speyer, *Haggahot Maimoniyot*,

obligation: men are obligated to *read* the *Megilla*; women, however, have a lesser obligation, that is, only to *hear* the reading of the *Megilla*.[32] This distinction in obligation bears direct halakhic repercussions with regard to the question of whether women can read the *Megilla* for men. As a rule, one Jew can assist another in fulfilling his/her obligations only if the former has an obligation that is equal to or greater than that of the latter.[33] Thus, Rosh[34] writes:

And *Ba'al haHalakhot* ruled that women are only obligated to *hear* the *Megilla*; however, her reading [of the *Megilla*] cannot assist the men in fulfilling their obligation. For the men are obligated to *read* [and do not fulfill their obligation] until they hear the *Megilla* read by men, who are obligated in *reading* like them - and hearing [the reading] from women is not equivalent [i.e., is of a lower level of obligation] to the men's reading for themselves...And according to *Halakhot Gedolot* and *Tosefta*, the statement in *Arakhin*, "All are empowered to read the *Megilla*...to include women" needs to be explained [as follows]: not that women are empowered to read for men, but [rather they are empowered to read] only for women. [And the significance of this statement is] that one should not suggest that women cannot fulfill their obligation until they hear an important [i.e., high level obligation] reading of men. [*Arakhin*] teaches us that a woman can indeed assist her fellow [woman in fulfilling her obligation].

As far as the *Tosefta* is concerned, this school maintains that the last sentence which reads "Women...are exempt and cannot assist the masses in

---

Hilkhot Megilla, 1:1; R. Eliezer ben Yoel haLevi (Ra'avya), *Sefer Ra'avya*, II, *Hilkhot Megilla*, sec. 569.

[32] The first and second schools argued that as a result of "*she-af hen hayu be-oto ha-nes*," there is no longer any difference between men and women and both genders share the *maximal* obligation. The third school notes that *mikra Megilla* is a time-determined rabbinic commandment, in which women should not have been obligated at all; as a result, perhaps the obligation placed upon them because of "*she-af hen hayu be-oto ha-nes*" assumes a minimal form. Interestingly, such analysis with regard to *neirot Hanukka* and *arba kosot* is absent in the halakhic literature. Indeed, there is no dissenting opinion to the ruling that a woman can light *Hanukka* candles for the men of the home; see: *Shabbat* 23a; *O.H.*, sec. 675, no. 3; *Encyclopedia Talmudit*, XVI, *Hanukka*, p. 248 note 106. This may result from the fact that there is no simple way to divide the obligation into minimal and maximal forms.

[33] See, for example, *Berakhot* 20b "*le-afukey rabim yedei hovatam*."

[34] R. Asher ben Jehiel (Rosh), *supra*, note 18.

fulfilling their obligation" should be understood to mean "Women are exempt [from the obligation to *read* the *Megilla* – though they are obligated to hear it, as indicated by R. Joshua ben Levi] and cannot assist the masses [of men] in fulfilling their obligation"

We would like to reiterate that, as presented above, there are two distinct traditions as to the position of Behag. Both agree that women cannot read *Megillat Esther* for men; the rationales for this, however, are fundamentally different. *Tosafot* in *Sukka*[35] places Behag in the Second School according to whom women are obligated equally with men - but cannot read for them because of a side consideration of *zila milta*. *Tosafot* in *Arakhin* and Rosh,[36] on the other hand, place Behag in the Third School maintaining that women's obligation is on a lower level than that of men – and, hence, women cannot read for them either. Both positions, however, would agree that women can indeed read for other women in accordance with the statement in *Arakhin*: "All are empowered to read the *Megilla*...to include women."[37]

Korban Netanel, in his commentary on Rosh,[38] suggests that the two traditions in Behag can be unified. As indicated by *Tosafot* in *Arakhin* and Rosh, Behag maintains that women have a lesser obligation than men and, hence, cannot read *Megilla* for them. The seemingly contradictory statement of *Tosafot* in *Sukka* - according to which women cannot read for the community because of the side consideration of *zila be-hu milta* – is in fact not referring to men (for that possibility is already excluded because of women's lesser obligation). Rather it is referring to the impropriety of having a woman read for a community of *women!* Thus, while "a woman can indeed assist her fellow [woman]" (as Rosh himself states above[39]), according to *Korban Netanel, Tosafot* in *Sukka* is teaching us that it is improper (*zila be-hu milta*) for her to do so for a *group* of women.

---

[35] *Supra*, note 25

[36] *Supra*, note 31.

[37] *Supra*, note 16.

[38] R. Nathanel Weil, *Korban Netanel*, Rosh, *Megilla* (4a), Chap. 1, sec. 4, notes *mem* and *samekh*.

[39] *Supra*, note 18.

This novel suggestion of *Korban Netanel* runs counter to the understanding of *Magen Avraham*,[40] *Ateret Zahav*,[41] and *Arukh haShulhan*[42] that *zila be-hu milta* clearly refers to the case of a woman reading for men. More importantly, however, the *Tosafot haRosh*[43] – the version of the *Tosafot* in *Sukka* that was used by Rosh – reads as follows: "Alternatively, *zila be-hu milta* for women to assist *men* in fulfilling their obligation." Thus, it is clear from this reading that *zila be-hu milta* invoked by *Tosafot* in *Sukka* refers to a woman assisting men - not a woman for a group of women, as suggested by *Korban Netanel*. We will return to the opinion of the *Korban Netanel* later, but it would seem, for the time being at least, that his unified interpretation of the position of Behag is problematic.

III. Shulhan Arukh and *Posekim*

We turn now to the codification of the above discussion of a woman's obligation in *mikra Megilla* as found in the *Shulhan Arukh*. R. Joseph Caro (*Mehaber*) writes as follows:[44]

(1) All are obligated in the reading of the *Megilla*: men, women and freed slaves. Children, too, are educated to read it.

(2) Both one who reads [the *Megilla*] and one who hears it read by another have fulfilled their obligation – provided one hears it from one who is obligated to read it…. And there are those who maintain that women cannot assist men in fulfilling their obligation.

To this R. Moses Isserles (Rema)[45] comments:

"Gloss: And there are those who maintain that, if a woman reads for herself, she should recite the benediction "…*lishmoa* [to hear] *Megilla*" - for she is not obligated to read it."

---

[40] R. Abraham Gombiner, *Magen Avraham*, O.H., sec 271, no.2 – as noted by *Korban Netanel* himself.

[41] R. Menahem Mendel Auerbach, *Ateret Zahav*, O.H., sec. 689, no. 2, *s.v.* "*sheNashim*."

[42] R. Jehiel Mikhel Epstein, *Arukh haShulhan*, O.H., sec. 271, no. 5, and sec. 689, end of no. 5.

[43] *Tosafot haRosh*, *Sukka* 38a, *s.v.* "*be-Emet Amru*."

[44] R. Joseph Caro, *Shulhan Arukh*, O.H., sec. 689, parag. 1–2. "*Mehaber*" literally means "the author [of the *Shulkhan Arukh*]."

[45] R. Moses Isserles, *Mapah* to *Shulkhan Arukh*, O.H., sec. 689, parag 2.

The first view cited by the *Mehaber*, appearing in paragraph 1 and the beginning of paragraph 2, reflects the opinion of the "equal obligation" school of Rashi (see section II.1). According to this first opinion, women are obligated equally with men in *mikra Megilla* and, hence, can read for them. The second view, cited by R. Caro at the end of paragraph 2, would seem to be the view of Behag who prohibits women to read for men - though it is not clear which of the two traditions (see section II.2 *vs.* II.3) is being referred to.[46] Finally, the third view, cited by Rema in his gloss, is based on the "lesser obligation" school attributed to Behag, according to which a women's obligation is only to hear the *Megilla* (see section II.3).

These rulings of the *Mehaber* and *Rema* raise several practical issues discussed below.

A. Can Women Read *Megillat Esther* for Men?

As a general rule, Sefardic practice follows the ruling of R. Caro (the *Mehaber*), whereas Ashkenazic practice follows the opinion of Rema. Regarding the former, we need to determine which of the two opinions, cited by R. Caro in the *Shulhan Arukh,* actually reflects the *Mehaber*'s own position. Some scholars[47] have argued that R. Caro sides with the more stringent second opinion of Behag, which prohibits women from reading for men – though, as already noted above, it is not clear which of the two traditions in Behag is being referred to. R. Ovadiah Yosef,[48] on the other

---

[46] This point is a dispute between *Magen Avraham* note 5 and *Be'ur haGra s.v* "*veYeah omrim she-haNashim*," both *ad. loc.* See also *Mishnah Berurah* note 7.

[47] R. Yosef Hayyim al-Hakham, *Ben Ish Hai, Shana Rishona, Tetsave,* no. 2; R. Yaakov Hayyim Sofer, *Kaf haHayyim,* O.H. sec. 689, no. 14; R. Isaac Ben-Shushan, *Toldot Yitshak,* sec. 12, no. 2; R. Hayyim David Halevi, *Mekor Hayyim haShalem,* IV, sec. 232, no. 5 and note 22; R. Mordechai Eliyahu, cited by R. Moshe Harari, *Mikraei Kodesh: Hilkhot Purim,* Chap. 6, no. 8, note 28, p. 115. See also the comments of R. Aaron Cohen, *supra* note 1, endnote 10 therein.

[48] R. Ovadiah Yosef, *Resp. Yehaveh Da'at,* III, sec. 51, p. 159 and IV, sec. 34, note 2, p. 162. R. Ovadiah Yosef, *Me'or Yisrael,* I, *Megilla* 4a, *s.v. "Tosafot d"h Nashim."* R. Ovadiah Yosef, *Halikhot Olam,* I, *Tetsave - Hilkhot Purim,* sec. 2, note 2, p. 225. See also *MiShiurei Maran haRishon leTsiyyon Rabbeinu Ovadiah Yosef Shelita,* I, *Gilyon* 19, *vaYera* 5756, sec. 2, where R. Ovadiah Yosef permits a woman to read *Megilla* for a man (when absolutely necessary and only according to Sefardic usage), concluding: "And this is not, perish the thought, a Reform innovation, since this is the law and the halakha." See also: R. Yitshak Yosef, *Yalkut Yosef,* V, pp. 287–289 and R. David Yosef, *Torat haMo'adim, Hilkhot Purim veHodesh Adar,* sec. 5, no. 9, p. 138.

hand, is one of the leading proponents of the opinion that Rashi's position (section II.1) is presented first as the primary view (*stam*); this is then followed by Behag's view - merely as a dissenting minority position (*yesh omrim*).[49] In such a case, maintains R. Yosef, the *Mehaber* would seem to be ruling with the former - more lenient - opinion and, hence, would allow women to read for men. In practice, however, and in deference to the second opinion, R. Yosef only allows Sefardic women to read for Sefardic men *be-she'at ha-dehak* - when no suitable male is available.[50] We note that the scholars of the second *"kevod ha-tsibbur"* school would agree with this latter ruling, since the consensus of *posekim* is that *kevod ha-tsibbur* can be set aside *be-she'at ha-dehak*.[51]

By contrast, the view of Rema in his gloss would seem to be rather clear: women, whose obligation in *mikra Megilla* is a lesser one than that of men, cannot read the *Megilla* for the latter.[52] In a case where there is no male available to read for a man, the *posekim* rule that a woman should read for him (without *berakhot*) so that he will fulfill his obligation at least according to the first two schools. If at some later hour on Purim a capable male becomes available, the *Megilla* should be heard again.[53]

---

[49] For a discussion of *stam ve-ahar kakh yesh omrim*, see: R. Ben Tsiyyon Abba Shaul, *Or le-Tsiyyon*, II, *Teshuvot*, pp. 5–10; *Yalkut Yosef*, IX, pp. 5–44.

[50] See references in note 48 *supra*.

[51] For documentation of this point, see: Aryeh A. Frimer, *"Ma'amad haIsha beHalakha - Nashim uMinyan,"* Or haMizrah 34:1, 2 (*Tishrei* 5746), pp. 69–86 – page 73, note 29. This was confirmed recently by R. Shlomo Fischer in a conversation with R. Meir Schweiger.

[52] See discussion at note 34 *supra*. Apropos, R. Yosef Adler (Personal communication, March 10, 1996) recalls that R. Joseph B. Soloveitchik, the Rav, often commented on his difficulty in accepting the view of Behag. Nonetheless, the Rav acknowledged that since Rema cites *Halakhot Gedolot's* ruling approvingly, it has become normative halakha. Consequently, women could not read *Megilla* for Ashkenazic men. Interestingly, though, in the winter of 1977, our sister-in-law Mrs. Sabina Frimer asked the Rav whether she could read the *Megilla* for her grandmother and home-bound grandfather – since no one else was available to do so. The Rav responded that it would be preferable to find a male to read for them, but if she were not successful, *be-she'at ha-dehak*, she could read for them herself. The Rav also suggested that the grandfather should make the *berakhot*.

[53] *Kaf haHayyim*, O.H., sec. 689, note v12 and 14; R. Shaul Yisraeli and R. Mordechai Eliyahu, cited in R. Moshe Harari, *Mikraei Kodesh – Purim*, chap. 6, note 28.

Nevertheless, there are those who have recently suggested, that even according to the Behag, women can *in practice* read for men at the nighttime reading of the *Megilla*.[54] In support of this position, these authors cite the writings of the early twentieth century Lithuanian scholar R. Hanokh Henikh Agus, in his renowned work *"Marheshet,"* and several others who adopt a similar view.[55] In their attempt to explain the Behag's distinction between the obligation of men and women, many scholars have proposed that the obligation of *Megilla* reading is actually composed of two facets. All agree that the first of these is *pirsumei nisa* (publicizing the miracle) – an obligation in which men and women share equally. Various suggestions have been put forward as to the second, e.g., *zekhirat Amalek* (remembering to destroy Amalek), *keriat haHallel* (equivalent to reciting *Hallel*), or *talmud Torah* (learning the laws of the Holiday). Since women are not obligated in the second facet, they cannot assist men in fulfilling their *Megilla* obligation – which involves both facets. The school of the *Marheshet* notes, however, that the second facet in each case is only applicable during the day. Hence, regarding the *Megilla* reading at night, men and women are equally obligated in only one facet (*pirsumei nisa*). Women can, therefore, read for men at that time.

Several basic arguments seriously undermine reliance on this lenient approach in practice.[56] Firstly, the explanations of the *Marheshet* and others

---

[54] R. Moshe HaLevi Steinberg, *Hilkhot Nashim*, sec. 15, no. 2; R. Avraham Weiss, "Women and the Reading of the Megilla," *Torah u-Madda Journal*, 8 (1998–1999), pp. 295–397; R. Daniel Landes, "The Reading of the Megilla on Purim Night," found through website www.pardes.org.il.

[55] R. Hanokh Henikh Agus, *Marheshet*, I, sec 22, no. 9; R. Tsvi Pesah Frank, *Mikraei Kodesh, Purim*, sec. 29; R. Samuel Grunberger, *Hedvat Hashem, be-Inyanei Purim*, sec. 5, no. 3; R. Simcha Elberg, *"Im Isha Motsi'a Ish beKeriat haMegilla,"* *HaPardes* 51:6 (*Adar* 5737) sec. 40, p. 9 – reprinted in R. Simcha Elberg, *Shalmei Simha*, I, sec. 62; R. Simcha Elberg, *"be-Din Im Isha Motsi'a Ish beKeriat haMegilla,"* *HaPardes* 63:6 (*Adar* 5749) sec. 31, p. 4 – reprinted in R. Simcha Elberg, *Shalmei Simha*, V, sec. 44; R. Moshe Shternbuch, *Mo'adim uZemanim*, VII, addenda to II, sec. 171; R. Zevulun Sacks, *"Keri'at haMegilla al Yedei Nashim,"* *Tehumin*, XVIII, pp. 357-369 – see last section. For a review see: R. David Aurbach, *Halikhot Beitah*, sec. 24, no. 12, note 23.

[56] See the excellent and lengthy discussion of these points by R. Aaron Cohen, "Women Reading Megillah for Men: A Rejoinder," *The Torah U-Madda Journal*, 9 (2000), pp. 248–263.

may have been stated only in theory, but not in practice (*halakha le-ma'ase*).[57] In this regard it is important to distinguish between two very different categories of halachic scholarly activity. The first is *hiddush* – the development and/or advocacy of a novel or creative position; the second is *psak* – the halakhic decision making process. When one *paskens*, one must be cognizant of and take into account all the varying positions of the leading halakhic authorities throughout the generations.[58] We note as well, that consciously to adopt one particular approach simply because it yields the desired result, without grappling with the argument and the standings of the other halachic positions, is foreign to the halachic process and may lack intellectual integrity.[59]

Secondly, the suggestion that women can read *Megilla* for men at night was never mentioned or even hinted by any of the *rishonim* or the codes – this despite their extensive discussion of the topic of women reading for men under various conditions. The omission of such a major and obvious point surely indicates its rejection.[60]

Furthermore, the position of *Marheshet* and his colleagues resulted as an offshoot of a possible explanation of Behag – yet many other explanations are possible and have been proposed.[61]

Finally, the position of the *Marheshet* has been explicitly rejected by many

---

[57] See, R. Shlomo Zevin, *Sefarim veSoferim*, p. 181 who includes this discussion of R. Agus among the "*teshuvot ha-ma'asiyot*" (practical responsa) in the *Marheshet*. R. Aaron Cohen, *supra*, note 56 and R. Chaim Jachter, *infra*, note 60 maintain otherwise.

[58] See R. Yitshak Herzog, *Resp. Heikhal Yitshak, E.H.,* II, sec. 43, no. 3, who notes that we do not generally implement intricate and creative *pilpul* style explanations against the consensus of the traditionally accepted authorities.

[59] See Dov I. Frimer, "Letter to the Editor," Jerusalem Post, October 14, 2002, p. 5. See also R. Aharon Lichtenstein, "The Human and Social Factor in Halakha," *Tradition* 36:1 (2002) who writes: "Commiseration is acknowledged as a legitimate factor stimulating the posek's quest for a solution, but it is barred as a component of the halachic process proper, once that has been set in motion" (p. 11, top).

[60] See: R. Isaac Ben-Shushan, *Toldot Yitshak*, sec. 12, no. 2; R. Tsvi Shapira, *Tsivyon haAmudim* to *Sefer Mitsvot Katan*, V, sec. 148, end of note 9; R. Chaim Jachter, *Gray Matter* (2000), "May Women Read the *Megilla*," p. 227, note 8.

[61] For example, R. Joseph B. Soloveitchik himself gave many different explanations of the Behag. See: *Mesorah*, 12 (*Tammuz*, 5756), p. 14; R. Michal Zalman Shurkin, *Harerei Kedem*, sec. 174, p. 200; R. Zvi Joseph Reichman, *Reshimot Shiurim* (New York, 5749), *Sukka* 38a, pp. 184–5.

posekim.[62]

B. Can Women Read *Megillat Esther* for Women?

Above,[63] we cited the Talmud's statement in *Arakhin:*[64]

'All are obligated in the reading of the *Megilla;*' 'All are empowered (*kesheirin*) to read the *Megilla* – ['All'] to include what? To include women.

As we noted, the *Rishonim* who discuss women's obligation in *mikra Megilla* indicate that this statement empowers women to read for *men*, according to the school of Rashi,[65] or at least for *women*, according to the schools of Behag.[66] Nevertheless, two major hurdles stand in the way of women's *Megilla* readings for women. The first is the aforementioned *Korban Netanel,*[67] who argues that it is a breach of propriety (*zila milta*) for a woman

---

[62] For a variety of reasons, R. Pesah Eliyahu Falk, *Resp. Mahaze Eliyahu*, sec. 22, R. Isaac Leibis, *Resp. Beit Avi*, V, sec. 47, R. Isaac Ben-Shushan, *Toldot Yitshak*, sec. 12, R. Yehuda Lavi ben-David, *Shevet miYehuda*, Part 1, p. 155, and R. David Auerbach, *Halikhot Beitah*, sec. 24, note 23, subsec. 15 all explicitly disagree with the position of *Marheshet*. Moreover, *Marheshet's* assumption that *Megilla* reading is in lieu of *Hallel*, is disputed by R. Hayyim Joseph David Azulai, *Birkei Yosef*, sec. 693, no. 4, and by R. Moshe Shternbuch, *Resp. Teshuvot veHanhagot*, IV, sec. 177, no. 2. His assumption that there is *pirsumei nisa* at night is disputed by R. Joseph Rosen ("The Rogatchover"), *Tsafnat Panei'ah*, M.T., *Hilkhot Megilla*, 1:1. Similarly, his distinction between day and night with regard to the recitation of *Hallel* is in disagreement with the position of R. Samuel Eliezer Edels (Maharsha), *Hiddushei Aggadot*, Megilla 14b (cited by R. David Yosef, *supra*, note 48, p. 136). *Marheshet's* suggestion that women are freed from the obligation of *zekhirat Amalek* is also the subject of major disagreement; see: *Encyclopedia Talmudit*, XII, "Zekhirat Ma'ase Amalek," sec. 3 (p.222); *Resp. Yabia Omer*, VIII, sec. 54; *Resp. Yehave Da'at*, I, sec. 84; *Halikhot Beita*, sec. 9, no. 5, note 8; *Halikhot Bat Yisrael*, sec. 22, no. 1, notes 1-4; *Hilkhot Hag beHag: Purim*, sec. 3, no. 3 note 8 and end of addendum to sec. 3, no. 2 note 7, p. 214; *Nitei Gavriel – Dinei uMinhagei Purim*, sec. 4, no. 4, notes 5–8, and no. 10, note 14. R. Aryeh Pomeronchik, *Emek Berakha, vaYelekh beTokh haEmek* (collection at end of volume), *Keriat Megilla*, no. 3 takes the opposite position – that it may be possible for women to read for men but only at the *day* reading. Thus, the statements of R. Daniel Landes, *supra* note 54: "This is *conclusively demonstrated* by R. Hanoch Henech Agus..." and "Thus...it is *incontestable* that women may fulfill the obligation for men...." (emphasis mine) – are unfounded.

[63] Text at note 16, *supra.*

[64] *Arakhin* 2b-3a.

[65] See, for example, quote from Rashi at note 21.

[66] See, for example, quote from Rosh at note 34.

[67] *Supra*, note 38.

to read *Megilla* for a *group* of women. The view of *Korban Netanel* is cited approvingly in the noted halakhic woks *Mishna Berura*[68] and *Kaf haHayyim*.[69]

The second ruling is that of *Magen Avraham*[70] who, based on the kabbalistic *Midrash Ne'elam Rut*, indicates that it is preferable that women not read for themselves but hear the *Megilla* from men. *Mishna Berura* cites this view of *Magen Avraham*.[71] Many contemporary authors also cite *Korban Netanel*, *Magen Avraham* or both of these stringent opinions, at least *le-khathila*.[72]

Despite the stature of the scholars in the above "stringent school," a large number of *posekim* (the "lenient school") have permitted women's *Megilla* readings,[73] the rulings of both *Korban Netanel* and *Magen Avraham*

---

[68] R. Israel Meir haKohen Kagan, *Mishnah Berurah*, O.H., sec. 689, no. 2, *Sha'ar haTsiyyun* note 15.

[69] *Kaf haHayyim*, O.H. ibid., no. 17.

[70] *Magen Avraham*, O.H. sec. 689, no. 6

[71] *Mishnah Berurah*, O.H. sec. 689, no. 8 and *Sha'ar haTsiyyun* no. 16.

[72] Both of the past Chief Rabbis of Israel have published opinions against women's *Megilla* readings: Former Sefardic Chief Rabbi Mordecai Eliyahu is quoted by R. Moses Harari, *Mikra'ei Kodesh - Hilkhot Purim*, chap. 6, parag. 8, note 30. Former Ashkenazic Chief Rabbi Abraham Kahana Shapira is quoted by his assistant R. Zalman Koitner, in a letter distributed by a group called "Women of Efrat for the *Achdut* of *Halakhah*" and published in the newspaper *Yom ha-Shishi*, 15 *Adar* 5791 (March 1, 1991), p. 8. R. Shapira's letter indicates that although "...*halakhically*, a woman can read for other women," nevertheless "one should not change the prevalent custom" which has followed the more stringent ruling of the *Mishnah Berurah* (*Korban Netanel*). R. Menashe Klein, *Mishneh Halakhot, Mahadurah Tanyana*, vol. 1, O.H. sec 550 and R. Efraim Greenblatt, *Resp. Rivevot Efrayyim*, VII, 548, no. 3, also dissent. As mentioned below in notes 73c and 106, the *Rav* (Rabbi Joseph B. Soloveitchik) preferred that women be *machmir* in order to be *yotzei kol ha-de'ot*. See also: R. Yoel Schwartz, *Adar u-Furim*, sec. 8, no.3.A.1; R. Tsvi Cohen, *Purim veHodesh Adar*, Sec. 10, no. 17; *Nitei Gavriel, Dinei uMinhagei Purim*, sec. 13, no. 1, p. 65; R. Isaac Ben-Shushan, *Toldot Yitshak*, sec. 12.

[73] (a) Published responsa: Beersheba Chief Rabbi Elijah Katz, *haEshel* (*Bita'on haMoetsa haDatit Be'er Sheva*), XIII (Nissan 5736), pp. 41, 42 and 48 – see also Letter to the Editor, Shirah Leibowitz Schmidt, *Tradition*, 33:2 (Spring 1999), p. 80–82; Ma'ale Adumim Chief Rabbis Joshua Katz and Mordechai Nagari, *Ma'alot*, no. 185, *Parshat Tetsave* 5756, *Halakha Sedura*, sec. B, no. 5 and conversation with Dov I. Frimer, March 23, 1996 – this ruling was reprinted the following year as well in *Ma'alot, Parshat VaYikra* 5757, *Halakha Sedura*; R. Raphael Evers, *Resp. vaShav veRafa*, O.H., sec. 31; R. Ariel Pikar, *Tehumin* 18 (5758), pp. 361-368; R. Yehuda Herzl Henkin, "*Mahu Kevod haTsibbur*," *HaDarom* 55 (*Elul* 5746), pp. 33-41 (see especially top of page 37) – expanded and revised in *Resp. Benei Vanim*, II, no. 10; R. Yehuda Herzl Henkin, *Tsibbur Nashim biKri'at haMegilla, Keshot*, 4 (*Adar II/Nisan* 5755), sec. 14, pp. 8–10 – reprinted in *Resp. Benei Vanim*, III, sec. 7; R. Yehuda Herzl Henkin, *Equality Lost: Essays in Torah, Halacha and Jewish Thought* (Jerusalem: Urim Publications, 1999), pp. 54–65; R. Yehuda Herzl Henkin, "*Keriat haMegilla al Yedei Nashim – haMahloket eina be-Halakha*," *HaTsofe*,

notwithstanding. Regarding the *Korban Netanel*, the "lenient school" schol-

---

14 *Adar* 5759 (March 2, 1999), p. 9; R. Gedaliah Felder, cited by R. Henkin in *HaDarom*, *ibid.* In a conversation with Aryeh A. Frimer, April 29, 1992, R. Henkin reaffirmed the accuracy of this citation, despite its omission in the revised *Benei Vanim* presentation of this responsum.

(b) Similar opinions have been orally expressed by (in alphabetical order): R. Moshe Feinstein, as reported to R. Chaim Spring by R. Mordechai Tendler, October 1985; R. David Cohen, conversation with R. Shael I. Frimer, March 1979, and to Aryeh A. Frimer, March 1980; R. David Feinstein, conversation with Aryeh A. Frimer and Noach Dear, March 26, 1991, and to Aryeh A. Frimer, Dov I. Frimer and Noach Dear, March 19, 1995; and R. Levi Yitzchak haLevi Horowitz, The Bostoner *Rebbi*, conversation with Mr. Noach Dear, March 1990 – however, on April 13th, 1997, the *Rebbi's gabbai*, Nesanel Peterman, wrote the following: "Since the *Rebbi* considered this issue in the early 1990's, the whole question of women's 'rights' has become more complex and the *Rebbi* would like to consider the wider issues further."

(c) R. Aharon Lichtenstein, conversation with R. Chaim Brovender, March 1992 and February 1994, and to Dov I. Frimer, October 21, 1992 and February 19, 1994, also permits a women's *Megilla* reading. Nevertheless, R. Lichtenstein does advise Jerusalemite women not to hold such a reading when the fifteenth of *Adar* falls on *Shabbat* (known as *Purim me-shulash*). In such an instance, Jerusalemites read on the fourteenth, and, as noted below (see section III.D), many *posekim* maintain that since this reading is not on its normally designated date, a *minyan* is an absolute requirement. (In all other years, a *minyan* is advisable but not a prerequisite to fulfillment.) While most authorities agree that ten women do constitute a *minyan* for *mikra Megilla* even on *Purim meshulash*, a minority dissent (see *infra*, end of note 94). R. Lichtenstein maintains, therefore, that it is best to be stringent so as to be sure that one's obligation has been fulfilled. R. Lichtenstein noted that his father-in-law, Rabbi Joseph B. Soloveitchik ("the *Rav*"), preferred that women be *machmir* for the same reasons (to be *yotzei kol ha-dei'ot lekhathila*) every year. Hence, the *Rav* preferred that women did not have their own service for *mikra Megilla* at all; see note 106, *infra*.

(d) R. Ahron Soloveichik, in a taped conversation with Dov I. Frimer, July 8, 1997, ruled that in those communities, such as in Israel, where there is already an established custom to have a second *Megilla* reading for women, it is irrelevant whether the reader is male or female. Elsewhere, where such a *minhag* is not so common, a special women's *Megilla* reading should not be permitted (for *hashkafic* and public policy reasons). Should the local rabbi be afraid, however, that a rift in the community might result, he should refrain from taking any position whatsoever on the matter. Similarly, R. Jacob Ariel maintains that while basically women can read for other women they should not specifically break off from the rest of the community to do so (because of *pirsumei nisa*) unless necessary or in an instance where a separate reading for women will take place anyway; see: R. Jacob Ariel, *Resp. beOhalah shel Torah*, II, O.H., sec. 105 and his comments in Moshe Stern, *Megillat haAtasma'ut*, Mekor Rishon, 7 *Adar* 5761 (March 2, 2001) p. 16–17.

(e) R. Ovadiah Yosef, *Yabia Omer*, VIII, O.H., sec. 56, end of no. 4 writes: "...the custom of women who make a *minyan* by themselves for *mikra Megilla*...should be encouraged." Indeed, his son R. David Yosef, *Torat ha-Moadim: Hilkhot u-Minhagei Purim ve-Hodesh Adar*, sec. 5., note 9, p. 139, s.v *ve-ha-Rema*, indicates that despite the rulings of *Magen Avraham* and *Korban Netanel*, Ashkenazi (and certainly Sefardi) women can read for women.

ars note that authorities of the stature of *Magen Avraham*, *Ateret Zahav*, and *Arukh haShulhan*[74] do not view a women's reading of the *Megilla* as unseemly. Even more importantly the scholars of this school, as well as many others,[75] argue that *Korban Netanel* erred in his understanding of the *ba'alei haTosafot*, who were in fact discussing the impropriety of a woman's reading of the *Megilla* for *men*. Neither *Mishna Berura* nor *Kaf haHayyim* were aware of the reading in the relatively recently discovered[76] manuscript of *Tosafot haRosh*[77] which confirms that *Korban Netanel* erred.

The ruling of *Magen Avraham*,[78] based on *Midrash Ne'elam Rut*, is also quite surprising since it flies in the face of the above cited talmudic statement in *Arakhin*: "All are empowered (*kesheirin*) to *read* the *Megilla*."

---

[74] *Supra*, notes 40–42.

[75] Thus, R. Jacob Zev Kahana, *Resp. Toledot Ya'akov*, sec. 5; R. Jehiel Michel Tucazinsky, *Lu'ah Erets Yisrael, Purim dePrazim*; and R. Shlomo Zalman Auerbach, cited in *Halikhot Beita, Petah haBayyit*, sec. 25 – all maintain that one woman may make *berakhot* for many others. (We note, however, that R. Shlomo Zalman Auerbach, as recorded in a personal written communication from his nephew, R. Yitshak Mordechai Rubin, to R. Asher Viner (*Kislev* 5794), was nevertheless unwilling to permit a women's Megilla reading, though he does not state why.) Similarly, in *Kiryat Sanz*, it is the wont of the *Alter Rebbetsin* to recite *kiddusha rabba* for the women. (Shira Schmidt, personal communication, January 19, 2001). Rabbi Isaac Liebis, *Resp. Beit* Avi, V, sec. 15 indicates that the ruling of the *Shulhan Arukh, O.H.*, 199, sec. 7, that women can make a *zimmun* for themselves also speaks against the position of *Korban Netanel*. The following *posekim* also set aside the view of *Korban Netanel*: R. Tsvi Shapira *Tsivyon haAmudim* to *Sefer Mitsvot Katan*, V, sec. 148, note 9; R. Gavriel Zinner, *Nitei Gavriel – Dinei uMinhagei Purim*, sec. 13, no. 9, note 14; R. Simha Israel Blum, "*beInyan Keriat haMegilla leNashim*," *Sefat haOhel* (*Nisan* 5743), sec. 15, p. 98; R. Zvi Kohen, *Purim veHodesh Adar*, sec. 10, no. 17; R. Haim David Halevi, *Mekor Hayyim liBnot Yisrael*, sec. 34, nos. 6 and 7; and R. Moses Mordechai Karp, *Zer Aharon – Inyanei Purim* (Jerusalem: Oraysa, 5749), sec. 21, no. 7, who writes: "All the *posekim* have stated simply that a woman can read for other women, and it would seem so even for many women." See also R. Karp's *Hilkhot Hag beHag: Purim*, sec. 7, no. 3, note 7, p. 60, where he states: "See the *Sha'ar haTsiyyun*, who writes in the name of *Korban Netanel* that a woman should not read for many women because of *zila milta*. This does not seem to be the view of other *posekim*." These four authors indicate, however, that because of *Midrash Ne'elam*, a women's *Megilla* reading is not preferred; it is, nevertheless, permitted if necessary. See also R. Ben-Tsiyon Lichtman, *Benei Tsiyyon*, IV, *O.H.* sec. 271, no. 3, *s.v.* "*veRa'iti*," who disagrees with *Korban Netanel*'s understanding of *Tosafot*, though his stance on a women's *Megilla* reading is unknown. See also the critique appearing in *Tehilla leYonah* (Machon Be'er haTorah, Lakewood NJ, 5759), *Megilla* 4a, *s.v.* "*Ulam beKorban Netanel*," p. 23.

[76] Discovered by R. Solomon Aaron Wertheimer and first published in Jerusalem 1903.

[77] See text at note 38.

[78] *Magen Avraham, O.H.* sec. 689, no. 6

Although, as noted above, *Mishna Berura* cites *Magen Avraham*, he takes serious issue with him in *Sha'ar haTsiyyun*.[79] Indeed, *Midrash Ne'elam Rut* is not accepted as normative halakha by the above the "lenient-school" decisors, as well as many other *posekim*.[80]

C. What Benediction (*Berakha*) Should Women Recite Before Reading *Megillat Esther*?

The Rabbis instituted the benediction "...*al mikra Megilla*" to be recited prior to the reading the *Megilla*.[81] Since according to the "equal obligation" and "*kavod ha-tsibbur*" schools (see secs. II.1 and II.2 above) women share equally with men in the obligation of *mikra Megilla*, there is no logical reason to distinguish between the genders in the preliminary *berakha*. The above ruling of Rema indicates, however, that according to the "lesser obligation" school, which maintains that a woman's obligation is to *hear* the *Megilla* and not to *read* it – a woman should recite a different benediction, namely, "...*lishmoa* [to hear] *Megilla*." The origin of Rema's ruling is an innovation of R. Eliezer ben Yoel haLevi (Ra'avya, d. 1224).[82] This ruling, however, has been subject to serious challenge by R. Hezekiah de Silva (*Pri Hadash*)[83] and R. Elijah Kramer of Vilna (Gra).[84] The latter maintain that there is no justification to change the *berakha* from what originally appears in *Hazal*, *Geonim* and other *Rishonim* without any gender distinction.

The issue of what Ashkenazi women should do in practice is also a matter of major dispute among the modern *posekim*. Some cite the Rema's

---

[79] *Mishna Berura*, O.H. sec. 689, no. 8 and *Sha'ar haTsiyyun* no. 16.

[80] *Arukh haShulhan*, O.H. sec. 689, no. 5; former Chief Rabbi Mordechai Eliyahu, cited by R. Moses Harari, *Mikra'ei Kodesh – Hilkhot Purim*, 6:8, note 29; several other *posekim* cited by R. Nahman Kahana, *Orhot Hayyim*, O.H. sec. 689, no. 2, note 6.

[81] *Masekhet Soferim*, 14:1; Shulkhan Arukh, O.H., sec. 692, no. 1.

[82] Ra'avya, *Megilla*, end of sec. 569; "And it would seem to me that women should recite the benediction '*al mishma Megilla*' even if they read it themselves;" cited in Mordekhai, *Megilla*, no. 779.

[83] R. Hezekiah de Silva, *Pri Hadash*, O.H., sec. 689, end of note 2; see also "*Likutim*" at end of commentary.

[84] R. Elijah Kramer of Vilna, *Ma'aseh Rav, Hilkhot Purim*, sec. 246 (in some editions it is sec. 237, in others 243); R. Issacher Ber of Vilna, *Peulat Sakhir*, to *Ma'aseh Rav*, indicates that from the analysis of the *Turei Even* in his commentary on *Megilla* 4a, one can deduce that he too agrees that the *Berakha* should be "...*al mikra Megilla*."

ruling as is: "…*lishmoa Megilla*,"[85] while others cite the ruling of Rema with the variant text "…*lishmoa mikra Megilla*."[86] Yet a third group of scholars rule like the *Pri Hadash* and Gra that women like men should say "…*al mikra Megilla*."[87] What's more, R. Moshe Sternbuch argues that if a woman recites "…*lishmoa Megilla*" - she may well be reciting a *brakha le-vatalla*. A number of decisors have ruled that, even according to the view of the Rema, *be-di-avad* (ex post facto) all would agree that "…*al mikra Megilla*" is valid.[88] Finally, R. Hayyim Sonnenfeld is of the opinion that either of the benedictions is appropriate. To prevent confusion and error, he advises, therefore, that "…*al mikra Megilla*" should be preferred since that is the text which appears in all the siddurim and printed texts.

In light of the strong preference of some *posekim* to recite "…*al mikra Megilla*," and the sense of others that this formulation is valid *be-di-avad* according to all, it would seem that the best course of action is to recite

---

[85] R. Shlomo Zalman Auerbach cited by R. Nahum Stepansky, *veAleihu Lo Yibol*, I, *O.H.*, sec. 433; R. Jehiel Abraham Zilber, *Berur Halakha, Mahadura Tanyana*, *O.H.*, sec. 689. R. Gabriel Zinner, *Nitei Gavriel – Dinei Purim*, sec. 13, no. 5; R. Yehoshuah Yeshayahu Neuwirth, *Madrikh Hilkhati leAhayot beVatei Holim*, Chap. 10, *Purim*, no. 3; R. Jehiel Michel Tuketchinsky, *Luah Erets Yisrael, Purim*; R, Haim David Halevi, *Mekor Hayyim leBenot Yisrael*, sec. 34, no. 8; R. Moshe Harari, *Mikraei Kodesh- Purim*, sec. 9, no. 9.

[86] R. Abraham Danzig, sec. 155, no. 11 – cited by *Mishna Berura*, sec. 689, note 8 – note however, that in sec. 692, note 11, *Mishna Berura* uses the Rema's formulation *li-shmoa Megilla*; *Arukh haShulhan*, *O.H.*, sec. 692, no. 7; R. Isaac Ben-Shushan, *Toldot Yitshak*, sec. 12, no. 4; R. Eliezer Waldenberg, *Resp. Tsits Eliezer*, XIX, sec. 67, no. 2; R. Tsvi Cohen, *Purim veHodesh Adar*, Chap. 10, no. 48; R. Yoel Schwartz, *Adar uPurim*, sec. 8.3.4.

[87] R. Dov Ber Karasik, *Pithei Olam uMatamei haShulhan*, *O.H.*, 692, sec, 2, note 7; R. Ovadiah Yosef, *Resp. Yabia Omer*, I, *O.H.*, sec. 44 and VIII, *O.H.*, sec. 22, no. 27; R. Ovadiah Yosef, *Halikhot Olam*, I, *Tetsave - Hilkhot Purim*, sec. 1, note 1, p. 224; *Resp Yehave Da'at*, I, sec. 88; R. David Yosef, *Yalkut Yosef*, V, *Dinei Keriat haMegilla*, sec. 7, p. 284; R. Moshe Sternbuch, *Moadim uZemanim*, II, sec. 171; R. Moshe Sternbuch, *Teshuvot veHanhagot*, III, sec. 228 – at the end he cites that this is also the opinion of R. Aryeh Pomeronchik.

[88] See: R. Gabriel Zinner, *Nitei Gavriel – Dinei Purim*, sec. 13, no. 2; R. Dov Eisenberg, "A Guide for the Jewish Woman and Girl," Fourth Edition (Brooklyn, NY, 1986), *Halachos Pertaining to Purim*, p. 123, note 18. The latter notes as proof that when men are listening to the *Megilla* as well, "…*al mikra Megilla*" is recited and both genders fulfill their *berakha* obligation.

"...*al mikra Megilla*." Indeed, R. Yosef[89] and others[90] indicate that this is the prevalent custom.

D. Do Women Count for a *Minyan* for the Reading *Megillat Esther*?

In normal years when neither *Purim* nor *Shushan Purim* fall on Shabbat, a *minyan* is advisable for *mikra Megilla* because of *pirsumei nisa* (publicizing the miracle), although it is not a prerequisite to fulfillment.[91] A *minyan*, however, is required for the *berakha* "*ha-rav et riveinu*" said following the *Megilla* reading.[92] In addition, when the fifteenth of *Adar* falls on *Shabbat* (known as *Purim meshulash*), Jerusalemites read on the fourteenth; numerous *posekim* posit that, since this reading is not on its normally designated date, a *minyan* is an absolute requirement.[93] Many leading *aharonim*[94] maintain that ten

---

[89] *Supra*, note 87.

[90] R. Shimon Golan, *Hilkhot Purim* (*Moetsa Datit Efrat*, 5760), p. 4, sec. 8.

[91] *Shulhan Arukh, O.H.* 690:18 and Rema *ad loc.*

[92] Rema, *O.H.* sec. 692, no. 1, maintains that a *minyan* is always required to recite the "*ha-rav et riveinu*" blessing that follows the *Megilla* reading. For further discussion, see *Birur Halakha*, sec. 690, no. 18 and sec. 692, no. 1; R. Jacob Hayyim Sofer, *Kaf haHayyim* sec. 690, no. 124; *Yehave Da'at*, I, sec. 88 and sec. 90, no. 2; *Yalkut Yosef*, V, *Hilkhot Mikra Megilla*, no. 39, note 70, p. 300. There are, however, many dissenting opinions who permit the recitation of *ha-rav et riveinu* even in the absence of a *minyan*; see, for example, *Be'er Heitev*, sec. 692, no. 4; *Arukh haShulhan, O.H.* sec. 690, no. 25 and sec. 692, no. 5; R. Joseph Hayyim, *Ben Ish Hai, Tetsave* 13; R. Aaron Felder, *Mo'adei Yeshurun*, I, *Laws of Purim*, sec. 7, no. 9; R. Avraham David Horowitz, *Resp. Kinyan Torah beHalakha*, III, end of sec. 103. This is also the view of R. Moshe Feinstein, as quoted by R. Dovid Katz, "*A Guide to Practical Halakha – Chanuka and Purim*" (New York: Traditional Press, 1979), VIII, Laws of *Purim*, sec. 14, no. 15, p. 134, and former Chief Rabbi Mordechai Eliyahu, as quoted by R. Moses Harari, *Mikra'ei Kodesh – Hilkhot Purim*, sec. 9, no. 7, note 30. Although *Arukh haShulhan, ibid.*, states that the common *minhag* is to recite *ha-rav et riveinu* even in the absence of a *minyan*, apparently the Ashkenazic *minhag* in Israel is not so; see *Lu'ah Dinim uMinhagim*, Israeli Chief Rabbinate (5757), p. 60; *Lu'ah Erets Yisrael*, R. Jehiel Michel Tucazinsky (5757), p. 44. R. Isaac Ratsabi, *Shulhan Arukh ha-meKutsar*, III, sec. 122, nos. 9 and 11, indicates that according to Yemenite usage, *HaRav et riveinu* can be said privately.

[93] *Mishna Berura O.H.* sec. 690, note 61 and *Sha'ar haTsiyyun ad loc.* On whether *Megilla* reading on the fourteenth in walled cities (*e.g.*, when the fifteenth falls on the Sabbath) is considered *she-lo bi-zmano*, see: R. Ovadiah Yosef, *Yehave Da'at*, I, sec. 90, no. 2 and IV, sec. 40; *Resp. Yabia Omer* VI, *O.H.*, sec. 46; R. Shlomo Zalman Auerbach cited by R. Nahum Stepansky, *veAleihu Lo Yibol*, I, *O.H.*, sec. 425.

[94] R. Mas'ud Raphael Alfasi, *Resp. Mash'ha deRabvata*, addenda at end of II, sec. 689; R. Joseph Hayyim, *Resp. Rav Pe'alim, O.H.* II, sec. 62; R. Moses Hayyim Lits Rosenbaum, *Sha'arei Emet, Hilkhot Megilla*, sec. 4, *Hemdat Arye*, sec. 4, no. 5; *Hug haArets*, sec. 3; R. Joseph Hayyim Sonnenfeld, *Resp. Salmat Hayyim*, I, sec. 101; R. Tsvi Pesah Frank,

women alone indeed *do* constitute a proper *minyan* for both the reading of the *Megilla* (in a regular year and even on *Purim meshulash*) and the reciting of the *ha-rav et riveinu* benediction.[95]

It is important to distinguish in this regard between public prayer (*tefilla be-tsibbur*) rituals, e.g., the recitation of *kaddish, kedusha, bareku,* and *hazarat ha-shats* — where women do not count towards a *minyan*, and *Megilla* reading where the consensus of leading *aharonim* is that they do. *Tefilla be-tsibbur* ceremonies are essentially communal obligations that become incumbent

---

Mikra'ei Kodesh, Purim, sec. 35 and 50, note 3; R. Avraham Yeshayahu Karelitz, *Hazon Ish,* O.H. sec. 155, no. 2; R. Isaac Halberstadt, *Shenei Sarei haKodesh,* p. 16; *Purim Meshulash,* sec. 2, nos. 8 and 9 and addendum thereto; R. Hanoch Zundel Grossberg, *Iggeret haPurim,* first edition, sec. 7, no. 2, second edition, sec. 8, no. 3; *Resp. Yabia Omer,* VIII, O.H. sec. 23, no. 27 and sec. 56, end of no. 4; R. Ovadiah Yosef, *Likkutei Kol Sinai,* sec. 23, p. 47; *Yalkut Yosef,* V, *Hilkhot Mikra Megilla,* sec. 7, p. 284; *Kitsur Shulhan Arukh Yalkut Yosef,* O.H. sec. 692, nos. 4 and 10; *Resp. Tsits Eliezer* XIII, sec. 73; *Resp. Rivevot Efrayyim,* VIII, sec. 274, no. 2; R. Moshe Shternbuch, *Resp. Teshuvot veHanhagot,* IV, sec. 177, no. 2; R. Joseph Shalom Elyashiv (personal written communication to Aryeh A. Frimer, 27 *Adar* 5754, March 10, 1994); Sefardi Chief Rabbi Eliyahu Bakshi-Doron, cited in *Lu'ah Dinim uMinhagim,* Israeli Chief Rabbinate (5757), p. 122; R. Joel Schwartz, *Adar uFurim,* sec. 8, no. 5, par. 2 and 3 and note 11; *Halikhot Beita,* sec. 24, nos. 17-21 and notes 33, 34, 44 and 48; *Hilkhot Hag beHag: Purim,* sec. 8, no. 13 and 14, note 32 and addendum to sec. 8, no. 13, note 31, p. 218; Chief Rabbis of Ma'ale Adumim Joshua Katz and Mordechai Nagari, *Ma'alot,* no. 185, *Parshat Tetsave* 5756, *Halakha Sedura,* sec. B, no. 5 and conversation with Dov I. Frimer (March 23, 1996); R. Yehuda Herzl Henkin, *Tsibbur Nashim biKri'at haMegilla, Keshot,* 4 (*Adar II/Nisan* 5755), sec 14, pp. 8-10, reprinted in *Resp. Benei Vanim,* III, sec. 7; R. Yehuda Herzl Henkin, *Equality Lost: Essays in Torah, Halacha and Jewish Thought* (Jerusalem: Urim Publications, 1999), pp. 54–65; R. Yehuda Herzl Henkin, "*Keriat haMegilla al Yedei Nashim — haMahloket eina be-Halakha,*" *HaTsofe,* 14 *Adar* 5759 (March 2, 1999), p. 9

Other *posekim* dissent; see R. Shlomo Kluger, *Hokhmat Shelomo,* O.H. sec. 689, no. 5; *Kaf haHayyim,* O.H. sec. 690, no. 120; *Arukh haShulhan,* O.H. sec. 690, no. 25; *Resp. Mishne Halakhot, Mahadura Tinyana,* I, O.H. sec. 550; and R. Moshe Feinstein as quoted by R. Dovid Katz, "*A Guide to Practical Halakha — Chanuka and Purim*" (New York: Traditional Press, 1979), VIII, Laws of *Purim,* sec. 14, no. 15, p. 134; R. Shlomo Zalman Auerbach cited by R. Nahum Stepansky, *veAleihu Lo Yibol,* I, O.H., sec. 431. R. Raphael Evers, *Resp. vaShav veRafa,* O.H., sec. 31 suggests that the *minhag* is to be stringent. Surprisingly, in *Halikhot Shlomo, Hilkhot Tefilla,* chap. 23, *Dvar Halakha,* no. 3 and note 13, R. Shlomo Zalman Auerbach maintains that while women count towards a *minyan* for reading the *Megilla* on *Purim meshulash,* they do not recite "*ha-rav et riveinu.*" This is also the position cited by R. Yeshayahu Shapira, *Tseida laDerekh,* (Jerusalem: Machon Zomet, 2001), Chap. 67, secs. A1, C1 and C2, pp. 157 and 158. Note, however, that both *Arukh haShulhan* and R. Feinstein, like many other leading *posekim,* maintain that the *HaRav et riveinu* benediction can be said even in the absence of a *minyan;* see *infra,* note 92.

[95] It should be emphasized that the *posekim* of note 94 are referring to a women's *Megillah* reading exclusively and no generalization can be made regarding women's services. See: Aryeh A. Frimer and Dov I. Frimer, *supra,* note 1.

once a community of ten is established; since women lack the obligation of public prayer they cannot count towards the requisite *minyan*. In contradistinction, the obligation of *Megilla* is essentially a personal one in which women *are* obligated. Furthermore, the purpose of the *minyan* is not to create the obligation, but to enhance the element of *pirsumei nisa*.[96]

E. Are Women's *Megilla* Readings Advisable?

The last, and perhaps most difficult issue to tackle is whether women's *Megilla* readings are advisable. Clearly many contemporary women need venues of personal religious expression. Where this can be clearly done within the halakhic guidelines, women desiring this expression should be encouraged to do so.[97]

However, this should not be done at the expense of the community. There is after all a clear sense in the halakhic literature that the *Megilla* reading should be carried out in a large group for two reasons. One is the general consideration of "*be-rov am hadrat melekh*" - "In the multitude of people is the King's glory."[98] From this passage, the Rabbis derived that it is preferable to perform commandments and rituals together with or in the presence of large numbers of people.[99] A second consideration, more particular to Purim and *Megilla* reading, is *pirsumei nisa* (publicizing the miracle) – which also leads the codifiers to the conclusion that it is preferable to read and hear the *Megilla* in the presence of large numbers of

---

[96] For documentation of the various points raised in this paragraph and an analysis of the issue of women and *minyan*, see: Aryeh A. Frimer, "Women and *Minyan*," *Tradition* 23:4 (Summer 1988), pp. 54–77 – available online through http://mail-jewish.org; and Aryeh A. Frimer, "*Ma'amad haIsha beHalakha – Nashim uMinyan*," *Or haMizrah* 34:1, 2 (*Tishrei* 5746), pp. 69–86.

[97] R. Ovadiah Yosef, *Yabia Omer*, VIII, O.H., sec. 56, end of no. 4 writes: "...the custom of women who make a *minyan* by themselves for *mikra Megilla*...should be encouraged." See also R. Aharon Soloveichik, *Od Yisrael Yosef Beni Hai*, end of sec. 32, p. 100, who writes regarding the recitation of mourner's *kaddish* by women: "Nowadays, when there are Jews fighting for equality for men and women in matters such as *aliyyot*, if Orthodox rabbis prevent women from saying *kaddish* when there is a possibility for allowing it, it will strengthen the influence of Reform and Conservative rabbis. It is therefore forbidden to prevent women from saying *kaddish*."

[98] Proverbs 14:28.

[99] *Encyclopedia Talmudit*, IV, "*BeRov Am Hadrat Melekh*," p. 195; R. Abraham Isaiah Pfoifer, *Ishei Yisrael*, sec. 8, no. 9.

people.[100] Clearly, breaking off from the community at large to organize a women's *Megilla* reading contravenes the spirit of these guidelines.

It is true that many noted halakhicists rule that women, unlike men, are not required to hear a *public* reading of the *Megilla* – arguing that women are obligated in neither *be-rov am hadrat melekh* nor in *pirsumei nisa*.[101] Indeed, it is a prevalent custom worldwide[102] for men to read for their wives and daughters at home, or to have a second *Megilla* reading for women; yet no provisions are made to have a *minyan* of ten men present. Nevertheless, many *posekim* dissent, suggesting that women like men need to be concerned with both *be-rov am* and *pirsumei nisa*.[103]

---

[100] See sources in note 101.

[101] *Magen Avraham,* in his gloss to the statement of *Shulhan Arukh*, O.H. sec. 689, no. 1, that "women, too, are obligated to hear the *Megilla*," writes, "'Women' – Therefore one must read the *Megilla* at home for the unmarried women." To this, *Be'er Heitev* and *Mishna Berura* add: "In some places, the unmarried women go to the women's section of the synagogue to hear the *Megilla*." R. Menashe Klein, *Resp. Mishne Halakhot, Mahadura Tinyana*, I, O.H. sec. 550, understands from the above citations that it was not the obligation nor the wont of the unmarried women, and certainly of the married women, to hear a public reading of the *Megilla*. R. Mordechai Jacob Breisch, *Resp. Helkat Yaakov*, III, sec. 144 (O.H., sec. 232 in the 1992 edition) concurs. (See, however, *Halikhot Beita, Petah haBayyit*, no. 25, who suggest an alternate understanding of *Magen Avraham*). R. Yehuda Herzl Henkin, *Tsibbur Nashim biKri'at haMegilla, Keshot*, 4 (*Adar II/Nisan* 5755), sec 14, pp. 8–10, reprinted in *Resp. Benei Vanim*, III, sec. 7, suggests that this is the meaning of the cryptic suggestion of Behag, *Halakhot Gedolot, Hilkhot Megilla, s.v. "haKol hayyavin"*; cited in *Rema*, O.H. sec. 689, no. 2, that women are obligated in hearing the *Megilla* [in private] and not in reading it [in public]. R. Mordechai Jacob Breisch, *ibid.*, argues that women are obligated in neither *be-rov am hadrat melekh* nor in *pirsumei nisa*. A similar position is maintained by: R. Moses Sternbuch, *Mo'adim uZemanim*, II, sec. 173; R. Raphael Evers, *Resp. vaShav veRafa*, O.H., sec. 31; and R. David Auerbach, *Halikhot Beita, Petah haBayyit*, sec. 25. This also seems to be the view of R. Shlomo Zalman Auerbach cited by R. Nahum Stepansky, *veAleihu Lo Yibol*, I, O.H., sec. 431.

[102] R. Sraya Devlitsky, *Purim Meshulash*, Chap. 2, note 20, for example, refers to these second *Megilla* readings for women as the *"takana gedola"* (important innovation) of Bnei Brak.

[103] R. Israel David Harfeness, *Resp. VaYvarekh David*, I, O.H. sec. 82, and R. Gavriel Zinner, *Nitei Gavriel – Dinei uMinhagei Purim*, sec. 13, no. 3, note 6, maintain that women are obligated in *be-rov am*. At first blush, this would also seem to be the view of *Hayyei Adam, kelal* 155, no. 7, who writes, "...Even if one can gather a *minyan* in his home, it is still highly preferable (*mitsva min ha-muvhar*) to go to the synagogue – he, his wife and his children – to hear the *Megilla*." Similar language is found in *Bah*, O.H., end of sec. 687 and *Ateret Zekenim*. Nevertheless, one could well argue that *Hayyei Adam, Bah* and *Ateret Zekenim* maintain that children and certainly women contribute by their presence to the *be-rov am hadrat melekh* of others, though they themselves are not obligated therein. See R. Joshua M.M. Ehrenberg, *Resp. Devar Yehoshua*, I, sec. 96.

Unity and togetherness is the message of Purim, argues R. Jonathan Eybeschutz.[104] The weakness of the Jews at the time of Mordechai and Esther is clearly delineated by none other than Haman, who refers to them as: "…a nation – dispersed and divided…" (Esther 3:8). Esther's antidote was "Go gather all the Jews" (Esther 4:16). Little wonder, then, that "*be-rov am hadrat melekh*" carries such weight in the practice of this day of joy.

In this light, a balanced approach would seem to be the correct one. Thus, it would certainly seem preferable that women should not break off from the general community unnecessarily for the sole purpose of organizing their own special reading of the *Megilla*.[105] However, where a second *Megilla* reading is held anyway for the women (as is often the case Purim morning), there are then excellent grounds for having a women's *Megilla* reading for the women.[106] Additionally, such readings may well be encouraged in educational settings such as women's *ulpanot* and *midrashot*. As a rule, the local rabbinic leadership should be involved in such *halakha le-ma'ase* evaluations and determinations.

Alternatively, these *posekim* may consider the presence of women and minors preferable because of *pirsumei nisa* (even in the absence of *be-rov am*). This is in fact the implication of *Or Zaru'a*, *Hilkhot Megilla* sec. 368, who states that one should be accompanied to the reading of the *Megilla* by his wife and children because of *pirsumei nisa*.

[104] R. Jonathan Eybeschutz, *Ya'arot Dvash*, II, p. 37; reprinted in *Perush Rabbenu Yehonatan* (Machon Yerushalayim, Jerusalem, 5753), *Shemot, Megillat Esther*, 3:8.

[105] See the related comments of R. Aharon Soloveichik and R. Jacob Ariel in note 73d, *supra*.

[106] We have noted in note 73c above that R. Joseph B. Soloveitchik preferred that women not have their own *Megilla* reading [Conversations with R. David Gorelik, R. Jacob J. Schacter and R. Binyomin Walfish; see also: R. Jacob J. Schacter, "Facing the Truths of History," *The Torah U-Madda Journal*, 8 (1998–1999), note 97, pp. 260–261]. Both R. Schacter and R. Walfish noted, however, that the Rav indicated that if necessary, there was room to be lenient. Consequently, R. Soloveitchik advised R. Walfish that where the women of a particular congregation insist on having their own *Megilla* reading, the rabbi should not object. Similarly, in a telephone conversation with R. Bertram Leff, R. Shmuel Goldin and Mr. Nathan Lewin (in 1980 or 1981), the Rav permitted a women's *Megilla* reading by Mr. Lewin's daughter, Alyza, for those women who were unable to attend the regular congregational, early morning, *Purim minyan*. R. Soloveitchik emphasized, however, that the women's reading should not be held in *shul*, that the *ba'alat keria* could read only for women, and that this reading was not meant to replace the more preferred regular reading with a male *minyan*. See also: R. Bertram Leff, *Tradition* 33:1 (Fall 1998), pp. 135–136. The issue of motivation and public policy considerations is beyond the scope of this paper. The reader is referred to our discussion of these issues in Aryeh A. Frimer and Dov I. Frimer, note 1, *supra*.

III. MEANINGFUL PREPARATION

THROUGH ACTIVE PARTICIPATION

WOMEN AND TORAH STUDY*

RABBANIT MALKE BINA

In Haftez Hayyim's famous *teshuvah* on Torah study for women, he posits that, ideally and historically, Jewish women need to study Torah only insofar as they need to know about belief in God and practical *halakhah*. They naturally learned from their mothers and gracefully accepted the yoke of Torah through observance. "All that has changed today," he wrote about his own generation. Although less than thrilled with the choice, he saw that social and religious realities dictated that unless women began to study *Humash*, Prophets, *mussar*, and Jewish philosophy, they would drift away from Torah and *klal Yisrael* would be weakened. He saw that women must be fortified with sufficient Torah knowledge to meet the intellectual challenges of the outside world. He, of course, intended that proper Torah educational institutions should be set up to strengthen Torah and *yirat shamayim*. After a while, his less-preferred option [*bedievad*] became the standard for even the most pious sectors in schools such as Beit Yaakov.

Today, Orthodox communities face much of a similar situation regarding the study of rabbinic texts. Rather than fight the desire of women to learn, rabbis and leaders should structure educational frameworks that would advance the basic goals of strengthening Torah and *yirat shamayim*. Many women who "leave the fold" are intelligent and honest but uninspired Jewishly on an intellectual level comparable to their abilities and secular exposure. The *halakhic* approval given by Hafetz Hayyim could certainly apply to our question regarding rabbinic texts. In a couple of generations, schools that teach rabbinic texts to girls and women will probably seem no more radical that Beit Yaakov appears today.

I will not review here the permissibility of women studying rabbinic texts.[1] Instead, I would like to broach a "hasidic" approach to the

* This essay was originally published in *Women and the Study of Torah: Essays from the Pages of Tradition*, ed. Joel B. Wolowelsky (Ktav: New Jersey, 1992), pp. 67–71.

significance of outside forces and new trends in general. Rather than view secular feminist concerns as the enemy, why not see them as the guiding hand of Providence trying to reveal a new face of Torah? We know that in the area of *mitzvot*, "even if the original intent is wrong, performing the *mitzvah* brings with it proper intent" – *mitokh she-lo lishma ba lishma*. In this case, secular concerns can be seen as an impetus to deepen and broaden understanding of Jewish texts and, more importantly, to challenge the superficiality of Jewish commitment prevalent in our generation. This outside force can be utilized to strengthen and revitalize Jewish women's ties to Torah through greater learning. It is upsetting to think that today, when women are leaders in fields such as psychology or math, they often remain ignorant of the body of Jewish study which is its essence: *Torah she-be'al peh*, the Oral Law.

Ultimately, I would like to see the establishment of institutions of Torah study for women that extend from preschool age through adulthood, and which will set high standards of learning in both the Written and the Oral Law, *halakhah* as well as Jewish philosophy. As this has not been tried until now, I cannot foresee clearly what difficulties will arise in this type of girls' school system. This is not to ignore the important body of research that has been done on the differences between men and women in terms of intellectual and psychological development. However, I would aim to get beyond the current situation and then see what adjustments need to be made.

Differences in the needs of individuals or groups in such schools should be taken care of by tracking within the schools. Girls would not be forced into one particular mold; some would excel in *Tanakh* while others would concentrate on *Torah she-be'al peh*. The basis for advancement would be personal capabilities maximized and nurtured by careful instruction.

The traditional interpretation of *kol kevuda* is simply not adhered to anymore by any sector of the religious community; witness, for example, *kollel* wives working in busy offices, and *haredi* women teaching, running

---

[1] See, for example, R. David Auerbach, *Halikhot beita*, pp. 389–391, and R. Aharon Lichtenstein, "Torah Study for Women," *Ten Da'at* 3:3 (Spring, 1989), pp. 7–8. [The subject is also discussed in essays in this volume by Erica Brown and R. Aryeh Strikovsky – editor's note.]

schools and managing charities. In the past many women were home most of the day, but all that has changed today.

Realistically, the only difference between the "approved" jobs held by women outside the home and those jobs whose legitimacy are questioned is the status that comes with the latter. For instance, a woman who wishes to serve on a shul board or a religious council would be no more "visible" that a female principal in a girls' school. A woman who runs a prosperous business to support her husband who learns is no less involved in the outside world than a lawyer. Yet the first set is already accepted as a necessity even though it runs counter to the classical interpretation of *kol kevuda*. I think that women's participation in decision-making bodies, such as a religious council or appearing for a client in court, is also necessary so that both the social and religious needs of women are met and the needs of *klal Yisrael* are better served. If a woman is more competent to fill a particular position than a man, the jewish people lose out if she does not fill it.

Our challenge today must therefore be to preserve the inner sanctum even while operating in public spheres. The question of how to educate for *tzeniut* in an age of promiscuity and for inner values in an age where externals are so highly valued is a serious one for both men and women. Such education can only be based on personal examples and *mesirut nefesh* as exemplified by role models like Nehama Leibowitz or Miriam Adahan, women whose whole beings speak of internal values and modesty but whose voices are heard far beyond the confines of their own homes.

In order to serve both home and outside in a practical way, two factors are essential. First, husband and wife must work together by mutual consent; second, both must realize that neither will have all their needs met – for example, a woman will either need house help or lessen household expectations. Priorities must be clearly set, such as time spent with children as opposed to cleaning house.

I have always believed that women are released from positive time-bound *mitzvot* in order for them to have more flexibilities and more choices. There should be many different models for schools for women. Women should not be pressured to feel that they must assume public roles, but should feel that they have the option to do so. I do not think that either studying Talmud or assuming public roles is cause for fear that we will lose something or tarnish some ideal. Quite the opposite. Whatever path we choose, we need only fear if Torah and fear of heaven are not our primary focus.

BAT MITZVAH: JEWISH WOMEN THROUGH THE AGES

RABBANIT OSHRA KOREN AND TIRZA KELMAN (GARBER)

MaTaN Program for Mothers and Daughters

R. Eliezer asked: What does this verse in Proverbs 31:26 mean? "She opens her mouth with wisdom, and on her tongues is a Torah of *hesed* (loving-kindness)." Is there a Torah of *hesed* and another Torah not of *hesed*? Rather, Torah learned for its own sake (*lishmah*) is Torah of *hesed*, while Torah learned not for its own sake is Torah without any *hesed*.[1]

> Torah *lishmah* – this means for the sake of the Torah itself. For it is God's will that divine wisdom be actualized in our world.... Each person who learns Torah draws that divine wisdom from potentiality into real existence. And, undeniably, the light engendered when one individual's soul connects with the Torah is totally different from the light born of another person's connecting. Thus, each individual really affects the greatness of Torah through her learning....[2]

Every person, male as well as female, should find expression for his or her "letter in the Torah." The *bat mitzvah* program we developed at MaTaN is founded on this idea and on Rav Kook's conviction that each person should study Torah in his or her unique way.

The program began in 1995 in response to the feeling many had that girls approaching the age of full acceptance of the *mitzvot* should mark their

---

* translated by Judith Weil

[1] *Sukkah* 49b.

[2] R. Avraham Yitzhak Hacohen Kook, *Orot ha-Torah* (Jerusalem 5733) 2.1.

rite of passage into Jewish adulthood in some meaningful way. MaTaN of Ra'anana launched a pilot program entitled "Getting Ready to become *Bat Mitzvah*: Jewish Women Through the Ages." The following pages describe some of the concepts underlying that program, which spawned many similar ones taking place today throughout Israel.

The guiding force of the program is that becoming *bat mitzvah* is not a one-time event, but the culmination of a process. A girl's *bat mitzvah* day is more than just another birthday; it is the day she enters a wholly new category, ceases to be a child, and becomes a Jewish woman obligated to perform the *mitzvot*. Our goal was that, when her *bat mitzvah* day arrived, each girl would have full understanding of her responsibilities, aware of the significance of her joining the community of Jewish women of all generations; this event would be carved in her memory as a turning point in her life. The program was built as a learning process for girls to experience together with their mothers, and involved encounters with outstanding female personalities of Jewish history.

The Community of Women

Jewish women have played an important role in the dynamic development of the Jewish people throughout the generations. In addition, each individual woman makes her own unique and extensive contribution to the Jewish experience. One purpose of the program is to enhance girls' awareness of women who lead active, dynamic Jewish lives; this helps them identify with the women they encounter and, hopefully, to see themselves as part of this female chain. Each girl then feels linked to the values that guided these women, and that enables her to pass them, in her turn, to the next generation of Jewish women.

A variety of techniques are used to create the sense of connection to past generations. The program involves a series of meetings each of them focusing on one leading female Jewish personality, presented in chronological order. The choice to put figures of women at the axis of the program expressed our aspiration that the girls would identify with values they represented. We assume that values are more accessible when embodied in actual people, whether of the present or of the past, than as abstract concepts. In addition, attention to the qualities and values that guided the figure under discussion aids the girl in her own encounter with those qualities and values – despite the differences in circumstances – and enhances her ability to internalizes them.

The various meetings introduce a wide range of figures with various roles, each of them with her unique attributes and strengths. In the course of learning, the girls see that any quality can be directed in different ways. To give an example: Miriam's daring and even audacity empowered her to offer Pharaoh's daughter a Jewish wet nurse for the baby that she had taken from the river. That enabled Moshe's own mother to raise her own son during his infancy, and hasten the redemption. Yet when Miriam showed the same audacity in speaking against her brother, now leader of the people, it caused her downfall and brought her to sin. Internalizing the principle that every trait can serve for good and for bad is essential in the character development of girls as they approach the stage of accepting the yoke of the *mitzvot* and responsibility for their own actions.

The girls encounter a wide range of personalities whole lived in different historical ages. Beginning with the Matriarchs and other biblical characters, they include women of the rabbinical period, the Middle Ages, the modern period, and contemporary women alive today. A range of personalities is presented, with a variety of occupations. Among them: Rebecca, who embodied *hesed*, or loving-kindness, Beruriah the scholar, Hannah, who taught us the power of prayer, and Donna Grazia, a businesswomen with manifold interests. Also included are women who won the Israel Prize for various fields – Nehama Leibowitz, on one hand, and Rabbanit Kappah, for her grass-roots acts of *hesed* throughout Jerusalem, on the other.

The girls gain insight into the rich world of women. The image of "the ideal Jewish woman," they realize, can be embodied in many different ways, all of them legitimate. As they reach maturity, those answers can be used as a basis for each one's unique response.

Another fundamental aspect of the program is the way it relates to the continuity from one generation to the next. The entire program involves daughters and mothers studying and learning together; mother-daughter *hevruta* learning is a central component of the program. Other activities are planned with a similar intention to enhance the ties between the mother and daughter on the threshold of adulthood. One evening a week over a

period of several months is devoted to creating a new, unique bond between the two. The ramifications this has for the future is very great,
especially in terms of the new avenues of communication it develops
between them.[3]

So far, we've focused on the temporal aspect of the girl's entrance into
the feminine continuum. The program works in another direction as well:
an additional circle of women opens for her through the encounter with the
program leader, female lecturers and guest-speakers, such as craftswomen
and figures active in public life. This draws the girl into the circle of Jewish
women surrounding her. The face-to-face, immediate encounter with
women who fulfil their unique potential, each in her own way, aids her yet
further in internalizing the principles we have discussed, and guides her in
choosing the way in she will actualize her own personality.

The involvement of a large number of mother-daughter pairs enables
the girls in the program to meet contemporaries, both her own age and
older than she. This creates a heterogeneous female community and
provides a strong, positive group with which the girl can identify.

The Learning Experience

Torah learning is central to Jewish life. It is only natural, then, that Torah
should play a central role in preparing a girl for her *bat mitzvah*. Each
meeting is centered on structured mother-daughter learning. The
participants prepare together for the *shiur* (frontal lecture and discussion)
that follows later in the session. This helps both of them reach greater
proficiency in coping with sources and become familiar with part of the
vast corpus of Jewish literature. The girls gain understanding of the
concepts of *pshat* and *drash* (literal meaning and interpretation) and realize
the connection between a text's superficial meaning and the more profound
messages the Rabbis draw from it.

At each meeting, the learning session is accompanied by an experiential
activity related to the relevant figure or subject. Each activity creates a
different atmosphere and invites different modes of self-expression, such as
creative dance, acting, crafts using various materials. The underlying

---

[3] An example of the fruits of this mother-daughter study within the framework of
MaTaN can be seen in Rachel Adelman's essay in this volume [ed.]

principle is that a successful learning experience is based not on the intellect, but draws on other realms of the personality, among them emotions and creativity. The world of the senses enriches and harmonizes the learning experience. Our use of experiential activities as a means of learning is founded on the conviction that there are many ways to express one's Judaism and many ways to serving God – each of them is important and meaningful. Leading the girls into the atmosphere of the subject or personality experientially, before they encounter the text itself, enhances their textual study, as they have already identified with the issues. Another goal of this sort of activity is to spark questions and generate ideas that are not central to the text, but are nevertheless important.

The meeting focused on the figure of Queen Esther could serve as an example of the way experience and study can complement one another. First of all, groups of a few mother-daughter pairs draw their vision of the ideal Jewish woman. Then the groups break up into *hevrutot* and each mother and daughter pair learns selected passages from *Megillat Esther*, to be discussed in the lecture that follows. When they have finished learning, everyone gathers and each group describes the ideal woman they drew. The lecture then begins with a portrait of the ideal woman from Ahasuerus's perspective, proceeding to a consideration of Esther's role in that system and the transition she underwent from passive presence in the king's harem to active involvement in becoming savior of the Jewish people.

The Celebration

At the completion of the *bat mitzvah* preparatory program a party is held, integrating the entirety of elements and values learned throughout the course. It is the high point, experientially and spiritually, of the program.

Each girl presents a project she has prepared on an outstanding woman of her choice. That figure can be historical, or someone she is drawn to personally; it must, though, be a personality not discussed during the program. This enables each girl to apply the process she experienced and give expression to her internalization of it.

Aside from presentation of the projects, the party consists of two main parts:

The first part includes a game summarizing the ideas learned from each personality, *divrei Torah* given by mothers and girls, and a *shiur* on "*Eshet Hayil*," the "woman of valor" described in the last chapter of Proverbs. The girls then stand before the *aron hakodesh* (the Ark) and say a special *bat mitzvah* prayer that was traditionally used in Italian communities. The second and final part of the party and the program as a whole, women sing and dance.

Conclusions

The *bat mitzvah* program is not meant to substitute for each girl's marking her own acceptance of the *mitzvot*. Rather, its purpose is to prepare the girl and her family for her becoming *bat mitzvah* and to heighten their awareness that the date should be distinguished in some meaningful way.

After more than six years' experience, we can say the program has met with success in many senses. A good number of girls who participated decided to continue their learning in a serious way – alone or with their mothers – as it had been an important aspect in preparing for their bat mitzvah. Requests are many to hold additional meetings even after the program has ended.

The very existence of the program aroused awareness in the community as a whole that investing religious and spiritual content in *bat mitzvah* celebrations is of crucial importance. The influence of the program permeates community consciousness more and more, and the circle of participants and their families widens from year to year. Demand for the program, which has led to its expansion from MaTaN Jerusalem throughout Israel, testifies clearly to a real need the program answers with great success.

INSCRIBE THIS IN A BOOK AS A REMEMBRANCE[#]

BRYNA JOCHEVED LEVY

"And all replied, 'Study is greater, for study leads to action!'" (*Kiddushin* 40b)

These words of the Sages affect our religious lives in many ways. Learning not only spurs us on to observe *mitzvot*, it develops our overall attitude toward accepting the yoke of the commandments. At crucial points in the course of our lives, such as a son or daughter's reaching the age of *mitzvot*, the learning experience can accompany the young girl or boy through this important rite of passage by laying a meaningful foundation. It was this idea that guided us, as parents and educators, when our children reached *bar* and *bat mitzvah* age.

When our oldest daughter, Shira Leah's *bat mitzvah* approached, we deliberated for a long time about how to mark this important passageway in her life – 'from voluntary to compulsory observance of mitzvot' [*mi-eina metzuvah ve-osah le-metzuvah ve-osah*].

In the absence of established ceremonies marking a girl's acceptance of *mitzvot*, we sought other ways to make the event significant. We began by embarking upon a course of study. Every Shabbat Shira would spend time learning with her father Daniel. Since when Shira was younger she and Daniel had concentrated on *Tanakh* study, Daniel chose the study of Mishna for this next formative stage in Shira's educational development. Since the goal was to complete an entire *seder* of Mishna and a tractate of Gemara, the project began several years before the year of *bat mitzvah*.

Shira's learning project with me was of a different nature. We began the process on her eleventh birthday. Instead of concentrating on a specific text, we chose to explore the biographies of great Jewish women. The message was clear. In addition to the *halakhic* aspect of *bat mitzvah*, our study was designed to emphasize entry into the ranks of the Jewish com-

---

[*] translated by Ora Wiskind Elper

[#] Exodus 17:14.

munity and assumption of both responsibility and leadership. Since the specific nature of the public and communal role of Jewish women is an open question, our study opened new vistas highlighting a wide variety of possible leadership models.

Each month we chose a different woman for our focus. We began with the biblical period, learning about Devorah the Judge and Hulda the Prophetess. From the Hellenistic period, we chose Yehudit, and from the talmudic period we studied Beruriah and Shlomtzion Hamalkah. Sarah Shneirer and Henrietta Szold were the women we chose to meet from the modern period. In addition to prominent women from the various historical periods, Shira interviewed her two grandmothers to learn from them about their own mothers (her great-grandmothers) for whom she is named.

So that our learning could be considered:

"כתב חזון ובאר על הלחות למען ירוץ קורא בו (חבקוק ב:ב)" "Write the prophecy down, inscribe it clearly on tablets, so that it can be read easily" (Habakuk 2:2), Shira wrote an essay on each of these figures. We included these essays in the booklet we distributed at her *siyyum*. We decided to call the booklet, Shira's personal creation, by the title:

"חן ושכל טוב בעיני אלהים ואדם" – "Favor and wisdom in the eyes of God and man." The choice of title encapsulated the blessing we hoped Shira would represent for the Jewish people.

Another advantage of this project was the priority time I devoted exclusively to my oldest daughter. In families blessed with many children, it often happens that much time is spent with the younger children, in the hope the older ones will manage. Throughout the year before her *bat mitzvah*, many precious hours each month were devoted exclusively to Shira. I remember fondly, as the end of Kislev approached, that we hadn't had the chance to finish learning the *Book of Yehudit*. We decided to go out to a café where we stayed until we completed the book.

Our *bat mitzvah* resolution was complete. The choice of learning, the *siyyum* and the publication of the booklet answered our needs and proved gratifying on many levels. That should have been the end of the story, at least for a while, since Shira's next two siblings are brothers. But to my surprise, when our son Aharon turned twelve, he approached me and asked what kind of booklet he could compile. I explained to him that there really wasn't any need for that. When his *bar mitzvah* came he would be able to officiate as a *hazan* and read from the Torah. He, too, had finished a *seder* of Mishna and a tractate of Gemara. But he insisted that he wanted to learn with me and write a booklet. I realized he had seen the project as an opportunity to learn and spend quality time with *Imma*, as well as studying topics he enjoyed. His enthusiasm, of course, was contagious. Because his *bar mitzvah parashah* is *Vayigash*, we decided to prepare for it by learning the stories of Yosef and his brothers. Our study began with *parashat Vayeshev* and culminated with *parashat Vayigash*. This time, as well, the spiritual and personal planes dovetailed. Our learning opened up precious opportunities to talk about relationships within the family, about dreams and aspirations, about self-image, and about the meaning of the verse:

"רבות מחשבות בלב איש ועצת ה' היא תקום" – "Man toils and God foils."

In Aharon's booklet, we collected pearls of wisdom from the assorted commentaries on the Yosef stories. He chose comments and insights from the giants of biblical exegesis throughout the generations, organized and explained them. We also included two important essays written by Aharon Dov Mordechai's forefathers. The first was an essay on *bar mitzvah* written by his maternal grandfather and namesake, R. Aharon Dov Seidman *z"l*. The other is a chapter on the figure of Yosef from a book on great Jewish personalities authored by Aharon's paternal great-grandfather, Mordechai Levy *z"l*, whose name Aharon also bears. Again the messages of leadership was explicit. In addition, the specific essays written by Aharon's family members communicated the important question of Aharon's place in the chain of Jewish heritage. This message was also articulated by the juxtaposition of Aharon's own writings with those of his elders. The title we gave Aharon's booklet was "A man's wisdom lights up his face"

"חכמת אד"ם (אהרן דוב מרדכי) תאיר פניו".

Next in line was Naftali Zvi. By this time, it was self-understood that in addition to his seder Mishna, he and I would compile a booklet. When I asked him what he wanted to learn, he chose *Navi* (Prophets). Each month we studied a different prophet, most of them from *Trei Asar*, the "minor prophets." Here, as well, I felt the medium spoke for itself in terms of the centrality of the concept of leadership. The prophets of Israel throughout the generations represents magnificent role models. Despite adversity, their tenacious and passionate adherence to their divine misssion serve as a source of limitless inspiration. All of them were lovers of God and the Jewish nation, as we pray Naftali himself will continue to be. Naftali's booklet was entitled "ואקים מבניכם לנביאים ומבחוריכם לנזירים" – "And I raised up prophets from among your sons."

Naftali is followed by three sisters, which left three additional *sedarim* of Mishna to be covered and three more booklets to be written. Elisheva Yehudit was next in line. She is the most musical and dramatic of my children. I wanted her to appreciate that her special gifts can also be directed to serving God. And so we decided to study biblical poetry, the *Book of Psalms* and *Zemirot Shabbat*. We called her booklet יזמירות היו לי חקך׳ – "Your laws are like songs" in the hope she would keep the Torah's commandments wholeheartedly, with intense enthusiasm and passion.

A year prior to Leora Malka's *bat mitzvah* we began learning *Pirke Avot* together. The topic was a reflection of her wonderful *middot* and her desire to study more about ethics. To my surprise, in the course of our study we discovered that there was something else she preferred studying. She expressed great interest in delving into the *Book of Samuel*. Since the motivating factor in our study was to find material the *bat mitzvah* girl found inspirational, we immediately switched gears. Our study focused on the theme of families in the *Book of Samuel*. Leora herself is very connected to her family and found learning about King Saul's and King David's respective families eye-opening. Her booklet was called: "שתי המשפחות אשר בחר ה׳" – "The two families that the Lord chose." Ayelet Eliana's seder of Mishna – *Taharot* – is a function of her being sixth in line, but her study for her booklet will, with God's help, be of her own chosing.

In all the experiences I have described here, our learning together brought us deep satisfaction. With each child, fruitful discussions developed on subjects concerning maturation, leadership, *mitzvot,* and community responsibility. Compiling the booklets added an important dimension. As our study took written form, it metamorphosed into "learning in order to teach others." Our daughters and sons took pride in the fruits of their labors. We are hopeful that they will be able to use their booklets as a foundation for future compositions, but more importantly that they will use their experience of family learning as a springboard for continued spiritual and intellectual growth.

REFLECTIONS OF A *BAT MITZVAH* TUTOR*

ILANA FODIMAN-SILVERMAN

This year I had the privilege of studying Torah with Jenny Feldstein in preparation for her *bat mitzvah*. Jenny and her family strongly felt that the *bat mitzvah* primarily represents initiation into the world of Torah and *mitzvot*. What better way to prepare for such an experience than by intense study of Jewish texts? Jenny and I spent approximately four to six hours a week studying a chapter of Talmud. We chose the Drisha *beit midrash* as our place of study, as it was important for us to be surrounded by other women studying Torah. I wanted Jenny to be introduced to the sense of ownership and connectedness with Jewish texts that full time students at Drisha experience after years of study.

We studied Talmud for no other purpose than to explore what our ancient traditions and laws offer. In preparation for the event, many girls choose to focus upon female role models, or upon topics relating to the time-period in which their *bat mitzvah* falls. Jenny and I strongly felt that a *bat mitzvah* represents the embracing of an entire tradition of law and interpretation, and thus chose to study Talmud, a strong link in the chain of transmission of *halakhah*. Our one-on-one study sessions afforded us the opportunity to question, reflect and internalize the material. We did not focus upon the *bat mitzvah* ceremony or speech, but upon our role as students and interpreters of traditional texts. My primary goal was to instill in Jenny a sense that learning is fun, exciting and interesting. We celebrated occasions on which we found solutions to difficult problems, remembered difficult words, or recognized a *tanna* or *amora* whom we had met before.

One of the greatest problems of many *bar-* and *bat mitzvah* preparation programs is the sense that the *bar-* or *bat mitzvah* celebration is a culminating event, a sort of graduation experience to which there is little or no

* This essay was previously published in *The Orthodox Jewish Woman and Ritual: Options and Opportunities*, Jewish Orthodox Feminist Alliance (www.jofa.org).

follow-up. The *bar-* or *bat mitzvah* ceremony all too often ends up representing the celebration of the conclusion of a learning process, rather than celebration of its beginning. Jenny's *bat mitzvah* ceremony was true testimony to the fact that a *bat mitzvah* represents entrance into a tradition and acceptance of life-long commitments. Jenny made a *siyyum*, a ceremonial conclusion of the chapter of Talmud we had studied by presenting a well constructed lesson on the last topic we had dealt with. However, the most important element of a *siyyum* is recitation of the *hadran*, a text that affirms our eternal commitment to study: "We have concluded this text, but we will return to it, and it will return to us." Returning to study became the theme of Jenny's *bat mitzvah*, as she completed one text, but reaffirmed her commitment to study more and delve ever deeper.

The seriousness of her commitment was evident in the first week following Jenny's *bat mitzvah*. I received a phone message from her mother explaining that despite Jenny's busy schedule of piano lessons and extracurricular activities, Jenny was anxious to get back to her *Gemara*. Jenny truly viewed her *bat mitzvah* as an introduction to the world of Torah study and initiation into a community of women who are actively engaged in Torah texts. In a sense, Jenny had learned the path to the *beit midrash*. And so months after her "official" *bat mitzvah* celebration, the real celebration takes place; Jenny and I continue to study with the promise of *hadran alakh ve-hadrakh alan* – "if you return to the text, it will return to you."

Jenny Feldstein is a sixth grader at the Ramaz School in Manhattan.

SENSE AND SENSIBILITIES: WOMEN AND TALMUD TORAH

BRYNA JOCHEVED LEVY

There is a quiet revolution taking place today in classrooms and halls of study, in synagogues and homes, in Israel, in America, and throughout the world. Far from the hue and cry of the sometimes acrimonious debate about the involvement of women in public Jewish life, the study of Torah is changing the way Jewish women view themselves and their connection to Jewish tradition.

In the early years of women's Torah education, women were offered a basic school curriculum stressing practical halakhic knowledge and other morally edifying studies.[1] This itself was a concession to the changing times. Fearing that women would leave the religious fold, the *Chafetz Chayim* rendered his famous *pesak* that women should learn Scripture and ethics.[2] This ruling served as the basis of Orthodox Jewish women's schooling, starting a process which has continued unabated to this day.

Today, in many circles, the initial limits on the scope of women's Torah learning have faded. Recent years have seen the inclusion of Talmud and

---

* previously published in *Jewish Action*, the magazine of the Orthodox Union (Winter, 1998).

[1] דבורה וייסמן, חינוך בנות דתיות בירושלים בתקופת השלטון הבריטי: התמסדותן והתגבשותן של חמש אידיאולוגיות חינוכיות, (ירושלים, תשנ"ד).

Shoshana Zolty, *And All Your Children Shall be Learned: Women and the Study of Torah in Jewish Law and History* (NJ, 1993).

[2] R. Israel Meir HaKohen (Kagan), *Likkutei Halakhot*, Sotah 20b: "It seems that all of this [prohibition against women learning Torah] applies only to times past when everyone lived in her father's house and tradition was very strong, assuring that children would pursue their parents' path, as it says, 'Ask your father and he shall tell you.'" On that basis we could claim that she needn't learn Torah but merely rely on proper parental guidance. But nowadays, in our inquity, as parental tradition has been seriously weakened and they moreover regularly study secular subjects, it is certainly a great mitzvah to teach them Chumash, Prophets and Writings, and Rabbinic ethics, such as *Pirke Avot, Menorat Hamaor*, and the like, so as to validate our sacred belief; otherwise they may stray totally from God's path and transgress the basic tenets of religion, God forbid."

other subjects which were hitherto considered to be the exclusive province of men's Torah study. However, the major change is that now women have the opportunity to study Torah on a high level, not only in practical preparation for a career in teaching, but as *Torah lishma*.

While women's precise halakhic obligation *vis a vis* Torah study is a complex question,[3] it was not the desire to technically address this particular issue which led to the establishment of *batei midrash* for women. The recent surge in the involvement of women in serious Torah learning may have begun in some quarters as a statement of feminism. However, the constant growth in this important trend comes not from contentious motives, but rather from women's deep desire to achieve spiritual fulfillment through *talmud Torah*.

This profoundly positive development has yielded interesting fruit. In the course of seeking quantitative parity in the study of Torah, women have discovered that there is a qualitative difference in the way they learn Torah. In a very short time, we have progressed from imitation to innovation – innovation in search of tradition.

Today women are talking Torah. We are finding our voices, conversing with other women in a new spiritual dialogue, one whose point of departure is the halachic way of life. We are discovering that the emotional and intellectual themes which animate texts of Torah resonate deeply within our own lives.

This realization has found expression across the entire range of Torah learning. It appears in the world of *Aggadah* – in which the emotional undertones of a tale or a parable may be uniquely perceived by ears sensitized to human emotion through years of nurturing and care-giving. It

---

[3] Moshe Meiselman, "Torah Knowledge for Women," *Jewish Woman in Jewish Law* (New York, 1978) pp. 34–43; Naomi Cohen, "Women and the Study of Talmud," *Tradition* 24(1), (Fall 1988), pp. 28–37; "Symposium on Women and Jewish Education," *Tradition*, 28(3), (Spring 1994); see Seeman, ibid., particularly notes 21 and 26; Susan Handelman, "Women and the Study of Torah in the Thought of the Lubavitcher Rebbe," *Jewish Legal Writings by Women* (Urim Publications, Jerusalem, 1998).

אליקים ג' אלינסון, בין האשה ליוצרה: האשה והמצוות ספר ראשן (ירושלים, תשמ"ז), פרק יג: תלמוד תורה, עמ' 143-163. עיין עוד הרב אהרן ליכטנשטיין, "בעיות היסוד בחינוכה של האשה, בתוך בן ציון רוזנפלד (עורך), האשה וחינוכה (ישראל, תשמ"ם) עמ' 157-165; דוד גולינקין, "תשע גישות למעמד האשה בהלכה במאה העשרים," (כתב יד); הרב מנחם מנדל שניאורסון, ליקוטי שיחות, (כפר חב"ד, תש"ן).

appears in the perception of a halakhic distinction – one which might seem to the male reader to be purely formalistic, but is revealed to a woman's inspection to be deeply rooted in psychological subtleties which bring new meaning to a familiar law.

Allow me to describe to you this dynamic meshing of text with life. The following vignettes are telling indicators of the power of Scripture and tradition to strike responsive chords in their readers. They illustrate the experience of *talmud Torah* for women students and teachers, and demonstrate that women today have the potential of effecting an important new development in the spiritual life of the Jewish People.

All of the episodes described here are true. They are experiences which I have shared with my students at Matan (*Machon Torani LeNashim*), where women of all ages and all walks of life come to actively engage in *talmud Torah*. Here the women of Jerusalem leave politics behind, seeking to uphold the blessing of *la'asok bedivrei Torah* – to immerse themselves in study to enable them to live enriched Torah lives.

The following are but a few journal entries in the life of one privileged to teach in such an institution:

It is a few days before *Rosh Hashanah* in the city of Jerusalem. The room is overflowing with women who have come to prepare themselves for the Days of Awe. Together, we begin our study of the opening section of the Book of Samuel, which we women will hear recited as a *Haftarah* on Rosh Hashanah. Today we will read it ourselves.

We read of Channah's childlessness, and how she is taunted by the jealous Peninah. Hannah grows used to her rival's harsh words. Paradoxically, it is her husband Elkanah who causes her grief. He says, compassionately: "Channah, why are you crying and why aren't you eating? Why are you so sad? Am I not more devoted to you than ten sons?"[4]

One of the women in the class points out that even Elkanah's expressed concern for his wife demonstrates his lack of understanding of her pain: There is no substitute for the children she does not have; she lacks not only children, but motherhood.

---

[4] NJPS translation. An alternate reading might be: "I am more valuable to you than ten sons."

Another student adds that there is an additional dimension present in the dialogue. What Channah suddenly realizes is that Elkanah is resigned to her childlessness.[5] Her despair at being utterly alone in her hope of deliverance pushes her to make a bold move.[6] She will go alone to the House of the Lord. There she will pour out her heart. She will say out loud what has been left unspoken. She will express what is in every woman's heart:

> Master of the Universe! All that you have created in woman is purposeful. You have created eyes with which to see, ears with which to hear, a nose for smelling, a mouth for speech, hands for toil, legs for walking. These breasts which you have given me – are they not for nursing? Give me a son so that I may nurse him!
> (*Berakhot* 31b)

I propose to the class that the thrust of this *midrash* is that motherhood for Channah is the ultimate expression of *spiritual* self-actualization. It is through her physical being that her spirit will find expression. She longs not only for a child, but for purpose and fulfillment.[7]

As I make this statement I weigh each word carefully. I stand before a group of women both like and unlike myself, teaching about childbirth, motherhood and self-actualization, through the agency of a Biblical text. I empathize with the pain of our heroine, and delight in her joy. But there are women in the class who identify with her even more closely than I.

I look up from my books and I see two sisters, whom I know personally; the older – childless, the younger – pregnant with her fifth child. I wonder how they relate to this chapter. It is a story which they have read and re-read. How, I wonder, are they reading it now? I ask myself how they

---

[5] אוריאל סימון, "סיפור הולדת שמואל – המבנה, הסוג והמשמעות," בתוך עיוני מקרא ופרשנות ב, עורך אוריאל סימון, (רמת גן, 1986); אברהם וולפיש, "חנה: תפילת תערומת וענווה," מגדים כ (תמוז תשנ"ג).

[6] שמות רבה יט:א: ד"א לב יודע מרת נפש היא לעצמה. כיון שנפקדה לא פקדה האלהים אלא לעצמה שנא' ובשמחתו לא יתערב זר וכתיב עלץ לבי בה' כי שמחתי בישועתך, אני לעצמי שמחתי אבל אחר לא ישמח עמי.

[7] The Rabbinic expression for this is מי שאין לו בנים חשוב כמת found in *Nedarim* 64b:

אריב"ל: כל אדם שאין לו בנים חשוב כמת, שנאמר: (בראשית ל) הבה לי בנים ואם אין מתה אנכי.

The example cited by the Gemara with regard to barrenness being equivalent to death is, of course, Rachel who explicitly makes this statement.

---

relate to each other. They are not rival wives vying for the love of one husband, but the fulfillment of the one and emptiness of the other are very real parts of their lives. It must be difficult for them to relate to each other; so much must remain unsaid between them.

I have known these sisters for years, yet not well enough to get close to their wounds. I would like to share words of encouragement, yet I fear to say that which might offend or hurt. However, by learning the story of Hannah together with them, I can offer hope and comfort. I know, too, that other women in the class are thinking of and silently praying for their childless classmate, and for other friends and relatives who have not been blessed with children. Scripture gives expression to things which they dare not say.

As I close my *Tanakh*, I ponder the awesome responsibility inherent in teaching words of Torah which touch souls so deeply. I recall the teacher's prayer of R. Nechuniah b. Hakannah (*Berakhot* 28b):[8]

יהי רצון מלפניך ה׳ א-להי שלא יארע דבר תקלה על ידי –

"May it be Thy will, My Lord, that no mishap be caused by my teaching...." This classroom session has made me realize the relevance of this prayer beyond the realm of halakhic ruling. We have studied a chapter of *Tanakh*, and I pray that my friends shall find joy, comfort and hope in the words which the biblical text directs me to say. This Rosh Hashanah we will sing Channah's song in our hearts, transformed, as prophecy for all those not yet blessed with motherhood.

Another class draws to a close. The women file out. As I put my books away I am approached by a woman in her mid-fifties. She, too, is on her

---

[8] ברכות כח ע״ב: בכניסתו מהו אומר? יהי רצון מלפניך ה׳ אלהי שלא יארע דבר תקלה על ידי, ולא אכשל בדבר הלכה, וישמחו בי חברי, ולא אומר על טמא טהור ולא על טהור טמא, ולא יכשלו חברי בדבר הלכה, ואשמח בהם.

"On entering what does a man say? May it be Thy will, O Lord my God, that no offence may occur through me, and that I may not err in a matter of Halachah, and that my colleagues may rejoice in me, and that I may not call pure impure or impure, pure and that my colleagues may not err in a matter of Halachah, and that I may rejoice in them." Note that the standard translation of this passage is based on Rashi, who connects the phrase ישמחו בי חברי with ולא אכשל בדבר הלכה thereby interpreting it: "So that my colleagues may rejoice over me, i.e., over my discomfiture, and so bring sin upon themselves." I suspect (as my translation shows) that these two phrases are a request that the Torah one teaches and learns should bring only joy to speakers and hearers alike.

way out, but first she says: "I must thank you – your class was a great comfort to me."

I think to myself: What kind of comfort? I had just finished teaching וחי אחיך עמך – a biblical injunction[9] which the Rabbis apply to a fascinating moral dilemma:

Two men are traveling in the desert. They have only one canteen between them. If they share it, they will both die. If one drinks, he will survive, but his companion will not. What are they to do? Ben Petura contends that they should share their water, so that neither will witness the death of his fellow. R. Akiva argues that the owner of the canteen shall drink, in accordance with this biblical ordinance: "Let him live by your side," – with you, not instead of you. Your life takes precedence over that of your fellow.[10]

We had considered and debated the divergent views. Whose life takes precedence? What if one is a child and the other an adult? What if one is a person of greater religious stature? What if the travelers are a man and a woman? How do we measure the relative value of life?[11]

Our discussion was animated and, no doubt, intellectually stimulating, but this woman found it comforting. Before I can consider what she meant, she provides the explanation.

"You see, I work for Yad Sarah, a volunteer organization which lends medical equipment. Of course, we never have enough to go around. My job is to make life and death decisions. Should this respirator go to an 8-month old baby or to an 80-year old woman? *A part of me dies every day.* I never

---

[9] Leviticus 25:37. The literal sense of the text is about loans: "Do not exact from him advance or accrued interest, but fear your God. Let him live by your side as your kinsman."

[10] Bava Batra 62b:

"ורבי יוחנן וחי אחיך עמך מאי עביד ליה? מבעי ליה לכדתניא: שנים מהלכין בדרך וביד אחד מהן קיתון של מים אם שותין שניהם מתים ואם שותה אחד מהן מגיע לישוב. דרש בן פטורא: מוטב שישתו שניהם וימותו ואל יראה אחד מהם במיתתו של חברו, עד שבא ר' עקיבא ולימד: וחי אחיך עמך – חייך קודמים לחיי חבריך."

[11] עיין הוריות ג:ז–ח, רמב"ם פירוש המשניות שם, מנחת חינוך מצוה רצו,ירושלמי תרומות ח:ד, רמב"ם הל' יסודי התורה ה:ה ; שו"ע יו"ד קנז:א ; תפארת משה שם ; חזון איש יו"ד סט, סני לקוטים סי' כ"ו ; הרב א"י אונטרמן, *שבט מיהודה*, שער א' פרק ח; א"מ פייבלזון, ספר פיקוח נפש, סי' ה' אות קי"ע ; ישראל שחור, "סדר עדיפויות בטרפיאה", *תחומין* 7, עמ' 397–402

know if I've made the right choice. Our study of the sources has taught me that there is no single absolute right decision. I find comfort in that."

I am stunned by the passion in her words. I had taught the various *midrashim, gemarot,* and *teshuvot* bearing on the verse as a theoretical study; here was a woman who was living the *Halakha* every day. By reading the texts in the light of her experiences, she has revealed a new facet of the Torah.

On another day we begin our class elsewhere. We find ourselves in Poland in the late 16th century. The following case is under consideration:[12]

A Jew and his driver took to the road. The young coachman rode ahead on the horses pulling the wagon; his master sat in the carriage. He passed the time by cleaning his pistol. Although he intended to empty the barrel and shoot into the air, his hand slipped and he killed his faithful servant. He immediately made his way to the town sage, asking how to atone for his tragic error. Eventually he found his way to the *Rema* in Cracow, who ruled that he was to go into exile for a full year, never sleeping in the same place for two consecutive nights, in addition to fasting, making confession, and observing the anniversary of the death every year as if it were the anniversary of his own father's death.

We consider similar cases in the responsa of R. Abraham b. Isaac of Narbonne,[13] R. Jacob b. Judah Weil,[14] R. Yair Hayim Bakhrakh,[15] R. Joseph Hayim of Bagdad[16] and R. Isaac Jacob Weiss.[17] I brought these sources to our classroom in an effort to gain some understanding of the biblical and rabbinic philosophy of Halakha regarding *'Arei Miklat*, the cities of refuge, the institution designed to deal with accidental homicide. Are these cities of refuge simply safe-havens from relatives thirsty for blood-vengance? Are they a form of punishment, a type of exile? Perhaps they are a method of

---

12 ר' משה איסרליש מקראקא, שו"ת הרמ"א (ירושלים, תשל"א), סי' לז.

13 אברהם בן יצחק מנרבונה, ספרן של ראשונים (ירושלים,תרצ"ה), סימן מי"א.

14 ר' יעקב בן יהודה וייל, שאלות ותשובות והלכות שחיטה ובדיקה וחידושי דינק (ירושלים, תשמ"ח), סי' קכג.

15 יאיר חיים בכרך, שו"ת חות יאיר (רמת גן, תשנ"ז), סי' קע.

16 יוסף חיים מבגדד, ספר רב פעלים שאלות ותשובות בענין הלכה (ירושלים, תשי"ם), או"ח ח"ג, סי' לו.

17 יצחק יעקב וייס, *לקוטי תשובות מנחת יצחק* (תשנ"ו), סמי קד.

atonement.[18] As we turn the pages, we traverse the globe and travel through time. The women of the class are struck by the recurrence of the issue throughout Jewish history: accidental homicide, in a world with no biblical cities of refuge. What operative principles for such cases can be derived from the Torah and the teachings of *Chazal*?

The women concur that of the above-mentioned approaches to the problem, the opportunity for atonement offered by the Cities of Refuge is of paramount importance. This process is linked by rabbis of later times to other practices, so that a person responsible for accidental homicide might make amends.

As class ends, students leave our hall of study with much food for thought. One of them approaches me. "Thank you so much!" she says as she hugs me, and leaves without another word. She has left the interpretation of her words up to me.

What was it that moved her so? I pause to think; then, it all becomes clear. Her husband, a building contractor, was involved in a renovation project. A terrible mishap took the life of a child – a case of accidental homicide. For her, there was nothing theoretical about our discussion. It was a live issue, a raw nerve. For this student our class was a form of atonement, resolution, closure.

"ויהי המה הולכים הלוך ודבר והנה רכב אש וסוסי אש ויפרדו בין שניהם ויעל אליהו בסערה השמים (מל״ב ב:יא). במה היו עוסקין? אף אליהו לא נפטר מאלישע אלא מתוך דבר של תורה בקריאת שמע היו עוסקין...".

"As they kept on walking and talking, a fiery chariot with fiery horses suddenly appeared and separated one from the other; and Elijah went up to heaven in a whirlwind." (II Kings 2:21) – What were they talking about?... Eliyahu took leave of Elisha with words of Torah...they were reciting the Shema...."[19]

---

[18] See for example:

רמב״ם מו״נ ח״ג פי״מ, שד״ל במד׳ לה:יב, רמב״ם הל׳ רוצח ושמירת נפש ז:ג, ח,יג; תוספות מכות יא ע״ב ד״ה מיד גלות מכפרת; ר׳ דוד צבי הופמן בפירושו לדברים פרק יט, עמ׳ שסט; ספר החינוך מצוה תי.

[19] JT *Berachot* 5:1:

אף אליהו לא נפטר מאלישע אלא מתוך דבר של תורה: ויהי המה הולכים הלוך ודבר במה היו עוסקין? ר׳ אחווא ברי זעירא אמר בקרית שמע היו עוסקין היך מה דאמר (אמר) ודברת בם. ר׳ יודה בן פזי אמר בבריאת עולם היו עוסקין היך מה דאמר בדבר ה׳ שמים נעשו. ר׳ יודן בריה

It is Eliyahu's final hour on this earth. He must pass his mantle on to Elisha, his disciple. They walk together engrossed in discussion. What was it that they were discussing? *Keriyat Shema.*

What possessed the rabbis to offer this suggestion? A student surmises that this opinion is simply a function of the final hour; the recitation of the Shema is the final religious act performed before death. Another student points out how the Rabbis cleverly interpret the phrase *"Veshinantem Levanecha VeDibarta Bam... Uvlekhticha VaDerech."* Yet another woman looks for a deeper meaning, unpacking the fundamentals of religious dogma contained in the *Shema*, which Eliyahu the Master reviews with his student before his final departure. But our discussion has not ended. Another voice is heard:

"You know, Bryna, I haven't thought about it in years.... I was only a child.... It was the summer of 1944. My mother and I had fled from Poland to Czechoslovakia, from there to Hungary, and then we found ourselves in Rumania. It was in Rumania that we managed to obtain British certificates allowing us to leave for Palestine, by way of Turkey. Three ships were waiting at the port. Although my mother and I were booked on the second ship, my mother bribed an official to let us on the first, to be with our only surviving family, for fear that we would once again be separated. The ships set sail and we felt as if we were finally on our way to some sort of secure destination. Suddenly we were attacked by a German submarine. Two of the three ships sank, leaving no survivors. Ours was next. The captain jumped ship. We all got together on the deck, held hands, and said: *"Shema Yisrael Hashem Elokenu Hashem Echad."* We were preparing to die.... Miraculously, we sailed along unmolested and reached our destination."

She glanced at the Tanach before her, and then up at me, and continued. "It has been over 50 years... suddenly our study of the final journey of Eliyahu and Elisha, of *Keriyat Shema*, of the fiery chariot which separated them, unearthed a memory which time had long since buried...."

What was it about our story which awakened this long-suppressed memory?

דר׳ אייבו אמר בנחמות ירושלים היו עוסקין כמה דאמר דברו על לב ירושלם. ורבנן אמרין במרכבה היו עוסקין היך מה דאת אמר והנה רכב אש וסוסי אש וגו׳.

Was it a yearning of an orphan of the Holocaust for the immortality of Eliyahu which stirred her? Perhaps it was the continuity embodied by Elisha, by his ability to pick up the mantle of his father[20] and start again, without turning back to search for a past he knew he could not retrieve. What is clear is that this biblical episode had leapt twenty-eight hundred years into the future, enabling one woman to experience a catharsis of spirit which had been denied her for most of her life.

I turn away from the class, knowing now that the midrashic account of Eliyahu's parting from Elisha poses another question as well: With what does a teacher leave a pupil?

The Rabbis have enriched me with their insight, and as a teacher I have passed it on to this student. How moving it is that she has in turn offered me an additional dimension of this lesson which I had never imagined.

As our class begins, the women open to the thirty-ninth chapter of Genesis. Joseph is pursued by the wife of Potiphar. Although the Bible fully describes the external events, the Rabbis suggest what was going on at the time in Joseph's heart.

Joseph, finding himself alone with Potiphar's wife, is about to fall into the alluring clutches of sin when he is halted in his tracks by the image of Jacob his father, his mentor, his conscience. He sees his father's face; he hears his voice:[21]

באותה שעה באתה דיוקנו של אביו ונראתה לו בחלון אמר לו יוסף עת ידין אחיך שיכתבו על אבני אפוד ואתה ביניהם רצונך שימחה שמך מביניהם ותקרא רועה זונות...

At that moment, he beheld his father's countenance through the window. "Joseph, your brothers' names will be inscribed on the stones of the *ephod*. It is your choice: Will you be inscribed among them, or will your name be erased and you remembered as a companion of harlots?"

Joseph's father suddenly appears in the window, in the opening in the wall which has separated Joseph from his family, and which might separate him forever from the destiny of *Benei Yisrael*. His actions now will determine his place in the roster of *Shivtei Kah*. Will he become one of the stones of the *ephod*, engraved forever on the mantle of holiness?

---

[20] Elisha calls Eliyahu his father in II Kings 2:12.

[21] *Sotah* 36b.

A woman sitting on the left explicates this midrashic text.

"My brother and I were taken from Belgium to Auschwitz. Just before we were parted my brother said, 'We will never see each other again, so let me teach you one *midrash* about Joseph and Jacob. Whenever life will present you with moral dilemmas, see my face and you will know what to do.'" It is this *midrash* which served to guide me through many lonely and difficult ordeals, the student explains.

I find myself amazed by the power which this *midrash* has given to this woman. Joseph for her was a survivor, one whose world was held together through his moral resolve which he transported from his father's house. It is tempting to view this midrashic text as classic example of Freudian superego, but in fact it goes far deeper. Jacob was the moral anchor which neither temptation, loneliness nor evil could destroy.

In the silence which envelopes our classroom following this moving recollection, we realize that our friend has captured the power of Torah. This *midrash* served as her anchor, her link with her brother who was taken from her, with her forebears, perhaps; but it was also her bridge into the future, a future which, in Auschwitz, could only be considered a wild dream. It was Joseph the slave who left Europe with her; Joseph the dreamer who accompanied her to her new life; but Joseph the stone in the *Ephod* who sits in our *shiur* today.

The Midrashic prayer of the midwives, Shifra and Puah, is our point of departure. The midwives – women who bring life into the world – find themselves commanded by Pharoah to be the agents of death. They are caught between a rock and a hard place. The death of innocent babies, or their own. Their recourse is to prayer.

‏"היו עומדות בתפילה ואומרות להקב"ה רבונו של עולם תלה להם עכשו ותן להם נפשותיהם..."‏

"And they gave life to the babies…." They stood in prayer and said to the Holy One, Blessed Be He, "Master of the Universe, give them their lives!"[22]

The silence of the classroom is shattered by a sudden outburst of tears. What was it I said? I have taught this *midrash* dozens of times. It is most certainly poignant, but I had never thought of it as painful. The student

---

[22] *Shemot Rabbah* 1:15.

explains about her baby with a congenital heart defect, and as she does we witness her becoming an inseparable part of the text. She cries as she utters the prayer of the midwives, "Master of the Universe, give them their lives!"

After class the student comes to seek advice to help her through her ordeal. I immediately realize that I have nothing to add. In our Beit Midrash she has already found what she needs. The spiritual fortitude of Shifra and Puah described by the Sages has inspired her to find strength, to shoulder her burden and to go forward in life.

I am haunted by the silent stare of the woman still mourning the death of her first child. We are studying II Samuel 12: Batsheva gives birth to a son who, as the fruit of David's iniquity, will not survive. The Bible describes the weeping and penitence of David,[23] yet the mourning and pain of Batsheva, twice the victim of David's tragic weakness, is not portrayed. Did she not mourn?

The silence of the student fills the vacuum in the text.

A key chapter in the tale of the downfall of the House of David is the story of Amnon's rape of Tamar. This is indeed a "text of terror";[24] women readers are deeply affected by Tamar's fear, pain and anguish. We are gripped by Tamar's desperate and masterful attempts to ward off Amnon's advances. In her last pathetic plea she says: "Please speak to the king; he will not refuse me to you." Tamar has tried all else; her final attempt is to appeal to Amnon suggesting that she will *marry* him and that King David will approve!

Chazal have great difficulty understanding the logic of this appeal. If Tamar was Amnon's half-sister, as the text maintains,[25] how could such a union be approved?

---

[23] Although most commentators explain David's grief as an authentic expression of pain, remorse, penitence and even prayer, Abravanel is the lone dissenting voice:

ואני אחשוב שעשה דוד זה להעלים הענין מהאשה ומאנשיו ולכן לא ביאר להם שהיה זה בענשו ואחרי מות הילד בא אל בית ה' והשתחוה שמה להיותו מקבל עליו את הדין. (אברבנאל שמ"ב יב:כ עמ' שמט).

[24] Such is the name of Phyllis Trible's well know volume of biblical studies; *Texts of Terror: Literary-Feminist Readings of Biblical Narratives* (Philadelphia, 1984), in which Tamar is one of the women discussed.

[25] *Sanhedrin* 21a:

The Rabbis claim that Tamar was the daughter of a captive woman (*yefat toar*) and therefore halachically not Amnon's sister.[26] In this attempt to avoid the horrifying conclusion that Amnon's sin entailed incest in addition to rape, the Rabbis adduce Tamar's very own statement "Please speak to the king; he will not refuse me to you" as a proof text.

As women of Jerusalem, we read the annals of the Davidic dynasty in our Beit Midrash, located near the City of David. We share the pain and humiliation of our sister of generations ago; we might walk on the same stones which long ago were wet with her tears. The ingenuity of *Chazal*'s interpretation is clear, but we continue to discuss the passage, straining to hear Tamar's own voice, pleading, across the chasm of the ages.

"It's clear," suggests one student, "that Tamar's statement is her final attempt to ward off Amnon's heinous attack. Rape is a fear that women live with. Don't many of us envision that if we ever found ourselves in such a position, we would negotiate with the rapist, that we would offer ourselves in some other way, to avert his violence? Tamar's proposal has nothing to do with her halakhic status vis a vis Amnon; She's just grasping at her last straw!"[27]

Glances are exchanged among the students; we all feel that Tamar's voice has been heard in our classroom. We reread the verse, and her words cry out to us from across the generations. The Rabbis seek a halakhic

---

אמר רב יהודה אמר רב: תמר בת יפת תואר היתה, שנאמר (שמואל ב' י"ג) ועתה דבר־נא (על) (מסורת הש"ס: אל) המלך כי לא ימנעני ממך. ואי סלקא דעתך בת נישואין הוא־אחתיה מי הוה שריא ליה? אלא שמע מינה בת יפת תואר היתה.

וכן דעת הרמב"ם, הל' מלכים ח:ח: נתעברה מביאה ראשונה הרי הולד גר, ואינו בנו לדבר מן הדברים מפני שהוא מן העכו"ם, אלא בית דין מטבילין אותו על דעתם, ותמר מביאה ראשונה של יפת תואר היתה, אבל אבשלום נולד מאחר הנישואין, נמצאת תמר אחות אבשלום מאמו ומותרת להנשא לאמנון, וכן הוא אומר דבר נא אל המלך כי לא ימנעני ממך.

[26] Tosafot ibid:

על כן נראה למימר דתמר לא היתה בת דוד שאמה כבר היתה מעוברת כשבאת למלחמה והיא דכתיב (שמואל ב יג) כי כן תלבשנה בנות המלכים מעילים מתוך שגדלה בחיקו של דוד קרי לה בת מלך.

[27] Indeed, Abravanel is of this opinion:

מה שאמרה תמר דבר נא אל המלך כי לא ימנעני ממך לא אמרה כי אם להנצל מידו ומהצד שאבאר ותנחומני של הבל היו ורצתה לדחותו בקש. אף כי בדבריה על העירה על אמיתת הדבר באמרה כי לא יעשה כן בישראל אל תעשה הנבלה הזאת ר"ל היותה ערותו..." (אברבנאל שמ"ב יג:א עמ' שנא)

solution to the halakhic problem; Tamar's problem is survival. There is no deeper *omek peshuto shel mikra* than that.

„ויהי אחר הדברים האלה והאלהים נסה את אברהם"

"Some time afterward, God put Abraham to the test."

I have so much to say about the *Akedah*, but my class has been taken over by one of my students. Her questions are probing; her comments rich in insight. This woman and her husband, like many other Israeli parents, have walked the long and lonely road to their own personal *Akedah* – and returned without their son. I have spent years studying this biblical text, yet nothing I can say approaches the depth of this woman's understanding. Her Yitzhak, a soldier in the Israeli army, fell in Lebanon – he will never laugh again. Her husband reads this Torah portion in shul every Rosh Hashana; today she teaches it to us all.

„וירע הדבר מאד בעיני אברהם על אודות בנו"

„ויאמר אלקים אל אברהם...כל אשר תאמר אליך שרה שמע בקלה..."

"And the matter greatly troubled Abraham for it concerned his son."

We learn about yet another trial of Abraham, this time a domestic conflict affecting the greater good of the family. Sarah is certain that Ishmael must go. His negative influence on her son Isaac is clear. Abraham, a father at long last, is terribly pained by the thought of banishing his son.[28] The decision to heed Sarah's demand is rendered by the Almighty. Only He has the perspective and objectivity necessary to make this judgment. Was this the only resolution possible?

A lively discussion ensues. I am attacked with angry and difficult questions: not textual, but moral. They are being asked by a woman with a retarded son. The expulsion of Ishmael is a test case for her. She and her husband are grappling with the question of whether they should institu-

---

[28] The two classic explanations are supplied by Rashi:

על אודות בנו. על ששמע שיצא לתרבות רעה. ופשוטו, על שאומרת לו לשלחו.

But the most poigniant explanation is that of Yaakov Zvi Meklenberg, in his commentary *HaKetav VeHakabbalah* Gen. 21:11:

...כי חשב אברהם כי לסבה זו בעצמה היה יותר טוב להניחו בביתו שיוכל להוכיחו ולהוליכו בדרך טוב אולי ישוב.

His despair was great since no one was more capable than Abraham to counsel a wayward son, yet as his parent he was unable to do so.

tionalize their son or keep him at home. They fear the effect of his behavior on their other child. They have not been privileged to receive the word from on high: the story of Genesis 21 is the closest they will come to revelation.

These stories are moving, but women's Torah learning is not composed only of such moments. We also spend long hours poring over *Midrash Tanhuma* or reading a *teshuva* of *Radbaz*, in our efforts to understand the basic meanings of the texts. These accounts, however, demonstate a striking and somewhat radical point: it is precisely the subjective, emotional, "feminine" cognitive style, which for years was asserted to be a barrier to women learning Torah properly, which is precisely what has yielded such deep and moving insights into the Word of God. We have only now begun to discover the contribution which we can make to each other and to all those who love Torah and seek its inspiration.

All of the women I have described here – and countless others – have found their way to the Beit Midrash. It is here that they become part of a new generation of *Talmidot Chakhamim,* women who are the students of the Rabbis, who are mastering the wisdom of Torah not only by analyzing the sources but by engaging them; by apprenticing themselves to the Sages.

There are serious questions regarding the role of Jewish women in the public arena. Issues of *Halakha, tzeniut,* and tradition need to be considered in redefining the place of women in the Torah community today.[29] But one thing has become clear: our sacred space is in the Beit Midrash. There is no *mechitzah* between women and *Divrei Torah.* Women are incapable of spiritual passivity in the world of learning. We may listen to the *haftarot* or the *parshiot* passively in shul before we have studied them, but not after. This remarkable transformation is the legacy of all those women who don *Keter Torah,*[30] which is available to all those who seek it. There are many

---

[29] See Joel Wolowelsky, *Women Jewish Law and Modernity* (Hoboken, 1997).

דוד אויערבאך, ספר הליכות ביתה (ירושלים, תשמ״ג), סי׳ כח, ״תלמוד תורה, עמ׳ שפח ואי׳.

[30] בשלשה כתרים נכתרו ישראל, כתר תורה וכתר כהונה וכתר מלכות, כתר כהונה זכה בו אהרן שנאמר והיתה לו ולזרעו אחריו ברית כהנת עולם, כתר מלכות זכה בו דוד שנאמר זרעו לעולם יהיה וכסאו כשמש נגדי, כתר תורה הרי מונח ועומד ומוכן לכל ישראל, שנאמר תורה צוה לנו משה מורשה קהלת יעקב, כל מי שירצה יבא ויטול, שמא תאמר שאותם הכתרים גדולים מכתר תורה הרי הוא אומר בי מלכים ימלוכו ורוזנים יחוקקו צדק בי שרים ישורו, הא למדת שכתר תורה גדול משניהם. (רמב״ם הל׳ תלמוד תורה ג:א)

338

realms of *mitzvot* and ritual in which Jewish women may find inspiration and fulfillment, but *Talmud Torah keneged kulam*–Torah learning is matchless.

What about those of us who are blessed "*Shesam Chelkenu Bein Yoshvei Beit Hamidrash*" – women who teach Torah to other women? We have been entrusted with the role of explicating divine commands, elucidating the omnisignificance of sacred literature, and of interpreting the eternal prophecies so that they continue to offer perspective to our lives. The responsibility is overwhelming; the spiritual challenge – formidable.

And yet for me, as for every teacher of Torah, nothing could be more fulfilling. How can I explain the spiritual exaltation which I experience every Rosh Hashanah hearing *Shirat Channah*, as I look around the *Ezrat Nashim*, recollecting the classroom scene I described above, holding the hand of my little one sitting beside me; or every Yom Kippur when we say "*Hashem Hu HaElokim,*" knowing how many students have stood with me on Mount Carmel; or how I sit down to the Seder every year, exhausted like every other Jewish homemaker, but bolstered by the knowledge that students to whom I have taught *Sefer Shemot* over the last twenty years will read the *Haggadah* and explain it to their families in a way their mothers and grandmothers could not?

I am strengthened in my labors by the knowledge that with each passing year there are more and more learned women who join the ranks of Torah teaching.[31] I can think of no nobler occupation.

For an enlightening discussion of the position of the Rambam on women and Talmud Torah see Marvin Fox, "Torah Study for Women: Prohibited, Permitted, Commanded," Lecture taped by Maayan (Boston, 1996).

[31] A great Torah teacher of our times who was an inspiration for thousands of women involved in Torah learning was Nechama Leibowitz *z"l*. First and foremost, Nechama taught us how to learn and how to teach. Perhaps more than any other figure of this century she engendered a renaissance in the study of *Tanakh* and classical commentaries.

As an indefagitable teacher she traversed the Land of Israel teaching all who thirsted for words of Torah: observant and non-observant, Ashkenazim and Sepharadim, young and old, soldiers, Rabbis, kibbutzniks and moshavniks, new immigrants in development towns, university professors and laymen alike – truly *Kehal 'Adat Bnei Yisrael*. Every shiur with Nechama was a moving experience. There was rarely a lesson which did not include a story – a slice of life – which breathed new meaning into ancient sources. In interpreting the eternal words of Torah, Nechama saw the life experiences of all those in the classroom as being relevant to the text in the same way that the text was relevant to their lives. Her *chiddushei Torah* and inimitable

I have argued that women learning Torah are making a unique contribution to the way Torah unfolds in our generation - to the *peshatot hamitchadshim bekhol yom*.[32] Perhaps women, using their special sensitivities, will best be able to reveal the hitherto hidden spiritual valences of Torah still awaiting discovery.[33] This power of innovation is captured beautifully by a *drashah* in *Pesikta deRav Kahana*:

"On this day they arrived at Sinai" (Exodus 19:1). Was it on this day? Rather, when you study My teachings let them not seem worn in your eyes; let them be as fresh as the day they were given. It does not say 'on that day;' it says *"On this day"* (*Bayom hazeh*), since in this world only a few engage in Torah study, but on that day – in the days to come – I will teach it to *all of Israel* and they will study and shall not forget it, as it says: "But such is the covenant I will make with the House of Israel after these days – declares the Lord; *I will put My teaching into their inmost being and inscribe it upon their hearts. Then I will be their God, and they shall be My people"* (Jer 31:33).[34]

When Torah is learned by all of Israel – men and women alike – then it will be a Torah which enters our innermost being and is inscribed deeply upon our hearts.

---

methodology are preserved for posterity in her *Studies* which have appears in dozens of editions and many languages. Yet, above and beyond her scholarship and creativity, Nechama was a towering example of *Torah VeYirat Shamayim*. Though relentlessly critical in her pursuit of *peshuto shel mikra* she was a woman of genuine humility and deep spirituality. She was and will always be a magnificent role model for all women who aspire to become *Talmidot Chakhamim*.

[32] This is the phrase used by Rashbam in Genesis 37:1 quoting his grandfather Rashi about the commentary he wished to compose if only he had the time.

[33] See the commentary of Meir Leibush Malbim, *Nachal Eshkol*, Lamentations 3:23.and most recently a modern treatment of the issue in:

תמר רוס ויהודה גלמן, "השלכות הפמיניזם על תיאולוגיה יהודית אורתודוקסית", בתוך *ספר זכרון לאריאל רוזן-צבי*, (תל אביב, 1998).

[34] ביום הזה באו מדבר סיני (שמות יט: א). וכי ביום הזה באו, אלא כשתהא למד דברי לא יהו בעיניך ישנים אלא כאילו היום ניתנה תורה, ביום ההוא אין כת' כן, אלא ביום הזה (שם שמות י"ט). בעולם הזה נתתי לכם את התורה והיו יחידים יגיעים בה, אבל לעולם הבא אני מלמדה לכל ישר' והן למידין אתה ואינן שכיחים, שנ' כי זאת הברית אשר אכרות את בית ישראל אחרי הימים ההמה נאם ה' נתתי את תורתי בלבם ועל לבם אכתבנה והייתי להם לאלהים והמה יהיו לי לעם (ירמיה לא: לב). ולא עוד שאני מרבה ביניהם שלום, כשאמר ישעיה וכל בניך למודי ה' ורב שלום בניך. (פסיקתא דרב כהנא יב:כא)

CONTRIBUTORS

Rachel Adelman has an M.A. in Tanakh from MaTaN. She heads the MaTaN branch in Beit Shemesh, whose *Bat Mitzvah* program she runs, and teaches Tanakh and midrash to adults in Jerusalem and Beit Shemesh. She writes poetry as well, and is presently studying Hebrew literature at the Hebrew University in Jerusalem.

Rabbi Ya'akov Ariel studied at Merkaz Harav Yeshivah and the Harry Fishel Institute, and received *semikhah* from Rabbi Yitzhak Arieli, Rabbi Avraham Adler, and Rabbi Avraham Shapira, Chief Rabbi of Israel. He served as rabbi of the moshav Kefar Maimon and headed the high school yeshivah there; from 1980 he headed the Hesder Yeshivah of Yamit, and has been Chief Rabbi of Ramat Gan since 1990.

Rabbanit Malke Bina is the educational director of MaTaN, the Women's Institute for Torah Studies in Jerusalem. She holds a B.A. from Michlalah Jerusalem and an M.A. in Bible from Yeshiva University.

Erica Brown completed the Jerusalem Fellows program and is the former scholar-in-residence of the Combined Jewish Philanthropies (Federation) of Boston. She is the author of the upcoming book *Sacred Canvas: The Hebrew Bible in the Eyes of the Artist* and writes and lectures on topics of Jewish interest. She currently lives in Silver Spring, Maryland with her husband and four children.

Dr. Gabriel H. Cohn has a Ph.D. from Amsterdam University, Holland. He teaches in the Department of Bible at Bar Ilan University, and is former head of the Gold College for Women. He is author of *Studies in the Five Megilloth* (Hebrew), Ministry of Education and Culture, Jerusalem 5774–5784. He is co-editor of *Prayer in Judaism: Continuity and Change* (eds., Gabriel H. Cohn and Harold Fisch), Jason Aronson, 1996, and of *Pirkei Nechama – Prof. Nechama Leibowitz Memorial Volume* (eds., A. Ahrend, R. Ben Meir, G.H. Cohn) The Jewish Agency: Jerusalem, 1991 (Hebrew), and editor of *Deoth*, a religious-academic periodical, from 1957-1987 (Hebrew).

Yardena Cope-Yossef is the director of MaTaN's Advanced Talmudic Institute and assistant director of MaTaN, where she teaches Talmud and *halakhah*. She has taught at the Pelech High School, the Pardes Institute, and an online course for the Jewish Agency's Jewish University in cyber-space. Ms. Cope-Yossef holds a law degree from Hebrew University and is a member of the Israeli bar association. She is currently studying for an advanced degree in Talmud and Jewish Law.

Rabbi Dr. Seth (Shaul) Farber recieved *semikhah* from the Rabbi Isaac Elchanan Theological Seminary and his Ph.D. from the Hebrew University of Jerusalem. He is the co-founder of Ma'ayan in Boston and the co-founder of Kehillat Moriah in Jerusalem. He is presently the founding director of ITIM: The Jewish-Life Information Center (www.itim.org.il). Rabbi Farber's book on Rabbi Joseph B. Soloveitchik's Maimonides School will be published by the University Press of New England in the fall of 2003. Rabbi Farber lives in Raanana with his wife, Michelle and their three children.

Ilana Fodiman-Silverman is the coordinator of Rabbinic Literature at the Jewish Community High School in San Francisco. She has studied in the Drisha Scholars circle and the Bernard Revel Graduate School of Yeshiva University.

Sara Friedland Ben Arza is editor of the Hebrew edition of *Bat Mitzvah* upon which this volume is based. She teaches Hasidism and midrash at MaTaN, Beit Morasha, and Beit Midrash Elul in Jerusalem. She has a B.A. in Hebrew and Musicology from Bar Ilan University and an M.A. in Hasidism from the Department of Literature at Hebrew University, and is a member of the editorial board of *Dimui*, a Hebrew journal of literature and Jewish culture. She is a writer and editor, married and mother of three.

Rabbi Prof. Aryeh A. Frimer received rabbinical ordination from Rabbi Yehudah Gershuni *zt"l* and served as Rabbi of the Harvard Radcliffe Hillel Orthodox Minyan. He has a Ph.D. in Chemistry from Harvard University, and is presently the Ethel and David Resnick Professor of Active Oxygen Chemistry at Bar Ilan University and Senior Research Associate at NASA's Glenn Research Center in Cleveland, Ohio.

Baruch Kahana is a clinical psychologist, and is currently writing his doctoral dissertation on psychology and Hasidism at the Hebrew University, Jerusalem.

Felice Kahn Zisken has an M.A. in English Literature from Hebrew University, Jerusalem. She is editor of *The Pardes Reader* (The Pardes Institute: Jerusalem, 1997), and English editor of *Drawings of Bruno Schulz* (The Israel Museum: Jerusalem, Winter 1990) and *The Fire and the Light* by Herman Kahan (Yad Vashem: Jerusalem, 2003).

Tirza Kelman (Garber) is a graduate of MaTaN Ha-Sharon's *Matmidot* program. She has taught in MaTaN's *Bat Mitzvah* programs and is involved in education and teaching.

Rabbanit Oshra Koren is the director of MaTaN Hasharon and other MaTaN branches, and has a B.A. in Jewish Thought and Hebrew Literature from the Hebrew University, Jerusalem. She founded the MaTaN *Bat Mitzvah* program, leads the group *Bat Kol*, is a member of the Community Council of Ra'anana, and initiated the Hebrew edition of *Bat Mitzvah*.

Rabbi Dr. Benny Lau is a former member and Rabbi of Kibbutz Sa'ad. He heads the Women's *Beit Midrash* of Beit Morasha, Jerusalem and serves as Rabbi of the Himmelfarb high school for boys in Jerusalem, as well as in a community of Jerusalem. He received his Ph.D. from the Department of Talmud at Bar Ilan University, and *semikhah* from the Israeli Rabbinate. Rabbi Lau is married and has six children.

Dr. Yael Levine holds a Ph.D. from the Talmud department of Bar-Ilan University. She has published numerous articles in scientific journals, focusing on issues related to women and Judaism. She has also composed several prayers, among them *Tehinnat ha-Nashim le-Vinyan ha-Mikdash* (The Supplication of the Mothers for the Rebuilding of the Temple), which is recited in various communities on Tisha Be'Av as an extra-liturgical text.

Dr. Bryna Jocheved Levy is the director of MaTaN's Graduate Program in Biblical Studies. She was the first woman to receive a Ph.D. in Bible at Yeshiva University.

Rabbanit Malka Puterkovsky has a B.A. from the Integrated Jewish Studies Program of Bar Ilan University and an M.A. in Talmud from Tel Aviv University. For the past fifteen years she has taught Talmud, *halakhah*, and Jewish thought in various frameworks, in recent years at Midreshet Lindenbaum, Jerusalem.

Rabbanit Rivka Rappoport has a B.A. in Psychology from Barnard College. She is founder and director of Ahavat Yisrael Elementary Schools in Jerusalem and Beit Shemesh.

Chana Ross Friedman teaches in the "Hevruta" *beit midrash* and is currently studying for a Ph.D. in Rabbinic Thought at Hebrew University.

Rabbi Dr. Aryeh Strikovsky has a Ph.D. in Bible from Yeshiva University, and teaches at the Pardes Institute and at Machanayim in Jerusalem. He is the editor of publications in the Torah Culture Department at the Ministry of Education and has published numerous essays and books on Jewish subjects.

Manuel Weill has an M.A. in Philosophy from the University of Nanterre, Paris and studied law at Bar Ilan University. His primary interest lies in the question concerning the relevance of the Orthodox world-view to modern life.

Dr. Ora Wiskind Elper has an M.A. in Comparative Literature and Ph.D. in Hebrew Literature from Hebrew University, Jerusalem. She teaches Jewish thought at Michlalah College and Touro College, Jerusalem. Her publications include *Tradition and Fantasy in the Tales of Reb Nahman of Bratslav* (State University of New York Press, 1998) and co-editor of *Torah of the Mothers: Contemporary Jewish Women Read Classical Jewish Texts* (Urim Publications, 2000). She has also translated works from Hebrew, French and German, and is editor of this volume.

Rabbi Dr. Joel B. Wolowelsky is Dean of the Faculty at the Yeshivah of Flatbush and associate editor of *Tradition*, the journal of Orthodox Jewish thought published by the Rabbinical Council of America. He is also author of *Women, Jewish Law and Modernity: New Opportunities in a Post-feminist Age* (Ktav, 1997).